From Party Politics
to Militarism in Japan,
1924–1941

Published in association with the
Japan Publishing Industry Foundation for Culture

From Party Politics

to Militarism in Japan,

1924–1941

Kitaoka Shinichi

LYNNE
RIENNER
PUBLISHERS

BOULDER
LONDON

Published in the United States of America in 2021 by
Lynne Rienner Publishers, Inc.
1800 30th Street, Suite 314, Boulder, Colorado 80301
www.rienner.com

and in the United Kingdom by
Lynne Rienner Publishers, Inc.
Gray's Inn House, 127 Clerkenwell Road, London EC1 5DB
www.eurospanbookstore.com/rienner

First published in Japanese as *Nihon no kindai 5: Seitō kara gunbu e 1924–1941*
© 2013 by Kitaoka Shinichi

Library of Congress Cataloging-in-Publication Data
A Cataloging-in-Publication record for this book
is available from the Library of Congress.

ISBN 978-1-62637-857-5 (hc)

British Cataloguing in Publication Data
A Cataloguing in Publication record for this book
is available from the British Library.

Printed and bound in the United States of America

The paper used in this publication meets the requirements
of the American National Standard for Permanence of
Paper for Printed Library Materials Z39.48-1992.

5 4 3 2 1

Contents

Illustrations

1

The Beginning of
the Shōwa Period

~

This book is concerned with the history of slightly more than seventeen years: from June 1924, when a coalition cabinet of three parties was established, to December 1941, when Japan commenced its war with the United States. At first glance, it would seem that two different historical periods are encompassed in these seventeen years: the 1920s, characterized by party politics and international cooperation; and the 1930s, marked by the rising influence of the military and war.

During the 1920s, Japan achieved a certain affluence and freedom. Particularly in urban areas, a prosperous and vibrant society and culture had taken root, anticipating postwar developments. But in the 1930s, and the latter years of that decade in particular, Japan entered a dark and oppressive era of warfare. The references to "party politics" and "militarism" in the title of this book are emblems of these two distinct periods.

Yet it would be a mistake to stress only the discontinuity between the two. The 1930s were born out of the 1920s; and the developments of the 1920s were not only inherited by the 1930s but also passed on to serve as the foundations of Japan's postwar rebirth. Yet the military was far from impotent during the period of party politics—it was, in fact, a powerful presence. Nor did the political parties slip into insignificance in the 1930s. Until the end of the decade, as before, they wielded considerable power.

In this regard, it is important to note that neither the political parties nor the military existed as monolithic entities. Among the political parties, the Rikken Seiyūkai (Friends of Constitutional Government), Rikken Minseitō (Democratic Party), and proletarian parties were engaged in strenuous conflict with one another, and frequently riven by internal conflicts nearly as fierce.

1

Similarly, within the military, there were divisions between the army and navy; between the Ministry of Army and Army General Staff Office; between the Ministry of Navy and Navy General Staff Office; between the operations and intelligence bureaus of Army General Staff Office; and so on—and there were frequent conflicts and contention among and between almost all of them. In addition to the usual bureaucratic rivalries, there were also fierce disagreements over ideology and policy. And in fact, these internal conflicts within the parties and the military would play a major role in shaping the history of this period.

As the title makes clear, the focus of this book is on politics. A number of political decisions—or absence thereof—brought about immense disaster on Japan and its neighbors. The history of prewar Japan exemplifies the horrific damage that can result when a modern nation-state goes off course. Because of this, it seems obvious to place politics at the center of our discussion of this period.

But of course we cannot ignore economics, society, or culture. Politics cannot exist without an economic base. The failure of Japan's prewar politics, in a sense, originated in the attempt to leap beyond the country's actual economic foundations. Politics is also impossible without the support or at least the tacit acquiescence of the majority of the people. Because of this, it is important to understand exactly what sort of society and culture the Japanese people inhabited. The pages I can devote to them are limited, but I will do my best to give attention to economics, society, and culture as they relate to the politics of the period.

A History of Ideas

One of the most important aspects of politics is the interaction of foreign affairs with domestic policy. The question of "What if?" is generally taboo in the study of history—but if there had been no Great Depression, and if there had been no rise of Nazi Germany, then it seems likely that Japan would have pursued a far different course. It is impossible to adequately understand the history of modern Japan without paying close attention to the relationship between domestic politics and foreign policy.

So the fundamental aim of this book is to provide a comprehensive look at the two periods of the 1920s and the 1930s in Japan, paying particular attention to the interaction of domestic and foreign affairs and to the conflict not only between the political parties and the military, but also among the parties themselves and the factions within the military, while also devoting appropriate space to developments in the economic, social, and cultural spheres. In this sense, it is a completely ordinary history of prewar Japan, centered on the political history of the era. But in fact there are not so many such "ordinary" books available to the general public—which is perhaps an indication of the shallowness of Japanese culture.

This book is not only a political history, but also one that focuses on the actions of political elites. When people hear the phrase "political elite," many think of a handful of people with little relationship to the majority of the citizens. Many also regard politicians as individuals motivated by nothing other than their own interests. And to be sure, the actions of most people—not only politicians—seem to center on their own interests. But the real issue here is that it is not as easy as one might think for these people to discern what is advantageous or disadvantageous for themselves, their organizations, or Japan as a whole. When people look at their surroundings, they always see them through a particular framework or conceptual lens. To put it another way, people are motivated by their interests, and these interests are defined in large part by ideas. In the 1930s, as decisions were being made regarding the advantages of allying with Germany or with Britain and the United States, the value systems leaders embraced had perhaps as great an impact as their ability to read the changing international situation. When considered in this way, the history of prewar Japan is, to a surprising extent, a history of ideas.

Most significant among these ideas or ideologies were choices between a free or controlled economy; whether or not to cooperate with the United States and Britain; and whether or not the emperor should be regarded as an organ of the Japanese state—that is, as a limited, constitutional monarch—or as a more absolute and sovereign authority. On almost every occasion that a new prime minister was appointed, the emperor explicitly instructed him to exercise caution in foreign policy and to respect the constitution. The former was tantamount to ordering the prime minister to prioritize relations with the Anglo-American powers and respect the principles of the free-market economy. The latter was a recommendation that the cabinet, the Diet, the military, and the other organs of government all cooperate with one another in the policymaking process. Yet despite this clear statement by the emperor as the sovereign power, these two policies were ignored and swept aside. Why? This is the most important question in Japan's prewar history, and one that we will encounter again and again in the pages of this book.

Japan at the End of the Taishō Period

When Does the Shōwa Period Begin?
As noted earlier, this book deals with the period from the three-party coalition cabinet of 1924 to the attack on Pearl Harbor in 1941—in other words, the prewar years of the Shōwa period.

The Shōwa period is ordinarily thought of as beginning on 25 December 1926 with the death of Emperor Taishō and the accession to the throne of Crown Prince Hirohito, later to be known as Emperor Shōwa. But it is also possible to place this starting point a bit differently.

For example, it might be possible to see the end of World War I on 11 November 1918 as the beginning of Shōwa. The Great War changed the world, and had a powerful impact on Japan. From an economic perspective, the development that took place during the war laid the foundations for the economy of the early Shōwa years down to the outbreak of World War II. And in terms of political thought, the victory of democracy in the Great War and of the revolution in Russia formed the basis for Japanese thought in the interwar period.

Politically, the Shōwa period might be regarded as beginning in November 1921, a month in which three epoch-making events occurred: the assassination of Prime Minister Hara Takashi on 4 November; the opening of the Washington Naval Conference on 12 November; and the appointment of Crown Prince Hirohito as regent for the ailing Emperor Taishō on 25 November. Moreover, all three events were interrelated.

The Constitution of the Empire of Japan (popularly known as the Meiji Constitution) articulated a very clear separation of powers. It declared that "the Emperor . . . combin[es] in Himself the rights of sovereignty, and exercises them," but of course the emperor could not make all decisions by himself. If he did, and made a major error of judgment, he might be held responsible, and endanger the imperial house itself. Because of this, the emperor's conduct of policy was fundamentally based on accepting the counsel of various institutions advising him: his cabinet, the Diet, and the military. But what happened when these advisory bodies contradicted or conflicted with one another? From the Meiji period onward, the elder statesmen, or genrō, had played an important role in coordinating and unifying these opinions. But as the original genrō aged and departed the political scene, it was the political parties that emerged as potential heirs to this responsibility.

The last genrō who could effectively wield such power was Yamagata Aritomo (1838–1922), and the first party politician to do so was Hara Takashi (1856–1921). For a number of years before Hara's death, these two men were the most powerful forces in Japanese politics, vying with one another for leadership but also cooperating with one another when necessary. Hara was killed in November 1921; Yamagata died in February 1922. From this point of view, one could see November 1921 as the end of one era and the beginning of another.

It happens that the last issue on which Hara and Yamagata cooperated was one that ended in failure. A serious incident had arisen within the imperial court when it was alleged that Princess Nagako, the fiancée of Crown Prince Hirohito, might be a hereditary bearer of the gene for color blindness. Yamagata and his associates argued that Nagako's family, the Kuninomiya, should withdraw her engagement on the grounds that the purity of the imperial family bloodline must be preserved. Hara supported Yamagata in this position. But there were others who attacked Yamagata and company vigorously, using the ethical argument that the sovereign must be a moral exemplar, and thus should not break a solemn vow. Since the Kuninomiya family was related to the Shimazu, former rulers of Satsuma domain, and Yamagata was a leader from the domain of Chōshū, old rivalries between the domains that had engineered the Meiji Restoration also came into play, increasing the gravity of the incident. In the end, the engagement stood, and Yamagata was defeated so bitterly that for a time he declined all honors due to him as an elder statesman. This incident concerning the imperial house was one that the two most powerful political figures of their time proved powerless to resolve.

Moreover, Emperor Taishō was sickly and frail. According to Makino Nobuaki, minister of the imperial household, in July 1921, not long before the decision was made to establish a regency, the emperor had to be supported by two retainers holding his hand on either side when he went on summer retreat at the Shiobara Imperial Villa in Tochigi prefecture, and despite having visited there every year when he was crown prince, did not remember having been there. He was also unable to recognize the crown prince of Korea when the latter paid him an official visit. The situation was grave.

Thus the Achilles' heel of the constitutional order was the imperial court. Under the Meiji Constitution, whose institutional framework possessed aspects of both a constitutional and an absolute monarchy, the imperial court was a very delicate issue. Hara believed that the court should stand apart from the political disputes of the day, and be maintained as a locus of a healthy political and international sensibility. This was why he arranged a European tour for Crown Prince Hirohito (the first ever for a member of the imperial house), and decided to have him installed as regent upon his return. Hara's opening move in this strategy had been to appoint his close friend Makino Nobuaki as imperial household minister in February 1921, in an effort to introduce Makino's open-minded and internationalist spirit into the atmosphere of the imperial court. The crown prince's European visit was a major success, and preparations for his regency began immediately upon his return to Japan.

Hara's leadership was also crucial to the other major event of November 1921, the convening of the Washington Naval Conference. This conference, along with the Paris Peace Conference of 1919, was essential to the creation of the international order following World War I, but there were many in Japan who were apprehensive about their country's participation. For many years the United States had been fiercely critical of Japan's expansion into continental Asia, and it was true that during the course of

Crown Prince Hirohito, later Emperor Shōwa
Hirohito in the midst of his five-nation European tour in May 1921, with British prime minister David Lloyd George and family. (© The Mainichi Newspapers Co., Ltd.)

the Great War, Japan had engaged in policies on the Asian mainland that were open to such criticism.

However, Hara was one of the earliest among Japanese statesmen and diplomats to perceive the power and influence of the United States. He was convinced that cooperation with the United States was of utmost importance for Japanese foreign policy, and worked hard to steer the country in that direction. It was primarily the groundwork laid by Hara Takashi that made it possible for Japan to maintain cooperation with the United States at the Washington Conference without seriously damaging its own interests, with regard to either naval disarmament or the issue of China.

So by November 1921, two major goals Hara had pursued—a pragmatic policy of cooperation with the United States and an imperial court with a more enlightened perspective on international affairs—had been realized. But in that month, Hara was assassinated. This was a harbinger of the difficult fate awaiting these two major themes of Hara's. And Japan would have to confront these difficulties without powerful leaders such as Hara and Yamagata.

The Political Situation After Hara

If we can consider November 1921 as a possible alternative beginning for the Shōwa period, then let's briefly review the situation of late Taishō Japan from 1921 to 1924, the year with which this book actually commences.

The cabinet formed in September 1918 (just prior to the end of World War I) by Hara Takashi and his party, the Rikken Seiyūkai, was an unusually strong cabinet for prewar Japan. In 1919, Hara's government successfully revised the electoral law to introduce a single-member constituency system, and in the snap general election called in 1920 won an overwhelming victory. Outside the House of Representatives, the largest parliamentary faction in the House of Peers, the Kenkyūkai (Study Group), was also favorable to Hara, and the Privy Council did not oppose him. The mainstream factions in both the army and navy were also well disposed toward Hara, and tried to avoid conflict.

But when Hara was assassinated in November 1921, the Seiyūkai suffered from a leadership vacuum. Takahashi Korekiyo (1854–1936) took over the prime ministership and leadership of the party after Hara, but he was a newcomer to the Seiyūkai (joining in 1913), and because he seemed to lack either the ambition or the ability to unify the party, it split into two factions—one supporting him, the other opposing his leadership. This internal factionalism led to a conflict over a cabinet reorganization, and in June 1922 the Takahashi government collapsed after only a little over half a year in office.

The second largest party in the House of Representatives was the Kenseikai (Constitutional Party), led by Katō Takaaki. Although the Kenseikai had an absolute majority in the House of 197 seats (out of a total of 381) upon its formation in October 1916, it had now fought two elections as the opposition party and its total number of seats in the House had slid to 108 (out of 464). This number did not bode well for the party's ability to form a government, even if a general election were called and it had an opportunity to increase its seats. Moreover, as foreign minister in the second cabinet of Ōkuma Shigenobu, Katō had damaged relations with both China and the United States by pressing the "Twenty-One Demands" against China in 1915, losing the confidence of Japan's elder statesmen in the process. For these reasons, the prospects for a Kenseikai cabinet were remote.

The Yamagata clique had shared political power with the Seiyūkai, but Yamagata Aritomo died in February 1922, seeming to follow Hara in death, and other political figures who might have unified the clique were also gradually fading from the scene. Taking advantage of this situation, and amassing considerable power in the late Taishō period, was the Sappa, or Satsuma faction, a group of politicians from the former domain of Satsuma that included Matsukata Masayoshi, Makino Nobuaki in the imperial court, Tokonami Takejirō in the Seiyūkai, and Yamamoto Gonnohyōe, then biding his time outside public life. However, since it was their geographical origins that united them rather than shared ideals, principles, or even a party organization, they were unlikely to be able to extend their reach. The power of the Satsuma faction could never be more than temporary or supplementary in nature.

From the Takahashi Cabinet to the Katō Cabinet

When the Takahashi cabinet collapsed in June 1922, the figure proposed as his successor, Katō Tomosaburō, was not affiliated with either the Seiyūkai, the Kenseikai, or the Yamagata clique. In fact, he had no particularly powerful background in civilian politics—but he was a career naval officer who had reached the rank of admiral, and had served as navy minister. Katō had been instrumental in the success of the Washington Naval Conference, and was expected to be a steady hand in implementing the arms reductions it called for.

But the Seiyūkai expressed dissatisfaction with the idea of a cabinet headed by Katō. In response, Matsukata and Makino, the imperial household minister, began considering Katō Takaaki of the Kenseikai as a second choice. Learning of this, and determined to prevent their rival party from forming a government, the Seiyūkai suddenly threw its support behind Katō Tomosaburō, and a cabinet was formed.

At the time, the biggest issue in the world of politics was universal manhood suffrage. The third largest party in the Diet, the Kakushin Kurabu (Reform Club), had come out in favor of it. Katō Takaaki of the Kenseikai was a conservative and a very wealthy man who originally had opposed universal suffrage, but around 1920 shifted to a position supporting it. In 1919, under the Hara cabinet, the Seiyūkai had reformed the electoral law (introducing single-member constituencies and lowering the tax-payment qualification for voting to ¥3 or more in direct national tax), and in 1920 it dissolved the Diet, saying it would seek the judgment of the people in an election in which the party declared its opposition to universal manhood suffrage. In other words, despite some internal dissension, the Seiyūkai was generally negative toward the introduction of universal manhood suffrage. This was clearly a major and divisive issue, but there was no political force in sight that was powerful enough to make universal suffrage a reality. In this regard as well, party politics was reaching a dead end.

Arms reduction was another critical concern. The Washington Naval Conference placed limitations on new construction of battleships and brought about reductions in the number of existing capital ships. And in 1922–1923, during Yamanashi Hanzō's tenure as army minister, the army undertook various arms reduction measures, including a reduction in overall troop strength. In a Europe that had witnessed the horrors of the Great War, a great longing for peace was born, and its influence extended as far as Japan. If there was ever a time when military men felt uncomfortable walking about in uniform, it was the 1920s.

The Genrō and the Imperial Court

In the power vacuum following the assassination of Hara Takashi, the role played by the genrō was crucial in determining the direction of the government. The appointment and removal of the prime minister was ultimately one of the sovereign powers of the emperor, but in practice it was the genrō who made the recommendations. The genrō were not an official institution, nor did their recommendations have institutional status. The figure officially charged with advising the emperor on affairs of state and conveying the imperial will to his subjects was the *naidaijin* (lord keeper of the privy

Table 1.1   A List of the Genrō

Name	Origin	Date of Imperial Decree According Them Status of Elder or Senior Statesman	Died	Government Offices Held	Peerage
Itō Hirobumi	Yamaguchi	Nov. 1889	Oct. 1909	Councilor, prime minister, others	Prince
Kuroda Kiyotaka	Kagoshima	Nov. 1889	Aug. 1900	Councilor, prime minister, others	Count
Yamagata Aritomo	Yamaguchi	May 1891	Feb. 1922	Councilor, prime minister, others	Prince
Matsukata Masayoshi	Kagoshima	Jan. 1898	July 1924	Councilor, prime minister, others	Prince
Inoue Kaoru	Yamaguchi	Feb. 1904	Sep. 1915	Foreign minister, finance minister, others	Marquis
Saigō Tsugumichi	Kagoshima	—	July 1902	Councilor, navy minister, others	Marquis
Ōyama Iwao	Kagoshima	Aug. 1912	Dec. 1916	Councilor, army minister, others	Prince
Saionji Kinmochi	Court nobility	Dec. 1912	Nov. 1940	Prime minister	Prince

Source: Kokushi daijiten (Encyclopedia of Japanese History), Yoshikawa Kōbunkan.

seal). When consulted by the emperor on such matters, the *naidaijin* would then seek the opinions of the genrō and report to the emperor.

After Yamagata's death, only two of the genrō remained: Matsukata Masayoshi and Saionji Kinmochi. Matsukata was born in 1835 and was eighty-six years old when Yamagata died; Saionji, born in 1849, was fourteen years his junior. Neither of the two possessed the powerful political base that Yamagata had established for himself. But Matsukata was from Satsuma, and was surrounded by Satsuma men. As a result, even if he did not particularly strive to advance the interests of the Satsuma clique, it shaped the information he received and biased him in that direction. Something similar was true of Saionji, who had deep ties to the Seiyūkai and had served as its president. Even if Saionji subjectively believed himself to be impartial, his sources of information were largely people associated in some way with the Seiyūkai.

Matsukata served as *naidaijin* from 1917 to September 1922, when he was succeeded in the post by Hirata Tōsuke. This meant the office was no longer occupied by one of the genrō, and Hirata was a powerful politician in his own right, unlikely to be completely subservient to Saionji's leadership. If anything, he was also somewhat more sympathetic to the Kenseikai than was Saionji.

Another post of importance in terms of relations with the imperial court was that of president of the Privy Council. This position had long been occupied by Yamagata. In other words, both this post and that of *naidaijin* had traditionally been held by genrō. After Yamagata's death, Kiyoura Keigo, who had served as vice president of the council, was promoted to president.

The Concept of Normal Constitutional Government

On what basis did the genrō make their recommendations for the selection of the prime minister? Here we must consider the "theory of normal constitutional government" frequently debated at the time as the model for changes in government. Simply stated, this theory held that when a government collapsed, it should be replaced by one formed by the largest opposition party in the lower house (the House of Representatives) of the Diet. This seems reasonably clear and straightforward, as a concept. But in actual application, it proved to be quite complicated.

For example, if a cabinet collapsed as a consequence of the illness or death of the prime minister, there was no real reason for a new government to be formed by the opposition party. Nor should this apply to cases in which cabinets collapsed for reasons other than misrule or political failure. But when a cabinet did collapse, there might be ample room for debate as to whether this was the case.

The definition of "opposition party" was also unclear. For example, when the cabinet of Terauchi Masatake collapsed in 1918, the Seiyūkai could not really be regarded as an opposition party, for it had maintained a more or less amicable neutrality toward his government. But it did not support him on the two issues—the Siberian Intervention and the Rice Riots of 1918—that became the source of his cabinet's failure, so the Seiyūkai could not be regarded as the ruling party, either.

In the end, the most vocal supporters of the theory of normal constitutional government—aside from journalists and pundits (and even they were not unanimous)—were the opposition-party politicians who stood to take power if and when there was a change in government. In other words, when a Seiyūkai cabinet fell, the Kenseikai would proclaim the theory of normal constitutional government; but once in power themselves, they would not think of simply handing it back to the Seiyūkai once again if the Kenseikai cabinet should falter.

Speaking somewhat cynically, the theory of normal constitutional government was an opposition argument. No politician had a consistent stance on this theory. But this is not to say that it was completely meaningless. The history of party politics in prewar Japan is, in fact, largely a history of the Seiyūkai. Hara Takashi's strategy was to establish the Seiyūkai as a permanent ruling party, securing its position to determine the budget and the distribution of other benefits, and using this to cultivate an unshakeable power base in the countryside, making it nearly impossible for any political force outside the parties to form a government without the cooperation of the Seiyūkai.

As a result, Hara's concept of party politics did not envision the transfer of power between parties; in fact, it worked to prevent it. Yet, as noted earlier, cohesive groups representing political forces outside the parties (such as the genrō) were gradually declining. If party politics was to move to the next level—where the parties alone would be responsible for the formation of governments—then a theory of normal constitutional government was meaningful indeed.

Yet by 1922, even Yoshino Sakuzō (1878–1933), formerly one of the most vocal advocates of the theory of normal constitutional government, had ceased to speak in favor of it. This was because, he said, money politics had rendered all of the parties incapable of expressing the will of the people. The dominant argument of the day was universal manhood suffrage, and that its reflection of the will of the people was the surest route to normal constitutional government. The argument for universal suffrage had gone beyond a simple issue of civil rights and was being propounded as a new and indispensable condition for achieving political unity. While not a particularly fresh perspective, the reason this book begins with the three-party coalition cabinet of 1924 is to emphasize the importance of universal manhood suffrage as a new phase in Japanese politics.

Saionji and Normal Constitutional Government

If we think about it in this way, then Saionji's relationship with normal constitutional politics becomes a major issue—because as the figure most able to determine the formation of new governments, his views on the rules for cabinet successions were of crucial importance. It is well known that Saionji, at least at one time, was skeptical of the theory of normal constitutional government. For example, on 9 March 1922, he said to Matsumoto Gōkichi, "We hear a lot about 'reason' and 'normal practice,' but I'd like to know what books this is written in, and which countries are actually doing this at present. Sometime soon I intend to invite some scholars to tell me about this." (Hayashi Shigeru and Oka Yoshitake, eds., *Taishō demokurashī-ki no seiji: Matsumoto Gōkichi seiji nisshi* [The politics of Taishō democracy: The political diary of Matsumoto Gōkichi]).

Yet this was not necessarily a consistent position of Saionji's, who changed his stance on a variety of issues many times. For example, during the Taishō period he frequently called the Seiyūkai a party of national significance, but in the Shōwa period stopped making such assertions. Moreover, while he was clearly antipathetic to Katō Takaaki and the Kenseikai in the period 1922–1924, after that he began to express strongly favorable sentiments toward them. Saionji was a man who made many mistakes, learned from them, and changed.

Saionji's most consistent criterion for selection of a prime minister was his commitment to peaceful diplomacy grounded in cooperation with Britain and the United States. Second was support for a candidate who could skillfully unify and aggregate the various organs and agencies of the government. But government is shaped by legislation and the budget, and without a majority in the lower house, neither was feasible. Because of this, a cabinet had to have the support of one of the stronger parties in the House of Representatives. Moreover, the budget and legislation also had to pass the House of Peers, and certain legislation as well as treaties and other international agreements required the approval of the Privy Council as well. But this was not too tall an order for a popularly elected party with the qualifications to form a government. In other words, the theory of normal constitutional government could be thought of as a powerful method for fulfilling the conditions necessary to meet Saionji's second criterion—a candidate who could unify the institutions of government. And in fact, Saionji's actual selections for the post of prime minister tended to accord with the theory of normal constitutional government.

Saionji Kinmochi (1849–1940)
Saionji's contacts with Katō led him to reevaluate the capabilities of both Katō and the Kenseikai. Photo courtesy of Kyodo News Images Inc.

The Great Kantō Earthquake and the Yamamoto Cabinet

Formation of the Yamamoto Cabinet

On 24 August 1923, Prime Minister Katō Tomosaburō died of an illness, and his cabinet resigned. Both the Seiyūkai and the Kenseikai had hopes of forming a party cabinet in the name of normal constitutional government. However, on 27 August, the genrō (Saionji, with the agreement of Matsukata) appointed Yamamoto Gonnohyōe, a navy admiral on reserve duty, as the next prime minister. Their rationale was that the term of the members of the House of Representatives was ending the following year, and in order to ensure that the upcoming general election would be implemented fairly, it would be better to avoid a party cabinet at that time.

Yamamoto had been prime minister once before; in 1913–1914 he led a cabinet that cooperated with the Seiyūkai to implement a series of bold reform measures intended to blunt the political ascendency of the Yamagata clique and the army: a revision of the rule that required the ministers of both the army and navy to be active-duty officers, allowing reserve officers to serve in these capacities (though none were actually appointed); a revision of the civil service appointment ordinance that relaxed the requirements for appointments to senior bureaucratic positions; and a liberalization of personnel policy for semi-governmental corporate entities in Japan's colonial sphere of influence, such as the South Manchurian Railway Company and the Oriental Development Company. However, the eruption of the Siemens scandal (involving bribery in navy armaments procurement) led Yamamoto to resign the prime ministership and be placed on the reserve list by the navy.

The second Yamamoto cabinet was a choice welcomed by Matsukata, since Yamamoto was also a Satsuma man. And Makino Nobuaki, minister of the imperial household, wrote in his diary for 27 August, "Personally I am delighted by the baron's [Yamamoto's] restoration." And in an entry for 29 August, Makino wrote that while people around Yamamoto had never stopped advocating for his return to public life, such sentiment broadened "as the current situation [became] more conflicted and popular feeling more agitated." He noted that it is human nature to seek strong and dependable leadership in times of social unrest, and concluded that "both genrō seem to have decided to recommend the baron's appointment for quite fair and honest reasons."

Having received the imperial command to form his second cabinet, Yamamoto ambitiously set about assembling a government of national unity comprising some of the most powerful politicians in Japan, figures who were themselves potential candidates for the prime ministership. These included the presidents of the three major parties (Takahashi Korekiyo of the Seiyūkai, Katō Takaaki of the Kenseikai, and Inukai Tsuyoshi of the Kakushin Kurabu); Gotō Shinpei, who had previously served as president of the South Manchurian Railway Company, as home minister, and as minister of foreign affairs; Den Kenjirō, former governor-general of Taiwan and a bureaucrat affiliated with the Yamagata clique; and former army minister Tanaka Giichi. But the presidents of both the Seiyūkai and Kenseikai refused to participate, making the process of cabinet formation difficult. And at that juncture, the Great Kantō Earthquake occurred.

The Shock of Natural Disaster

The earthquake struck the area of Tokyo and Yokohama just before noon on 1 September 1923. Damage was widespread throughout the Kantō region and extended even into Yamanashi and Shizuoka prefectures. Dead and missing totaled 142,807 people; 576,262 houses and other structures collapsed, burned, or were swept away.

Simply in terms of the numbers of dead and missing, this was a greater disaster than the Russo-Japanese War of 1904–1905; twenty times the number in the Great Hanshin-Awaji Earthquake of 1995; and seven times that of the Great East Japan Earthquake of 2011. The number of victims was almost as large as that of the atomic bombings of Hiroshima and Nagasaki combined, and more than that resulting from the terrible firebombing of Tokyo on 10 March 1945.

The monetary value of damages was estimated at ¥5.5 billion. This was 5.4 percent (8.0 percent excluding land) of Japan's total national wealth at the time, which was estimated at ¥102.3 billion (¥69.1 billion excluding land). If we consider that the three and a half years of the Pacific War (1941–1945) resulted in 3 million dead and the loss of a quarter of the national wealth, this gives a sense of how immense was the damage caused at a single stroke by this natural disaster (Nakamura Takafusa, *Shōwa shi* [A history of Shōwa Japan, 1926–1989], abridged translation).

Tokyo was plunged into anarchy, in the midst of which baseless rumors proliferated accusing Koreans of poisoning wells, resulting in the tragic massacre of what is believed to have been more than a thousand Korean

Crown Prince Hirohito surveys the earthquake damage
Photo taken 15 September 1923 on the main avenue of Ginza in Tokyo, with the scars of the quake still clearly visible. (From Kokusai shashin jōhō *[The international graphic], September 1927)*

residents. Martial law was declared to restore order, but the police and troops charged with this mission themselves engaged in illegal acts. In addition to the Koreans, a number of Chinese residents were murdered. A dozen or more workers regarded by certain elements in the military as a threat to the established order were murdered in the Kameido Incident. And on 17 September, army lieutenant Amakasu Masahiko murdered anarchist Ōsugi Sakae, his wife, Itō Noe, and Ōsugi's six-year-old nephew. Newly appointed home minister Gotō Shinpei protested to the army and placed known socialists under protective custody.

Formation of the Yamamoto Cabinet

Confronted with this disaster, a cabinet was quickly organized, and at 8:00 P.M. on 2 September 1923, the ceremony of imperial investiture was conducted, in the midst of aftershocks of the quake and without electric power. The cabinet lineup was as follows:

Prime minister: Yamamoto Gonnohyōe
Minister of foreign affairs: Ijūin Hikokichi (Prime Minister
    Yamamoto concurrently held this post until 19 September)
Minister of home affairs: Gotō Shinpei (House of Peers, Sawakai
    [Tea Talk Club])
Minister of finance: Inoue Junnosuke
Minister of the army: Tanaka Giichi
Minister of the navy: Takarabe Takeshi
Minister of justice: Hiranuma Kiichirō (Minister of Agriculture and
    Commerce Den concurrently held this post until 6 September)
Minister of education: Okano Keijirō (House of Peers, Kōyū Kurabu
    [Friendship Club]; Minister of Communications Inukai
    concurrently held this post until 6 September)
Minister of agriculture and commerce: Den Kenjirō (House of Peers,
    Sawakai; to 24 December); Okano Keijirō
Minister of communications: Inukai Tsuyoshi (House of
    Representatives, Kakushin Kurabu)
Minister of railways: Yamanouchi Kazuji (House of Peers,
    Kōyū Kurabu)
Chief cabinet secretary: Kabayama Sukehide
Director-general of the Cabinet Legislation Bureau: Baba Eiichi
    (to 19 September); Matsumoto Jōji

Here I should say a word about the composition of cabinets at this time. As we can see, there were a total of eleven cabinet ministers, including the prime minister. The posts of chief cabinet secretary and director-general of the Cabinet Legislation Bureau, which in today's cabinets are held by ministers, were in those days seen as positions equivalent to ministers, for a total of thirteen cabinet offices in all.

Among them, the posts of minister of the army and minister of the navy had to be filled by individuals with the rank of general or lieutenant-general (admiral or vice admiral). Since the reform of 1913, these could also in theory be officers on reserve or secondary reserve duty, but appointment of active-duty officers remained customary. For this reason, there was no chance for members of political parties to hold these posts.

Moreover, since the concept of the foreign minister as a nonpartisan post was well-established, it was also customary to appoint someone without party affiliation. This did not pertain, however, to career diplomats who later became party members, such as Katō Takaaki, who served as foreign minister in the second Ōkuma cabinet (a career diplomat, but then president of the Rikken Dōshikai [Constitutional Association of Friends]). There were also cases in which the prime minister would concurrently hold the post of foreign minister, as in Tanaka Giichi's cabinet in the late 1920s.

There were eight other ministerial posts besides the three just mentioned. Of them, that of minister of home affairs was of particular importance, since this ministry controlled the police and appointed and supervised the governors of all the prefectures. Next in importance was the minister of finance, usually selected from among career bureaucrats in the ministry itself or from among the business elite. The minister of agriculture and commerce was also seen as an important post, for its role in the development of industry. The remaining ministerial positions—justice, railways, communications, and education—were seen as less significant, though this could be affected by the stature of the appointee.

The Yamamoto cabinet was an impressive lineup. Tanaka Giichi was serving for the second time as army minister and regarded at the time as a future candidate for the prime ministership. Den Kenjirō was a trusted associate of Yamagata Aritomo, had served as governor-general of Taiwan in Hara Takashi's government, and was also seen as a possible future prime minister, as was Minister of Finance Inoue Junnosuke. Inukai Tsuyoshi was a veteran politician since the opening of the first Diet session, and would also have been a reasonable choice for the top post. And Hiranuma Kiichirō was a powerful and capable justice ministry bureaucrat.

The posts equivalent to ministers were also filled by able individuals. Kabayama Sukehide, a Satsuma man, was a graduate of Yale and of Yale Law School, where he earned a doctorate in law, after which he worked in the Ministry of Colonial Affairs and the Ministry of Education, and served as executive director of the South Manchurian Railway Company. Matsumoto Jōji was a professor of commercial law at Tokyo Imperial University who in addition worked for the Cabinet Legislation Bureau and served as vice president of the South Manchurian Railway Company. He is famous in the postwar period for his role in drafting a proposed revision of the constitution as a member of Shidehara Kijūrō's cabinet.

Planning for Universal Manhood Suffrage

Thus the Yamamoto cabinet was a cabinet of major political figures—almost all potential prime ministers in their own right—presided over by Yamamoto himself. In 1913, when the Katsura Tarō government was paralyzed by opposition from the Movement to Protect Constitutional Government, Yamamoto pressed him to resign and took over the reins of government himself, presenting a bold challenge to such strongholds of the Chōshū clique as the army, the office of the governor-general of Korea, and the South Manchurian Railway Company.

Now it was the Seiyūkai that Yamamoto was challenging. The Seiyūkai had won an absolute majority in the general election of 1920, but the party was riven with internal discord and not as strong a force politically as it might have been. Moreover, at a time when public opinion was turning decisively in favor of universal manhood suffrage, its stance continued to be that the time was not yet ripe for such reform.

Inukai was publicly criticized for agreeing to join the Yamamoto cabinet despite the refusal of the leaders of the other parties to participate, but said that his own participation was for the purpose of implementing universal suffrage. Gotō Shinpei made similar claims. Gotō had previously managed the general election campaign supporting the Terauchi cabinet, challenging the current Kenseikai majority as "unnatural," and deftly fighting to demolish it. Now he appeared poised to use universal suffrage as the standard around which to rally a similar demolition of the Seiyūkai majority. And in fact, the political program announced by the Yamamoto cabinet in October 1923 included the implementation of universal suffrage.

Yokota Sennosuke of the mainstream faction of the Seiyūkai is said to have anticipated that Yamamoto's cabinet would dissolve the Diet and seek new elections, and remarked that "if there is a dissolution, the combination of Yamamoto's strength after having awaited this opportunity for a decade, Gotō's surging popularity, Inukai's latent power, and pressure from Hiranuma will probably mean that the Seiyūkai majority will be completely destroyed." Even after the collapse of the Yamamoto cabinet, Yokota still said it was the most formidable he had seen, and lamented the fact that the old guard of the Seiyūkai did not seem to comprehend that the political parties not only had to change with the times, but in fact needed to lead such change (Oka Yoshitake, *Tenkanki no Taishō* [Taishō: Period of transition]).

The Issue of Reconstruction

The most pressing challenge facing the Yamamoto cabinet was that of reconstruction after the great earthquake. And it was Gotō Shinpei who was assigned primary responsibility for this task. Gotō had shown extraordinary skill as a colonial bureaucrat, serving as the chief civil administrator of the Government-General of Taiwan and as president of the South Manchurian Railway Company, and had then accepted new challenges as chief of the national Railway Bureau and minister of communications. From 1920 to 1923, Gotō had been mayor of Tokyo (now the governor of Tokyo), and he invited American historian and authority on urban administration Charles A. Beard to come to Japan to consult on an ambitious plan for urban renewal, beginning a relationship of deep mutual respect.

Gotō's plan for reconstruction was a bold one: simply put, he proposed using public bonds to buy up the devastated sections of the city, implement land readjustment and public infrastructure development, and, when the reconstruction projects were completed, sell or lease them as necessary to the private sector. To achieve this ambitious vision, Gotō created the Imperial Capital Reconstruction Council with Prime Minister Yamamoto as president, Gotō himself as director-general, and a membership that included the cabinet ministers, members of the Privy Council, and representatives of the two major political parties. The Bureau for Reconstruction of the Imperial Capital was also established, with Gotō as its director, to oversee the practical implementation of Gotō's plan.

However, there was fierce opposition to Gotō's plan from landlords and other stakeholders. No matter how beneficial this urban planning might be from a long-range perspective, it meant that even in the short term their land was expropriated, and also that issuing a large volume of government bonds to acquire land would almost inevitably lead to a sudden drop in the value of the bonds themselves.

Moreover, landholders had strong ties to the Seiyūkai. As noted, the Seiyūkai feared the Yamamoto cabinet and disliked Gotō. The result was that the Reconstruction Council cut Gotō's original proposal for a reconstruction budget of ¥3 billion (approximately ¥1.2 billion exclusive of land purchase costs) to ¥597 million, saying that rather than a hundred-year plan, what was needed were immediate relief measures. This represented less than one-fifth of what Gotō had asked for in total, and about half of the net costs.

Collapse of the Yamamoto Cabinet

Thus the Yamamoto cabinet experienced a serious blow to its plans in the Reconstruction Council, but took the resulting reconstruction budget to the Diet anyway. An extraordinary Diet session was convened on 11 December 1923, and there again the Seiyūkai opposed the budget bill, claiming that the amount was still excessive. As a result, the budget was cut by another ¥130 million, to ¥466 million.

During a press conference in his later years, Emperor Shōwa would remark on the fact that Gotō's master plan for recovery after the Great Kantō Earthquake had failed to be realized, and that if it had been, the devastation caused by the war would probably not have been as great. The earthquake was the first major incident that had confronted Crown Prince Hirohito in his new role as imperial regent, and as Emperor Shōwa he looked back with regret on the failure of Gotō's plan, for which he had entertained high hopes (Takahashi Hiroshi, *Heika, otazune mōshiagemasu* [Your highness, a question please]).

Another point of contention in the Diet was the problem of earthquake insurance. Normal insurance policies stipulated that damages incurred from major natural disasters such as earthquakes of this magnitude would not be covered. But the government wanted to provide subsidies that would allow insurance claims to be paid at a rate of 10 percent of the total. This, too, did not pass the Diet, and as a result Minister of Agriculture and Commerce Den Kenjirō resigned.

In addition, the Satsuma faction in the cabinet wanted no further conflict with the Seiyūkai, and put the brakes on introduction of a bill for universal manhood suffrage. Yamamoto had an opportunity to fight the Seiyūkai by dissolving the Diet and calling for an election—which might shift things in a direction more advantageous to both the recovery budget and earthquake insurance. But Yamamoto was seventy-one years old, and the vigor of his earlier days was waning. Nor was he strongly convinced that passage of universal suffrage was necessary.

The extraordinary session of the Diet concluded on 23 December, leaving the cabinet battered and bruised. Two days later, the ordinary session of the Diet was convened. But on 27 December, the imperial procession of Crown Prince and Regent Hirohito, who was on his way to attend the ceremony opening the Diet session, was attacked by a young anarchist with a pistol just as it was passing the Toranomon intersection. This assassination attempt failed, but the Yamamoto cabinet resigned en masse to take responsibility for what came to be known as the Toranomon Incident. Among the cabinet ministers, Inukai had been especially vocal in calling for a mass resignation. Inukai joined the Yamamoto cabinet intent on achieving universal manhood suffrage and, discontented by the lack of enthusiasm for this goal among the other members of the cabinet, had been looking for a way out.

2

Japan in the Era of Party Politics

~

Establishment of the Kiyoura Cabinet

With the collapse of the cabinet of Yamamoto Gonnohyōe, genrō Saionji Kinmochi, after consultation with fellow genrō Matsukata Masayoshi, petitioned the emperor to appoint Kiyoura Keigo, chairman of the Privy Council, to succeed Yamamoto as prime minister. Kiyoura was an influential member of the Yamagata clique, and had deep connections with the Kenkyūkai, long the dominant faction within the House of Peers. Kiyoura's first cabinet-level position was in 1896 as minister of justice in the second Matsukata cabinet. And in 1914, after the collapse of Yamamoto Gonnohyōe's first cabinet, Kiyoura had received the imperial order appointing him prime minister, but he was unable to secure the cooperation of the navy and the Seiyūkai in forming a cabinet and declined the post. After having served for many years as the vice chairman of the Privy Council, Kiyoura was promoted to chairman in 1922, succeeding Yamagata Aritomo after the latter's death. Thus, after a decade, Kiyoura finally had a second chance to become prime minister—and coincidentally, once more as successor to Yamamoto.

But the Seiyūkai was shocked by the appointment of Kiyoura as prime minister. Despite the fact that the party had an overwhelming majority in the House of Representatives, after the collapse of the cabinet of Takahashi Korekiyo in 1922 the party had been passed over in the process of nominating three prime ministers in a row—Katō Tomosaburō, Yamamoto, and

21

Kiyoura. So it was not surprising that members of the party were strongly opposed to the Kiyoura government. Despite this resistance from the Seiyūkai in the lower house, Kiyoura succeeded in receiving an official endorsement from the Kenkyūkai, the leading faction in the House of Peers, on 4 January 1924, and organized a cabinet on 7 January:

Prime minister: Kiyoura Keigo
Minister of foreign affairs: Matsui Keishirō
Minister of home affairs: Mizuno Rentarō (House of Peers)
Minister of finance: Shōda Kazue (House of Peers, Kenkyūkai)
Minister of the army: Ugaki Kazushige
Minister of the navy: Murakami Kakuichi
Minister of justice: Suzuki Kisaburō (House of Peers)
Minister of education: Egi Kazuyuki (House of Peers)
Minister of agriculture and commerce: Maeda Toshisada (House of
    Peers, Kenkyūkai)
Minister of communications: Fujimura Yoshirō (House of Peers,
    Kōseikai)
Minister of railways: Komatsu Kenjirō (House of Peers, Kenkyūkai)
Chief cabinet secretary: Kobashi Ichita
Director-general of the Cabinet Legislation Bureau: Matsumoto Jōji
    (to 10 January); Satake Sango

Rift in the Seiyūkai and the Movement to Protect Constitutional Government

On 15 January, at a meeting of the party's executives, Seiyūkai president Takahashi Korekiyo set forth a policy of staunch opposition to the Kiyoura cabinet, but this met with resistance from some party leaders, who argued that the Seiyūkai should be patient and support Kiyoura and wait for another opportunity to form a party cabinet. On 16 January this developed into a full-scale split in the party, with Yamamoto Tatsuo (former minister of finance and former minister of agriculture and commerce), Tokonami Takejirō (former minister of home affairs), Nakahashi Tokugorō (former minister of education), and Motoda Hajime (former minister of communications and former minister of railways) all declaring their intention to leave the party. The background to this was a long-standing division in the party reaching back to Takahashi's cabinet of 1921–1922, which fell as a result of conflict between his supporters who wanted to reorganize the cabinet and a faction that was against the reshuffle.

On 18 January the leaders of the Seiyūkai, Kenseikai, and Kakushin Kurabu met for talks that resulted in an agreement to coordinate their efforts

The Kiyoura Keigo cabinet (7 January–11 June 1924)
Kiyoura is on the right of the first row. This picture does not show Ugaki Kazushige, minister of the army. (From Kokusai shashin jōhō *[The international graphic], February 1924)*

toward achieving the goal of a true party cabinet. Meanwhile, on 29 January the group that had left the Seiyūkai organized itself as the Seiyū Hontō (True Seiyū Party). Although it began as a splinter group, the Seiyū Hontō faction immediately became the largest in the lower house, with 149 members, while only 129 members remained loyal to the Seiyūkai.

The coalition of the other three parties called themselves the Kenseikai (Movement to Protect Constitutional Government), styling itself after the earlier movement of 1912–1913 that went by the same name. But it did not display the spirit and enthusiasm of its predecessor.

The lack of enthusiasm was due to the fact that the Kenseikai was, at best, a fragile alliance of three parties without a common mission. While they spoke of establishing party government, they did not have a firm consensus on the key issue of the day, universal manhood suffrage. The Seiyūkai avoided taking a position on universal suffrage, and as a result had decided to let its candidates freely determine their own individual positions on this issue, and to pass a party resolution after the election. On the other hand, the Kenseikai wanted to avoid the reform of the House of Peers, a topic often discussed in tandem with proposals for universal suffrage. The president of the Kenseikai, Katō Takaaki, a viscount and former foreign minister, and Wakatsuki Reijirō, its de facto vice president, were both members of the House of Peers. The party itself was largely led by career bureaucrats.

In January 1924, Prime Minister Kiyoura dissolved the Diet before the end of a full term. Due to the effect of the Great Kantō Earthquake of 1923, however, a general election was postponed to 10 May, the scheduled expiration date of the term. It was exactly four years since the previous election. The result was a major victory for the three-party coalition, with the Seiyū Hontō reduced to a modest 114 seats.

In itself, the victory of this three-party coalition (termed the Goken Sanpa) was unsurprising. What was unexpected was the fact that the elitist Kenseikai became the party with the largest representation in the lower house, winning 154 seats. The Seiyūkai had been certain that it would emerge as the leading party, or, if not, that it could merge with the Kakushin Kurabu (Reform Club) to come out on top. But the Seiyūkai captured only 101 seats, so even a merger with the Kakushin Kurabu (29 seats) would leave it short of a majority.

So it was Kenseikai president Katō Takaaki who received the emperor's order to form a new cabinet. The Kenseikai had originally formed as a merger of the Rikken Dōshikai, the ruling party under the second Ōkuma Shigenobu government, with two other parties after the resignation of the Ōkuma cabinet in October 1916, giving it a majority in the Diet, but it was denied the opportunity to form a government at that time. After enduring almost eight years in the political wilderness, the party now had its chance.

Formation of the Katō Cabinet

Katō Takaaki, president of the Kenseikai, became the new prime minister. Born in 1860, Katō graduated from the University of Tokyo and joined the Mitsubishi group, whose founder, Iwasaki Yatarō, saw his potential, sending Katō overseas to study in England (1883–1885) and appointing him as an assistant manager at the Mitsubishi head office. Katō married Iwasaki's eldest daughter in 1886. In 1887, he was invited by Mutsu Munemitsu to join the Ministry of Foreign Affairs. Later, Katō shifted to the Ministry of Finance, where he served as a counselor and then as a bureau chief. In 1894 he was named Japan's envoy to Great Britain and became a staunch advocate of Anglo-Japanese cooperation. After serving as foreign minister in the fourth Itō Hirobumi cabinet in 1900 and the first Saionji Kinmochi cabinet in 1906, he became ambassador to Great Britain in 1908. He served as foreign minister twice more, in the third Katsura Tarō cabinet (1913) and the second

Leaders of the three-party coalition, the Goken Sanpa
(Front row, from left) *Katō Takaaki, Inukai Tsuyoshi, Takahashi Korekiyo. On 18 January 1924, the leaders of the three parties met and agreed to establish a coalition cabinet. The original caption for this photo, in* Kokusai shashin jōhō *(International Graphic), March 1924, satirized the meeting, saying, "It's great the dogs and monkeys are sitting down at the same table to chat about protecting the constitution, but how long will this last?"*

Ōkuma Shigenobu cabinet (1914–1915). In 1913, he joined Katsura's Rikken Dōshikai, becoming president of that party upon Katsura's death that autumn, and in 1916 became president of the newly formed Kenseikai.

Katō could pride himself on an illustrious career and his status as a key figure in the pro-British faction within the Ministry of Foreign Affairs. His self-confidence, however, was also his chief weakness. With the exception of his positions in the short-lived Itō and Katsura cabinets, he was prone to resign posts based on his principles and policies. He lacked the commitment or the patience to see anything through to the end.

Katō's most dubious legacy was as the author of the "Twenty-One Demands," notoriously forced on the Yuan Shikai government of China in 1915. At the time there was nothing especially ambitious or aggressive about this policy, which actually amounted to little more than an effort to confirm rights and privileges that Japan had already achieved in fact. But under Katō's leadership, the diplomacy was clumsy, and clever lobbying by the Chinese made the Japanese seem particularly aggressive and treacherous. Moreover, as foreign minister in the Ōkuma cabinet, Katō angered the genrō by ending the custom of sharing important diplomatic documents with them, in an attempt to consolidate the control of foreign policy within the foreign ministry itself. Katō's major diplomatic failure and the deterioration of his relationship with the genrō were factors that kept Katō from the prime ministership before this.

Katō's political skills were nothing like Hara Takashi's. Under Katō's leadership, the number of seats held by the Kenseikai in the lower house declined steadily, from 198 (52 percent) in October 1916 when the party was formed, to 108 (23 percent) in the fourteenth general election in May 1920 under the Hara cabinet. As might be expected, this was a source of discontent within the party. Katō survived as the party leader primarily because of his financial power. He was almost solely responsible for funding the party.

In this era of party politics, opposition parties played an important role. For example, when Matsukata Masayoshi proposed Katō Tomosaburō to succeed Takahashi Korekiyo as prime minister, Katō Takaaki was his second choice. It was the opposition to Katō Takaaki and the Kenseikai that made the choice of Katō Tomosaburō acceptable to the opposition parties. While it is true that this eagerness to divine the will of the genrō and prevent the majority party from forming a government was indicative of the immaturity of party politics in Japan, it also suggests the latent concern about Katō Takaaki and the Kenseikai. As the relative importance of the parties to the political system grew, the role of the opposition parties also became more important. Moreover, as the Seiyūkai gained strength in the Diet, even the conservative Katō Takaaki began to adopt policies that had more mass appeal, including support for universal manhood suffrage.

Because Katō was a committed Anglophile who played an important role in the establishment of the Anglo-Japanese alliance, he regretted the fact that the alliance was terminated at the Washington Conference of 1921–1922. Katō was critical of the Four-Power Treaty among Japan, the United States, Britain, and France that replaced the alliance, comparing it to watered-down whiskey. While it is true that the Four-Power Treaty was not as powerful a diplomatic instrument as the Anglo-Japanese alliance, it is doubtful that Katō could have secured a continuation of the alliance even if he had been prime minister, and we may assume that he also eventually came to understand the necessity of terminating the alliance with the British and seeking greater cooperation with the United States.

The lineup of Katō's cabinet, which included Takahashi Korekiyo, president of the Seiyūkai, and Inukai Tsuyoshi of the Kakushin Kurabu, was as follows:

Prime minister: Katō Takaaki (House of Peers, Kenseikai)
Minister of foreign affairs: Shidehara Kijūrō
Minister of home affairs: Wakatsuki Reijirō (House of Peers, Kenseikai)
Minister of finance: Hamaguchi Osachi (House of Representatives, Kenseikai)
Minister of the army: Ugaki Kazushige
Minister of the navy: Takarabe Takeshi
Minister of justice: Yokota Sennosuke (House of Representatives, Seiyūkai)
Minister of education: Okada Ryōhei (House of Peers)
Minister of agriculture and commerce: Takahashi Korekiyo (House of Representatives, Seiyūkai)
Minister of communications: Inukai Tsuyoshi (House of Representatives, Kakushin Kurabu)
Minister of railways: Sengoku Mitsugu (Kenseikai)
Chief cabinet secretary: Egi Tasuku (House of Peers, Kenseikai)
Director-general of the Cabinet Legislation Bureau: Tsukamoto Seiji

The army and navy ministers, the foreign minister, and the education minister were all drawn from outside the political parties; of the other ministers, five (including the chief cabinet secretary) were from the Kenseikai, two were from the Seiyūkai, and one was from the Kakushin Kurabu.

Enactment of Universal Manhood Suffrage

The first item on the agenda of the Katō cabinet was universal manhood suffrage. Even the Seiyūkai had abandoned its opposition, so passage of universal suffrage legislation in the House of Representatives was almost assured—but securing the assent of the House of Peers and the Privy Council was another matter. Approval of the Privy Council was the first hurdle for the revision of the electoral law, but the council believed that suffrage should be conditional upon an individual's capacity to earn an independent living, and wanted language inserted that would exclude anyone "receiving assistance from others." But this would prevent the vote from being given, for example, to university students receiving support from their parents. The government altered this to "receiving relief from others"—wording that could not be construed as parental assistance—and that the Privy Council accepted.

During the Diet deliberations, however, there was a protracted struggle over language, with the House of Peers wanting "relief" restored to "assistance" to exclude people such as university students. In the end, the wording adopted gave voting rights to "all males over the age of twenty-five, with the exception of individuals receiving public or private assistance for reasons of poverty"—thus giving students the right to vote because assistance to them by, say, their parents, was not for the reason of poverty. This compromise was finally arrived at on 29 March 1925, after three extensions of Diet session.

But passage of universal manhood suffrage was accompanied by enactment of the Peace Preservation Law. Politicians such as Hiranuma Kiichirō (later prime minister) argued that while many European countries had laws banning communist agitation, Japan did not, and that enacting universal suffrage without outlawing the Communist Party would invite the spread of "dangerous social movements." The result was the Peace Preservation Law, enacted on 19 March 1925, which established harsh penalties for individuals advocating the destruction of Japan's "national polity" (*kokutai*; i.e., the imperial system) or the abolition of the system of private property.

Tanaka Giichi Named President of the Seiyūkai

When the Diet adjourned, Takahashi Korekiyo called on Prime Minister Katō and gave his resignation from the cabinet. On 1 April 1925, the Ministry of Agriculture and Commerce had been split into two separate ministries, and Takahashi had been serving jointly as minister of commerce and industry as well as minister of agriculture and forestry. Takahashi also informed Katō of his intention to resign as president of the Seiyūkai, anticipating that Tanaka Giichi would take his place as party head. Katō strongly urged Takahashi to remain in his posts, but Takahashi would not change his mind, and on 10 April a meeting of the executives of the Seiyūkai resolved to appoint Tanaka as the new party president, a move confirmed at a special general assembly of the party on 14 April.

Takahashi had apparently reached his decision to retire from the party presidency sometime in the autumn of 1924. Gotō Shinpei, Itō Miyoji, Den Kenjirō, and Tanaka were all considered possible successors. But Itō had withdrawn from the center stage of politics some time before, and Takahashi regarded Gotō as too unpredictable in thought and behavior to serve as president. Age was also an issue. Someone younger than the retiring Takahashi was desirable. But at the end of 1924, Takahashi was seventy, Den was sixty-nine, and Gotō and Itō were both sixty-seven. Only Tanaka, at sixty, was relatively youthful. Tanaka was a career military man from Chōshū, but he had served as army minister in Hara Takashi's Seiyūkai cabinet (1918–1921), and enjoyed friendly relations within the party. When the Hara cabinet was having budgetary difficulty funding increases in defense spending for both the army and the navy, Tanaka played a key role by agreeing to an arrangement in which the navy would be given priority, on the condition

Crowd celebrating the enactment of universal manhood suffrage
A rally celebrating universal suffrage, held on the grounds of the Seiyōken restaurant in Ueno Park, Tokyo, on 5 May 1925, was attended by a cheering crowd of several thousand people and headed by dignitaries that included Prime Minister Katō Takaaki and the members of his cabinet, the speakers of both houses of the Diet, and the leaders of the Goken Sanpa three-party coalition. Photo courtesy of Kyodo News Images Inc.

that the army would receive an increase in funding in following years. Tanaka was aware of the fact that the navy's warships had specified service life-cycles and that planned expenditure for such ships could not be easily cut, so he deferred to the navy in these negotiations. His statesmanship in this situation greatly impressed Hara and the other Seiyūkai leaders. Genrō Saionji Kinmochi also appeared to have a favorable impression of Tanaka. Nor did it hurt that Tanaka was a cheerful sort who seemed suited to the role of party leader.

Tanaka was also well known as a founder of the Imperial Military Reservists Association, an organization that could serve as a potential ally for the Seiyūkai. And as we shall see, Tanaka was believed to have amassed a fairly substantial war chest of political funds.

The very fact that Tanaka had joined a political party was an indication of how strong the parties had become at this time. Even among Tanaka's elders in the Chōshū clique in the army, Katsura Tarō had also taken the plunge into party politics. But Katsura had founded his own party; in contrast, Tanaka had simply joined the Seiyūkai.

When Tanaka was confirmed as president of the Seiyūkai, Prime Minister Katō invited him to join the cabinet as a replacement for Takahashi. But Tanaka firmly declined the offer. As a result, Noda Utarō (Seiyūkai) was named minister of commerce and industries and Okazaki Kunisuke (Seiyūkai) was named minister of agriculture and forestry. But the solidarity of the coalition cabinet was weaker without the presence of the party president.

On 10 May, the Kakushin Kurabu decided to merge with the Seiyūkai. Then, on 26 May, Inukai Tsuyoshi announced his retirement from political life. The reason given was that he felt himself no longer able to adequately care for the friends and colleagues who had supported him for so many years (despite this attempted retirement, Inukai remained immensely popular with his constituents, who continued to vote him into office). With Inukai's resignation from the cabinet, Adachi Kenzō of the Kenseikai became minister of communications.

As a result of the merger, the Seiyūkai controlled 136 seats in the lower house, surpassing the Seiyū Hontō to become the second largest party, and diminishing the lead held by the Kenseikai. The Seiyūkai was now bent on toppling the Katō cabinet and forming its own government.

The Second Katō Cabinet

By the summer of 1925, two members of the cabinet affiliated with the Seiyūkai came into conflict with the Kenseikai members over the issue of tax reform. Unable to reach a consensus, the entire cabinet resigned. Forcing the resignation of the cabinet was an intentional, strategic move by the Seiyūkai. But Saionji Kinmochi, charged with recommending the next prime minister, once again saw that the imperial order went to Katō Takaaki. Although Saionji was usually indecisive, in this case even he could see the obvious manipulations by the Seiyūkai.

In the past, Saionji had not held Katō in especially high regard. For one thing, Katō had resigned his post as foreign minister in Saionji's first cabinet—but Saionji also was immensely displeased by the damage the "Twenty-One Demands" inflicted on China and on Japan's reputation in diplomatic relations. Saionji's view of Katō improved after his first term as prime minister. Later, in 1936, when Saionji bemoaned the absence of capable advisers to Emperor Shōwa, he included Katō when he said, "Looking back, Kido [Takayoshi], Ōkubo [Toshimichi], Itō [Hirobumi], and Katō Takaaki or, though somewhat less so, Hara Takashi were all outstanding men." (Harada Kumao, ed., *Tōan-kō seiwa* [Memoirs of Prince Saionji]). The fact that Saionji would include Katō and rank him above Hara is sur-

Tanaka Giichi with Gotō Shinpei and Tokonami Takejirō

Tanaka Giichi (right, 1864–1929), with Gotō Shinpei (center) and Tokonami Takejirō (left). During his army career, Tanaka worked tirelessly to establish and maintain the Imperial Military Reservists Association and the Young Mens Associations (Seinendan). When he became president of the Seiyūkai, Kojima Kazuo asked him if Tanaka thought the party could win the next election, and Tanaka boasted, "I have the support of three million military reservists."

prising, unless we realize that Saionji was an aristocrat, and he probably preferred the arrogant and stiff Katō to the clever and slightly unscrupulous dealmaker Hara.

Having been appointed prime minister a second time, Katō moved to fill the cabinet posts vacated by Seiyūkai members with members of the Kenseikai, organizing a single-party cabinet. But because the Kenseikai still did not command a parliamentary majority, overtures were made to the Seiyū Hontō. The latter was also being courted by the Seiyūkai, but as far as Tokonami Takejirō, president of the Seiyū Hontō, was concerned, if he returned to the Seiyūkai or his party merged with it again, it was likely that he would have to wait in line behind Tanaka Giichi for a chance at the prime ministership. He probably calculated that if he allied with the Kenseikai, it was possible that he might have a chance to become Katō's successor. Moreover, Yamamoto Tatsuo, one of the party elders of the Seiyū

Hontō, was also originally a Mitsubishi man, and was quite friendly with Katō. Before the opening of the Diet session in December, relations between the Seiyūkai and Seiyū Hontō were troubled, and they failed to reach consensus on the election of the chairmen of the standing committees. When the Diet opened on 26 December, the Seiyū Hontō appeared to be much more cooperative with the Kenseikai. Incensed by this, a faction of the Seiyū Hontō that had been hoping for a merger with the Seiyūkai, led by Nakahashi Tokugorō, bolted the party on 29 December, forming a group called the Dōkōkai (Association of the Like-Minded). Twenty-five members of this group returned to the Seiyūkai on 11 February 1926, giving it a total of 161 seats—which meant that the newly combined total for the Seiyūkai was only a few shy of that of the Kenseikai.

Even before these complex political maneuvers, Katō's health had been failing. When the Diet session opened in December 1925, he already appeared frail, and immediately after the Diet reconvened after the New Year's recess, he died on 28 January 1926.

Formation of the Wakatsuki Cabinet

The imperial order to form a new cabinet was handed down to Wakatsuki Reijirō, a member of the Kenseikai who had served as Katō's deputy prime minister. Saionji did not want Katō's death to produce a complete change in government. On 30 January 1926, Wakatsuki immediately formed a cabinet with the same lineup of ministers as the Katō cabinet.

Wakatsuki was born in 1866, graduated from the University of Tokyo, and entered the Ministry of Finance in 1892. He became director of the Bureau of Taxation in 1904, and in 1906 served as a vice minister of finance in the first Saionji cabinet. He later was posted to Britain and France in the capacity of vice minister of finance for international affairs, and served once again as vice minister of finance in the second Katsura Tarō cabinet. Since Katsura himself held the post of finance minister concurrently with the prime ministership, it would not be an exaggeration to state that Wakatsuki was the de facto minister of finance.

The close relationship between Wakatsuki and Katsura continued, and in 1911, when Katsura traveled to Russia and Europe, Wakatsuki accompanied him. When Katsura organized his third cabinet in 1912, Wakatsuki was named minister of finance, and in 1913 participated in the founding of the Rikken Dōshikai. After Katsura's death, Wakatsuki remained a member of that party, and served as finance minister in Ōkuma Shigenobu's second cabinet.

Wakatsuki was an unusually competent administrator, and one of the sharpest minds among the past prime ministers. Yet this was offset by a lack of persistence and decisionmaking ability. Max Weber once wrote that "politics is a strong and slow boring of hard boards" and in this respect Wakatsuki was not an ideal politician.

The Seiyūkai went on the warpath against the Wakatsuki cabinet. The party had been passed over for a total of six times in the formation of new governments—the cabinets of Katō Tomosaburō, Yamamoto Gonnohyōe, Kiyoura Keigo, first and second Katō Takaaki, and now the Wakatsuki cabinet.

The first opportunity to go after the Kenseikai was a bribery scandal involving the relocation of the Matsushima red-light district in Osaka, which came to light in February 1926. Both Seiyūkai and Kenseikai party executives were arrested, including Minoura Katsundo, one of the Kenseikai party elders. Even Prime Minister Wakatsuki was questioned in relation to the incident, and it was rumored that he might have to take political responsibility for the scandal and resign. And what made things worse, he was indicted for perjury by Minoura in November.

An even more serious problem arose with an incident involving Korean anarchist Park Yeol and his Japanese wife, Kaneko Fumiko, who were charged in September 1923 with possession of explosives and accused of plotting to assassinate the regent. In March 1926 the Supreme Court sentenced the couple to death, but their sentences were commuted by the emperor in April to life imprisonment. Kaneko, however, protested this commutation by committing suicide in prison in July.

Toward the end of July, a photograph of the couple in a casual embrace in an interrogation room at the courthouse somehow leaked to the press, and the Seiyūkai took this opportunity to attack the Wakatsuki cabinet for being lax in its handling of the case and being deficient in protecting the "decorum of the national polity (*kokutai*)." It was actually a fact that the authorities, in an effort to gain the cooperation of the accused, had permitted Park and Kaneko to see one another and even to have the photograph made.

In opposition to these attacks, in March, Nakano Seigō of the Kenseikai raised questions in the Diet about the large amounts of money that appeared to have changed hands at the time Tanaka Giichi was appointed president of the Seiyūkai, suggesting that when Tanaka had served as army minister at the time of the Siberian Intervention, a large quantity of gold bullion had gone missing, and that this was what Tanaka had used for political funds. The Seiyūkai countered by accusing Nakano of being a spy in the pay of the Soviet Union—a complete fabrication that soon became clear. Nonetheless, Minister of Army Ugaki Kazushige strongly opposed the accusations against Tanaka, so the Kenseikai dropped any further pursuit of the matter.

What were the facts? The Siberian Intervention was a military action that involved unusually large amounts of covert funds, and there was considerable suspicion about how these funds had been deployed. There had also been some internal whistle-blowing regarding covert funds during

Tanaka's tenure as army minister, which, with support from elements within the army who were opposed to Tanaka and Ugaki, eventually served as the basis for Nakano's accusations in the Diet. Documentary evidence available to us today confirms that covert army funds were in fact used for political purposes (Itō Takashi, *Shōwa-ki no seiji* [Politics of the Shōwa period]). It is thus highly probable that Tanaka misappropriated army covert funds.

Prosecutors continued to pursue this issue, and in the autumn of 1926 they appeared to be making progress. But public prosecutor Ishida Motoi, chief investigator on the case, died under mysterious circumstances at the end of October. Writer Matsumoto Seichō examined this incident in great detail in his *Shōwa-shi hakkutsu* (Unearthing the Shōwa period), concluding that it was likely that Ishida was murdered by an extra-parliamentary group affiliated with the Seiyūkai.

Wakatsuki Reijirō (1866–1949), minister of home affairs
As minister of home affairs in the cabinet of Katō Takaaki, Wakatsuki won high marks for his skill in maneuvering the law on universal manhood suffrage and the law on peace preservation through the Diet, and was appointed prime minister upon Katō's death in office. However, he was unable to successfully address the financial crisis of 1927, and resigned. During the period of the Pacific War he was one of the voices of moderation among Japan's elder statesmen. Photo by Nihon Denpō Tsūshinsha, courtesy of Kyodo News Images Inc.

Park Yeol (1902–1974) and Kaneko Fumiko (1903–1926)
Following the suppression of the March First Independence Movement in Korea in 1919, Park came to Japan and engaged in anarchist activities that included publication of a magazine whose name, Futei senjin *(Korean outlaws), played on a common epithet used against the Korean minority in Japan. In the wake of the Great Kantō Earthquake in 1923, Park and his wife, Kaneko, were arrested. Examining magistrate Tatematsu Kanekiyo fabricated a case of high treason against the couple, accusing them of conspiracy to assassinate the regent. When this photo of Park and Kaneko embracing in a courtroom was leaked, the incident blew up to even greater proportions, including the proposal of a vote of no confidence against the Wakatsuki cabinet. It is said that right-wing activist Kita Ikki was responsible for making the photo widely available. Photo courtesy of Kyodo News Images Inc.*

Compromise and Collapse

By the end of 1926, the conflict between the Seiyūkai and Kenseikai had become serious. The Kenseikai leadership was poised to dissolve the Diet. Adachi Kenzō, nicknamed the "God of Elections" for engineering the landslide victory of the ruling party at the time of Ōkuma Shigenobu's second cabinet in 1915, had been temporarily appointed as the interim minister of home affairs and began preparing for a new election. Genrō Saionji Kinmochi was also secretly hoping that dissolution of the Diet followed by a decisive general election would serve to end the political deadlock.

But it was precisely at this juncture, on 25 December 1926, that Emperor Taishō died. Prime Minister Wakatsuki, who was prone to indecision and had been unenthusiastic about dissolving the Diet, saw the death of the emperor as an opportunity for a political truce. He called for a temporary suspension of the disputes with the Seiyūkai and Seiyū Hontō on the grounds that such bitter political infighting was inappropriate for the commencement of the new era of Shōwa (Enlightened Peace), and the two parties accepted Wakatsuki's proposal, contingent upon his "serious and due consideration"—which strongly implied that they expected him, once the Diet session had ended, to choose an appropriate time to resign the prime ministership. As Wakatsuki later hinted in his memoirs, what may have led him to avoid dissolution of the Diet at this time was the fact that he was short of campaign funds, mainly because of his own inadequacy as a political fundraiser (Wakatsuki Reijirō, *Kofūan Kaikoroku* [Memoirs of Wakatsuki Reijirō]).

Other leaders of the Kenseikai were furious over Wakatsuki's move. Adachi, the "master of elections," was aggressively in favor of continuing the struggle, and asked Wakatsuki point-blank if he really intended to resign after the Diet session ended. In order to prevent a transfer of power to the Seiyūkai, negotiations to forge an alliance with the Seiyū Hontō were started in late February 1927. The idea was that the Kenseikai and Seiyū Hontō would keep the government out of the hands of the Seiyūkai by trading power back and forth between themselves. On March 1, a meeting of the lower-house members of the Kenseikai voted to approve this alliance.

The Financial Crisis of 1927

The Seiyūkai were isolated, and in order to topple the Kenseikai cabinet they seized upon two major issues—the financial crisis and problems in China. Let's examine the background of the financial crisis first.

Beginning with the post–World War I downturn in 1920, Japan slid into a chronic recession punctuated by a series of sharper economic panics. Then, in 1923, came the tragedy of the Great Kantō Earthquake. Immediately after the quake, the government issued a moratorium on loan repayments and set about providing relief to financial institutions in the areas impacted, issuing an ordinance that permitted the Bank of Japan to rediscount the commercial loans that had become unrecoverable as a result of the earthquake. The government, in turn, provided up to ¥100 million to cover the Bank of Japan's potential losses.

In the end, Bank of Japan rediscounts amounted to ¥430 million, and even though about half the amount was recovered, the shortfall was still about ¥200 million. Although it was not public knowledge at the time, the largest debtors were major trading companies such as Suzuki Shōten and Kuhara Shōji, two companies that had long been rumored to have questionable management. The government regarded this ¥200 million as unrecoverable, and after indemnifying the Bank of Japan for ¥100 million as per the ordinance, the idea was to have the Bank of Japan extend long-term loans to banks, which in turn would allow debtors to redeem their obligations over a ten-year period. This was the gist of the legislation the government introduced into the Diet in 1927 to try to solve the issue of the "earthquake bills." And indeed, it was a solution of sorts, but one that would mean bailing out Suzuki Shōten as well as the Bank of Taiwan, which had extended most of the questionable loans.

This financial crisis became an issue in hearings in the Diet at the time that the Kenseikai cabinet was under fierce attack from the Seiyūkai. At a hearing in the House of Representatives on 14 March, Minister of Finance Kataoka Naoharu rose to answer a question and mistakenly read aloud the contents of a memo passed to him by his staff, saying that the Tokyo Watanabe Bank had gone bankrupt that morning—which was actually not true at the time. The government legislation passed, but Kataoka's slip of the tongue triggered the failure of six small banks, including Watanabe. This was the first stage of what became a major financial crisis.

The shockwaves soon reached the Bank of Taiwan, which had extended nearly half of its outstanding loans, about ¥350 million, to Suzuki Shōten and its affiliated companies, and, as now became clear, most of the amount was not recoverable. On 26 March, the Bank of Taiwan announced that it was refusing any further credit to Suzuki Shōten, but this was too late.

On 13 April the government decided to issue an extraordinary imperial ordinance permitting the Bank of Japan to bail out the Bank of Taiwan. But when this was brought before the Privy Council for deliberation on 17 April, it was rejected.

The Seiyūkai used its full force to take advantage of this controversy in the Privy Council. But the decisive factor in the Privy Council was more the issue of China than that of the financial crisis itself. Itō Miyoji, the de facto power-holder in the Privy Council, was deeply dissatisfied with the way the foreign minister, Shidehara Kijūrō, had handled the anti-foreigner riots in Nanjing triggered on 24 March 1927 by the entry of Chiang Kaishek's Northern Expeditionary Army into the city. In a plenary session of the Privy Council, in the presence of the emperor, Itō openly criticized the government—not for the financial problems that were ostensibly the subject of the deliberations, but for the way in which the Wakatsuki cabinet was dealing with China policy and the riots, which were endangering the lives of Japanese civilians in China.

As a result of the failure of the extraordinary ordinance to pass the Privy Council, the Wakatsuki cabinet resigned, and the Bank of Taiwan and a number of other banks failed and were forced to suspend operations. Dissatisfaction in the Privy Council with the direction of the nation's foreign policy had led to rejection of an extraordinary imperial ordinance and invited major economic disorder. This was an unprecedented event.

From the time of its formation in January 1926, the Wakatsuki cabinet had been plagued by scandal. The erstwhile coalition that had somehow managed to accomplish the collective goal of promulgating universal manhood suffrage had now fallen into an intense, three-way power struggle. The Seiyūkai, in a fight for its life, was using desperate measures including taking advantage of political scandals. But in the midst of this struggle, it became obvious that the Kenseikai, not the Seiyūkai, had the upper hand. Wakatsuki, as prime minister and president of the Kensaikai, was at fault for not using the most powerful weapon in the arsenal of a democratic system—an election. But it also had become abundantly clear that these power struggles among the parties had disgusted the general public. As a result, it is ironic that after the passage of universal manhood suffrage, the curtain in Japan rose on a period of disastrous party politics.

The China Problem and Japan

The history of the Shōwa period was shaped by problems related to China. This includes the interests Japan had acquired on the Chinese mainland, as well as Manchuria, and the way in which these interests affected Japan's relations with the Western powers.

The Washington Treaty System and China

The history of the Shōwa period moved within the context of the interests Japan had acquired on the Chinese mainland and Manchuria, including not only the type of relations Japan was to establish with China, but also Japan's relations with the Western powers.

At the Washington Conference of 1921–1922, the Nine-Power Treaty concerning China was signed by Japan, Great Britain, the United States, France, Belgium, Portugal, Italy, the Netherlands, and China. This treaty, while tacitly acknowledging the existing rights and interests and concessions of the powers in China, broadly rejected any further expansion of special rights or privileges, calling for strict adherence to the principles of the Open Door and equality of opportunity. Here we must pause to review the situation pertaining in China at that time.

When the Washington Conference concluded in February 1922, the government in Beijing was regarded as the legitimate government of China.

But this government was in fact an uneasy coalition of various warlord factions that were almost continually in conflict with one another, and at best controlled only the territory in the vicinity of Beijing. The pro-Japanese Anhui clique (led by Duan Qirui) and the Zhili clique (led by Cao Kun and Wu Peifu), which was sympathetic to the Anglo-American powers, fought the brief Zhili-Anhui War in 1920, before the Washington Conference. Zhang Zuolin, the warlord of Manchuria and the leader of the Fengtian army, struck an alliance with the Zhili clique that led to their victory. For a time, a Zhili-Fengtian coalition government ruled Beijing, but conflict between the two cliques eventually deepened into open warfare in the spring of 1922. The result was another Zhili victory, and Zhang Zuolin and his Fengtian army retreated north of the Great Wall, back to Manchuria. This incident is now known as the First Zhili-Fengtian War.

Civil War and Nonintervention

In October 1924, the Second Zhili-Fengtian War broke out. Zhang Zuolin, who had been keeping an eye on the situation from his base in Manchuria, was the one who challenged the Zhili clique to renewed conflict, despite being the weaker of the rivals. It soon appeared that if things were allowed to run their course, the army of Wu Peifu of the Zhili clique would emerge victorious and pursue Zhang Zuolin back into Manchuria. Many Japanese wanted to avoid this outcome.

At the time, Katō Takaaki was prime minister of the three-party coalition cabinet, and his foreign minister, Shidehara Kijūrō, was famously dedicated to a noninterventionist policy in China. But many opinion leaders were calling for Japan to assist Zhang Zuolin, and even Katō, who had placed great confidence in Shidehara, as well as Takahashi Korekiyo, minister of agriculture and commerce, were contemplating sending troops in support of Zhang.

However, on 23 October a Zhili-clique general named Feng Yuxiang led a revolt against Wu Peifu, which caused the collapse of the Zhili clique and saved Zhang and his army. It appeared that Shidehara had been correct not to intervene. When news of the victory of Zhang Zuolin reached Tokyo, Takahashi vigorously shook Shidehara's hand to congratulate him for saving Japan's honor. Shidehara was deeply moved by both Takahashi's response and his own success in sticking to his principles.

However, Ugaki Kazushige, who was present in the cabinet room as minister of the army, viewed this scene with sarcasm. Ugaki knew that Zhang's victory and Feng Yuxiang's betrayal of the Zhili clique had been engineered by Lieutenant-Colonel Doihara Kenji, a Japanese military intelligence officer stationed in China. As Ugaki wrote in his diary, "It is both pitiable and completely ludicrous to see how smug they [Shidehara and

Takahashi] are about Feng's betrayal and Zhang's victory—without having a clue as to how this came about." (Tsunoda Jun, ed., *Ugaki Kazushige nikki* [Diary of Ugaki Kazushige])

November 1925 brought another incident in which Guo Songling, a Fengtian-clique general, revolted against Zhang Zuolin and attacked Zhang's headquarters at Fengtian, but was defeated with the assistance of Japanese forces garrisoned in that city. At the time, Zhang Zuolin was expanding his power south of the Great Wall (south of Shanhaikuan, the symbolic wall between Manchuria and China) after emerging victorious from the Second Zhili-Fengtian War. But he was coming into conflict with Feng Yuxiang. Meanwhile, Guo Songling did not feel he had been sufficiently rewarded for supporting Zhang and the Fengtian clique in the war, and was also being courted by the Kuomintang (KMT; Chinese Nationalist Party) and Feng Yuxiang, and so on 22 November 1925, Guo mobilized his troops against Zhang.

The Kwantung Army, which was the Japanese army group responsible for the protection of Japanese interests in Manchuria and thus deeply concerned with the situation in North China, saw Guo Songling as a threat, because he both was pro-Kuomintang and also close to the Chinese Communist Party (CCP). They saw the possible entry of Guo's forces into Manchuria as harmful to Japanese interests and called for intervention. In addition, on 27 November, Japanese residents in Manchuria requested additional troops or reinforcements to be sent from Japan.

Minister of Foreign Affairs Shidehara Kijūrō, once again, stated his position of nonintervention in China's internal affairs. But after consultation with Prime Minister Katō on 7 December, it was decided to increase the troops of the Kwantung Army and issue a warning on 8 December in the name of General Shirakawa Yoshinori, commander in chief of the Kwantung Army, to the effect that any disturbances in the peace and order of the railway zone of the Japanese-owned South Manchuria Railway or its vicinity would not be permitted. This in fact prevented Chinese forces from entering the railway zone on 15 December, aiding Zhang Zuolin's forces and frustrating those of Guo Songling, who was soon defeated and killed.

During this time, Ugaki vacillated. He had met Guo, and had friendly feelings toward him. Ugaki felt that Guo represented a new generation of Chinese leadership. But after brief hesitation, Ugaki finally chose to protect Zhang Zuolin. There are several points to be noted concerning this important turn of events.

First, Shidehara Kijūrō's well-known commitment to a policy of nonintervention in China did not apply in the north, where the Kwantung Army intervened to protect what they perceived as Japan's interests, which in this case was the support of Zhang Zuolin. Second, the situation was changing as the impact of Chinese nationalism started reaching North China. The Anhui clique, which had been supported by Japan during World War I, was now heavily influenced by the May Fourth Movement of 1919. With the rise of Chinese nationalism, support from Japan had become a liability. Wu Peifu, whose ascendance had been favored by the United States and Great Britain, and Guo Songling with his revolt, now derived their strength from the nationalistic Chinese groups, while the power of the self-serving warlords began to wane. Third, as the clashes between Chinese warring factions came closer to the border with Manchuria, the Japanese became even more interventionist, beginning first with the problem of Zhang Zuolin in Beijing, then next with the movement of the battle toward the Manchurian border, and finally with the battles along the corridor of the South Manchurian Railway. In short, as conflict gradually spread to northeastern China, the local Japanese troops on their own initiative intervened in an attempt to defend Japanese interests.

Ugaki Kazushige (1868–1956)
Ugaki, a career army officer and politician, served in a number of important posts, including minister of the army, governor-general of Korea, and minister of foreign affairs. In 1925, during his tenure as army minister in the Katō cabinet, he eliminated four infantry divisions in an effort to shift operating expenses to investments in state-of-the-art artillery and modern equipment for the remaining forces. His diary, Ugaki Kazushige nikki *(Misuzu Shobō, 1968, 1970, 1971) provides an uncompromising expression of his stance on army politics and his views on China. Photo courtesy of Kyodo News Images Inc.*

Shidehara Kijūrō (1872–1951)
*Serving two terms as foreign minister, Shidehara ushered in a unique period in the
history of foreign relations known as "Shidehara diplomacy," which emphasized international cooperation based on the framework of the Washington Treaty System. He
was later appointed to serve as prime minister after World War II (1945–1946).
Photo courtesy of Kyodo News Images Inc.*

The Tariff Conference in Beijing

A special conference on the Chinese customs tariff, an important international
meeting, was convened in Beijing just before the outbreak of the Guo
Songling incident. At the Washington Conference in 1921–1922, the great
powers had agreed on a policy of nonintervention in China. The intent was to
respect Chinese sovereignty and provide it with an opportunity for independent development, without active intervention from outside powers. But the
absence of intervention also meant that the Chinese government was deprived
of sources of funds it had previously been receiving from the great powers.

In order to stabilize China as a unified nation-state, the great powers
agreed that China should be granted the right to collect its own tariffs. This
was particularly important for a large country like China, where the central
government lacked the ability to collect taxes from remote areas. During the
later years of the Qing dynasty (1644–1911), customs administration had

Zhang Zuolin (1875–1928)
Warlord of the Fengtian clique, Zhang rose to prominence as a protégé of Yuan Shikai, and developed close relations with the Japanese military. Defeated in the First Zhili-Fengtian War, he was victorious in the second, winning control, for a time, of the government in Beijing. Photo courtesy of Kyodo News Images Inc.

come under the control of the British, largely as a lien on duties to recover loans and reparations. Thus, the ability of China to collect its own tariffs would immediately improve the finances of the central government.

The special conference on the Chinese customs tariff was originally supposed to convene immediately after the conclusion of the Washington Conference, but among the signatory countries, France asked to delay ratification because of a sudden drop in the value of the franc vis-à-vis gold. The Chinese still had outstanding debts to France incurred before World War I, and the French refused to convene the conference unless the Chinese agreed to repay debts in gold, rather than devalued in francs.[1]

Eventually the Chinese made concessions that allowed the conference to open in Beijing on 26 October 1925. In the original Nine-Power Treaty signed at the Washington Conference in 1922, an ad valorem tariff increase of 2.5 percent was permitted, as well as a 5 percent increase on luxury items. But there was also a condition to abolish the inland transit duties known as *lijin* that were charged at provincial borders as goods traveled through the inland of China. Naturally, this was a difficult issue, because tariff autonomy would increase the revenue of the fledgling central government at the expense of the regional governments, which often had considerable power. Yet the abolition of the *lijin* was also an important step toward the transformation of China into a centralized, modern nation-state.

At the tariff conference, Great Britain and the United States refused to recognize China's tariff autonomy, but thought a tariff hike to the level of 12.5 percent was acceptable. However, for Japan—which unlike the Anglo-American powers depended on the sale of cheap cotton textiles—a rise in tariffs of this proportion would be a major blow.

China asserted its right to tariff autonomy from the beginning of the conference, conflicting with Britain and the United States, which insisted this should be predicated on an abolition of the *lijin*. But Japan took the position to support tariff autonomy for China as long as tariffs on inexpensive products (in fact, Japanese products) were kept low. This policy pitted Japanese interests against those of Britain and the United States, and had the possibility of currying favor with the Chinese. Shidehara diplomacy is commonly known for its emphasis on cooperation with the United States and Britain, but there were times when it adopted independent policies in an effort to draw closer to China.

Shigemitsu Mamoru, first secretary of the Japanese legation in Beijing, is said to have taken the lead in articulating this policy. Shigemitsu sometimes had pan-Asianist ideas that put him at odds with Shidehara's tilt toward the Anglo-American powers. This would later be demonstrated at the Greater East Asia Conference of 1943, and at a number of points in the early postwar period.

In any case the tariff conference was one of the few hopes to implement an agreement from the Washington Conference that could give assistance to China. But the conference was unable to reach an agreement, and broke up in the summer of 1926. For the great powers, it was a significant missed opportunity.

The United Front

While these events were occurring, Sun Yat-sen's Kuomintang was active in South China. In 1917, Sun organized a military government of constitutional protection in Guangdong, followed in 1920 by a Guangdong government, but these were dependent upon the power of warlord factions in the Guangzhou (Canton) region, and foreign observers largely dismissed Sun Yat-sen as an isolated idealist and dreamer.

But the situation began to change significantly with the establishment of a united front between the KMT and the Chinese Communist Party in

1924. In January, Sun convened the first national congress of the Kuomintang in Guangzhou, shifting the party to a program that included alliance with the Soviet Union, acceptance of the CCP, and support for workers and peasants. The aim was a nationalist revolution, unifying the national bourgeoisie, intellectuals, peasants, and workers for the unification of China and its liberation from imperialism and warlordism.

In June 1924, a Nationalist military academy was established at Whampoa Military Academy (Huangpu) in Guangzhou, with Chiang Kai-shek as its commandant, and a training institute for the peasant movement was attached to it. The ideology of the KMT was founded upon Sun's "Three People's Principles" (nationalism, popular rights, and people's livelihood), but now communist organizing principles were being added to this, and cooperation with the CCP was also bringing in support from the Soviet Union. The Whampoa Military Academy aimed at training military men who would not hesitate to sacrifice their lives in service to the revolution; in less than two years it had produced 2,300 new officers. Funding and weapons were provided by the Soviet Union, which also sent advisers, among the most powerful of whom was Mikhail Markovich Borodin.

In November 1924, Sun Yat-sen departed Guangzhou to attend a conference on national reunification, stopping over in Japan on his way. There he advocated what he called a "Greater Asianism," arguing that instead of acting in concert with the Anglo-American powers, Japan should align itself with China.

But Sun was seen in Japan as a revolutionary dreamer. Minister of Foreign Affairs Shidehara and other Japanese leaders had their eyes on the conflicts among the northern warlord factions, and looked coldly upon Sun's alliance with the Soviets. But there were people in Japan who had longstanding friendships with Sun, among them Inukai Tsuyoshi.

After leaving Japan, Sun went to Beijing, where he made an appeal at a conference for abrogation of the unequal treaties China had signed with the Western powers and Japan. Sun died in Beijing, away from home, in March 1925. Sun had been willing in many respects to compromise, and had attempted to find common ground with both the northern warlords and Japan. But in the meantime, the power of the Chinese Communist Party continued to grow.

The May Thirtieth Movement was indicative of the new power of the CCP. In February 1925, a strike that began at a Japanese cotton spinning factory in Shanghai escalated into a movement, and by May the protests developed into a demonstration of more than 2,000 people calling for the end of Japanese and British imperialism and a return to China of the foreign concessions (residential and commercial areas leased by the foreign powers from China that possessed extraterritorial administrative and legal rights). When about a hundred of the demonstrators were arrested, a much larger demonstration of more than 10,000 people occurred on 30 May. British police fired into the crowd, killing ten and wounding fifteen others, and fifty-three people were arrested. After this, a wave of demonstrations spread to other Chinese cities—Wuhan, Wuchang, Hankou, and Guangzhou. Behind the demonstrations was agitation by the CCP, demonstrating its differences with the right wing of the KMT, which preferred a more moderate and incremental approach.

Progress of the Northern Expedition

On 9 July 1926, the Kuomintang in Guangzhou, with Chiang Kai-shek as commander-in-chief of its National Revolutionary Army (NRA), commenced its Northern Expedition. The initial goal of the northward march was to capture the area around Hankou, held by Wu Peifu of the Beiyang clique, and then Nanchang, where Sun Chuanfang had his forces. By mid-August the Nationalists had taken Changsha, the capital of Hunan. They

Chiang Kai-shek (1887–1975)
After training in artillery at Baoding Military School, Chiang went to Japan for further studies. It was there he met Sun Yat-sen while he was serving in a field artillery regiment of the Imperial Japanese Army at the time of the Revolution of 1911, which brought his immediate return to China. After being appointed commandant of Whampoa Military Academy he gained de facto control of the KMT, and initiated the Northern Expedition. (© The Mainichi Newspapers)

seized Hanyang on 6 September, Hankou on 7 September, and Wuchang on 10 October—the three cities now known as Wuhan. In November, they fought and defeated Sun Chuanfang's army and controlled Nanchang.

Chiang Kai-shek spent the Chinese New Year (early February) of 1927 in Nanchang. By 20 March, the Northern Expedition forces had reached the outskirts of Shanghai—where the foreign concessions and foreign population were concentrated. He wanted to avoid serious fighting in this area. The Nationalist army was able to negotiate its entrance into the foreign concessions, but the Communist Party was powerful in the Chinese areas of the city.

The Northern Exhibition now headed from Shanghai to Nanjing. It met with little resistance, but when the army entered the city, it ran amok, resulting in a rash of attacks, lootings, and violence and arson against foreign consulates and residents, and a number of foreigners were shot. This was in March, and the incident dealt a serious shock to Britain, the United States, and Japan.

Behind these incidents was a long smoldering anger at the imperialist powers—fanned by the agitation of forces under Communist Party influence. Foreign Minister Shidehara responded at this time with considerable restraint, permitting only a minimal landing force to be dispatched. As a result, in the course of the Nanjing Incident, while the Japanese consulate and other facilities were attacked and a hundred or so Japanese residents were subjected to violence, there was not a single fatality. In the case of the Hankou Incident on 3 April as well, Shidehara responded with great patience, and did not accede to a British proposal for a joint military intervention. Shidehara was well aware that these incidents were supported by CCP agitation. He reasoned that if a hard-line approach were adopted in response, not only would there be greater loss of Japanese lives, but Chiang Kai-shek's position would be endangered as well, which, he calculated, would result in greater expansion of Communist power.

Somewhat before this, the left wing of the Kuomintang had joined with the CCP to create the Wuhan National Government. Shidehara demanded that Chiang Kai-shek take charge of the situation as supreme commander. On 12 April, Chiang initiated a coup d'état in Shanghai, and set about suppressing the CCP. On 18 April, Chiang set up a rival government in Nanjing and, not long afterward, in July 1927, the left-wing faction of the KMT under the leadership of Wang Jingwei broke off its ties to the CCP and agreed to merge with the Nanjing government. As a result it can be said that Shidehara's policies were reasonable.

However, before these events took place, on 17 April 1927, the cabinet of Wakatsuki Reijirō collapsed under a concerted attack from the Seiyūkai and the Privy Council for this reasonable and restrained China policy, and on 20 April, Tanaka Giichi formed a new cabinet.

48

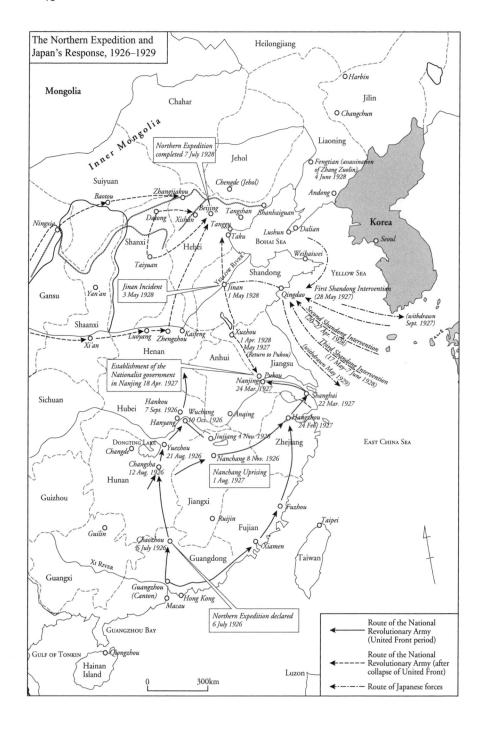

The Northern Expedition and
Japan's Response, 1926–1929

Mongolia

Heilongjiang

Chahar

Harbin

Jilin

Changchun

Inner Mongolia

Liaoning

Northern Expedition
completed 7 July 1928

Jehol

*Fengtian (assassination
of Zhang Zuolin)
4 June 1928*

Suiyuan

Chengde (Jehol)

Andong

Korea

Baotou

Zhangjiakou

Beijing

Tangshan *Shanhaiguan*

Lushun *Dalian*

Seoul

Ningxia

Datong *Xishan*

Tanggu

Taku

BOHAI SEA

Shanxi

Hebei

Weihaiwei

YELLOW SEA

Taiyuan

YELLOW RIVER

Shandong

Gansu

Yan'an

Jinan Incident
3 May 1928

*Jinan
1 May 1928*

Qingdao

*First Shandong Intervention
(28 May 1927)*

*(withdrawn
Sept. 1927)*

Shaanxi

Luoyang *Kaifeng*

Zhengzhou

*Xuzhou
1 Apr. 1928
May 1927
(Return to Pukou)*

*Second Shandong Intervention
(20–27 Apr. 1928)*

Xi'an

Henan

Anhui

Jiangsu

*Third Shandong Intervention
(17 May–June 1929)*

(withdrawn May 1928)

Establishment of the
Nationalist government
in Nanjing 18 Apr. 1927

*Nanjing
24 Mar. 1927*

Pukou

*Shanghai
22 Mar. 1927*

Sichuan

Hubei

*Hankou
7 Sept. 1926*

*Wuchang
10 Oct. 1926*

Anqing

*Hangzhou
24 Feb. 1927*

Hanyang

Jiujiang 4 Nov. 1926

Zhejiang

EAST CHINA SEA

DONGTING LAKE

Changde

*Yuezhou
21 Aug. 1926*

Nanchang 8 Nov. 1926

*Changsha
12 Aug. 1926*

Nanchang Uprising
1 Aug. 1927

Hunan

Guizhou

Jiangxi

Ruijin

Fuzhou

Taipei

Guilin

Fujian

*Chaozhou
6 July 1926*

Guangdong

Xiamen

Taiwan

XI RIVER

Guangxi

*Guangzhou
(Canton)*

Hong Kong

Macau

Northern Expedition declared
6 July 1926

GUANGZHOU BAY

GULF OF TONKIN

Qiongzhou

Hainan
Island

Luzon

0   300km

Route of the National
Revolutionary Army
(United Front period)

Route of the National
Revolutionary Army (after
collapse of United Front)

Route of Japanese forces

The Tanaka Giichi Cabinet

The New Cabinet Members

The entire Wakatsuki cabinet resigned on 17 April 1927, partly to take the blame for a financial crisis caused when the Privy Council had opposed issuing government bonds to prevent multiple bank failures. Makino Nobuaki, lord keeper of the privy seal, was immediately queried by the emperor concerning who should be chosen as the next prime minister; Makino responded that the emperor should consult with Saionji Kinmochi. Makino was of the opinion that "in conformity with the normal procedures of constitutional government, it was quite logical for Baron Tanaka to receive the imperial appointment," and Saionji also approved the appointment of Tanaka. Saionji had been extremely disappointed by the weakness of Wakatsuki's leadership. The determination of the Seiyūkai to overturn the cabinet had been crudely blatant, and Saionji had been displeased by the criticism of Shidehara's diplomacy. But he found Tanaka himself to be more moderate than the party rank and file—something that often happens in political parties—and had hopes for him.

Tanaka organized his cabinet on 20 April. The lineup was as follows:

Prime minister and minister of foreign affairs: Tanaka Giichi (House of Peers, Seiyūkai)

Minister of home affairs: Suzuki Kisaburō (House of Peers, Seiyūkai, Kenkyūkai)

Minister of finance: Takahashi Korekiyo (House of Representatives, Seiyūkai)

Minister of the army: Shirakawa Yoshinori

Minister of the navy: Takarabe Takeshi

Minister of justice: Hara Yoshimichi

Minister of education: Mitsuchi Chūzō (House of Representatives, Seiyūkai)

Minister of agriculture and forestry: Yamamoto Teijirō (House of Representatives, Seiyūkai)

Minister of commerce and industry: Nakahashi Tokugorō (House of Representatives, Seiyūkai)

Minister of communications: Mochizuki Keisuke (House of Representatives, Seiyūkai)

Minister of railways: Ogawa Heikichi (House of Representatives, Seiyūkai)

Chief cabinet secretary: Hatoyama Ichirō (House of Representatives, Seiyūkai)

Director of the Cabinet Legislation Bureau: Maeda Yonezō (House of Representatives, Seiyūkai)

A total of ten ministers in the Tanaka cabinet (including the two ministerial-grade posts) were members of the Seiyūkai. The other important feature of this cabinet was that Tanaka held the posts of prime minister and foreign minister concurrently, and that Suzuki Kisaburō was appointed home minister.

We will leave discussion of Tanaka as foreign minister aside for now, to look at the significance of Suzuki as home minister. Suzuki Kisaburō was a graduate of the University of Tokyo, after which he joined the Ministry of Justice and rose swiftly through the ranks, eventually serving as vice minister of justice during the second Ōkuma, Terauchi, and Hara cabinets, and was made a member of the House of Peers by imperial appointment in 1920. In 1921 he became the public prosecutor-general, and in 1924 was named minister of justice in the Kiyoura cabinet. He joined the Seiyūkai in 1925.

What gave weight to a figure with a career like Suzuki's was the fact that enormous sums of money were circulating in party politics and election fraud was endemic. As a result, the judiciary could be a great threat to a political party—or a great source of power. Hara Takashi had realized this early on, and in order to curb the independence of the judiciary had experimented with the introduction of a jury system (Mitani Taichirō, *Kindai nihon no shihō to baishinsei* [The judiciary and the jury system in modern Japan]). While working to restrain the judiciary in this way, Hara also forged close relationships with powerful figures in the ministry of justice such as Hiranuma Kiichirō and Suzuki Kisaburō, in an effort to bring the judicial branch of government into a well-disposed neutrality—or at least an absence of animosity—toward the Seiyūkai.

That a figure such as Suzuki, who did not have a particularly favorable opinion of the parties to begin with, was led to join the Seiyūkai, tells us much about what a powerful force the parties had become. Conversely, Suzuki's elevation to the crucial post of home minister so soon after joining the party indicates the degree of importance he was accorded. The chief cabinet secretary, Hatoyama Ichirō, was Suzuki's brother-in-law. It was rumored that in 1921, when Mori Tsutomu, then parliamentary vice minister of foreign affairs, seemed in danger of being indicted in a bribery scandal involving the South Manchuria Railway, Hatoyama had called on Suzuki to lend his support to extricate himself from the crisis. The new political force represented by Suzuki, Hatoyama, and Mori seemed to be overtaking that of the post-Hara leaders of the Seiyūkai such as Ogawa Heikichi and Mochizuki Keisuke.

Aftermath of the Financial Crisis and the First Shandong Intervention

The first order of business for the new cabinet was dealing with the aftermath of the financial crisis. After the Privy Council refused to approve its extraordinary ordinance and the Wakatsuki cabinet collapsed, there was a run on the banks, and the Bank of Taiwan was forced to temporarily suspend all transactions at its branches in Japan.

The new cabinet called on banks nationwide to participate in a two-day voluntary closure, during which it implemented an extraordinary ordinance mandating a three-week moratorium on payments. This time, the Privy Council swiftly approved the measure. In the meantime the Bank of Japan printed an enormous volume of new banknotes that it lent to banks across the country. This was so hastily done that one run of ¥200 notes was printed on only one side.

On 10 May 1927, when the banks reopened, the tellers' windows were armed with a mountain of fresh banknotes, and further panic was averted. Minister of Finance Takahashi Korekiyo had ordered that the Bank of Japan be authorized to make special advances of up to ¥500 million under government guarantee, aimed at quieting the crisis. Even so, forty-four banks were forced to cease operations, including Jūgo Bank, which served the Ministry of Imperial Household and whose president was Matsukata Iwao, eldest son of the genrō Matsukata Masayoshi, and Ōmi Bank, who had deep ties to the Osaka textile industry.

As soon as Takahashi had completed this cleanup of the financial crisis, he resigned as finance minister. He was replaced in that post by Mitsuchi Chūzō, who had been serving as minister of education, and Mizuno Rentarō was appointed to replace Mitsuchi as minister of education. Mitsuchi was a confidant of Takahashi's who had previously served as chief cabinet secretary in Takahashi's cabinet. Mizuno was a home ministry bureaucrat with close ties to Hara Takashi and had served as home minister in the Terauchi, Katō Tomosaburō, and Kiyoura cabinets. He had joined the Seiyūkai in 1926. With the financial crisis more or less under control, Tanaka embarked on the Shandong Intervention.

The biggest public promise Tanaka had made in the campaign concerned continental policy. The Seiyūkai, which had savagely criticized Shidehara's diplomacy in 1926–1927, had to provide the public with a viable alternative. Tanaka aimed at accomplishing this single-handedly, serving simultaneously as prime minister and foreign minister.

The result was the First Shandong Intervention. On 28 May 1927, the government sent troops to the Shandong Peninsula in China, in the name of protecting Japanese residents during the unrest created by the Kuomintang's Northern Expedition. But the government exercised extreme caution to avoid a collision with Chinese forces, and it looked for the first opportunity to withdraw the troops. The withdrawal was completed on 8 September, without major incident.

The Eastern Conference (Tōhō Kaigi)

After these emergency measures were concluded, Tanaka invited Japanese diplomats and military officials stationed in China to come to Tokyo on 27 June for what was called the Eastern Conference, a high-level reexamination of Japanese policy in continental Asia. Participants included Prime Minister Tanaka and his cabinet ministers; Yoshizawa Kenkichi, minister to China; Yoshida Shigeru, consul-general in Fengtian; the counsel-generals in Hankou and Shanghai; the governor-general of the Kwantung Leased Territory; the director of the Police Administration Bureau; the government-general of Korea; Mutō Nobuyoshi, commander of the Kwantung Army; Mori Tsutomu, parliamentary vice minister of foreign affairs; Debuchi Katsuji, vice minister of foreign affairs; and the chiefs of relevant bureaus and departments in the foreign ministry, finance ministry, and the ministries of the army and navy. A similar conference had been held once before, during Hara Takashi's cabinet, but this one was convened with even greater fanfare.

On 1 July 1927, after a full week of discussions, Minister of Foreign Affairs Tanaka announced his "Tai-Shi seisaku kōryō" (Outline for a policy toward China), consisting of the following points: first, Japan would observe a policy of neutrality regarding China proper, but would take resolute measures of self-defense to protect the Japanese concessions and the lives and property of Japanese residents whenever they were threatened; and second, Japan's special position in the Manchuria-Mongolia region (i.e., South Manchuria and eastern Inner Mongolia) would be respected, with aid and support given to individuals or groups making constructive efforts to stabilize the political situation. Thus, while clearly distinguishing between China proper and the Manchuria-Mongolia region, this document attempted to deal with them as a unified whole.

I have previously explained the term "continental policy" as connoting Japan's China policy plus its Manchurian policy. In other words, "continental policy" was the overall term for two different but intimately related policy lines: those concerned with how to relate to China, and those concerned with how to develop the interests and concessions Japan had established in Manchuria. This was certainly the nature of the foreign policy of the Tanaka cabinet.

A document that saw wide circulation in connection with this conference was the so-called Tanaka Memorial. Supposedly a memorial from Prime Minister Tanaka to the emperor outlining a detailed plan for Japanese conquest of Manchuria and Mongolia, it was later taken up at the International Military Tribunal for the Far East, but today is regarded as a forgery.

In fact, it is clear from even a cursory examination that the memorial is bogus; what is peculiar is that debate over its veracity went on for as long as it did. First of all, the style is completely different from that of other documents prepared for submission to the emperor. Second, there are too many fundamental factual errors in its content. Third, the original Japanese source has never come to light (the memorial was originally published in Chinese). Despite this, there are people who claim that the clearest proof that the memorial is genuine is the fact that Japan's later invasion of the continent fundamentally advanced along the lines that it described. But simply because events unfolded in a manner similar to those described in the document does not mean that the document was a genuine secret plan on the part of those involved. If Japan was intending to conquer China, the pathway to doing so was largely predictable. But it is the nature of forgeries that they are largely true, with a small admixture of fiction. If they were mostly lies, no one would believe them. The "Tanaka Memorial" is a forgery—no more, no less. To make a great fuss over it is foolish.

Japan's Manchurian Policy

Concrete policy decisions made at the Eastern Conference included not to interfere in Chiang Kai-shek's efforts to unify China proper; not to seek new concessions, but to affirm Japan's intention to defend existing interests in China; and in Manchuria and Mongolia, to lend firm support to Zhang Zuolin while not merely defending but expanding Japanese interests in the region.

Tanaka's policies differed from those of Shidehara, but they were not a major deviation from the line traditionally followed by the foreign ministry. However, Yoshida Shigeru (consul-general in Fengtian and son-in-law of Makino) told Lord Keeper of the Privy Seal Makino Nobuaki that "too much weight is being given to past statements by the Seiyūkai, with a failure to give overall consideration to the nation's long-term interests; the result is a truly deplorable state of affairs that has placed the vice-minister [of foreign affairs, Debuchi Katsuji] and the bureau chiefs in a very difficult position" (Itō Takashi and Hirose Yoshihiro, eds., *Makino Nobuaki nikki* [Diary of Makino Nobuaki], 8 July 1927). Yoshida felt that this was largely due to the fact that a full-time foreign minister had not been appointed, and that Tanaka was unable to adequately oversee the affairs of the foreign ministry in addition to his duties as prime minister.

As the standard-bearer for policy toward Manchuria and Mongolia, Tanaka appointed Yamamoto Jōtarō of the Seiyūkai as president of the South Manchuria Railway Company on 20 July 1927. Yamamoto had spent twenty years in China as a representative of the Mitsui trading company, and later continued to be active in China-related business.

As soon as Yamamoto was appointed, he began tough negotiations with Zhang Zuolin that resulted in an agreement on 15 October to build five additional railways in Manchuria and Mongolia. The Yamamoto-Zhang agreement specified a line from Dunhua to Laotougou to Tumen; a line from Changchun to Dalai; a line from Jilin to Wuchang; a line from Taonan to Suolun; and a line from Yanji to Hailin. Japan would undertake the construction of these railways and provide loans, on the condition that the Chinese would not extend the existing Dafushan-Tongliao line past Tongliao, or build a line between Kaitong and Bueyo, as these would threaten the interests of the South Manchuria Railway Company. Zhang Zuolin put up a good deal of resistance, but by May 1928 construction contracts were signed for all of the proposed railways except the Jilin-Wuchang line. In short, in exchange for supporting Zhang Zuolin, Tanaka was working to expand Japan's interests and concessions in Manchuria.

On the other hand, Yoshida Shigeru, who as consul-general in Fengtian was at the front lines of Japanese diplomacy in Manchuria, was proposing what was in a sense an even more hard-line policy. He wanted to prevent the Beijing-Fengtian railway, which served as a feeder line for Zhang Zuolin's arsenal, from crossing the South Manchuria Railway main line. Moreover, there was no rapport between Yoshida and Zhang, and Yoshida made no attempt to foster any. In this regard, Yoshida was tougher than Tanaka. But he was also defending what he considered legitimate interests.

As for policies toward the China mainland, Tanaka was in accord with Chiang Kai-shek. Chiang had been defeated in the Battle of Xuzhou (31 July–4 August 1927) by the armies of the Fengtian clique and had retreated to Jiangnan. In August, the Japanese minister to China, Yoshizawa Kenkichi, returned from Tokyo to meet with Chiang and convey to him a personal message from Prime Minister Tanaka. The contents of that message remain unknown, but on 13 August, Chiang announced he was resigning from his official posts, and at the end of September he traveled to Japan. On 5 November, Tanaka met with Chiang and told him he thought no one other than Chiang was capable of unifying China. He advised Chiang to spend some time mustering his forces in South China, and that it would work to his advantage not to involve himself in the factional infighting of the northern warlords. He also expressed the hope that Chiang would suppress the Chinese Communist Party. For his part, Chiang requested that Tanaka not give aid to Zhang Zuolin, but support the southern forces instead.

The First Election Under Universal Manhood Suffrage

As the year 1927 drew to a close, the focus of the political world turned to the dissolution of the Diet and the next election. In May 1927, immediately after the establishment of the Tanaka cabinet, the Kenseikai and Seiyū

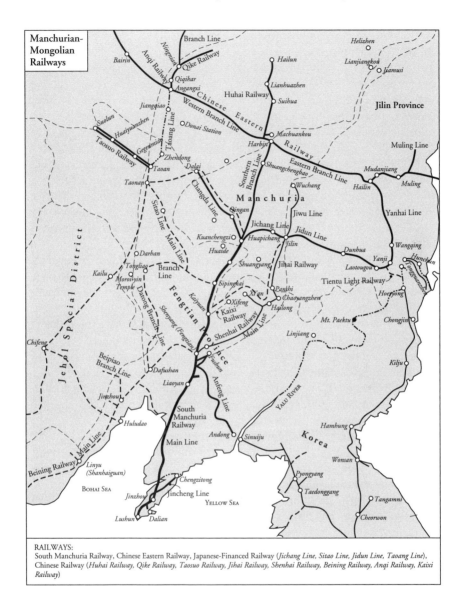

Manchurian-Mongolian Railways

RAILWAYS:
South Manchuria Railway, Chinese Eastern Railway, Japanese-Financed Railway (*Jichang Line, Sitao Line, Jidun Line, Taoang Line*), Chinese Railway (*Huhai Railway, Qike Railway, Taosuo Railway, Jihai Railway, Shenhai Railway, Beining Railway, Anqi Railway, Kaixi Railway*)

Hontō established a party called the Shintō Kurabu (New Party Club). In the coalition between the two parties that had supported the Wakatsuki cabinet, the agreement had been that a Seiyū Hontō cabinet would follow Wakatsuki's, which was dominated by the Kenseikai. But the advent of the Tanaka cabinet had made this impossible, and as a result the two parties decided to take a step further and merge. Thus, in June 1927, the Rikken Minseitō (Constitutional Democratic Party) was born. Hamaguchi Osachi became its president, while Wakatsuki Reijirō (former prime minister and former president of the Kenseikai) and Tokonami Takejirō (former president of the Seiyū Hontō) were named as the supreme advisers. However, twenty-four parliamentary members of the Seiyū Hontō were disgruntled with this merger and left the party to return to the Seiyūkai. Even after this, however, the Minseitō was the largest party in the House of Representatives, controlling 221 seats.

The thirty-nine prefectural assembly elections, taking place in September and October 1927, were closely watched as a prelude to the impending general election. They were the first elections under universal manhood suffrage, and the advantage went to the party in power: out of 1,488 elected officials, Seiyūkai accounted for 818, while 572 were affiliated with the Minseitō.

Despite this, when the Diet session opened, the Seiyūkai still controlled only 189 seats compared to the newly formed Minseitō's 221. The Seiyūkai campaigned on a traditional platform of transfer of the land tax from central to local government and decentralization of authority. It also worked to pack local governments with sympathetic officials and engaged in strenuous meddling in the election itself. On the eve of the election, Minister of Home Affairs Suzuki Kisaburō published a statement asserting that the order to form a cabinet was a prerogative of the emperor, not of a majority of Diet members, and that the Minseitō's advocacy of parliamentarianism was a violation of the spirit of the Constitution of the Empire of Japan, founded on the sovereign rights of the emperor. This was later heavily criticized as a statement denying the legitimacy of party politics, but it suggests how alarmed the Seiyūkai was at the prospect of losing the election.

When the election was finally held on 20 February 1928, out of 9.87 million valid votes cast, the Seiyūkai took 4.25 million and won 218 seats; the Minseitō took 4.27 million, winning 216 seats. So despite losing to the Minseitō in the total number of votes cast, the Seiyūkai barely managed to become the largest party in the lower house—though still short of a majority in the 466-seat chamber (see Table 2.1).

The fifty-fifth Diet, convened after the general election, was the first elected by universal manhood suffrage and the first after the establishment of a system that would be dominated by two major parties. Aside from the two main parties, six independent Diet members formed the Meiseikai (Association for Enlightened Government) to coordinate their activities, and another eight Diet members from the Shakai Minshūtō (Socialist People's Party) and other proletarian parties united with the aim of toppling the government.

While the Minseitō strategy was to initiate a vote of no confidence, among the minor parties there was a movement pursuing the responsibility of Suzuki Kisaburō, the home minister, for interference in the election. After a good deal of political maneuvering, Suzuki resigned on 3 May, the

Table 2.1   Results of the First Election Under Universal Manhood Suffrage, February 1928

Party	Candidates	Elected	Number of Votes
Seiyūkai (Friends of Constitutional Government Party)	432	218	4,250,848
Minseitō (Constitutional Democratic Party)	437	216	4,270,497
Independent	143	17	607,229
Kakushin Kurabu (Reform Club)	17	3	91,250
Jitsugyō Dōshikai (Businessmen's Association)	31	4	166,250
Shakai Minshūtō (Socialist People's Party)	17	4	120,044
Proletarian parties			
Rōdō Nōmintō (Labor-Farmer Party)	40	2	193,027
Nihon Rōnōtō (Japan Labor-Farmer Party)	15	1	91,170
Nihon Nōmintō (Japan Farmers Party)	9	0	35,750
Other regional proletarian parties	5	1	40,133
Total	1,146	466	9,866,198

Source: Shiryō ni yoru Nihon no ayumi: Kindai hen (Japan's progress as seen through historical documents: Modern times), Yoshikawa Kōbunkan, 1951.

Minseitō's no-confidence motion expired before being brought to a vote, and the Tanaka cabinet squeaked through to the end of the Diet session.

However, Suzuki's resignation shook up the Seiyūkai power structure. After the Diet closed on 23 May, Prime Minister Tanaka installed Mochizuki Keisuke, who had been serving as minister of communications, in Suzuki's vacated post of home minister. Kuhara Fusanosuke, who became communications minister, was a financier of Chōshū origin and a close associate of Tanaka's. He was a problematic individual who had just entered politics by winning a Diet seat in the recent election; he left the running of his businesses to his brother-in-law, Aikawa Yoshisuke,[2] who would later gain fame as the founder of Nissan and a developer of industry in Manchuria. Tanaka had wanted to make Kuhara the foreign minister and give him free rein with continental policy, but strong opposition from within the party forced Tanaka to rethink this and give him the communications ministry instead.

Even this compromise did not sit well with the old guard of the Seiyūkai, with strong opposition from Mitsuchi Chūzō, Mizuno Rentarō, and Koizumi Sakutarō. Koizumi left the party when his opinions were ignored, and Mizuno submitted his resignation as minister of education. This led to more confusion. Tanaka persuaded Mizuno to remain in his post with a personal message from the emperor. But this in turn was fiercely criticized as a manipulation of the emperor for political purposes, and Mizuno was forced to resign after all. He was replaced on 25 May by Shōda Kazue, a member of the Kenkyūkai in the House of Peers. This caused further repercussions, and on 2 June major parliamentary groups in the House of Peers published a joint statement censuring the government. When the government ignored this, criticism of the government in the House of Peers intensified, and in the 1928–1929 session of the Diet, the House of Peers passed a resolution of censure regarding the government's use of the emperor's message in the Mizuno affair.

Something else that should be mentioned concerning the Seiyūkai is the party's efforts to court Tokonami Takejirō. After the close of the Diet session, the Seiyūkai, in search of a parliamentary majority, began to make appeals to members of the former Seiyū Hontō within the Minseitō. On 1 August, Tokonami startled the public by suddenly announcing that he was leaving the Minseitō. He had been told that Saionji Kinmochi was dissatisfied with how both Shidehara and Tanaka had been handling China policy and, calculating that if he left the Minseitō he might attract as many as a hundred parliamentary followers from both the Minseitō and the Seiyūkai, he believed that he might stand a reasonable chance of becoming the next prime minister.

In the end, only twenty-seven Diet members followed him, with three more from minor parties joining in Tokonami's effort to form a new party. In September 1929, Tokonami ended up returning to the Seiyūkai, but by this time the Tanaka cabinet had resigned and a Minseitō cabinet under Hamaguchi Osachi had been formed.

The Second Shandong Intervention and the Jinan Incident

After having narrowly escaped intact from the 1928 Diet session, the Tanaka Giichi cabinet embarked on the Second Shandong Intervention. In China, Chiang Kai-shek had returned to his leadership posts in January 1928, and commenced the Second Northern Expedition in April. In response, Tanaka decided to send troops to the Shandong Peninsula once again, on the pretext of protecting Japanese residents. This was on 19 April. The following day, three infantry companies of the China Garrison Army stationed in Tianjin were sent to Jinan, and on 26 April the Sixth Division arrived from Kumamoto to Jinan, where these combined Japanese forces were soon to face forces of the Kuomintang's National Revolutionary Army. On the morning of 3 May, some NRA troops under the command of Feng Yuxiang looted a Japanese-owned store, sparking a military confrontation. A ceasefire agreement was quickly reached, but Japan sent reinforcements from the Kwantung Army, and the Army General Staff was determined to "chastise" the Chinese, making hard-line demands of the NRA for punishment of those responsible for looting the store, along with a formal apology. When these demands were not satisfied, Japanese forces, from 8 to 10 May, attacked the old walled city of Jinan, occupying it on 11 May. Some 5,000 Chinese were killed or wounded in this incident, known as the Jinan Incident, unleashing an explosion of Chinese resentment against Japan, and a nationwide boycott of Japanese goods. The Chinese government also made an official protest to the League of Nations. Meanwhile, on 9 May, the Tanaka cabinet approved a third dispatch of troops from Japan. By 17 May, withdrawal of Japanese forces had commenced, but slowly and with little progress. Negotiations concerning the incident dragged on into the following year before reaching a conclusion.

In fact, the Army General Staff had initially opposed sending more troops to China. The person really pushing for this is said to have been Mori Tsutomu, parliamentary vice minister of foreign affairs. In other words, the Second Shandong Expedition was a political decision, with little rational military value. And in the end, it turned out to be a major mistake.

In the aftermath of the incident, the National Revolutionary Army detoured around Shandong to avoid further conflict, and headed for Beijing. The armies of the northern warlords were believed to be at a disadvantage against Chiang Kai-shek's forces. If Zhang Zuolin were to fight against the NRA and lose, the conflict might expand to Manchuria, and Nationalist forces might establish a presence there. Alarmed by this, Japan warned that it would not permit such an incursion into Manchuria. The Nationalists were angered by this, and various foreign powers also voiced concern, albeit mutedly.

The Assassination of Zhang Zuolin

The progress of the Northern Expedition caused the Japanese army to completely change its viewpoint and policy stance. This was a major factor leading to the assassination of Zhang Zuolin, which delivered a fatal blow to the Tanaka cabinet and to Japan's China policies. This shift in viewpoint and policy was born out of a group of mid-level bureaucrats in the China department of Army General Staff headquarters in Tokyo.

In late October 1926, not long after the Northern Expedition had begun, Lieutenant-Colonel Sasaki Tōichi, an aide to the military attaché at the Japanese legation in Beijing, made a one-month inspection tour of South China. His assessment was that the old warlord factions were no longer enemies of the National Revolutionary Army, that the Kuomintang was deeply nationalistic and heavily influenced by the Chinese Communist Party, and that the result would be a Kuomintang seizure of power in China that would make Japanese relations with that country extremely difficult. In Sasaki's view, the Japanese army was underestimating the military power of the Kuomintang, while the Japanese diplomats did not understand the political danger posed by the party. According to him, the only person who shared this perspective was Yoshizawa Kenkichi, Japanese minister to China (Sasaki Tōichi, *Aru gunjin no jiden* [Autobiography of a soldier]). Yet this point of view was also held by Suzuki Teiichi, later a powerful figure in the Japanese army, who was also deeply involved in the issue of China (Nihon Kindai Shiryō Kenkyūkai, ed., *Suzuki Teiichi-shi danwa sokkiroku* [Transcripts of conversations with Mr. Suzuki Teiichi, vol. 1]).

This was clearly a different stance from that advocated by the Kwantung Army at the time of the Zhili-Fengtian Wars and the Guo Songling Incident, and from the policies of the Tanaka cabinet. In short, this new line of thought had concluded that Japan's interests could no longer be defended simply by supporting and manipulating Zhang Zuolin; what was needed was to place Manchuria directly under Japanese rule.

On 27 April 1928, Colonel Kōmoto Daisuke, a Kwantung Army staff officer, sent the following dispatch to Lieutenant-General Araki Sadao, chief of operations, and Lieutenant-General Matsui Iwane, chief of intelligence, at Army General Staff headquarters in Tokyo:

> Rather than wait for the southern faction to fail in the Northern Expedition, it is of the utmost importance to work toward the internal dissolution in the Manchuria-Mongolia region. If we simply wait passively for the advance of the Northern Expedition, I fear we will be missing a one-in-a-million chance; as someone who has always proclaimed the necessity of resolving the Manchuria-Mongolia issue, I cannot bear to sit idly by.
>
> Even if it is impossible to reverse the trends of the times, it is the duty of patriots to try to bend them toward advancing the fortunes of the nation. A voice ceaselessly assaults our ears from beyond the heavens, saying, 'Knowing what is right and failing to do it means a lack of courage.' (If it is necessary to sacrifice someone to resolve the issue of Manchuria and Mongolia, then I stand ready, sinful soul that I am, to be used as you see fit.). In light of the above, if through the good offices of your excellencies [Araki and Matsui] the will of the central leadership is secretly conveyed to me that some sort of action is required in the Manchuria-Mongolia region, I will exert all my efforts toward an appropriate resolution of the situation, and thus I make this special request to you (Tokyo Daigaku Hōgakubu Kindai Rippō Katei Kenkyūkai, ed., *Araki Sadao kankei monjo* [Papers of Araki Sadao]).

In other words, Kōmoto was proposing to use the advance of the Northern Expedition to create chaos within Manchuria and asking for either the tacit acknowledgment or active cooperation of the army leadership in this plan. On 4 June 1928, a special train from Beijing carrying Zhang Zuolin was blown up as it reached the crossing of the Beijing-Fengtian and South Manchuria Railways on the outskirts of Fengtian, and Zhang was killed in the explosion. Kōmoto had hoped that this incident would provoke Japan into all-out intervention in Manchuria, but this did not come to pass.

But as Kōmoto had also hoped, it did bring about a major shift of opinion within the military itself. And thus the assassination of Zhang Zuolin changed the direction of Japan.

The Kellogg-Briand Pact
and International Cooperation

Despite the situation just outlined, the Tanaka cabinet did not deviate from a fundamental policy line of international cooperation. Even the Shandong Interventions were not strongly criticized by the other great powers. In fact, though the Jinan was seen as an unfortunate incident, the Western powers too were having trouble with the rising tide of Chinese anti-imperialism, and there were even those who expressed envy at Japan's ability to take such a hard line with China (John Van Antwerp MacMurray, *How the Peace Was Lost*). In contrast to the declaration Japan issued regarding the preservation of stability in Manchuria, the great powers remained neutral with respect to the dispatch of Japanese troops to the Shandong Peninsula.

The representative example of the Tanaka cabinet's commitment to international cooperation was its participation in the General Treaty for the Renunciation of War as an Instrument of National Policy, also known as the Kellogg-Briand Pact. This treaty was proposed in 1927 by Aristide Briand, foreign minister of France, to US secretary of state Frank Billings Kellogg, and Kellogg advocated for its expansion into a treaty among the world's major powers. The main thrust of the treaty was conveyed in Article I: "The High Contracting Parties solemnly declare in the names of their respective peoples that they condemn recourse to war for the solution of international controversies, and renounce it as an instrument of national policy in their relations with one another." Article II, which promises the use of "pacific means" for "the settlement or solution of all disputes or conflicts," would later serve as the model for the first paragraph of Article 9 of the postwar constitution of Japan.

When invited to join the treaty negotiations in April 1928, Japan at first thought to try to gain an exemption for its activities in China, but in the end agreed to unconditional participation, contenting itself with a comment regarding the right of self-defense and an explanation of Japan's position toward China. The sponsoring powers had already affirmed that the treaty did not deny the right of self-defense, and so Japan participated without reservation.

In August, Japan dispatched Uchida Kōsai, a former foreign minister, as its commissioner plenipotentiary to the signing ceremony, at which he also explained Japan's position on the issue of China. This was not seen as significant. On the way home, Uchida visited the United States, where he met with Secretary Kellogg, but the Americans were indifferent to Japan's position. The Nine-Power Treaty signed previously in Washington, D.C., had committed the participating nations to frank discussions concerning any problems that might arise regarding China, but the United States did not seem to find the prevailing situation problematic. The figure who attempted to reconcile Japan's hard-line policy on the China question with a cooperative engagement with the United States and Britain was Yoshida Shigeru, who was appointed vice minister of foreign affairs on 24 July. It is quite telling that among the files Uchida carried with him on his international tour was one labeled "Shina mondai ni kansuru rekkoku kyōchō ikken" (Cooperation with the powers concerning the China issue).

Meanwhile, a major problem had emerged with the Kellogg-Briand Pact. Not with regard to its essential terms, but because of the phrase "in the names of their respective peoples" in Article I. In Japan, this was criticized as conflicting with the Constitution of the Empire of Japan, which located sovereignty in the person of the emperor, not the people. In fact, the government had become aware of this problem during the course of the treaty negotiations, and there was an exchange of memorandums that interpreted "in the names of" as being synonymous with "on behalf of," but this was not made public. At the end of September 1928, this phrase developed into a serious political issue in the Privy Council, and created lively discussions in the pages of the daily newspapers. In the end, a declaration was issued to the effect that this phrasing did not apply to Japan, and the issue was settled. But Uchida Kōsai found the issuance of this explanation regrettable, and he resigned from his position on the Privy Council.

This incident was in essence a trivial one, but could be seen as linked to the debate over the emperor as an organ of the state (*tennō kikansetsu*) because it touched upon principles such as imperial sovereignty and the nature of the national polity. As one might expect, legal scholar Minobe Tatsukichi, the leading proponent of the emperor-as-organ theory, did not see the language of the Kellogg-Briand Pact as conflicting with Japan's constitution.

The Beginning of Revolutionary Diplomacy in China

One reason that Prime Minister Tanaka was seeking closer contact with the United States and Britain in the summer of 1928 was because China had commenced a new diplomatic initiative. The Nationalist government was demanding revision of the unequal treaties, and on 19 July presented Okamoto Issaku, Japanese consul in Nanjing, with notification that it intended to abrogate the Sino-Japanese Treaty of Commerce and Navigation. At virtually the same time, on 25 July, the United States informed the Nationalist government in Nanjing of its approval for Chinese tariff autonomy—a response that was highly encouraging to China. On 9 June 1928, the National Revolutionary Army entered Beijing, and brought the Northern Expedition to a victorious conclusion. Beijing, whose name means "northern capital," was renamed Beiping, meaning "northern peace," and the nation was now declared to be united under the Nationalist government in Nanjing (meaning "southern capital").

On 7 August, Japan responded that it would not acknowledge such a unilateral abrogation of the treaty. But it responded fairly flexibly to China's unilateral tariff hikes and said that it was willing to sign a new treaty if the Chinese would agree to meet certain conditions.

In November 1928, the United States recognized the Nationalist government as the legitimate government of China, and the British and French followed suit in December. Also in December, Zhang Xueliang, son of Zhang Zuolin, raised the Nationalist flag (a white sun in a blue sky) over the three provinces of northeastern China—Fengtian (now Liaoning), Jilin, and Heilongjiang—the area that is commonly referred to as Manchuria. The Kuomintang unification of China was complete. Tariff talks continued, and on 30 January 1929, Japan agreed to China's revision of its import tariffs. But disputes continued, as Japan attempted to block collection of additional levies at three ports in Manchuria.

Meanwhile, Japanese special rights in Manchuria also became an issue. Zhang Xueliang was naturally not well-disposed toward Japan since Kōmoto Daisaku of the Kwantung Army had been behind the assassination of his father. An entry for 14 May in the *Diary of Makino Nobuaki* records an exchange between Zhang and Japanese consul-general Hayashi Kyūjirō. Hayashi was pressing strong demands on Zhang concerning a Jilin-Huining railway line, and declared, "I will stake my career on these demands," to which Zhang responded, "Then I must stake my life upon rejecting them." Makino treats this as an example of Hayashi's remarkable childishness, but it is also true that overall, what was described as an aggressive policy toward Manchuria and Mongolia bore little fruit. Makino went on to observe that when relatively unproblematic economic matters such as the Jilin-Huining line were blown out of proportion by politicians and the press, it stirred up alarm and suspicion on the part of the Chinese that could end only in failure.

Shortly thereafter, on 3 June 1929, the Tanaka cabinet finally recognized the Nationalist government. So we can see that the Tanaka cabinet did not adopt a consistently hard line toward China. If anything, it demonstrated a degree of flexibility. But the other powers were beginning to make concessions to China, and the careless diplomatic intransigence of the Seiyūkai and volatile public opinion had badly damaged the image of Tanaka's foreign policy. The Tanaka cabinet was not to blame for the assassination of Zhang Zuolin and other misfortunes, but overall its China policy had reached a dead end.

Collapse of the Tanaka Cabinet

The biggest issue at the end of 1929 was how to handle the aftermath of Zhang's assassination. Initially, Tanaka publicly acknowledged the incident and promised to severely punish those involved. But both the army and the Seiyūkai pushed back strongly against this policy. Ogawa Heikichi, who as railway minister was one of the first to learn of the incident, was vigorously opposed to revealing the facts to the public, and moved aggressively to try to prevent this.

For example, Ogawa had a lengthy talk with Tanaka on 8 December in which he said that if the incident were publicly announced, China would almost certainly, and understandably, demand a complete withdrawal of Japanese forces from Manchuria—something that Zhang Xueliang would definitely agree with, and that the foreign powers would also be likely to respond to positively. If this were to happen, it would mean that Japan would face a direct and fundamental threat to its concessions and interests in Manchuria.

During this talk, Tanaka was concerned about contradicting what he had already reported to the emperor (the exact contents are unknown). Ogawa comments on this in his diary:

> It is completely mistaken to say that it is impossible to conceal anything from the emperor. There is no need to conceal anything from the emperor. He can be spoken to frankly, and told the truth just as it is. It is just that he should also be told that the measures being taken at this time will have an important impact both at home and abroad, and must be approached with careful consideration and the best judgment. I quite forcefully explained that I hoped that the question of what should be done in this matter would be brought before the cabinet for a decision. Prime Minister Tanaka agreed to place a resolution before the cabinet. But it appeared that he could not bring himself to change his mind about how to proceed. He went on about how if the army minister would be more conciliatory, it might be possible to extend the Diet session by a bit, and so forth. Today I met with Yamamoto [Teijirō], the minister of agriculture and forestry, and talked for a bit. We both promised to try to prevent this incident from being made public. (Ogawa Heikichi Monjo Kenkyūkai, ed., *Ogawa Heikichi nikki* [Diary of Ogawa Heikichi], 8 December 1928)

On 11 December, Ogawa also met with Saionji Kinmochi because he suspected that Saionji was behind Tanaka's decision to publicly acknowledge the incident. And sure enough, Saionji said to Ogawa, "I agreed with Tanaka, and told him frankly that time was of the essence. I recall going so far as to say he should probably announce it before the Diet convened. Why don't you agree as well, and lend a hand in clearing away these abuses by the Army." Ogawa told him that this was impossible, and the two men argued back and forth for about an hour and a half, unable to reach agreement, before parting on a promise to think things over. Ogawa took the encounter as proof that Saionji was indeed behind Tanaka's decision to go public with the incident. "Yet Prince Saionji listened most intently to what I had to say regarding developments in the Diet and the situation in China, and made no effort to dispute it."

Two days later, on 13 December, Saionji sent a messenger to Ogawa, bearing a letter that read, in part: "I've given a great deal of thought to the things you discussed with me earlier, but I have been unable to find any grounds, moral or strategic, for changing my position. I simply thought I should let you know this." There was clearly a deep divide between Saionji and those who wanted to hush up the incident.

Eventually, Tanaka changed course. Minister of Imperial Household Makino Nobuaki, in his diary entry for 28 March 1929, recorded his astonishment at the change in Tanaka's attitude:

> [Prime Minister Tanaka] had stated that when the facts became clear and the necessary supporting documents were in order and the investigation complete, he was determined that a court martial would be convened, discipline restored in the army, and Japan's honor restored both at home and abroad. Moreover, he also said that while this might temporarily create animosity in China, in the long run the openness and honesty of the Japanese government would be recognized, and this might even provide an opportunity for the improvement of sentiment towards Japan. The eloquence with which the prime minister expressed this impressively high-minded attitude still rings in my ears. So I am absolutely astonished to hear him saying that we should announce to the public that the facts of the incident are unclear, that a few individuals should be subjected to administrative punishment, and the matter brought to a vague and ambiguous resolution. If he'd made this policy clear from the beginning, I would have been compelled to state my disagreement, but now that this fundamental reversal of position has been revealed, I find myself speechless. (Itō Takashi and Hirose Yoshihiro, eds., *Makino Nobuaki nikki* [Diary of Makino Nobuaki])

Makino predicted that the attempt to cover up the incident would inevitably be exposed, and create even larger problems. On 6 May, Makino said to Saionji that he had heard from the grand chamberlain that if Tanaka made his anticipated report to the emperor, the emperor intended to ask the prime minister to take responsibility for the incident by resigning, and since this was the situation, he asked Saionji to give due consideration to this matter. Saionji's response was that while this might lead to a change in government, further study was needed with regard to how this might affect the relationship between the emperor, as supreme commander, and the military.

However, on 25 June, two days before Tanaka was to meet with the emperor, Saionji suddenly said to Makino that there was really no precedent from the time of Emperor Meiji onward for what the emperor might say in this situation, and that he was opposed to the emperor explicitly asking for

Tanaka's resignation. Makino was taken aback, and asked Saionji to reconsider. But while Saionji called himself "a coward," he did not change his
mind. Makino allowed that Saionji had a point, but that informed opinion
was united in seeing that Tanaka had reached an impasse, that it was clear
he was trying to conceal the truth from the emperor regarding the problem
in Manchuria, and that in the present situation, with the political parties
seriously dysfunctional, the nation was depending upon the wisdom of the
emperor. Makino believed that the emperor's closest advisers could not risk
damaging this in any way, and wrote:

> If one thinks about it carefully, the situation at present is quite different
> from that of the Meiji era. This is not a case for painstaking research of
> precedent; the time has come when the emperor must express his own
> thoughts. Moreover, in the present circumstances. there is no need to fear
> that speaking out in this way might have a harmful impact upon the impe-
> rial house; I believe instead that healthy public opinion will receive this
> message gratefully and take it to heart. In any event, when I left Prince
> Saionji's residence today no conclusion had been reached. I have associ-
> ated with him for more than thirty years, and not once before has a matter
> been left unresolved in this way. (Itō Takashi and Hirose Yoshihiro, eds.,
> *Makino Nobuaki nikki* [Diary of Makino Nobuaki])

The shock experienced by Makino is palpable. Even more interesting is
the difference in how the two men, Makino and Saionji, interpreted the situation in relation to the institutions of constitutional monarchy. Makino had a
more idealistic and optimistic perspective on the role of the monarch. In contrast, Saionji was more cautious. And indeed, as Saionji feared, the genrō and
bloc of senior statesmen would come under increased criticism for what was
perceived as their role in the collapse of the Tanaka cabinet—something that
might actually have been averted if Makino's more forthright attitude had
prevailed. As it was, on 27 June 1929, Tanaka made his report to the emperor.
When the emperor remarked that it was different in content from what he had
been told previously, Tanaka was dumbfounded. His cabinet resigned en
masse, on the grounds that it had lost the confidence of the emperor.

Socialism and the Proletarian Parties

Toward Socialism

Now that the Cold War is over, it is difficult to explain the appeal socialism
once had. But it is impossible to speak of prewar Japan or any country in this
period without touching on socialism. This is not only because of the power
socialism possessed in its own right, but also because of the immense influence it exerted on anti-socialist ideologies and on the policies of the military.

The woes of the Tanaka cabinet

The Seiyūkai cabinet of Tanaka Giichi controlled a majority in the Diet through an alliance with the Shintō Kurabu formed by Tokonami Takejirō and other dissidents who had bolted from the Minseitō. But the cabinet was also faced with a number of thorny and pressing problems, not least of which was the assassination of Zhang Zuolin. The illustration is a political cartoon by Kitazawa Rakuten speculating satirically on the chances of the Tanaka cabinet making it through the fifty-sixth session of the Diet, convened in December 1928.

The first thing that must be stressed is that prewar Japanese society was one in which inequalities of income and wealth were much greater than they are today. Not just in Japan, but also throughout the world were work-ers like those depicted in Charlie Chaplin's *Modern Times*—either suffering from unemployment, or else forced to work brutally long days keeping up with the machines they tended. It was easy to see it as a society in which the rich were getting richer and the poor were getting poorer. Marxism was seen as providing the total answer to these economic and social problems. And not just in theoretical terms; the Russian Revolution of 1917 delivered a profound shock to Japan as well.

The period of Taishō democracy typified by political scientist Yoshino Sakuzō was relatively brief. His debut as a pundit came in 1913 (Taishō 2), but he really made his presence felt as the liberal champion of the era in November 1918, when he emerged victorious in a debate with members of the Rōninkai, an ultra-nationalist political group. But the students who supported Yoshino in this encounter had already begun leaning toward socialism by 1919 and 1920. Marxism was spreading rapidly among the elites of Japan's higher schools and imperial universities.

Formation of the Japanese Communist Party

It was in this context that a concrete movement arose to form a communist party in Japan. The initial impetus for this came from the Comintern (the Communist International, or The Third International), created in March 1919 to advance the cause of world revolution. The Comintern's first contact with Asia was in China, then experiencing a rising tide of nationalism. In early 1920, the year after the May Fourth Movement, the Comintern contacted Beijing University professors Li Dazhao and Chen Duxiu, who established cells in Shanghai in August and Beijing in September. The first national congress of the Communist Party of China convened in July 1921 in Shanghai.

In October 1920, a secret emissary from the Comintern arrived in Japan. As a result of the repression of the Meiji period, there were only a handful of socialists remaining in Japan, and they were kept under strict surveillance—figures such as Sakai Toshihiko (1871–1933), Yamakawa Hitoshi (1880–1958), and Arahata Kanson (1887–1981). The Comintern told Sakai and Yamakawa that it wanted them to travel to Shanghai to participate in the creation of a congress of Far Eastern socialists. But the High Treason Incident of 1910[3] and its suppression were still fresh in their memories, and they cautiously decided not to respond to this request.

It was Ōsugi Sakae (1885–1923), whose adventuresome personality led him to take up this dubious challenge, who ended up going to Shanghai. From the Comintern's standpoint, the anarchist Ōsugi was not an ideal partner, but it needed some point of contact with Japan. Ōsugi would not participate in the establishment of a Far Eastern socialist alliance, but he did agree to create a communication and coordinating committee. He returned to Japan with some funds given to him by the Comintern, and in January 1921 published the first issue of *Rōdō undō* (Labor movement), a weekly journal supported by both anarchists and Marxists.

One of those involved in *Rōdō undō* was Kondō Eizō (1883–1965), who belonged to a younger generation than Sakai and Yamakawa, and had been living in the United States until the Rice Riots of 1918 gave him hopes for revolution in Japan and he returned to his homeland. There he came into contact with Ōsugi, and traveled to Shanghai in May 1921. He returned with

¥6,500 in Comintern funds. In November he was arrested for distributing anti-military propaganda leaflets at the time of army field exercises, and a number of his comrades were arrested the following month in what is known as the Gyōmin Kyōsantō (Enlightened People's Communist Party) incident.

Somewhat before this, Comintern agent Zhang Tailei arrived in Japan with a request for a Japanese delegation to attend the Congress of Far Eastern Peoples (officially the First Congress of Communist and National Revolutionary Organizations for Far Eastern Countries), to be held in Irkutsk as a counterpoint to the Washington Conference scheduled for November 1921. The congress was eventually convened in Moscow in February 1922, with Tokuda Kyūichi (1894–1953) participating from Japan and Katayama Sen (1859–1933) and Suzuki Mosaburō (1893–1970) attending from the United States.

On 15 July 1922, the Japanese Communist Party (JCP) was illegally established as the Japanese branch of the Communist International. Sakai Toshihiko was chairman, and the members of the first Central Committee were Yamakawa Hitoshi, Arahata Kanson, Kondō Eizō, Takase Kiyoshi, and two others. The establishment of the party had largely been the work of Tokuda and Takase, recently returned from Moscow, who persuaded older activists Sakai and Yamakawa to participate.

Immediately afterward, Yamakawa wrote a famous article for the August issue of the journal *Zen'ei* (Vanguard) titled "Musan kaikyū undō no hōkō tenkan" (A change of course for the proletarian movement). As the title suggests, he wrote of the necessity for a shift "to the masses" and away from the movement of a small, self-satisfied elite. This was a direct contradiction of the philosophy of the "vanguard party" so influential at the time.

Two members of the JCP attended the fourth congress of the Comintern in November 1922 to announce the party's formation. The Comintern's 1922 draft program of the JCP (written by Nikolai Ivanovich) was drawn up at the fourth congress. At meetings of the JCP in February 1923 this document was fiercely debated. The key issue was its call for "abolition of the monarchy." The older Japanese socialists were strongly opposed to this policy. The result was that the JCP reported to the Comintern that the Bukharin program had been approved, and decided not to publish it anywhere within Japan, even for internal consumption. Three months later, in June 1923, the members of the JCP were all arrested. But because Takase, who had served as secretary, had not recorded any of the debate regarding abolition of the emperor system, they escaped being charged with serious crimes. The cautiousness of the Meiji-era socialists had proven to be a blessing. In February 1924 the JCP disbanded. Sakai wanted to save the lives of as many of its members as possible.

The Comintern would not accept the dissolution of the party, however, and ordered its reestablishment. In part this was because the Comintern overestimated the power of the JCP. This made it difficult to refuse the order to reconstitute the party.

In December 1926, a meeting—disguised as a company year-end party—was convened at Goshiki hot springs in Yamagata prefecture to rebuild the JCP. There were seventeen participants, including Sano Fumio (chairman) (1892–1931), Watanabe Masanosuke (1899–1928), and Fukumoto Kazuo (1894–1983), but veteran members such as Arahata and Tokuda were in prison.

The central figure was Fukumoto Kazuo. Born in 1894, he was an instructor at Matsue Higher School. He had recently returned in 1924 from studies in Germany and France, and was dazzling the intelligentsia with a series of essays written in his uniquely abstruse and pedantic style. The gist of his argument was for the construction of a vanguard party through theoretical struggle—the opposite of what was then known as "Yamakawaism."

But in May 1927, the Comintern's subcommittee on Japan met in Moscow and roundly denounced "Fukumotoism." The 1927 "Theses on the Japan Problem" produced by this meeting argued that while Japan's economy and society were still strongly colored by semifeudal remnants, capitalist elements were rapidly developing. Because of this, the objective conditions for a bourgeois-democratic revolution were already ripe—as were the conditions for transforming that revolution into a genuine socialist revolution. Therefore, the theses concluded, it was time to put aside theoretical struggle and shift to the practical struggle of winning over the broad masses of the people.

Universal Manhood Suffrage and the Peace Preservation Law

This brings us to government countermeasures against communism. The public figures earliest to seize upon this issue were Hiranuma Kiichirō and Suzuki Kisaburō. They believed that Japan should enact legislation prohibiting the Communist Party. Suzuki attempted to initiate such legislation as vice minister of justice in Hara Takashi's cabinet, but did not succeed. But as the implementation of universal manhood suffrage neared, these men became even more entrenched in their beliefs. As minister of justice in the Kiyoura cabinet, Suzuki had previously drafted this law. Then, in 1925, Ogawa Heikichi, who became minister of justice in the three-party coalition cabinet (following the death of Yokota Sennosuke), proved to be a strong proponent of the bill. And Hiranuma, a powerful figure in the Privy Council, is said to have declared that he could not support universal manhood suffrage unless legislation of this kind were passed. So the Peace Preservation Law was enacted as part of a two-piece set with universal manhood suffrage.

Hiranuma and Suzuki's fears that the JCP would make gains under universal suffrage proved to be accurate. In the 1928 election, the first under universal manhood suffrage, the JCP put up candidates, guided by the united-front policies articulated in the 1927 Comintern theses. The party could not do this openly, of course, but had its candidates stand for election as members of the legal proletarian parties. In its own name, the JCP posted placards calling for the abolition of the monarchy. Alarmed by this, on 15 March 1928 the Tanaka Giichi cabinet carried out mass arrests of suspected JCP members. In this March Fifteenth Incident, more than 1,500 people were arrested, of whom 488 were indicted. The Peace Preservation Law was revised by an extraordinary imperial ordinance to incorporate the death penalty as its most severe sanction.

The JCP rebuilt itself even after this, with an executive committee formed by Ichikawa Shōichi, Mitamura Shirō, and Nabeyama Sadachika. But the Tanaka cabinet continued the repression, and on 16 April 1929 another mass arrest ended in the indictment of 339 people on suspicion of violations of the Peace Preservation Law (the April Sixteenth Incident). This was a fatal blow for the Japanese Communist Party.

Conversion (*Tenkō*)

External repression was accompanied by the beginning of defections or conversions within the JCP. In 1929, Mizuno Shigeo issued a statement from prison in which he addressed the errors of the JCP up to that point and called for a dissolution and reformation of the party. Other party members such as Minami Kiichi and Nakamura Yoshiaki sympathized with this position, and proposed that the party abandon its demands for abolition of the monarchy and expropriation of the land owned by the imperial house. Later, Mizuno and Minami would secure military backing for a newspaper-recycling company they formed, and in the postwar era Mizuno became a leading figure in the Fuji-Sankei Communications Group, a major media conglomerate.

One of the most difficult problems for the JCP was its relations with the Comintern. And the policies of the Comintern changed frequently, in alignment with the interests of the Soviet Union. The domestic situation after Stalin's consolidation of power and international developments such as the Manchurian Incident led to changes in the directives issuing from Moscow. For example, the 1931 "Draft Political Theses" stated that the motive force of the revolution was the proletariat, allied with the poor peasants, and that the goal of the present struggle should be the overthrow of the bourgeois-landlord coalition of the emperor system, dominated by finance capital, and the establishment of a dictatorship of the proletariat. However, the "Theses on the Situation in Japan" and the "Tasks of the Communist Party," approved by the Comintern in 1932, returned to calling for overthrow of the emperor system, abolition of parasitic landlordism, and implementation of a seven-hour workday as immediate goals in a two-stage theory of revolution (a bourgeois-democratic revolution to be followed by a proletarian revolution).

Then, in 1933, the famous mass conversions of communists began. In June of that year, Sano Manabu and Nabeyama Sadachika announced their *tenkō* (literally, "change of course or direction"), and proposed that the slogan of overthrowing the emperor system be abandoned. They argued that veneration of the emperor was a sentiment of the people and that communists as well should take this position. They also rejected independence for colonies and ethnic minorities, which led them toward affirmation of the Manchurian Incident.

After this conversion of elite leaders such as Sano and Nabeyama, other former members of the party's central committee—Nakao Katsuo, Mitamura Shirō, Sugiura Keiichi, Takahashi Sadaki, and others—followed suit. This set off a wave of further defections, including members of the central party leadership in the period after the April Sixteenth Incident such as Tanaka Kiyoharu, Kazama Jōkichi, and Sano Hiroshi. Rank-and-file party members were influenced by copies of Sano and Nabeyama's *tenkō* declaration, which corrections officers from the Ministry of Justice distributed among the prisoners. Of prisoners awaiting trial, 415 (or 30 percent of the total of 1,370) recanted, as did 133 of the convicted prisoners (34 percent of a total of 393).

A survey of motives given for the *tenkō* found that 217 of the total (40 percent) cited love of family; 141 (26 percent), reflection while in prison; 58 (11 percent), reasons of lifestyle, health, or personality; 55 (10 percent), books they had read; and 25 (5 percent), religious instruction. Only 24 individuals (4 percent) cited an awakening to the spirit of the times and national identity (Nakamura Takafusa, *Shōwa-shi* [A history of Shōwa Japan, 1926–1989], abridged translation). As we can see, the major reasons for conversion had to do with personal feelings for family and relatives and the physical and mental hardships of prison life—Sano and Nabeyama's *tenkō* seems to have merely lit the fuse. The weak spot that led to conversion of the party elite would appear to have been their national consciousness.

Despite the scale of this repression, books on Marxism continued to be read. The years from 1932 to 1935 were the peak of the debate concerning the nature of Japanese capitalism, and the academic world was still a safe haven.

The Legal Proletarian Parties

The preceding is a simple sketch of the activities of the Japanese Communist Party. The reason for providing this first is that the proletarian movement in Japan was decisively born out of a neurotic relationship to the JCP. The left and right wings of the proletarian movement were determined by proximity to the JCP—the left closer, the right further away, from the communists. The schisms and mergers and alliances among the proletarian parties always took place with reference to the JCP and its positions. With this in mind, let's review the genealogy of the proletarian movement.

In August 1925, after the enactment of the law on universal manhood suffrage, representatives from major labor-farmer groups in Japan gathered together to convene an organizing council for the formation of a proletarian political party. But conflict between left and right ran high, and both the right-wing Nihon Rōdō Sōdōmei (Sōdōmei; Japan Federation of Labor) and the left-wing Nihon Rōdō Kumiai Hyōgikai (Hyōgikai; Japan Council of Labor Unions) eventually dropped out. A new party, the Nōmin Rōdōtō (Farmer-Labor Party) was formed in December 1925, but was forced to disband the same day.

In March 1926, the Rōdō Nōmintō (Labor-Farmer Party) was formed, excluding three left-wing organizations including the Hyōgikai. However, when opening the doors of the party to the left became an issue, Sōdōmei and other right-leaning members left the party en masse in December 1926, and formed the Shakai Minshūtō (Socialist People's Party). Centrists organized the Nihon Rōnōtō (Japan Labor-Farmer Party), confronting the Rōdō Nōmintō, chaired by Ōyama Ikuo. So from the beginning the proletarian parties were riven by conflict and schisms—the main point of which, it may be said without exaggeration, concerned their distance to or from the JCP.

The most active of these parties was the left-wing Rōdō Nōmintō. In the sixteenth general election, of February 1928 (the first under universal manhood suffrage), the Rōdō Nōmintō fielded forty candidates, won more than 190,000 votes, and sent two representatives to the Diet: Mizutani Chōzaburō and Yamamoto Senji, both from Kyoto (the party also had three runners-up in the election returns).

The centrist Nihon Rōnōtō was formed in December 1926 by a coalition of dissident members of Sōdōmei and the right wing of the Nihon Nōmin Kumiai (Japan Farmers Union). Its secretary-general was Miwa Jusō, followed in 1927 by Asō Hisashi. In the 1928 general election it put up fifteen candidates, electing Kawakami Jōtarō to a Diet seat (with four runners-up) and winning a total of 91,000 votes.

The right wing was represented by the Shakai Minshūtō. Formed in December 1926, with Abe Isoo (1865–1949) as chairman and Katayama Tetsu (1887–1978) as secretary, the party was active, from a reformist perspective, in the movement for enacting a labor union law. In the 1928 election it backed seventeen candidates, won 120,000 votes, and sent four representatives to the Diet (with one runner-up): Abe Isoo (Tokyo), Nishio Suehiro (1891–1981, Osaka), Suzuki Fumio (Osaka), and Kamei Kan'ichirō (1892–1987, Fukuoka).

Another right-wing proletarian party was the Nihon Nōmintō (Japan Farmers Party), led by Hirano Rikizō (1898–1981). In the 1928 election it put up nine candidates and won 36,000 votes. None of its candidates were elected, but it did have two runners-up. In addition, there were a handful of regional or local proletarian parties.

However, the Rōdō Nōmintō was forced to disband after the 1928 election and the March Fifteenth Incident. This was followed by the founding of the Shin Rōnōtō (New Labor-Farmer Party), with Ōyama Ikuo (1880–1955) as chairman, but opposition from the JCP to the founding of the new party threw it into disarray, and in July 1931 it merged into the Zenkoku Rōnō Taishūtō (National Labor-Farmer Masses Party). In the 1930 election, the Rōnōtō fielded thirteen candidates, won 79,000 votes, elected one candidate, and had two runners-up.

When the Rōdō Nōmintō was suppressed in 1928, dissident members (known as the Rōnō-ha, or Labor-Farmer, faction) formed the Musan Taishūtō in July, with Suzuki Mosaburō as chairman. Initially, it was a local Tokyo organization, but soon developed regional branches, and by September 1928 it had developed into a national party.

In December 1928, the Nihon Taishūtō (Japan Masses Party) formed. This was the result of a merger of the centrist Nihon Rōnōtō and Musan Taishūtō with five smaller parties. Hirano Rikizō became its chairman. But in 1929 internal disputes led to the ouster of Hirano and leftists Suzuki Mosaburō and Kuroda Toshio; Asō Hisashi became chairman and Kōno Mitsu was appointed secretary. In the 1930 election the party put up twenty-three candidates, won 160,000 votes, and had two successful candidates and five runners-up. On 20 July 1930, it merged with other proletarian parties into the Zenkoku Taishūtō (National Masses Party). Meanwhile, the rightist Shakai Minshūtō had thirty-three candidates in the 1930 election, winning 170,000 votes and two Diet seats (with four runners-up).

If we aggregate all of these election results, in the 1928 election there were a total of eighty-six proletarian party candidates who won a total of 480,000 votes, sending eight representatives to the Diet (and twelve runners-up). In the 1930 elections there were ninety-five candidates with 509,000 votes, five Diet seats, and twelve runners-up. Although somewhat fewer representatives were elected, the numbers were not much different in the two elections.

The Manchurian Incident had an enormous impact on the situation of the proletarian parties. The Shakai Minshūtō opposed the Shandong Interventions, but it supported the government's policies in Manchuria. Even before the incident, conflict had deepened between mainstream party leaders such as Katayama Tetsu, Matsuoka Komakichi, and Nishio Suehiro on the one hand, and a faction led by Akamatsu Katsumaro and Shimanaka Yūzō, who had become advocates of national socialism, on the other. They argued that Manchuria and Mongolia were Japan's "lifeline" and that Japan would have to occupy all of China, proclaiming "unconditional support" for the policies of the Army General Staff and the Ministry of Army. In October 1931, the Shakai Minshūtō dispatched a fact-finding mission to Manchuria that began to legitimize the incident as "a means to secure *lebensraum* for the broad masses of the Japanese people."

Liberal academic Yoshino Sakuzō pointed to two regrettable aspects of the Manchurian Incident: the hard-line stance taken by the mass media, and the support of the proletarian parties for the incident. Yoshino was especially distressed by the involvement of Akamatsu Katsumaro, his son-in-law.

Meanwhile, an alliance between left-wing and centrist factions, centering around the former Zenkoku Taishūtō, merged to form a new party called the Zenkoku Rōnō Taishūtō (National Labor-Farmer Masses Party). This party took action opposing the Manchurian Incident. But there was dissent within the party itself, with some members arguing that with domestic public opinion running so high, it was not a good strategy to be too vocal in opposition, while others actively supported Japan's involvement. The transformation of the proletarian parties would be interwoven with a reorganization of the more established parties, but I will cover this in greater detail when discussing the Manchurian Incident.

The Hamaguchi Cabinet

High Tide for the Party Cabinets

In July 1929, the Tanaka cabinet collapsed and was replaced by the Hamaguchi cabinet. From Saionji's perspective, Hamaguchi and the Minseitō would offer a more reliable foreign policy and seemed better capable of assuming the responsibilities of government. Since this was a model example of a party cabinet, let's examine the process of its formation in greater detail.

On the morning of 2 July, when Tanaka submitted the resignation of his entire cabinet to the emperor, the emperor queried Makino Nobuaki, lord keeper of the privy seal, as to what would happen next. Makino replied that Prince Saionji should probably be consulted. The emperor wondered aloud whether he should send the grand chamberlain or make a telephone call to Saionji, and decided in favor of the former. Makino agreed. At about 11:30 A.M., Saionji arrived at the imperial palace, and spoke with Makino. The two were in complete agreement. After Saionji's audience with the emperor, Makino was summoned and asked his opinion. Makino said that he favored Hamaguchi, and the emperor expressed his agreement.

At 1:30 P.M., Hamaguchi was summoned to the palace and received the imperial order to form a cabinet. Hamaguchi said to Makino that he was certain a cabinet could be formed quickly, and that he hoped to be ready

Establishing proletarian parties
With the first election under universal manhood suffrage coming up, a socialist organizing committee created the Nōmin Rōdōtō (Farmer-Labor Party) to defend the interests of the Japanese proletariat—but Minister of Home Affairs Wakatsuki Reijirō declared the party illegal on the day of its formation. The banner reads "Inaugural Meeting for the Formation of the Proletarian Party." (Kokkai Shūgiin and Kokkai Sangiin., eds., Me de miru gikai seiji hyakunenshi [Visual history of a century of parliamentary politics])

that evening for the ceremony of investiture by the emperor. Makino noted in his diary that "I felt reassured by his confidence."

Just after 5:00 P.M., Hamaguchi arrived at the palace bearing the official list of his cabinet ministers, which the emperor read attentively, and approved. The emperor then showed the list to Makino, and expressed his satisfaction, saying, "It's a good lineup." He said he was happy to see Ugaki Kazushige and Inoue Junnosuke on the list, and said that while he did not know them well, Matsuda Genji and Tawara Magoichi "seemed to have impressive credentials." After this, the investiture ceremony took place (Itō Takashi and Hirose Yoshihiro, eds., *Makino Nobuaki nikki* [Diary of Makino Nobuaki]).

As we see here, the selection of a new prime minister was determined through close cooperation between the lord keeper of the privy seal (*naidaijin*) and the elder statesmen (genrō). According to the normal procedures of constitutional government, power should be transferred to the leader of the majority party in the Diet, but it was through their hands that this transfer was implemented. The Hamaguchi cabinet represented the high-water mark for party cabinets, and its formation was the simplest. In fact, this was the last cabinet to be organized so smoothly. The composition of Hamaguchi Osachi's cabinet was as follows:

Prime minister: Hamaguchi Osachi (House of Representatives, Minseitō)
Minister of foreign affairs: Shidehara Kijūrō (House of Peers, Dōwakai)
Minister of home affairs: Adachi Kenzō (House of Representatives, Minseitō)
Minister of finance: Inoue Junnosuke (House of Peers)
Minister of the army: Ugaki Kazushige
Minister of the navy: Takarabe Takeshi
Minister of justice: Watanabe Chifuyu (House of Peers, Kenkyūkai)
Minister of education: Kobashi Ichita (House of Representatives, Minseitō)
Minister of agriculture and forestry: Machida Chūji (House of Representatives, Minseitō)
Minister of commerce and industry: Tawara Magoichi (House of Representatives, Minseitō)
Minister of communications: Koizumi Matajirō (House of Representatives, Minseitō)
Minister of railways: Egi Tasuku (House of Peers, Minseitō, Dōseikai)
Minister of colonial affairs: Matsuda Genji (House of Representatives, Minseitō)
Chief cabinet secretary: Suzuki Fujiya (House of Representatives, Minseitō)
Director-general of the Cabinet Legislation Bureau: Kawasaki Takukichi (House of Peers, Minseitō, Dōwakai)

Of these, Hamaguchi, Adachi, Egi, and Machida were all veterans of earlier cabinets and top executives of the Minseitō (as was Wakatsuki Reijirō). In addition, Inoue was also a veteran of the Yamamoto Gonnohyōe cabinet, and though he did not join the Minseitō until after being named a cabinet minister, he helped round out the list of the party's key leaders.

Aside from Inoue, there were only four members of the cabinet who did not belong to the Minseitō at the time of the cabinet's formation. Of these, Shidehara, Ugaki, and Takarabe were career bureaucrats and military men sympathetic to the Minseitō who had held the same ministerial posts in the Wakatsuki cabinet (Takarabe had also been a member of the Tanaka cabinet). Watanabe Chifuyu was the third son of Imperial Household

Minister Watanabe Chiaki and was also the adopted son of former finance minister Watanabe Kunitake, Chiaki's younger brother. Chifuyu had been selected for his post largely because he was an influential member of the Kenkyūkai in the House of Peers.

Other first-time Minseitō cabinet ministers (Inoue excepted) were Kobashi, Tawara, Koizumi, Matsuda, Suzuki, and Kawasaki. Tawara Magoichi had joined the Kenseikai from a career as a home ministry bureaucrat and had been elected to the Diet in 1924. His history as a party member was thin, but his bureaucratic credentials propelled him, after winning only one election, to the post of parliamentary vice minister for home affairs in the cabinets of Katō Takaaki and Wakatsuki Reijirō; after being elected a second time he became a minister in Hamaguchi's cabinet. Kobashi Ichita was also a veteran of the home ministry, appointed vice home minister in 1918. Elected to the House of Representatives in 1920, he left the Seiyūkai to join the Seiyū Hontō, and after serving as chief cabinet secretary in the Kiyoura cabinet, he joined the Minseitō.

Koizumi Matajirō (grandfather of the postwar prime minister Koizumi Jun'ichirō) was a veteran party politician, having joined the Rikken Kaishintō (Constitutional Reform Party) in 1887, and having been a member of the House of Representatives since 1908. Matsuda Genji was an attorney who had won his first election to the Diet in 1908 as a member of the Seiyūkai, and had then joined the Seiyū Hontō and then the Minseitō. This was his first experience as a cabinet minister.

Suzuki Fujiya was an attorney who had been elected to the Diet for the first time in 1917 as a member of the Kenseikai, and had served as parliamentary councilor to the home ministry, among other posts, before being selected as chief cabinet secretary. Kawasaki Takukichi was also a home ministry bureaucrat who had served as director of the Police Affairs Bureau and vice home minister before receiving an imperial nomination to the House of Peers in 1926 and joining the Kenseikai in 1927.

Career bureaucrats were the preponderant force in the Minseitō, while those without a bureaucratic background gathered around party veteran Adachi Kenzō (1864–1948). From the 1920s onward, young Diet members from urban districts had also made significant progress within the Kenseikai and Minseitō party. Hamaguchi's cabinet was a balanced representation of the composition of the party.

Return to the Gold Standard

Immediately after its formation, the Hamaguchi cabinet took on two major challenges. The first was the issue of abandoning the embargo against the export of gold and thereby returning the yen to the gold standard. The second was the London Naval Conference.

At the beginning of the twentieth century, a global economic network based on the gold standard had been established, but World War I caused nations to suspend gold exports and the convertibility of their currencies into gold. Later, to achieve a postwar recovery of the global economy, the currency systems of individual countries needed to be stabilized, and freedom of international currency exchange and capital transactions restored. For this reason, the United States led a return to the gold standard in 1919.

In 1920, a conference of experts met in Brussels to research stabilization of international exchange rates. Doubts regarding the gold standard were expressed, but the conference concluded that a return to the standard was desirable. Another conference held in Genoa in 1922 offered two recommendations for the reestablishment of the gold standard: first that it was not necessary to return to parity (the value of the various currencies prior to the suspension of gold exports), and second that a restoration via adoption of a gold-exchange standard would be acceptable. The first was an acknowledgment of the inflation caused by the Great War; the second made reestablishment of the gold standard a more realistic option by allowing countries on the gold standard to use their own currency to offer assistance to other countries (for example, aid from the United States would be received in dollars, not gold), thus enabling the settlement of accounts in

The Hamaguchi Osachi cabinet (2 July 1929–14 April 1931)
Welcoming Minister of Foreign Affairs Shidehara Kijūrō and Minister of Finance Inoue Junnosuke from outside the party, Hamaguchi's Minseitō cabinet aimed for international cooperation and fiscal reorganization and retrenchment, but was tripped up by issues such as the "supreme command" of the military and the global economic depression. Photo courtesy of Kyodo News Images Inc.

currency based on an exchange rate, rather than in actual gold itself. As a result, France returned to the gold standard in 1928, devaluing its currency to one-fifth of prewar parity. By 1929, of the thirty-two major countries, all but six—including Japan—had not returned to the gold standard.

The Minseitō was committed to orthodox economic policies, and had argued for some time that the gold embargo should be lifted. It was anticipated that a Minseitō cabinet would tackle this issue. The key official responsible for this task would be the finance minister, and Inoue Junnosuke was selected to fill this important position.

Inoue was born in 1869, and after graduating from the University of Tokyo entered the Bank of Japan. In 1913, he became president of Yokohama Specie Bank (a bank specializing in foreign exchange; after World War II it became the Bank of Tokyo, merging with Mitsubishi Bank in 1996 to become Bank of Tokyo–Mitsubishi and is now part of Mitsubishi-UFJ Bank), and in 1919 was appointed governor of the Bank of Japan. In 1923 he joined the second cabinet of Yamamoto Gonnohyōe, and as minister of finance made a major contribution to guiding Japan through the turmoil that followed the Great Kantō Earthquake. He was a figure who enjoyed the confidence of the entire financial community.

Inoue had not been a stalwart proponent of lifting the gold embargo. Therefore, it was a bit of a surprise when he was named finance minister in the Hamaguchi cabinet. He joined the Minseitō immediately afterward, and historian Nakamura Takafusa speculates that by successfully meeting this major challenge he hoped to dramatically lift his own fortunes as a politician (Nakamura Takafusa. *Keizai seisaku no unmei* [The fate of economic policy]).

There had been a number of opportunities to lift the gold embargo, but Japan had missed all of them. Then the Great Kantō Earthquake dealt the Japanese economy a heavy blow. Imports increased dramatically, and the value of the yen fell. The old rate had been 1 dollar = 2 yen (or more precisely, 100 yen = 49.875 dollars) but in the spring of 1924 the yen had dropped to 1 dollar = 2 yen 60 sen.

What Japan feared was a reversal of its trade balance and inadequate reserves of foreign currency. Thus the focus of Inoue's fiscal policy was retrenchment. He believed that deflation of commodity prices, reduction in wages, improving the competitiveness of exports, and the accumulation of foreign reserves were necessary. The Hamaguchi cabinet's 1929 working budget was cut by ¥90 million, and the 1930 budget proposal was even more severe: a ¥170 million cut (or minus 9 percent) compared to the preceding year.

One drastic proposal for accomplishing this was a pay cut for government officials. On October 15, the government announced a plan to reduce salaries by 10 percent. This met with strong opposition from almost all the government ministries (one of the leaders was a young Ministry of Commerce and Industry bureaucrat named Kishi Nobusuke).[4] Reaction from the judiciary was particularly vigorous, since the position of these officials was protected by the constitution. The strength of the opposition led the government to withdraw the proposal after only a week, on October 22. The cuts in salary, in a considerably modified form, would be implemented the following year by the second Wakatsuki Reijirō cabinet. Even so, officials of the judiciary were not subject to the pay cut, but were expected instead to make a voluntary contribution of a specified amount to the national treasury.

As noted earlier, public opinion generally favored lifting the gold embargo, but there were exceptions—among them Ishibashi Tanzan (1884–1973, prime minister 1956–1959), Takahashi Kamekichi, Obama Toshie, and Yamazaki Kiyosumi, who were strongly opposed to deflationary policies and argued for a return to the gold standard at a new parity appropriate to Japan's actual economic strength. And there were people in the business world who agreed with them. But on 21 November 1929, the Ministry of Finance issued an ordinance stating that the gold embargo would be lifted on 11 January 1930. This was a bold and decisive action taken only less than five months after the Hamaguchi cabinet took office.

Unfortunately, on 24 October 1929, a month before the Ministry of Finance ordinance was issued, the New York stock market crashed and the Great Depression began. US stock prices had been trending downward since the summer, and then a financial tightening had touched off the crash. But at that point, hardly anyone would have predicted that this would develop into a deep depression lasting for years. In fact, since initially interests rates in the United States fell, the general view was that this might even be advantageous in maintaining the value of the yen.

But the economic downturn spread like wildfire from the United States to Europe, and world trade sharply contracted. With the layering of a global recession over the retrenchment policies of the Hamaguchi cabinet, Japan was also struck by a major depression. From 1929 to 1932, wholesale prices fell by more than 30 percent, the price of raw silk on the Yokohama exchange fell by 50 percent, and stock prices slid to a third of their former value.

Farming villages were hit especially hard. In the same three-year period, income of farm families fell by more than half. The depression was particularly severe in rural villages of the Tōhoku region of northeastern Japan, where families were forced to sell their daughters into prostitution in order to feed their malnourished children. This situation contributed to the advancing power of the military in Japanese society, a point that will be considered in greater detail later.

Unrest in the Seiyūkai

After losing control of the government, the Seiyūkai was in disarray. Since the reason for the resignation of the Tanaka cabinet was that it had lost the confidence of the emperor, Tanaka was seen as incapable of forming another cabinet, and there was a movement afoot to install either Suzuki Kisaburō or Inukai Tsuyoshi as the new party president.

This situation was exacerbated by the surfacing of a series of bribery scandals. The first, which came to light in June 1929, involved Yamanashi Hanzō, who was governor-general of Korea under the Tanaka cabinet, and who was arraigned by the public prosecutor's office in November. In August 1929, a scandal surrounding the private Hokkaido Railway and Higashi Osaka Electric Railway was uncovered (later expanding into what became known as the Five Private Railways Bribery Scandal), along with a scandal in the Decorations Bureau in which meritorious service awards were exchanged for bribes. In September 1929, former railway minister Ogawa Heikichi and Amaoka Naoyoshi, former chief of the Decorations Bureau, were indicted. The timing of all of this suggests that rather than an ambush by the Minseitō, the eruption was due to the fact that a Seiyūkai cabinet was no longer in a position to suppress the scandals.

Just at the point this spate of scandals drastically injured public confidence in the Seiyūkai, Tanaka Giichi died suddenly of a heart attack on 29 September. Sentiment was running strong for him to be replaced as Seiyūkai president by Suzuki Kisaburō. Suzuki was relatively new to the party, but possessed powerful political skills and was believed to have the largest number of supporters. But there was considerable opposition from more traditional elements of the party discomfited by Suzuki's sudden rise to prominence. Their choice for president was Tokonami Takejirō. Tokonami had been seen within the party as a likely future president during the era of Hara Takashi, but he had left the party for a time and had only returned on 18 September—a significant weakness in his résumé. In the end, Inukai Tsuyoshi (1855–1932), acknowledged as an elder statesman throughout the political world, was chosen as a compromise, and named president of the Seiyūkai on 7 October at the age of seventy-four.

Although Inukai's presidency was the product of a compromise between the two main factions, his circle of advisers was actually dominated by members of the Suzuki faction. Ogawa Heikichi's fall from power as a result of the Five Railways Scandal was also a significant factor. Ogawa was a prominent member of the traditionalist faction, and had himself been a candidate for the party presidency. All of this had put the Seiyūkai in a weak position for the dissolution of the Diet, and the Minseitō took advantage of the situation by calling a snap election. The ordinary session of the Diet convened in December 1929, and on 21 January 1930, after the speech outlining the government's administrative agenda and subsequent debate, the House of Representatives was dissolved.

Voting took place on 20 February and resulted in a major victory for the Minseitō, which won 273 seats in the House—a gain of 100 seats. In contrast, the Seiyūkai lost 63 seats, ending with a total of 174. The Minseitō had won 5.47 million votes, 1.20 million more than the 4.27 million it had taken in the previous election. The Seiyūkai took only 3.94 million, down 300,000 from its previous 4.25 million.

At the time of this election, Japan was not yet feeling the effects of the recession that followed the lifting of the gold embargo. A majority of the electorate had given its support to the Minseitō and its program of austerity, and they were united around Hamaguchi, a leader of honesty and integrity. But as the economic situation worsened, it would begin to have a major impact on politics—a topic I will return to later.

The London Naval Conference

The other major test of the Hamaguchi cabinet was the London Naval Conference. The purpose of the conference was to continue the disarmament and arms limitation program begun by the Washington Conference of 1921–1922. The Washington Conference dealt with large battleships, and the London Conference was to extend the limitations to auxiliary vessels, including cruisers, destroyers, and submarines. An earlier conference on limitations for auxiliary vessels had met in Geneva in 1927, but ended in failure, with France and Italy not participating, and Japan, Britain, and the United States unable to reach an agreement (Japan's representatives to the Geneva conference were Saitō Makoto and Ishii Kikujirō).

After the failure in Geneva, there was increased momentum for disarmament. In 1928 the Kellogg-Briand Pact was signed in Paris. In the United States the newly elected Herbert Hoover administration proclaimed a policy of arms reduction and in Britain a Labour Party government was elected in June 1929 that vowed to cooperate with the United States on arms control. Preliminary talks between the United States and Britain had made progress, and in October the British foreign secretary, Arthur Henderson, issued invitations to a conference to Japan, the United States, France, and Italy.

The Hamaguchi cabinet had taken office on a platform of international cooperation and fiscal retrenchment, and favored arms reductions for both of these reasons, making it one of the ten major points in the policy program it issued soon after taking office. On the other hand, the Navy General Staff Office believed that Japan had to have a battle fleet that was at least 70 percent the strength of that of the United States to not be defeated by the latter, and insisted on maintaining this ratio. At the Washington Conference the Japanese delegation had proposed on a seven-to-ten ratio of capital ships versus the United States, but under the leadership of Katō Tomosaburō, who was a proponent of cooperation with the United States, the Japanese navy was persuaded to accept a six-to-ten ratio, in exchange for a commitment from the United States to limit its deployment in the Pacific. Two of the naval officers who objected to Katō Tomosaburō's 1921 compromise in Washington were Katō Kanji and Suetsugu Nobumasa, who were now chief and vice chief of naval operations, respectively, and who were determined not to see a repetition of the Washington Conference experience.

On the eve of the London Naval Conference, on 26 November, the government established three basic principles for the negotiations: achieving a 70 percent ratio in auxiliary ship tonnage versus the United States, securing a 70 percent ratio of heavy cruisers versus the United States, and maintaining submarine strength at a total of 78,000 tons. The Navy General Staff Office wanted the decision approved in an imperial council (*gozen kaigi,* a conference in the presence of the emperor) but Saionji rejected this, as he wanted to preserve some room for compromise.

The Japanese delegation to the conference was headed by former prime minister Wakatsuki Reijirō, accompanied by the navy minister, Takarabe Takeshi, and Japan's ambassador to Great Britain, Matsudaira Tsuneo. The conference ran into difficulties from the outset, but tough negotiations between US senator David A. Reed and Matsudaira led to a compromise proposal between Wakatsuki and the US chief delegate, Secretary of State Henry L. Stimson. In it, Japan would secure a 69.75 percent ratio in overall auxiliary ship tonnage. In heavy cruisers, it was promised only a 60 percent ratio, but the Americans agreed to defer the start of construction on three of its eighteen permitted vessels until after 1933, which meant that Japan would actually maintain a de facto ratio of more than 70 percent for the period covered by the treaty, which was to be renegotiated in 1935. A compromise was also reached on submarines, limiting total tonnage to a parity of 52,700 tons. It was agreed that the treaty would remain in force until the end of 1936, and that the moratorium on construction of battleships set by the Washington Conference would also be extended to that time. This compromise was reached on 13 March; on 14 March a cable signed by all senior members of the Japanese delegation was sent to Tokyo detailing this proposal and asking for final instructions (see Table 2.2).

This plan did not satisfy the Navy General Staff. Although it essentially preserved the overall 70 percent ratio versus the United States, they did not achieve their aims with regard to heavy cruisers, and were quite discontent with what amounted to a major reduction in Japan's submarine tonnage.

The cabinet, however, favored signing the treaty. It was essential both from a fiscal perspective and in terms of international cooperation. The support of Great Britain and the United States was essential to Japan's return to the gold standard—a policy already embarked upon by the government. Anglo-American cooperation was also needed in a second renegotiation of foreign loans Japan had taken to finance the Russo-Japanese War, which were soon coming due. The Ministry of Navy also took the long view, and believed some compromise of this kind was inevitable. Former navy minister and mil-

Table 2.2   The Compromise Proposal at the London Naval Conference, 1930

	Great Britain	United States	Japan
Heavy cruisers	15 ships, 146,800 tons	18 ships, 180,000 tons	12 ships, 108,400 tons
Light cruisers	192,200 tons	143,500 tons	100,450 tons
Destroyers	150,000 tons	150,000 tons	105,500 tons
Submarines	52,700 tons	52,700 tons	52,700 tons
Total	541,700 tons	526,200 tons	367,050 tons

itary councilor Okada Keisuke and others worked to persuade the Navy General Staff, and on 1 April the government issued an order adopting the compromise plan. The Navy General Staff was still opposed to the compromise, but let it be known that if the government was determined to adopt that line of policy, the navy would follow it. According to a diary entry by Okada Keisuke on 29 March, Prince Fushimi Hiroyasu, later chief of Navy General Staff, said: "The navy's argument is legitimate, and should be maintained to the end, but if the government decides to accept the American proposal—it may be misleading to call this a surrender—we must follow it. We should not repeat a mistake like that of the two divisions, years ago." Okada Keisuke and Okada Sadahiro, ed., *Okada Keisuke kaikoroku* [Memoirs of Okada Keisuke]. (The "two divisions" was a reference to an incident in 1913, during Saionji Kinmochi's second cabinet, when Minister of Army Uehara Yūsaku resigned when the army's demand for two additional divisions was not met, precipitating the collapse of the cabinet.)

Nevertheless, on 2 April, Katō Kanji, navy chief of staff, reported to the emperor that the treaty proposal would greatly compromise the navy's operational capabilities, and that serious deliberations were necessary before an agreement was signed. This was what turned the affair into a major political issue. Up to this point, Katō had openly expressed neither approval nor disapproval, though it was clear he did not approve. Now the government would be making decisions about the status of forces over the objection of Navy General Staff. Article 11 of the Constitution of the Empire of Japan stated that "the Emperor has the supreme command of the Army and Navy." Practically this meant that the emperor was to be counseled in his exercise of this power of supreme command by the Navy General Staff Office. Also, Article 12's "the Emperor determines the organization and peacetime standing of the Army and Navy" meant this prerogative was to be exercised with the counsel of the navy minister and of the cabinet in reality. Arms reduction was an issue involving both of these articles of the constitution, and inevitably raised difficult issues of constitutional interpretation.

The Issue of "Violation of the Supreme Command"

On 27 February 1930, as the special Diet session following the general election commenced, the defeated Seiyūkai used this issue to attack the government. The government's position was that, as in earlier disarmament conferences, it was the responsibility of the government (including the Ministry of Navy), in accordance with Article 12 of the constitution, to determine the strength of forces to be agreed upon by treaty, and that it was sufficient to consult, but not necessarily follow, the opinions of Navy General Staff.

In the Diet, the solid Minseitō majority meant the government's position prevailed, but the Seiyūkai's rhetoric had emboldened the hardliners in the navy. A meeting of the Conference of Military Councilors was also convened.[5] In this meeting, the Ministry of Navy and Navy General Staff clashed, and on 10 June, Katō Kanji submitted a personal report to the emperor and resigned as navy chief of staff. Okada Keisuke tried to mollify hardliners such as Fleet Admiral Tōgō Heihachirō by saying that the plan had demerits with regard to national security, but that if the government made a sincere effort to remedy them, it was still possible to defend the country. But the hardliners were not persuaded. As a result, they reached an agreement that in exchange for giving official approval to the government line and reporting to the emperor, Takarabe Takeshi should resign as navy minister. On 23 July the conference finally approved a formal report to the emperor.

Following this, on 24 July, deliberations began in the Privy Council. Initially, the council's attitude was one of opposition, but in the end Itō Miyoji, chairman of the committee reviewing the treaty, submitted a report on 17 September saying it should be "unconditionally ratified," thus settling the matter. This was because the government had taken an extremely hard line itself, making it clear that it was prepared to confront the Privy Council head-on, and dismiss the president and vice president of the council if necessary. Unlike the Wakatsuki cabinet at the time of the 1927 financial crisis, the Hamaguchi cabinet was determined to fight the Privy Council.

But the fire started by the hardliners in the navy was not readily extinguished. Right-wing groups, the military, and the Seiyūkai kept up a barrage of criticism of the cabinet, and on 14 November, Prime Minister Hamaguchi, as he was passing through Tokyo Station, was shot and gravely wounded by a right-wing assassin named Sagoya Tomeo.

This issue also left major scars in the navy, which was split into two competing factions based on their attitude toward the London Naval Treaty—the Treaty Faction and the Fleet Faction. Before long, supporters of the treaty—including navy minister Takarabe Takeshi, vice minister Yamanashi Katsunohin, chief adjutant Sakonji Seizō, and chief of the Military Affairs Bureau Hori Teikichi—found themselves removed from active service. Following this, Fleet Faction members such as Katō Kanji and

Suetsugu Nobumasa would advance into key positions. In the navy, the Ministry of Navy had always occupied the more important position because of the predominant importance of the naval budget, but now the primacy of the administrative chain of command was beginning to be challenged.

Among the army brass, Ugaki Kazushige had been of the opinion that the meeting of the Conference of Military Councilors prior to the Privy Council deliberations was unnecessary. In a diary entry for 23 July 1930, he wrote: "Imperial approval for the London Treaty should be secured as quickly as possible after Wakatsuki's delegation returns home, and we should precede Great Britain and the US in boldly expressing our passionate desire for peace and our intention to adhere faithfully to the treaty" (Tsunoda Jun, ed., *Ugaki Kazushige nikki* [Diary of Ugaki Kazushige]). From the standpoint of the army's sectional interests, naval arms reductions were a plus, but even if we set such factors aside, Ugaki appears to have been a strong supporter of the treaty.

Procedurally, Ugaki saw no need to bring the issue before the Supreme Military Council (Gensuifu)[6] or the Conference of Military Councilors prior to its deliberation by the Privy Council. He thought that if criticism arose in the Privy Council concerning deficiencies in national security as a result of the treaty, the government should take the stance that it saw no such deficiencies, and that the issue was being deliberated by experts; if defects were discovered, the government would take responsibility for correcting them, something that could be done in tandem or parallel with a meeting of the Conference of Military Councilors. If the Privy Council wanted to meddle with the content of such corrections, the government should refuse by saying the Privy Council was attempting to exceed its powers; if the Privy Council claimed its deliberations could not proceed without understanding more of the military's intentions, then this could be ignored, as any delays would be the responsibility of the Privy Council. The Supreme Military Council and the Conference of Military Councilors both had independent powers and opinions, and it was not their role to undertake prior investigation for the Privy Council. The government was mistaken in trying to get the navy to sign on before proceeding. As Ugaki wrote: "I feel intense regret that with the goal of this work in sight, the matter was not handled in a more bold and dignified manner" (Tsunoda Jun, ed., *Ugaki Kazushige nikki* [Diary of Ugaki Kazushige], 23 July 1930). Saionji Kinmochi also took a hard line on this issue, feeling that if the Privy Council kept up its opposition, the prime minister would be within his rights to remove the president and vice president of the council.

Ugaki and Saionji's stance was backed by popular opinion favoring the arms limitation treaty. All the major newspapers united in support of the treaty. However, as historian Itō Takashi has pointed out, what they supported on their editorial pages was not necessarily supported by their reporting

(*Shōwa shoki seijishi kenkyū* [A study of the political history of the early Shōwa period]). Something similar frequently happens today, when editorials may praise free trade, but news reports depict small businesses and farm families who are suffering as a result of trade liberalization.

The China Problem

Japan's diplomatic response to China foreign policy during its ongoing revolution had been relatively cooperative, even during the Tanaka government. Let's look now at further developments in China.

When the Northern Expedition ended in 1928, there were an estimated 2 to 2.5 million men at arms in China. The Northern Expedition had absorbed many local and regional armies as it had proceeded, and now the challenge was how to reorganize or disarm this collection of troops.

In addition to Chiang Kai-shek, the National Revolutionary Army had three other leaders: Feng Yuxiang, Yan Xishan, and Li Zongren. Chiang was said to command 500,000 men; Feng, 400,000; Yan, 200,000; and Li, 300,000. In July 1928, Chiang proposed to the others a plan for military reform. And in August, the fifth plenary session of the second Kuomintang national congress formally approved a plan for military reorganization.

Then, beginning in January 1929, sixty party and military leaders convened a month-long conference on national reorganization and demobilization, which produced a number of decisions, including division of the country into six reorganization and demobilization zones; reduction of the nation's land forces to sixty-five divisions, or about 800,000 men; and an annual military budget of 192 million yuan. Troop reduction had always been a major issue for China, and in this case, with the future course of the Kuomintang and the power of its various leaders riding on it, it attained even greater importance.

In March 1929, warfare broke out between Chiang Kai-shek and the Guangxi clique. Then in May, Chiang and Feng Yuxiang began fighting, followed in February 1930 by combat between Chiang's forces and those of Yan Xishan. In May 1930, the Central Plains War began between Chiang and a coalition of generals allied against him. It was Zhang Xueliang who turned out to determine the fate of these struggles. On 18 September 1930, he declared his support for Chiang, decisively tipping things in Chiang's favor. After this Chiang defeated a succession of other warlords and consolidated power with remarkable speed.

Meanwhile, in February 1929 the Nationalist government issued 50 million yuan in demobilization bonds, followed in September by an issue of 70 million yuan in treasury bonds for military reorganization. Revenues for repayment of which were to be derived from the tariffs managed by the central government. This made increasing tariffs all the more important. T. V. Soong, the Nationalist minister of finance, finally institutionalized the long-awaited nationwide annulment of the *lijin*, or internal tariffs, to be replaced with what was called a "consolidated tax," which was a form of freight tax charged at point of production. The shift from *lijin* to the consolidated tax essentially signified a centralization of tax collection and authority—an important change from China's tradition of decentralized taxes and tariffs.

On the diplomatic front, the Nationalist government also succeeded in 1929 in securing the return of the Belgian concession in Tianjin and the British concession in Zhenjiang, followed in 1930 by the British concession and leased territories in Xiamen and Weihaiwei. The revolutionary diplomacy mentioned earlier in relation to the Tanaka cabinet was producing real results.

The Return of Shidehara Kijūrō

In response to these developments in China, when the Hamaguchi cabinet took office it adopted as one of the ten major policies in its platform a friendly and cooperative attitude toward China with regard to the reform and abrogation of the unequal treaties, and promised that it would not casually send troops to China, it would prioritize economic development, and it would renounce any aggressive intentions.

In October 1929, Minister of Foreign Affairs Shidehara appointed Saburi Sadao as minister to China, hoping to achieve a fresh start for Japan's China policy. Saburi was a confidant of Shidehara's, who at the time of the special conference on the Chinese customs tariff in Beijing had taken the lead in proposing that tariff autonomy should be recognized in principle, increasing Japan's credibility with the Chinese. However, on a return visit to Japan in November 1929, Saburi died suddenly, under mysterious circumstances, at the Fujiya Hotel in Hakone. The death was ruled a suicide, but suspicions lingered, and little was known of the possible motive.

Obata Yūkichi was named as Saburi's successor. But Obata had served as the first secretary of the Japanese legation in 1915, at the time of Japan's "Twenty-One Demands" against China. One Japanese newspaper ran an article that praised his strength, saying that at the time of the negotiations he had taken a tough line and pounded the floor to drive home his point. This led the Chinese to withdraw their *agrément* to accept Obata as minister—something that happened occasionally in diplomatic affairs, but was traditionally kept from the public. Because this had been leaked to the public, China came under strong criticism in Japan. This was a case in which China's revolutionary diplomacy unfortunately caught both sides off-guard.

The government temporarily appointed Shigemitsu Mamoru, Japanese consul-general in Shanghai, as acting minister to China, and worked to improve Sino-Japanese relations. The most pressing issue was the tariff agreement—which, as we have seen, was quite important to the Chinese.

On 6 May 1930, a new tariff agreement was signed. There was vocal opposition in Japan to this, with fear that increased tariffs would mean a reduction in Japanese exports to China. But with the return of Shidehara diplomacy, the anti-Japanese boycott movement in China died down, and exports showed an upward trend. Emboldened by this, Shidehara began to make preparations for abandoning Japanese extraterritoriality in China.

So Sino-Japanese relations took a positive turn. One expression of this was an invitation to send a group of Japanese military training advisers to China. At the time, a military advisory group from Germany was quite influential in China, and the number of Japanese officers being invited was similar. However, Kamimura Shinichi, a Japanese diplomat stationed in China, observed that while the German advisory group was composed of high-ranking officers with considerable social skills, the Japanese training group was a much humbler and less effective presence, diplomatically speaking.

The Situation in Manchuria

The tide of nationalism in China proper was also making itself felt in Manchuria. One result of this was a famous clash between the Soviet Union and China in 1929. On 27 May, Zhang Xueliang ordered a search of the Soviet consulate in Harbin, and on 11 July forcibly repossessed the Chinese Eastern Railway. In response, on 17 July the Soviet Union announced it was breaking off diplomatic relations with China. A large-scale military offensive followed in October, with the Soviets swiftly defeating Zhang Xueliang's army. This conflict is remembered as the first significant violation of the Kellogg-Briand Pact. In the end, the Chinese gave in and signed the Khabarovsk Protocol on 22 December 1929, essentially restoring the status quo.

Minister of Foreign Affairs Shidehara took some initiative in resolving this conflict, acting as an intermediary between the Chinese and the Soviets and enhancing his international reputation. This incident also provided Japan with a few other important hints. First, it made at least a small group of Japanese specialists aware of the fact that despite the chaos of the Bolshevik revolution, the military capacity of the Soviet Union had recovered to a considerable level. Second, it made it clear that despite its anti-imperialist rhetoric, the Soviet Union was not eager to relinquish the concessions it had inherited from tsarist Russia. And third, it hardened the belief of some of the Japanese military and others that in the final analysis the only way to protect Japan's interests and concessions was military force.

Zhang Xueliang's attempts to oppose the Soviet Union had failed, and now he moved aggressively against Japan. From the mid-1920s onward, there had been voices in China calling for the construction of a network of Chinese railways to encircle and diminish the power of the Japanese-owned South Manchuria Railway. Japan had repeatedly protested this as a violation of the Treaty and Additional Agreement Relating to Manchuria (1905), in which the Chinese government had promised not to build parallel or branch lines that might adversely affect the South Manchuria Railway. But such construction proceeded, with the biggest impact coming from the Datong Railway (running from Dafushan to Tongliao), which opened in November 1927, and the Jihai Railway (from Jilin to Hailong), which opened in May 1929. In addition, Zhang Xueliang had contracted with a Dutch company to construct a major port at Huludao, southwest of Jinzhou, with an impressive groundbreaking ceremony held in July 1930. When completed, the Chinese railways and this port would become a major artery for transport and distribution of goods throughout Manchuria, which would clearly become major competition for the South Manchuria Railway and the Japanese-controlled port of Dalian.

On 19 December 1930, Shidehara announced a policy on Chinese railway development, basically stating that Japan would work to prevent construction of any lines that posed a major competitive threat to the South Manchuria Railway, but would cooperate with the construction of lines that did not pose such a threat. However, Zhang Xueliang's policies were fueled by the rising tide of nationalist feeling in China rather than by a calculation of interest, and left Shidehara with little room to maneuver. In fiscal 1929 the South Manchuria Railway was already running the first major deficit since its founding, though in part this was attributable to the effects of the global depression. Anxiety concerning the South Manchuria Railway, linchpin for the management of Japanese interests in Manchuria and Mongolia since the Russo-Japanese War, would come to have a major influence on Japanese policy. Just as Shidehara was laying out his policy on Chinese railways, Hamaguchi was shot by a terrorist and the Minseitō cabinet faced a major crisis. In less than a year, the Manchurian Incident would occur.

Society and Culture in the Early Shōwa Period

Newly Rising Forces

What kind of society had Japan become in the late Taishō and early Shōwa period? First, as mentioned in the earlier discussion of the proletarian political parties, Japan was a profoundly less egalitarian society than it is today. Corporate profits were distributed as shareholder dividends rather than held as retained earnings. Postwar Japanese corporations have a reputation for placing priority on employees among their stakeholders, but in prewar Japan it was the shareholders who were the priority. Inequality was also pronounced within the companies themselves; it was regarded as normal for top executives to draw huge bonuses, equivalent to 5 to 10 percent of corporate profits—an amount that would be unthinkably large today. In a survey conducted around 1929, the average after-tax annual salary for a company president was ¥151,000, while that for a newly employed male college graduate was ¥1,500—a hundred times less. That is greater than the same gap today by a factor of ten.

These facts lead us to several conclusions. The first is that many workers were caught in a condition similar to Charlie Chaplin's character in *Modern Times*—unable to make a decent living no matter how hard or long they worked. And at the opposite extreme were the wealthy capitalists. This was the sort of society described by Marx, and this became the basis for the powerful influence of socialism in prewar Japan.

The affluent strata of society had become ostentatiously rich. They began to possess wealth at a completely different level from that of the rich classes of the earlier Meiji period. And their standard of living was further transformed because they had access to conveniences that were beyond the reach of most Japanese. The first refrigerators were imported to Japan in 1923; domestic production began in 1930. The imports were mostly from General Electric in the United States, while the domestic models were made by Tokyo Electric Company (now Toshiba Corporation). In short, a limited stratum of Japanese society was already, in the prewar period, beginning to enjoy the affluence, symbolized by the electrical appliances that most Japanese would not experience until the postwar economic boom. It is important to understand this image of the early Shōwa period in prewar Japan.

A second important result of the rapid industrial development of the late Meiji period, especially after World War I, was the increase in the number of "salarymen" working for large corporations and living in cities (see Table 2.3). Lifestyles were transformed by the expansion of the urban population and the development of the transportation network. The population of the cities was both urban and suburban. In the cities, apartment blocks were built; and in the suburbs, new housing developments sprang up with a transportation network developed to facilitate commuting to the city centers. This separation between workplace and home also encouraged the development of urban entertainment districts.

Many of these new urban workers were relatively well-educated. Hara Takashi responded to the period of industrialization at the time of World War I by significantly increasing the number of secondary and higher educational institutions. And the universities became less a haven for the pursuit and refinement of knowledge than a venue for training the human resources

Table 2.3   Increase in Urban Population (as percentage of total population)

Year	Total Urban Population	Municipalities with Population of 50,000 or More	Cities with Population of 200,000 or More
1920	18.9	15.9	9.9
1925	21.7	20.5	11.2
1930	24.1	24.8	13.0
1935	32.9	30.8	21.2

needed for Japan's economic development. In the Meiji period there had been only eight high schools (*kōtō gakkō*) in the entire country; beginning with Hara's cabinet, twenty-six more were added. In short, the number of graduates from Japan's middle and higher schools, technical schools, and universities increased rapidly, and these graduates were beginning to form a core stratum of society. This stratum of relatively well-educated urban wage earners and salarymen was emerging in the early Shōwa period as a new force to be reckoned with.

Growth of the Cities

Next let's look at the pattern of Japan's urbanization. The Kansai region surrounding Kyoto, Osaka, and Kobe took the lead in suburban development. In 1910 the Minoo Arima Electric Tramway (now the Hankyū Takarazuka Line) opened, followed by the Hyōgo Electric Railway (now San'yō Electric Railway), the Keihan Electric Railway (now the Keihan Honsen Line), and in 1914 the Osaka Electric Tramway (now the Kintetsu Nara Line).

In the Tokyo area, the Keisei Electric Railway (now the Keisei Oshiage Line) opened in 1912, and the Keiō Electric Railway (now the Keio Line) in 1913. These were precursors of a railway boom that really took off after World War I. The Ikegami Electric Railway (now the Tōkyū Ikegami Line) opened in 1922, the Meguro-Kamata Electric Railway (later the Tōkyū Meguro-Kamata Line) in 1923, and the Tokyo-Yokohama Electric Railway (later the Tōkyū Tōyoko Line) in 1926. Existing railways such as the Musashino Railway (now the Seibu Ikebukuro Line) and the Tōbu Railway (still operating under that name) were renovated and electrified. In 1927 the Odawara Express Railway (now Odakyū Odawara Line) opened, and in 1930 the Shōnan Electric Railway (now part of the Keikyū Main Line) was completed. In a relatively short period of time, both the Kansai (Osaka-Kyoto) and Kantō (Tokyo-Yokohama) areas witnessed a boom in private railway construction, with a parallel development of high-class residential communities such as Ashiya in Hyōgo, and Den'en Chōfu and Seijō Gakuen in Tokyo. A related by-product of this boom was the private railway bribery scandals mentioned earlier.

As we have seen, urbanization was not a phenomenon limited to Tokyo alone; in fact, the Kansai region led the way in certain respects. In 1928 the population of Osaka reached 2.33 million, making it larger than Tokyo, with 2.21 million. The ranking reversed again in 1932, when a number of surrounding communities and rural areas were officially merged to form Greater Tokyo.

The private railway terminals of Tokyo also had nothing to rival the Umeda Terminal of Hankyū Railway in Osaka, where in 1929 the Hankyū Department Store became the first "terminal department store"—a combination that later became a defining feature of urban life in Japan. The Tokyo region also boasted nothing as impressive as the high-end suburban developments of places like Ashiya in Kansai—with large, landscaped standard lots equipped with water, sewer, city gas, buried electrical lines, paved streets, and well-appointed parks, tennis courts, and other conveniences. Historian Hara Takeshi appropriately described this as a "bourgeois utopia" (*"Minto" Ōsaka tai "teito" Tōkyō* [The "people's capital" of Osaka versus the "imperial capital" of Tokyo]).

The Transformation of Housing

Suburban development was accompanied by significant changes in the nature of Japanese homes. A home in a new development might have a lot of 120 *tsubo* (about 400 square meters) and a house of about 18 *tsubo* (60 square meters) and cost about ¥2,200, or about two years' salary for a mid-level salaryman. Compared to today, we might say that the lot was large, the house small, and the price inexpensive.

The main reason was that land was relatively cheaper than it is now. At the time, a *tsubo* of land (3.3 square meters) sold for ¥1,756 in Ginza, ¥600 in Yūrakuchō, ¥49 in Shiba Shirokane, and ¥5 in Koganei in Tokyo; ¥3–4 in Urawa in Saitama; and ¥3 in Ichikawa in Chiba. In 1999, land prices had fallen considerably from their bubble-era peak in the 1980s, but even so, current prices would probably be a hundred thousand times higher in most cases.

It is important to note that in prewar Japan the desire to own one's home was not strong, compared to today, and many more people lived in rental housing. A standard private-sector rental apartment might run ¥10–15 a month for a six-mat tatami room (about 9 square meters; a single tatami mat measures approximately 1 by 2 meters) with an alcove and closet, while city public housing might offer two six-mat rooms for ¥20 or a six-mat and a four-mat room for ¥15.

A major innovation of this period was the Dōjunkai apartments, the first reinforced concrete municipal housing complexes in Japan, built with ¥31 million in funds for recovery from the 1923 earthquake. A 138-unit complex opened in Honjo in August 1926, and a 136-unit complex in Aoyama in September of that year.

These changes in housing brought changes in lifestyle. As more homes were built with living/dining rooms, more families began eating together at a family dining table. Until the 1920s, kitchens where one kneeled or squatted to prepare food were the norm; the standing kitchen with modern appliances was an ergonomically liberating innovation that spread quickly. The year 1926 saw the advent of *bunka jūtaku,* or "cultured housing"—a new style of Japanese house incorporating Western features such as a parlor. In any case, the model for modern Japanese domestic architecture was established in the 1920s, at the end of the Taishō and beginning of the Shōwa eras.

Clothing and Food

A well-known image from the early Shōwa period is that of stylish *moga* (modern girls) and *mobo* (modern boys) striding down the streets of Tokyo's Ginza district. This fad seems to have peaked around 1927. A survey conducted by the cosmetic company Shiseidō of the clothing of passersby in the Ginza on 2 December 1926 showed that Western-style clothing was still much more prevalent among men than women: of the men surveyed, 797 were in Western dress and only 349 dressed in the Japanese style; for women, the numbers were 22 and 494, respectively. A similar survey conducted in front of Mitsukoshi Department Store in November 1928 found 61 percent of men dressed in Western style and 39 percent in Japanese style; for women, it was the opposite, with 16 percent in Western style and 84 percent Japanese.

Sugino Yoshiko opened her Women's Institute of Dressmaking in November 1926. This was predicated on the spread of Western-style clothing, much as English-language schools and cram schools proliferated in the postwar era, and computer-training schools exist in large numbers today. Schools are founded in response to social demand.

We should not forget that the background to the spread of Western-style clothing was the social advancement of women, who were now finding employment as typists, telephone operators, department store clerks, and bank tellers. In 1928, Dai-Ichi Bank hired its first female employees.

The Dōjunkai apartments in Honjo Nakanogō *(above)* and Asahi Housing Type 1 *(below)*

The Dōjunkai was a nonprofit government foundation established to build and manage public housing for victims of the Great Kantō Earthquake of 1923, and was headed by the minister of home affairs. It built wood-frame houses and reinforced concrete apartment buildings in various locations in the Tokyo-Yokohama area, and played a significant role in transforming the appearance of Tokyo in the period of recovery after the quake. (Nihon Kindaishi Kenkyūkai, Zusetsu kokumin no rekishi dai-15 *[Illustrated history of the Japanese people, vol. 15]* above; below, *Tonedachi Masao,* Asahi Jūtaku zuan-shū *[Collection of housing designs submitted to* Asahi shinbun*])*

This advancement into the workplace was supported by greater access to education. The year 1929 saw the founding of Tokyo Institute of Technology, Osaka Institute of Technology, Tokyo University of Literature and Science (later Tokyo University of Education, then University of Tsukuba), Hiroshima University of Literature and Science, and Kobe University of Commerce. These schools, along with various other established universities, began admitting female students. In the year of its founding, the Tokyo University of Literature and Science admitted five women. And the technical college affiliated with Meiji University added programs for women in its departments of law and commerce, accepting 160 new students.

Next let's look at food. What did people eat when they went out to have a meal with their family? The menu for the cafeteria in the building connected to the subway terminus at Asakusa around 1929 was as follows:

Rice, bread, coffee	5 sen
Tea with lemon, soda water	7 sen
Ice cream, cake, pineapple, fruit	10 sen
Fried prawns, curry with rice, kid's lunch	25 sen
Beefsteak, pork cutlet, croquettes, ham salad, stuffed cabbage, beef stew	30 sen
Lunch	35 sen

One sen was a hundredth of a yen, so if we multiply these figures by 5,000, we arrive at about what such things would cost today: ¥250 for rice, bread, or coffee; ¥500 for ice cream; ¥1,250 for curry rice; ¥1,750 for a full lunch. Perhaps because the subway itself was such a modern conveyance, this was also quite a modern menu. The children's lunch—an indispensable feature of a family outing in modern Japan—was pioneered in 1929 at a price of 30 sen by the Matsuzakaya Department Store in Ginza.

Wages and Prices

Now, let's look at the relationship between people's incomes and commodity prices. Salaries for university-educated public-sector employees ranged from ¥133 a month at the high end to ¥33 at the low end, with an average of ¥50–60. According to a 1927 Ministry of Home Affairs survey of household economics, the average monthly income per family was ¥131 and expenditures were 30 percent for food, 20 percent for housing, 10 percent for clothing, 25 percent for social life, and 15 percent for cultural pursuits. Of those surveyed, 85 percent lived in rental housing; salarymen spent an

Moga and *mobo*

The moga, *or "modern girl" abandoned the kimono for Western-style clothing and bobbed her hair. Long sideburns and bell-bottomed sailor pants were trademarks of the* mobo, *or "modern boy." So attired, they dashingly strode the streets of the Ginza like motion-picture stars. Photo courtesy of Kyodo News Images Inc. (Illustration by Hosokibara Seiki,* Gendai sesō manga *[Caricatures of contemporary culture])*

average of ¥22 a month on rent; wage workers, ¥17. Overall, salaried workers had a higher standard of living, as one might expect.

In 1926 a 10-kilogram bag of top-quality polished rice cost ¥3.20. In 1999, a similar bag of premium Koshihikari rice cost ¥9,000, or about 3,000 times as much. A meal of curry rice cost between 10 and 12 sen—and would be about 5,000 to 10,000 times more expensive at the end of the twentieth century.

In 1926, the monthly broadcast fee for radio reception was one yen. The Tokyo municipal streetcar system charged a 7-sen fare—2,000 times less than the ¥130 minimum fare on the Yamanote train line of Japanese Railways in 1999, and about 2,500 times less than the ¥160 fare charged on the Tokyo municipal subway lines. A different index is private university tuition, which was ¥140 per annum at Keiō University in the late 1920s, and now is about 7,000 times more expensive.

Development of Transportation

Major changes took place in transportation during the early Shōwa period. The first was the spread of automobiles, and especially taxis. The *entaku*, a "yen taxi" service that would take riders anywhere in city limits for a fare of one yen, debuted in Osaka in 1924. In 1927, you could also ride anywhere in Tokyo for one yen.

On the other hand, the rickshaws (*jinrikisha*) that had been a staple of urban transportation declined precipitously. In 1921 there were 10,659 rickshaws being operated in Tokyo; this had fallen to 8,776 by 1927. In the same period of time the number of automobiles more than tripled, from 4,097 to 13,163. The yen taxis were a major spur to this transformation. The number of bicycles in use also increased in this period from about 210,000 to 420,000.

The urban railway network was also expanding. After repairing the damage from the Great Kantō Earthquake, the construction of new lines began. On 1 November 1925, an elevated section of the Tōhoku Main Line opened between Kanda and Ueno in Tokyo, and service on the Yamonote Line circular route commenced. In November 1929, the time between trains on the Yamanote Line, the Chūō Line between Tokyo station and Nakano, and the Keihin Line between Kamata and Shinagawa was reduced to three minutes—which is about the same as today. And on 30 December 1927, Tokyo's first subway line opened between Asakusa and Ueno at a total length of 2.2 kilometers.

Long-distance trains were also popular. In September 1929, limited express trains named Fuji and Sakura began service between Tokyo and Shimonoseki at the western end of Honshū. The Japanese National Railways (now Japanese Railways) acquired its familiar abbreviation—"Kokutetsu"—about this time. The Fuji limited express train made the Tokyo-to-Osaka run in 10 hours and 52 minutes in 1929. By October 1930, the Tsubame limited express train was running between Tokyo and Kobe in 8 hours and 55 minutes.

An even newer phenomenon was civilian air travel. On 25 July 1925, the *Asahi* newspaper sponsored an aircraft named *Hatsukaze* (First Wind) and *Kochikaze* (East Wind) on the first flights to Europe. Departing from the Yoyogi parade ground in Tokyo, they arrived in Rome on 27 October. The journey took three months, but it was a splendid feat.

At the time, the main airfield in the Tokyo area was in Tachikawa, on the far western outskirts of the city. The site for land reclamation to build a new airport at Haneda in Tokyo Bay was purchased by the government in January 1930. It covered an area of 160,000 *tsubo* (530,000 square meters), and cost ¥130,000. Haneda Airfield was completed in August 1931, and the first flight to Osaka took off on 25 August at 7:20 A.M. Airplanes were now equipped for commercial travel. In March 1931, the Tokyo Air Transport Company hired its first stewardesses.

Transformation of the Mass Media

The mass media also underwent an enormous transformation. The biggest innovation was the commencement of radio broadcasting. Radio became the medium for transmitting some of the most familiar and widely remembered episodes of Shōwa history, such as the appeal in 1936 to the mutinous troops in the February Twenty-Sixth Incident to stand down; the announcer exhorting Japanese female swimmer Maehata Hideko—*Maehata, ganbare!* (Hang in there, Maehata!)—in her dead-heat race against a German rival in the 1936 Berlin Olympics; and the broadcast in December 1941 bringing news of Pearl Harbor and the outbreak of war: "Before dawn on the eighth, forces of the imperial army and navy entered into a state of war with American and British forces in the western Pacific."

The first radio broadcast in Japan took place on 1 March 1925, from the Tokyo Broadcasting Station, set up on the campus of the Tokyo Higher School of Arts and Technology. Not long afterward, Osaka and Nagoya Broadcasting Stations opened, and on 6 August 1926 the three stations merged to form the Nippon Hōsō Kyōkai (NHK; Japan Broadcasting Corporation).

The newspaper *Yomiuri shinbun* was running a radio guide as early as 1925; by 1927 live broadcasts of baseball games had begun. As a result, the school songs, fight songs, and dorm songs of Waseda University, Keiō University, and the First and Third Higher Schools were also introduced to a wider public and became something of a fad. And on New Year's Eve 1927, the radio carried the first live broadcast of the bell of the Kan'eiji temple in Ueno ringing out the old year. Radio had come a long way very quickly.

In the 1920s, Japan also saw the consolidation of newspapers into a form of oligopoly. The major papers vied with one another in sending large numbers of correspondents to major events such as the Washington Conference, and as a result it was the larger-scale, financially more powerful newspapers that prospered. In 1924, the *Ōsaka asahi shinbun* and the *Ōsaka mainichi shinbun* each announced circulations of more than one million. In the world of magazines, *King,* a general-interest monthly, was founded in 1925 with a print run of 770,000 copies.

Meanwhile, in 1929 Tokutomi Sohō retired from Kokumin Shinbunsha, the newspaper company he had founded in the 1890s. In the Meiji era, powerful editorial writers such as Fukuzawa Yukichi at *Jiji shinpō,* Tokutomi at *Kokumin shinbun,* and Kuga Katsunan at *Nippon* had shaped political opinion. This now changed to a more contemporary style of journalism emphasizing factual reporting and mass circulation.

Change came to the world of book publishing as well. In 1926, the first *enpon* ("yen books")—inexpensive multivolume series with individual titles selling for one yen each—were published and created an immediate sensation. In December 1926, the publishing house Kaizōsha began publication of the sixty-three-volume *Gendai Nihon bungaku zenshū* (Library of contemporary Japanese literature). In 1927, Shinchōsha commenced sales of the fifty-seven-volume *Sekai bungaku zenshū* (Library of world literature), with advance orders of 580,000 copies. Shun'yōdō began publishing its sixty-volume *Meiji Taishō bungaku zenshū* (Library of Meiji and Taishō literature) in 1927. This trend toward multivolume series extended into art book publishing as well, with Heibonsha beginning publication of its fifty-four-volume *Sekai bijutsu zenshū* (Library of world art) also in 1927.

The *enpon* boom reached politics and philosophy with a ten-volume edition of the collected works of Lenin, published by Hakuyōsha, and an eighteen-volume collected works of Immanuel Kant published by Iwanami Shoten, both in 1926, and a thirteen-volume series from Ueno Shoten published in 1927 titled *Marukusu-shugi kōza* (Lectures on Marxism).

Iwanami Shoten also launched its Iwanami Bunko (Iwanami Paperback Library) series in 1927—a phenomenon unthinkable without the spread of higher education and the cultured readership it created.

The Diffusion of Western Culture

It was the early Shōwa period that also saw the import of contemporary Western culture to Japan, with Western classical music as a representative example. After World War I, Western musicians of the first rank began to visit Japan frequently. In November 1923, violinist Jascha Heifetz came to Tokyo and gave a recital in the auditorium of the Imperial Hotel. In May 1928, Jacques Thibaud, the most popular violinist of the era, gave a recital at the Imperial Theater. Solo musicians such as this, and vocal artists who might travel with a single accompanist, were now able to make the long trip to Japan.

For obvious reasons, visits by larger-scale productions such as symphony orchestras and opera were less common than today. In their place, Japanese artists began to perform. In January 1926 the Symphonic Society of Japan mounted its first concert. It was for members only, who numbered a thousand people who had paid membership fees of either three to five yen. The program included Beethoven's Symphony No. 3 ("Eroica") and other works, and the orchestra was conducted by Prince Konoe Fumimaro's younger brother, Konoe Hidemaro, who made a gramophone record leading the Berlin Philharmonic before World War II, and had an active career in music into the 1970s.

In Japan, recordings were widespread and popular. They could also be quite expensive: a set of Beethoven's violin concertos recorded with Fritz

Kreisler sold for ¥35.50—at a time when the starting salary for a university graduate in a government job ranged from ¥33 to ¥133 a month. Slightly more affordable was ¥16 for Schubert's "Unfinished" Symphony (No. 8), conducted by the popular Leopold Stokowski. But this was still a lot of money, and the fact that there was a market at all is an indication of the level of interest in Japan for culture of this kind (Kurata Yoshihiro, *Nihon rekōdo bunka shi* [A history of Japanese records]).

Electric recording technology came to Japan in the late 1920s; "Defune no Minato" (Port of Departure) by Fujiwara Yoshie, recorded by Victor in February 1928, is said to have been among the first using the new technology. It also created a major scandal when Miyashita Aki—daughter of Nakamigawa Hikojirō, a powerful executive in the Mitsui zaibatsu and wife of prominent physician Miyashita Sōsuke—left her husband in pursuit of Fujiwara. Miyashita eventually parted from Fujiwara as well, but in the postwar period won renewed celebrity as a panelist on the popular NHK television show *Watashi no himitsu* (the Japanese version of the American program *I've Got a Secret*). In 1962 she was elected to the House of Councilors in one of the nationwide district elections, winning a large number of votes and making her a forerunner of later celebrity politicians.

The Growth of Sports

The burgeoning popularity of sports was also a phenomenon of the 1920s. In July 1924, at the Eighth Olympiad in Paris, nineteen Japanese athletes participated, and Oda Mikio placed sixth in the track-and-field events with his performance in the triple jump.

In July 1928, the Ninth Olympiad was held in Amsterdam. Triple-jumper Oda Mikio and 200-meter breaststroke swimmer Tsuruta Yoshiyuki won the first gold medals for Japan, while Hitomi Kinue captured the silver in the women's 800-meter race. Before this, Hitomi had participated in the Second International Women's Track and Field Competition in Sweden in August 1926, where she had set a new world's record in the broad jump, and also won the individual all-round event. She may still be the greatest female athlete in Japanese history.

But the sport that won the most passionate following was amateur baseball. In 1924 the Tenth National Secondary School Baseball Championship (now the National High School Baseball Championship) was held in the newly completed Kōshien Stadium in Osaka. The competition already had a decade-long history, but now it began to attract broader attention—especially after 1927, when the games began to be broadcast live over the new medium of radio.

The Intercity Baseball Tournament—now fallen on hard times, but once a very popular event—also began in 1927. The venue was Meiji Jingū Baseball Stadium, and the first tournament was won by the Mantetsu Club from the Japanese concession of Dalian in North China.

Golf also became popular in late Taishō and early Shōwa Japan. The diaries of government officials of the period frequently mention golf dates. When Kido Kōichi was serving as chief secretary to the lord keeper of the privy seal, it was not at all unusual for him to be golfing twice a week—taking either the morning or the afternoon off from office duties to do so. Golf was also developing into a competitive sport, and the first Japan Open Golf Championship was held on 28 May 1927.

The growth of sports during this period was symbolized by the development in 1926 of Meiji Jingū Gaien (the outer garden of Meiji Shrine) in Sendagaya into a major sports complex, with a baseball stadium, sumo wrestling arena, and other facilities.

Other Entertainment

Motion pictures developed into a major form of urban entertainment at this time. Beginning in 1924, dedicated movie theaters proliferated rapidly. In 1925, as the three-party coalition cabinet was replaced by the second Katō cabinet, Charlie Chaplin's *The Gold Rush* captivated large audiences.

At this point, films were still silent, and in Japan, entertainers called *benshi* accompanied them with live narration. In February 1931, the American film *Morocco* became the first "talkie" to be publicly screened, with Japanese subtitles.

Amusement parks were another innovation. In the Kansai region, Hamadera, which had been popular as seaside bathing resort since the Meiji period, was now developed into a more modern amusement park, and in 1926 the Ayameike Amusement Park opened in Nara prefecture. Also in 1926 the Ueno Zoological Gardens in Tokyo purchased a polar bear, which caused a great sensation. Night pleasure cruises along the coast to escape the heat of the summer also became a popular diversion in 1926.

The Shōwa Depression

The financial crisis of 1927 was abruptly followed by the global depression beginning in 1929, bringing major changes to Japanese society. In the two years after 1929, commodity prices fell by nearly 30 percent. Nominal gross domestic product (GDP) fell by 10 percent in 1930 compared to the previous year, and another 9.3 percent in 1931. For this period, the drop was even worse in Japan than in Britain, the United States, France, or Germany. The market for raw silk and cocoons collapsed, and prices for exports like cotton textiles, as well as for agricultural commodities like rice and soybeans, fell precipitously. About a million people lost their jobs, and social unrest increased, with a rapid surge in labor strikes and agrarian disputes beginning in 1930.

Looking at the situation sector-by-sector, the silk industry attempted to shift the burden of more than a 60 percent drop in prices to its female workers and the silk-raising farmers, but this strategy proved unsuccessful. Silk decisively lost its position as Japan's leading industry for earning foreign currency. On the other hand, the spinning industry, an oligopoly dominated by five major spinning companies, managed to recover from the depression relatively early by curtailing operating hours and laying off workers. But the weaving industry, dominated by small and medium-sized businesses, was hit hard. And the heavy industrial sector, which had been struggling since the 1920s, was also hit exceptionally hard.

The year 1929 was exceptionally bad for job-seeking university graduates: only 12 percent found work overall, and even graduates of the University of Tokyo—the most prestigious academic institution in the country—had slightly less than a 30 percent placement rate. But the gravest damage of the depression fell on farming villages.

First, the price of cocoons collapsed beginning in 1929. Raising silkworms was the biggest auxiliary source of income for many farm families, so this was a heavy blow. Then, in 1930, a bumper crop of rice sent rice prices down as well. The situation was dire: cocoon prices had fallen by 55 percent, and rice prices by 38 percent (see Table 2.4). And for the many farm households that supplemented income through part-time nonfarm work, wages fell sharply.

More than half of the country's independent owner-farmers and three-quarters of its tenant farmers were running deficits and piling up debts, with average indebtedness hitting between ¥800 to ¥900—significantly more than the average annual income of ¥600 to ¥700. Then in 1931 Japan was hit with a massive crop failure, exacerbating the disaster in rural areas.

One sign of this was undernourished children. In a 1931 survey in Akita prefecture, of 174,000 primary school students, 117,500 brought box lunches to school, 26,000 went home to eat, and 28,790 had no lunch at all. Many families were selling daughters into prostitution; many elementary school teachers in the countryside were not receiving their wages. Even in metropolitan Tokyo, some 6,000 primary school graduates were found to be working in geisha houses or in shops in conditions close to indentured servitude. Rural villages did not begin to recover until about 1935.

Table 2.4   Variation in Prices for Agricultural Commodities, 1921–1940
(base: 1934–1936=100)

Year	1934–1936 Weights		Agricultural Commodities Overall	Current Inputs (1918–1940 Weights)
	Rice	Cocoons		
1921	133.1	171.9	143.3	136.63
1922	97.2	251.6	127.8	143.59
1923	116.3	252.6	138.5	142.27
1924	140.9	198.8	148.5	151.46
1925	130.0	258.5	148.8	165.63
1926	120.2	202.9	134.1	139.66
1927	103.4	145.5	117.3	120.37
1928	98.5	156.3	115.6	127.33
1929	96.8	170.6	114.3	123.17
1930	60.8	76.0	75.3	93.20
1931	60.2	75.5	69.3	70.92
1932	74.4	88.1	77.8	82.92
1933	73.6	131.5	85.6	88.00
1934	97.2	62.2	92.2	91.58
1935	102.0	113.7	101.0	103.46
1936	100.8	124.1	106.8	104.89
1937	113.7	129.8	118.0	122.30
1938	120.0	122.3	126.8	134.46
1939	151.7	258.6	171.8	162.24
1940	152.6	262.0	190.2	176.57

Source: Umemura Mataji, et al., *Chōki keizai tōkei: Suikei to bunseki 9 nōringyō* (Estimates of long-term economic statistics of Japan since 1868: 9 Agriculture and forestry), Tōyō Keizai Shinpōsha, 1966.

Notes

1. The French had postponed the convening of the tariff conference for three years because of a disagreement over the payment of indemnities for the Boxer Rebellion. Britain and the United States offered to relieve the burden of the indemnities by converting them to funds for education and cultural development. The French insisted that the indemnities be denominated in gold, rather than the highly depreciated French franc, partly to compensate for the bankruptcy of a French bank related to Chinese investment.

2. Aikawa Yoshisuke (1880–1967) was born in Yamaguchi prefecture. After graduating from the Imperial University of Tokyo, he founded many businesses and became the leader of the Nissan group, which went on to develop into one of Japan's most powerful business groupings including present-day companies like Nissan Motors, ENEOS Holdings Inc., Hitachi, Ltd., etc.

3. In 1910, Kōtoku Shūsui (1878–1911) and twenty-four other people were indicted and sentenced to death for plotting an assassination of Emperor Meiji. Ultimately twelve of them, including Kōtoku himself, were executed while the rest

received reduced sentences of life imprisonment. It is now known that only five of them had any actual involvement in a vague, primitive plan to attack the emperor. For the most part, it was a frame-up orchestrated by the government.

4. Kishi Nobusuke (1896–1987) continued in the Ministry of Commerce and Industry to become a key figure in the industrializaiton of Manchuria. He was cabinet minister in the prewar cabinets of Prime Minister Konoe and Tōjō. He was imprisoned as a suspected war criminal after World War II and after his release played a key role in organizing the postwar Liberal Democratic Party, serving as prime minister from 1957 to 1960. Kishi was the grandfather of Prime Minister Abe Shinzō.

5. The Conference of Military Councilors provided advice to the emperor when requested to do so. It consisted of the army minister, chief of the general staff, a few senior generals, the navy minister, chief of the naval general staff, and a few senior admirals. Despite this, there was no joint meeting between the army and navy. This conference was a nominal one for senior military leaders without any particular roles or duties. However, it could exert influence when decisionmaking was at a stalemate.

6. The Gensuifu (Supreme Military Council), consisting of field marshals and admirals of the fleet, responded to consultations with the emperor. In reality, it was a place to show respect to the highest-ranking military leaders.

3

Japan in Crisis

~

Legacy of World War I

The Imperial Japanese Army had by far the greatest influence on the politics of prewar Japan. From the mid-1920s, when the Shōwa period began, the army started to transform into a very different and independent political power from that of the Meiji-Taishō period and began to exert enormous influence over foreign and domestic politics. This is why I call the army in the period from the mid-1920s to 1945 the "Shōwa army."

The roots of the Shōwa army can be traced to two sources, both originating with World War I. The first was the advent of modern military technology and the concept of preparing for a "total war," while the second was the rise of "pacifism" as will be discussed later.

World War I was the first war in decades in which the advanced nations threw themselves into an all-out conflict. After the Franco-Prussian War of 1870–1871, aside from a colonial skirmish or two, there was no major war among the Western powers (including the United States). And the Franco-Prussian War itself was brief. There had been no lengthy and truly murderous conflict among the advanced countries since the Napoleonic Wars.

Because of this, World War I saw a startlingly rapid modernization of military technology. Entirely new weapons such as tanks and poison gas were used for the first time, and even previously existing weapons such as airplanes and submarines evolved from prototypes into serious fighting machines. Machine guns and artillery, which had been around for some time, saw a dramatic improvement in deadly functionality. Moreover, the combating countries became totally focused on the military, devising ways to harness their entire modern production capacity for the war effort, resulting in systems of total national mobilization.

During this same period, the capabilities of the Imperial Japanese Army had deteriorated precipitously. At the time of the Russo-Japanese War of 1904–1905, the Japanese army was one of the most powerful in the world; by the end of World War I, it was third-rate among world powers.

A revision of the imperial defense policy undertaken in 1918, just before the end of World War I, was an attempt to cope with such development of military technology. The official text in this revision has not been found yet. But it is indisputable that this revision proposed a modernization of the army's equipment, the adoption of an army organizational structure, and increases in both firepower and mobility. In this new system, it was planned for an army to consist of two new divisions; a new division was 3/4 the size of an old division, therefore an army was 1.5 times the size of an old division (Kitaoka Shinichi, *Nihon rikugun to tairiku seisaku* [The Imperial Japanese Army and continental policy]). The driving force behind the adoption of this policy was Tanaka Giichi, deputy chief of general staff. As for the total mobilization system, such officers as Nagata Tetsuzan started serious studies.

The second legacy of World War I was a new type of pacifism. The results of one of the bloodiest conflicts in human history was a deep loathing of war among many, which gave rise to a new peace movement unlike any that had existed before. There is a well-known anecdote about Yamagata Aritomo—A military officer riding on a train accidentally stepped on the toes of a workingman standing beside him when the train lurched. The officer quickly apologized, but the worker retorted, "You think you can get away with that! Don't you know what's going on in Russia?"—clearly referring to the revolution. Overhearing this exchange, Yamagata was appalled by what he saw as the changes in the tenor of the times, and the contempt displayed for the military.

By the time of Yamagata's death in 1922, arms reduction bills had been introduced into the Diet. Previously, disarmament had been almost impossible for politicians to advocate if they wanted to maintain the favor of the genrō and the possibility of forming a cabinet. But this was now changing.

The Yamanashi and Ugaki Troop Reduction Plans

Following the naval arms limitations decided upon in 1921–1922 at the Washington Conference, it was now the army's turn, as the government began to grapple with reductions in its land forces. In 1922, Minister of Army

Yamanashi Hanzō implemented what came to be called the "Yamanashi troop disarmament," reducing the Imperial Japanese Army by 2,268 officers, 57,296 noncommissioned officers and soldiers, and about 13,000 horses. The number of divisions and infantry and cavalry regiments remained the same, but the number of companies in each division was reduced by attrition and other factors, eliminating 252 infantry companies (a division would normally have 12 companies), 29 cavalry companies, 7 companies of engineers, and 9 transport companies. The artillery lost six field artillery regiments and one mountain artillery regiment. Two new heavy field artillery regiments were created, but on the whole this meant a substantial reduction in firepower. In 1923 cuts were made to fortifications, military academies, and army administrative offices. This resulted in a total reduction in the army budget of ¥40.33 million for fiscal years 1922 and 1923.

But even this was not enough to satisfy public opinion. The army responded with the "Ugaki troop reduction" beginning in 1925, aimed at modernizing Japan's defenses. Pushed through by Ugaki Kazushige, army minister in the cabinet of Katō Takaaki, this plan sought to reduce the army by four divisions, and use the savings in the operating budget to invest in modern equipment for the army. Eliminating four divisions meant the elimination of sixteen infantry regiments, four cavalry regiments, four field artillery regiments, four regiments of engineers, and four transport regiments—or a total of 33,900 officers and men and some 6,000 horses.

To provide employment for some of the officers dismissed in this reduction of personnel, Ugaki assigned about 2,000 to military training programs in boys' schools (middle school and above). This would later form part of the system of total wartime mobilization. Ugaki also reduced the standard term of conscripted military service from two and a half years to two years. This would not only reduce the burden of service on conscripted personnel, but also create a larger number of army reservists.

However, the Ugaki troop reduction did not advance the cause of military modernization. The total number of field and mountain artillery pieces attached to a division would later rise to a peak of forty-seven, but even this fell short of the fifty-four that were standard at the time of the Russo-Japanese War. Despite the fact that the lesson of World War I had been, more than anything else, a need to increase and modernize firepower, the Yamanashi troop reduction in particular also cut expenses by cutting investments in artillery.

In 1926 the first independent tank company (comprising ten vehicles) had been created, but by 1928 the number still had not increased. Even by 1932, total annual tank production was only about twenty vehicles. In 1928 the army air corps was also stalled at the six air regiments to which it had been expanded during Ugaki's tenure as army minister (Bōei Kenshūjo Senshibu, *Rikugun gunsenbi* [Imperial Japanese Army war preparedness]; Yamada Akira, *Gunbi kakuchō no kindaishi* [A modern history of military expansion]). Ugaki was doing his best to meet the two challenges from World War I, but Japan's actual economic power was inadequate to achieve more than modest improvements in military equipment.

The Era of Ugaki

Yamanashi and Ugaki were both close to Tanaka Giichi. Yamanashi had served as vice minister when Tanaka was minister of the army in the Hara Takashi cabinet, and Ugaki had gone from vice minister under Tanaka in the second Yamamoto Gonnohyōe cabinet to become army minister in his own right in the cabinet of Kiyoura Keigo. This is especially noteworthy since Ugaki had been appointed army minister in the face of strong opposition from Field Marshal Uehara Yūsaku, chief of the Army General Staff. While Tanaka backed Ugaki, Uehara favored Fukuda Masatarō, and there was a clash between these two camps. Fukuda was a general and military councilor, two years older than Ugaki, and had also served as commandant in the Kantō area at the time that martial law was declared during the Great Kantō Earthquake. The previously noted massacre of Korean residents and other unfortunate incidents that occurred on his watch after the earthquake might have been one of the factors that prevented him from becoming army minister.

Ugaki's troop reduction plan was a brave experiment. Up to that point, elimination of entire regiments or divisions had not been attempted. The vote in the Conference of Military Councilors approving the Ugaki reduction had been close due to both factional and ideological conflict. The circle surrounding Army Chief of Staff Uehara tended to be rather old-guard in their thinking about armaments. For example, Lieutenant-General Tanaka Kunishige, a Satsuma man who graduated as a member of the fourth class of the Imperial Japanese Army Academy (IJAA), wrote a letter to Uehara on 4 September 1924 in which he observed that there was no nation in Japan's immediate vicinity that possessed modern armaments. Japan's neighborhood, according to the letter, consisted of a backward and inadequately armed China and a Soviet Union still in the throes of internal unrest. Modern armaments were not really necessary against such opponents. And Japan was a minor economic power, with few natural resources. Modern military equipment would be wasted on Japan, and Japan was not suited for protracted warfare. Japan should continue to aim for a quick victory, delivered at the early stage of a conflict by a large force of well-trained infantry (Uehara Yūsaku Kankei Monjo Kenkyūkai, ed., *Uehara Yūsaku kankei monjo* [Papers of Uehara Yūsaku]).

This argument had some logic from the perspective of Japan's immediate environment, limited economic strength, limited natural resources, and other factors at the time. But to adopt this policy would have opened up an insurmountable gap between Japan and the other great powers. And this was why Ugaki's insistence on the goal of military modernization won such strong support among the army elite at this time.

When the four divisions were eliminated in the implementation of the Ugaki troop reduction, a number of powerful high-ranking officers were placed on reserve duty (which in army culture was tantamount to punishment, unless it was for reasons of health or retirement). Among them were Generals Machida Keiu and Fukuda Masatarō (both military councilors) and Lieutenant-Generals Ishimitsu Maomi and Idogawa Tatsuzō. They were all men from Kyushu—Machida from Kagoshima, Fukuda from Nagasaki, Ishimitsu from Kumamoto, and Idogawa from Miyazaki—and all were close to Uehara. As noted earlier, a major scandal involving Tanaka Giichi's use of secret army funds from the Siberia intervention had arisen in the Diet in 1926, and it was Uehara who was behind this. The depth of outrage felt by Uehara and his faction is palpable. And it was Ugaki who suppressed their efforts. The Uehara faction saw Tanaka and Ugaki as a united force, which was not far from the truth.

In any case, Ugaki had won both the ideological and the factional struggle. Around him gathered officers such as Minami Jirō (6th class, IJAA), Hata Eitarō (7th class, deceased 1930), Abe Nobuyuki (9th class), Ninomiya Harushige (12th class), Sugiyama Hajime (12th class), Koiso Kuniaki (12th class), and Tatekawa Yoshitsugu (13th class), who occupied key positions in both the Ministry of Army and the Army General Staff Office.

But the power of the Uehara faction did not disappear. The attempt to pin the secret fund scandal on Tanaka had misfired, but the power of the faction lived on in figures such as Mutō Nobuyoshi (from Saga, 3rd class, inspector-general of military training, 1927–1932); Araki Sadao (Tokyo, 9th class, chief of the First Bureau [Operations] of Army General Staff, 1925–1928); Mazaki Jinzaburō (Saga, 9th class); and Hayashi Senjūrō (Ishikawa, 8th class), and remained a force to be reckoned with, especially in the Army General Staff Office.

I should mention that the reason I have indicated the graduating class at the Imperial Japanese Army Academy to which each of these officers belonged is because these class affiliations were extremely important in understanding the relationships among these members of the military elite. Even today, with the modern bureaucrats of the central government ministries in Kasumigaseki, knowing what year they entered their ministry is a crucially important piece of information. Bureaucrats—at least those belonging to the same ministry—are always well-informed about the years of entry and the curriculum vitae of their peers. Personnel assignments, and especially seniority and annual postings, are the core of a bureaucracy. And army officers are bureaucrats. In fact their sense of seniority was even more highly developed than that of their civilian counterparts. In the case of the Imperial

Japanese Army, where many officers went to army cadet school and then advanced to the Imperial Japanese Army Academy, members of the same graduating class would have been living, studying, and training together from the age of fourteen or fifteen until the age of twenty-two, which naturally resulted in a unique sense of both solidarity and competition. Knowing which class an officer belonged to is also very useful for understanding his relations with officers both senior and junior to him. As an additional comment, it is easy to remember Ugaki's lineage because he was a member of the first graduating class of the Imperial Japanese Army Academy, and he was born in 1868, the first year of the Meiji era.

Allow me to also add a line or two about the Army War College. After graduating from the Army Academy, graduates were assigned as officers for at least a few years. Some were given the opportunity to study at the Army War College for three years. Selection was highly competitive with only fifty to sixty officers, or about 10 percent of the Army Academy graduates, being admitted. These select officers made up the elite and would go on to be swifly promoted through the ranks. Between those who graduated from the Army War College and those who did not, there was a vast difference in terms of promotion.

In sum, the 1920s was the era of Tanaka and Ugaki in the Imperial Japanese Army. First and foremost, they prioritized military modernization. Second, as mentioned previously, they maintained cordial relations with the political parties. And third, they paid adequate attention to the issues of international relations. These were the essential characteristics of the Tanaka-Ugaki line. But before long, this line would come under criticism from several quarters.

The Futaba-kai and the Isseki-kai

One source of opposition was an association comprising graduates from the sixteenth class of the academy. The origins of the Shōwa army are often traced to a meeting in the German town of Baden-Baden on 27 October 1921 among three young officers to discuss plans for the reform of the army: Nagata Tetsuzan, military attaché to Switzerland; Obata Toshishirō, assigned as a military attaché to Russia but resident in Berlin at the time because the Soviets refused to admit him; and Okamura Yasuji, then traveling in Europe. Dubbed the "three crows" of the sixteenth class of the academy, and regarded as rising stars, they made "a secret agreement concerning the dissolution of cliques, personnel reform, military organization reform, and arrangements for general mobilization," according to an entry in Okamura's diary (Takamiya Tahei, *Gunkoku taiheiki* [A chronicle of militarism]; Tsutsui Kiyotada, *Ni niroku jiken to sono jidai* [The February Twenty-Sixth Incident and those times]). Many see this as the beginning of the Shōwa army.

Yet I think the importance of this meeting in Baden-Baden has been exaggerated. In 1921 all three of these men were about thirty-seven years old. It is not at all unusual for old friends who have not seen one another for some time, and who happen to meet in a foreign country, to stay up half the night talking—and perhaps talking big and boastfully. To characterize the contents of such talk as a serious secret pledge seems to be going too far. And historian Tsutsui Kiyotada has pointed out that the solidarity among these three figures commenced at a much earlier date than this (*Shōwa-ki Nihon no kōzō* [The structure of Shōwa-period Japan]).

Even so, the spirit of the meeting comes across clearly—especially from the fact that they identified the dissolution of cliques and personnel reform as the first points to be addressed. At that time, Yamagata Aritomo was still alive, and Tanaka Giichi and other members of the Chōshū clique were in robust good health, so the "three crows" shared a strong anti-Chōshū consciousness. Later, they agreed to prevent the admission of officers from Chōshū to the Army War College, and it is said that during the decade of the 1920s very few were admitted. In the 1920s, Tanaka Giichi and other Chōshū men held power at the top, but the men who were actually administering the entrance examinations at the college were of a much younger generation, and it seems likely they were able to implement the measures they envisioned. Even if they were acting out of a sense of victimization, it is surprising to see their sensitivity to factionalism.

After their return to Japan, they continued to get together from time to time—usually at a restaurant in Shibuya called Futaba-tei, which led the group to call itself the Futaba-kai. The men who assembled there, centered around the "three crows" of the sixteenth class, included Kōmoto Daisaku and Yamaoka Shigeatsu of the fifteenth class; Itagaki Seishirō and Kuroki Chikayoshi (retired) of the sixteenth class; and Tōjō Hideki of the seventeenth class. It is unclear when the name Futaba-kai began to be used, but Tsutsui Kiyotada believes that the group began to meet sometime in 1923. It is clear that by 1927 the group was gathering several times a year, and on 12 January 1929 there were a total of eighteen men in attendance: the eight already named were joined by Matsumura Masakazu (17th class), Isogai Rensuke (16th), Ono Hirotake (16th), Ogasawara Kazuo (16th), Okabe Naosaburō (18th), Nakano Naoharu (18th), Doihara Kenji (16th), Watari Hisao (17th), Kudō Yoshio (17th), and Yamashita Tomoyuki (18th). Two additional members—Iida Sadakata (17th) and, in an advisory capacity, Ogawa Tsunezaburō (14th)—were added in April 1929, bringing the total to twenty.

Following this, a slightly younger generation of staff officers formed another group, called the Mokuyō-kai (Thursday Club), centered around Suzuki Teiichi (22nd class). Participants in the first meeting were Suzuki, Ishiwara Kanji (21st), Murakami Keisaku (22nd), Nemoto Hiroshi (23rd), Numata Takazō (24th), Miyama Kamezaburō (24th), Hongō Yoshio (24th),

Tsuchihashi Yūitsu (24th), and Mutō Akira (25th). Tsutsui believes this first meeting took place on 3 November 1927. Nagata Tetsuzan attended the second meeting of this group, and eventually the Mokuyō-kai merged with the Futaba-kai to form the Isseki-kai. The leaders of the two groups, Nagata and Suzuki, were six years apart in age, and there was a decade between the most senior (15th class) and most junior (25th class) participants, but the establishment of this organization was a major step toward unifying the young staff officers serving in the nerve centers of the army: the Ministry of Army and the Army General Staff Office.

But how did these developments relate to the power of Ugaki and his associates? Suzuki Teiichi, leader of the Mokuyō-kai, later spoke of Ugaki's ascendency in the following, quite interesting terms: "Ugaki was someone the men of the army relied on and believed would accomplish something. When he took office [as army minister], his instructions to his subordinates were splendid. The officers all felt like, 'Yes, this is what we must do!' and backed Ugaki" (Nihon Kindai Shiryō Kenkyūkai, ed., *Suzuki Teiichi-shi danwa sokkiroku, jō* [Transcripts of conversations with Mr. Suzuki Teiichi, vol. 1]). In other words, it seems safe to assume that when Ugaki was appointed army minister in 1924, he was not criticized among the staff officers; rather he was redeemed by them. And this was true even when his troop reduction policy began to be implemented in 1925.

A Critique of the China Question

I believe there is another source for the origin of the Shōwa army. And that is a group who worked in or around the China Section of the Second Bureau (Intelligence) of the Army General Staff, which was passionately concerned with the issues of China, Manchuria, and Mongolia. The army placed extreme emphasis on grades and ratings, and many of the students with the best grades at the Army War College were sent abroad to study in Germany or France and returned to posts in the First Bureau (Operations) of the Army General Staff. Others, with perhaps more political skills and background, might be active in the Ministry of Army. Members of a sort of second-rate elite who did not fit into either of these first two categories ended up in the Second Bureau (Kitaoka Shinichi, "Shina-ka kanryō no yakuwari" [The role of the China Section bureaucrats]).

Even in the Second Bureau, the China Section was not a prized position. Despite the priority placed by the army on the issue of China, almost no chief of the China Section had ever risen to become bureau chief of the general staff. The army culture was such that officers with European language skills and experience studying abroad were the ones who were selected for advancement. Moreover, the China Section was a frustrating

Nagata Tetsuzan (1884–1935)
Known as "the army's greatest genius," Nagata was an elite graduate of the Army War College. His Futaba-kai was an organization of field-grade officers of the fifteenth to eighteenth graduating classes of the Imperial Japanese Army Academy, with about twenty members at its peak. Nagata had a rational approach to the establishment of a system of total mobilization, but he was seen by members of the rival Kōdōha (Imperial Way Faction) as the nucleus of the Tōseiha (Control Faction). On 12 August 1935 he was cut down in an assassination by Lieutenant-Colonel Aizawa Saburō, a Kōdōha sympathizer, while he was working at his desk in the Military Affairs Bureau. Photo courtesy of Kyodo News Images Inc.

place to work. Despite the opportunity to manipulate the various Chinese warlord factions, the officers working in the China Section felt constrained by Japan's policy to cooperate with the Western powers.

Meanwhile, among the China Section officers were many who were worried about the rising power of the Kuomintang. Unlike older China hands, they no longer believed that they could achieve their goals by simply manipulating the warlord factions. Those in the China Section were among the first to perceive that if Japan did not use its own forces to secure Manchuria, Japan's interests and rights would be at risk. It is not surprising that the combination of organizational and professional discontent coupled with frustration in the work itself led them toward a bold plan to break out of the status quo. Among the members of the Futaba-kai and Isseki-kai were more than a few with lengthy experience in the China Section—representative examples being Kōmoto Daisaku and Okamura Yasuji.

It took a surprisingly long time to build a consensus among various factions in the army on the resolution of the issue of Manchuria and Mongolia. There was nothing conclusive about this in the meeting at Baden-Baden. Minutes of the Mokuyō-kai show that resolution of the Manchuria-Mongolia issue was discussed at the March 1928 meeting, focusing on the question of whether or not Japan should take control of the region by force, but there did not appear to be passionate support for such a venture at that time. This would come afterward, in late 1928, following the assassination of Zhang Zuolin, in which their comrade Kōmoto played a key role. Calls to support Kōmoto probably strengthened their solidarity and contributed to the development of the movement. In this sense, the assassination of Zhang was significant in the final crystallization of Shōwa military factionalism.

The Isseki-kai was officially inaugurated on 19 May 1929. Three resolutions were agreed upon: there should be reform of army personnel and an aggressive pursuit of policy measures; priority should be placed on the resolution of the Manchuria-Mongolia issue; and Generals Araki Sadao, Mazaki Jinzaburō, and Hayashi Senjūrō should be supported in a campaign to restore the army to its proper state. This occurred right at the time that Prime Minister Tanaka Giichi was wrestling with the problem of whether or not to punish Kōmoto. Army General Staff officers were strongly critical of both Tanaka's foreign policy and his proposal for dealing with Kōmoto, and they entrusted the expression of their discontent to the three generals just mentioned, who were members of the Uehara faction, Tanaka's chief rivals.

The Second Ugaki Era

A little over a month after the formation of the Isseki-kai, the Tanaka cabinet resigned and the cabinet of Hamaguchi Osachi was formed, with Ugaki serving for the second time as minister of the army. Ugaki wrote in his diary that he alone could resolve the difficult problems facing the army—and then quickly added that this was hubris, and that perhaps even he was not up to the task.

Ugaki was certainly in an overwhelmingly strong position, but the road ahead was challenging. The first task was reform of military administration, which essentially meant pushing ahead with further downsizing and modernization. His list of reforms included: redeployment of certain divisions to the continent, disbanding of the Imperial Guards division, and closing of the Inspectorate-General of Military Training, with the expenses saved to be allocated to a buildup of the Army Air Service and an enhancement of the firepower of the army as a whole.

Kōmoto Daisaku (1882–1955)
Kōmoto's elder sister was the wife of General Hongō Fusatarō, and his younger sister married General Tada Hayao. In 1926, Kōmoto was promoted to colonel and became a staff officer of the Kwangtung Army. His role in engineering the assassination of Zhang Zuolin in 1928 radically altered the course of Shōwa history. Photo courtesy of Kyodo News Images Inc.

This was a bold plan, and naturally there was fierce opposition from conservatives in the army—especially concerning doing away with the Inspectorate-General of Military Training and the Imperial Guards, both institutions with long traditions. And the redeployment of military units to the Asian continent also met with considerable resistance. The regiments of the prewar Japanese army had strong ties to the districts of Japan in which they were based, and were the pride of their communities. The idea of stationing them on the continent was criticized for not giving sufficient consideration to these emotional—even spiritual—bonds between army units and their locale. Moreover, it was not clear whether the Hamaguchi cabinet, with its stated policy of budgetary austerity, would actually accept increased spending for military modernization. There was a strong chance that cuts would be made without the savings being invested in the promised modernization of forces.

The China issue had also become difficult. "Shidehara diplomacy" seemed to be reaching a dead end because of the rise of Chinese nationalism, and cooperation with the Anglo-American powers with regard to China was beginning to come unraveled.

As noted previously, Ugaki's strategy was to pursue modernization while maintaining cordial relations with the political parties and to pursue foreign policy through cooperative engagement with Great Britain and the United States. But first of all, there was opposition to modernization, mainly from the Uehara faction. Then there was opposition to cooperation with the British and the Americans. And there were those who favored modernization but thought it impossible within the framework of party politics, and who argued that the parties themselves must be shattered in order to move forward. There was deepening opposition to any cooperation with the political parties. Given the economic depression that followed the Hamaguchi cabinet's return to the gold standard and criticism of its signing of the London Naval Treaty as interference in the right of supreme command, the power of the parties appeared to be faltering.

Prime Minister Hamaguchi was shot in Tokyo Station in November 1930, which sent the Minseitō into shock. Just at the time of the shooting a new development occurred within the ranks of army staff officers with the formation of the Sakura-kai (Cherry Blossom Society), led by Lieutenant-Colonel Hashimoto Kingorō. Hashimoto was a graduate of the twenty-third class of the Imperial Army Academy and from 1927 to 1930 served as a military attaché in Turkey, where he was deeply impressed by Mustafa Kemal Atatürk and the Turkish independence war, which he studied carefully and wished to introduce to Japan. After he returned to Japan in 1930, he headed the Russian Section within the Second Bureau (Intelligence) of the Army General Staff, and recruited like-minded officers such as Sakata Yoshirō (21st class, head of the Intelligence Group, Military Intelligence Department of the Ministry of Army) and Higuchi Kiichirō (21st class, a staff officer at Tokyo Garrison headquarters) to join the Sakura-kai. This organization was formed sometime between August and October 1930, and numbered a dozen or so members: Hashimoto, Sakata, and Higuchi were joined by Nemoto Hiroshi (23rd class, chief of the China Group, China Section, Army General Staff), Chō Isamu (28th class, China Section, Army General Staff), and others. The members resolved that the purpose of their organization was national reform, for which they would not reject the use of force to achieve their goals, and that their members should be active-duty officers of the rank of lieutenant-colonel or below with a commitment to national reform and without ambition for personal gain, who would work to broaden awareness of the necessity for national reform, expand the membership of the organization, and craft concrete plans for such reform.

The Sakura-kai played a leading role, in concert with members of the civilian right wing such as Ōkawa Shūmei, in an abortive attempt in March 1931 to surround the Diet building and implement a coup d'état that came to be known as the March Incident. This was a very crude effort, but it is noteworthy because the coup's leaders planned to install General Ugaki as prime minister. Moreover, men seen as close associates of Ugaki, such as Koiso Kuniaki, director of the Military Affairs Bureau, and Tatekawa Yoshitsugu, chief of the Second Bureau of the Army General Staff, were implicated in the failed attempt.

It is doubtful that Ugaki himself was involved, but at the very least what we see here is that following the shooting of Prime Minister Hamaguchi, the movement to break out of the political deadlock had broadened from mid-level staff officers such as Hashimoto to higher-ranking military officials such as Koiso and Tatekawa. At this time, the army pinned its hopes on Ugaki, and then swiftly withdrew them. In April 1931, Ugaki resigned as army minister, claiming illness, thus ending the Ugaki era. It would be followed by the era of Shōwa military factionalism.

The Manchurian Incident

Ishiwara Kanji

The protagonist of the Manchurian Incident was Ishiwara Kanji. Without his ideology and resolution it would never have happened. Later, Ishiwara would oppose the widening of the Sino-Japanese War and come into conflict with Tōjō Hideki, and he has continued to enjoy a certain sort of popularity. His thought—an unusual mix of unique insight and bullheadedness, science and dogma, historical analysis and subjective prophecy—attracted not only many of his contemporaries, but also later generations of scholars. According to Ishiwara, humanity, which had recently experienced the unprecedented conflict of the Great War, was now poised on the brink of what he called the Final War—a thoroughgoing war of annihilation fought primarily with aircraft. This would be followed by an era of total world peace under the hegemony of a single country. By the time this Final War would commence, airplanes would be able to circle the globe on nonstop flights, and it would be fought between the United States as the representative of Western civilization and Japan as representative of the East. But before this, Japan would first have to overthrow the Soviet Union, and the key to the nation's development was Manchuria.

Considering the fact that at present the development of nuclear missiles has rendered all-out war between the great powers unthinkable, one might give Ishiwara some credit for prescient insight. But obviously his overall analysis of the international situation was extraordinarily full of dogma and prejudice and totally lacking in balance. Ishiwara was a fanatical believer in Nichiren Buddhism, and his speech and actions had an eccentricity that frequently surprised and confounded others. But this also made him attractive to many of his fellow soldiers.

Ishiwara was assigned to the Kwantung Army staff in October 1928. This was immediately after Kōmoto Daisuke had engineered the assassination of Zhang Zuolin but had failed to expand this incident into a full-scale conflict between Japan and China. In May 1929, Itagaki Seishirō was assigned as a high-level staff officer to replace Kōmoto, who had been forced out of his Kwantung Army post. Ishiwara and Itagaki then began to lay the groundwork for the Manchurian Incident.

By April 1931, their plan was nearly complete, though they believed another year or so should be devoted to working to sway public opinion. But two incidents occurred in the summer of 1931 that unexpectedly began to shift popular sentiment. The first was an incident involving two Japanese soldiers, Captain Nakamura Shintarō, an Army General Staff officer, and Isugi Nobutarō, a sergeant-major in the cavalry reserves who was operating a boarding house. They were traveling in the Taonan region from 9 June to conduct a topographical survey of strategic sites, but on 27 June they were attacked and killed by Chinese troops. When the news of this reached the Japanese, the Kwantung Army argued for a forcible response, but neither the central leadership of the army nor the foreign ministry approved. The incident nevertheless marked an upsurge in public opinion supporting the defense of Japan's interests in Manchuria and Mongolia.

The other famous incident of that summer was the Wanpaoshan Incident. Wanpaoshan was a small village in a marshy area on the outskirts of the city of Changchun in Manchuria, where a Chinese broker had subleased land without the consent of its owners to a group of Korean farmers. The Koreans had begun to dig an irrigation ditch running several kilometers to a nearby river, but its route crossed land owned by Chinese farmers. The Chinese farmers protested to the local authorities, who then dispatched police to order that work on the ditch stop. But the Japanese consulate in Changchun sent consular police to the scene to support the Koreans, and a confrontation ensued in which some 200 Koreans and about 300 Chinese farmers were involved.

The incident continued from June into July and, while relatively trivial, was widely reported. A particularly exaggerated report was published on 1 July, which sparked an anti-Chinese reaction in Korea, resulting in the murder of more than a hundred Chinese by an angry mob of Koreans. This incident remained unresolved at the time of the Manchurian Incident, and played a significant role in inflaming popular opinion on the issue of

Manchuria and Mongolia. Then, on 4 August 1931, Minister of Army Minami Jirō called for a "positive" resolution of the Manchurian-Mongolian situation, further stirring up popular sentiment.

In the midst of this atmosphere, the Kwantung Army made preparations for action. But rumors began to leak out. The high command in Tokyo dispatched Tatekawa Yoshitsugu, Army General Staff chief of operations, to prevent any rash action. But the Kwantung Army officers, aware that there had been an intelligence leak, spirited Tatekawa away to a banquet as soon as he arrived in Manchuria, and proceeded to get him drunk. It is likely that Tatekawa himself knew full well that the incident was about to occur and, secretly sympathetic to the plot, allowed himself to be plied with liquor. Meanwhile, the Liutiaohu Incident was taking place.

Ishiwara Kanji (1889–1949)
Ishiwara became an adherent of the Nichiren sect when he joined Tanaka Chigaku's lay Buddhist organization, the Kokuchū-kai. A student of Ludendorff's theory of "total war" and Hans Delbrück's writings on military history, he prophesied a decisive conflict between Japan and the United States as the world's "Final War." He engineered the Manchurian Incident and was instrumental in the founding of the puppet state of Manchukuo, but disagreements over policy direction eventually led to his transfer back to Japan as commander of the Fourth Infantry Regiment in Sendai. Photo courtesy of Kyodo News Images Inc.

Outbreak of the Manchurian Incident

About 10:30 P.M. on the night of 18 September 1931, a small section of South Manchuria Railway track was blown up near Liutiaohu, north of the city of Fengtian. Japanese army intelligence in Fengtian claimed this was the work of Chinese troops, and they called on Kwantung Army headquarters to send reinforcements while the local Japanese garrison troops were engaged in combat with the Chinese.

Of course the railway explosion had been engineered by Japanese forces. The central figure in the plot was Ishiwara Kanji. Ishiwara urged General Honjō Shigeru, commander-in-chief of the Kwantung Army, to dispatch more troops, hoping to escalate the incident into a full-scale conflict between Japan and China that would bring about an immediate resolution of the Manchurian question. Honjō, who had not been informed of the incident in advance, was hesitant, but at about 12:30 A.M. on 19 September approved the dispatch of troops to Fengtian, and departed Lushun about 3:30 A.M. as their leader. Arriving in Fengtian about noon, he found the city already occupied by Japanese forces.

The initial report of the incident came to Tokyo at 1:07 A.M. on 19 September, followed by two successive reports, and by 3:00 A.M. Minister of Army Minami Jirō and Kanaya Hanzō, chief of the Army General Staff, had been notified. A conference was convened at the General Staff Office at 7:00 A.M., where Koiso Kuniaki, chief of the Military Affairs Bureau, and others leaned toward approving the Kwantung Army's actions and sending further reinforcements. However, when a report came from Hayashi Senjūrō, commander-in-chief of Japan's Korean Army, that he was mobilizing his troops, he was ordered to desist, as it would create a major incident if he were to do so without receiving orders from the emperor. News of the incident also reached the foreign ministry very quickly. Hayashi Kyūjirō, Japanese consul-general in Fengtian, was convinced that it was a deliberate plot on the part of the Japanese army. Minister of Foreign Affairs Shidehara raced to the ministry and then called on Prime Minister Wakatsuki, urging him to convene an emergency meeting of the cabinet.

The cabinet met at 10:00 A.M. Minister of Army Minami took the position that the Kwantung Army had acted in self-defense, and he intended to propose sending the Korean Army into Manchuria, but when challenged by Minister of Foreign Affairs Shidehara as to whether there had been a plot, Minami found himself unable to propose a further dispatch of troops. As a result, the chief of the Army General Staff issued orders to the Kwantung Army that approved the actions taken on 18 September, but called for a local resolution, avoiding further expansion of the conflict.

The plotters within the Kwantung Army were disappointed by the orders from Tokyo. If things continued in this vein, the incident would not develop as they had planned. But they were convinced that the mid-level

officers in the Ministry of Army and the Army General Staff Office supported a widening of the conflict, and they decided to plunge ahead. At 3:00
A.M. on 21 September, the Kwantung Army sent troops into Jilin. Reports
of unrest in the province were used as a pretext to convince Honjō to commit troops. This unrest had also been manufactured and orchestrated by the
Kwantung Army itself. Then, at 1:00 P.M. on 21 September, a report came
that the Japanese forces in Korea had been mobilized of their own initiative, and the Kwantung Army commenced actions that completely ignored
the directive from Tokyo against expansion. The Kwantung Army was actually a very small force; it was impossible to expand the conflict without
reinforcements. By 22 September, the Kwantung Army had taken control of
the vicinity of the South Manchuria Railway line and the province of Jilin,
and convened a staff meeting at which a proposal for resolution of the
Manchuria-Mongolia problem was drafted and approved by General Honjō
to be sent to the army minister and chief of the general staff in Tokyo as an
official report. The audacious proposal called for Japanese occupation of
the four northeastern provinces of China—Liaoning, Jilin, Heilongjiang,
and Jehol (Rehe)—and Mongolia, and for the establishment of a new government headed by Puyi, last emperor of the Qing dynasty, who would in
turn cede the conduct of defense and foreign policy of the new government
to Japan. The next military objective was to take the city of Harbin.

At a cabinet meeting on 21 September, the army minister sought per-
mission to send the Japanese troops stationed in Korea into Manchuria, but
he was refused. The action was strenuously opposed by Minister of
Finance Inoue Junnosuke and Minister of Foreign Affairs Shidehara at
another cabinet meeting on 22 September. But when it surfaced that the
mobilization had already taken place, Prime Minister Wakatsuki gave his
post facto approval. In reaction, the emperor showed his displeasure, stating that the cabinet should adhere to the nonexpansion policy and take a
cautious approach. On 24 September the government released an initial
public statement saying that Japanese forces would be withdrawn to their
bases as soon as the security of the railway and of the lives and property
of Japanese residents could be guaranteed.

This meant that an advance to Harbin was not at all likely to be approved.
Harbin was in northern Manchuria, outside the Japanese sphere of influence.
It was only natural that the government and the army high command would
not approve an advance into that region, out of concerns for foreign reaction.

The Incident Widens

It had thus become difficult for the Kwantung Army to undertake further
military action. On 2 October, it reexamined its proposal of 22 September
and adopted a position that, at least on the surface, "looked towards the

Kasugachō Street in Fengtian
The business center of Fengtian bustles with rickshaws and pedestrians. Photo courtesy of Kyodo News Images Inc.

establishment of an independent state of Manchuria-Mongolia, placing it under our protection for the equal advancement of all the peoples of the region." Moreover, if the Japanese government was unwilling to accept such a policy, they envisioned a kind of declaration of independence on the part of the Kwantung Army, writing that "it may be necessary for members of the army in Manchuria committed to our cause to temporarily renounce their Japanese nationality in order to achieve the rapid advancement of our aims." This was in actuality a complete bluff, without basis in reality. But it was sufficient to throw the Japanese government on the defensive. And, as we shall see later, this was just at the time the October Incident, the abortive coup attempted by members of the Sakura-kai, had surfaced. By itself this plot was fanciful at best, but linking it with other events of the day made it a bigger threat.

On 4 October, the Kwantung Army announced its intention to confront the army of warlord Zhang Xueliang, and on 8 October, after securing the full cooperation of the South Manchuria Railway, began bombing the city of Jinzhou, where Zhang had his headquarters. When the newspapers ran headlines reading "Our Army Bombs Jinzhou," members of the press were reprimanded by Koiso Kuniaki, director of the Military Affairs Bureau, who claimed that the press reports were exaggerated, and that Japanese observation planes were merely responding in self-defense after they were subjected to anti-aircraft fire. This suggests that public opinion was already running ahead of the cabinet and army command, and the Kwantung Army was able skillfully to turn this to its advantage.

In the cabinet, Minister of Army Minami and Minister of Foreign Affairs Shidehara clashed vigorously, even though Minami and Kanaya Hanzō, chief of the Army General Staff, intended to halt Japanese forces east of the Liao River (in other words, east of Jinzhou) and south of Harbin. But the Kwantung Army was actually intent on plunging ahead into northern Manchuria.

The powerful anti-Japanese warlord Ma Zhanshan was established in the northern Manchurian province of Heilongjiang. The Kwantung Army, as a pretext for sending troops into Qiquhar, accused him of blowing up rail lines. High command initially acknowledged the pretext, but soon ordered the troops to withdraw as quickly as possible. However, once the Kwantung Army forces were sent in, they clashed with Ma Zhanshan's army, and the Kwantung Army used this as a further excuse to occupy the city. High command again ordered a withdrawal, but the Kwantung Army succeeded in political machinations that led Heilongjiang province to declare its independence.

The Kwantung Army now set its sights on Jinzhou. Already mobilized, on 27 November it received an order from Tokyo reading: "No matter what the situation, you must withdraw to east of the Liao River (short of Jinzhou)." But repeated negotiations with high command and the instability and collapse of the Wakatsuki cabinet on 11 December worked to the Kwantung Army's advantage, and it succeeded in a bloodless occupation of the city of Jinzhou on 3 January 1932.

Collapse of the Wakatsuki Cabinet

The Wakatsuki cabinet was devastated by the Manchurian Incident. Minister of Home Affairs Adachi Kenzō had written that, recognizing the gravity of the situation, he sought the cooperation of the Seiyūkai in an attempt to keep the army reined in, and it appears that Wakatsuki initially agreed to this plan. He had tried and failed during his first cabinet to reach a compromise with the opposition party, but he was willing to try the same method again to resolve the crisis. But Minister of Finance Inoue Junnosuke was vehemently opposed to this idea. There was no possibility of a policy compromise between Inoue, who had led the return to the gold standard, and the Seiyūkai, which had strongly opposed it. Minister of Foreign Affairs Shidehara was against this tactic as well. Swayed by the dissent of these two powerful members of his cabinet, Wakatsuki changed his mind.

The aims of the movement for a coalition cabinet were far from simple. The ostensible purpose was for the political parties to cooperate in restraining the growing power of the military, but it is questionable how many politicians were seriously committed to this cause. Most politicians felt that it would be difficult to keep the army under control without drawing closer to its position. If the policies of the Wakatsuki cabinet—including Inoue's fiscal policies and Shidehara's diplomacy—were to continue unaltered, the cabinet would lose its support, and if it fell, the Minseitō would become the opposition party. Those backing the idea of a coalition cabinet probably saw it as the best alternative for retaining power in this uncertain situation. If this came about, it was possible that Inukai Tsuyoshi of the Seiyūkai would become prime minister, with Adachi Kenzō in some cabinet position that would effectively make him a sort of deputy prime minister. From the perspective of the Seiyūkai politicians who supported a coalition cabinet, since the current Minseitō cabinet was under Wakatsuki, anything that could put the government in the hands of the Seiyūkai would be a victory.

Angered by Wakatsuki's change of mind, on 21 November 1931 Adachi made a public statement arguing for the necessity of a cabinet of national unity based on cooperation among the political parties and expressing his intention to challenge Wakatsuki. He stopped attending cabinet meetings, but would not submit his resignation. On 11 December, the Wakatsuki cabinet collapsed due to this failure of internal unity. On 13 December, Inukai Tsuyoshi of the Seiyūkai received the imperial order to form a new cabinet.

Inukai had supposedly retired from political life after the dissolution of the Kakushin Kurabu. But he was prevented from retiring due to the passionate support of his constituents, who continued electing him to office. Prior to Tanaka Giichi's death in September 1929, Inukai had been named as the president of the Seiyūkai as a kind of provisional measure in the midst of a struggle between Suzuki Kisaburō and Tokonami Takejirō to succeed Tanaka.

Prince Saionji had a very high opinion of both Shidehara's diplomacy and Inoue's fiscal policies. What he really wanted was for Wakatsuki to govern with a firmer hand. Before nominating Inukai, Saionji privately expressed doubts and expressed conflicted feelings on several occasions to his trusted aide Harada Kumao. He was particularly apprehensive that Japan's policy of cooperation with the Anglo-American powers might shift to something very different. But it was also apparent that Wakatsuki could not achieve national unity.

Yoshino Sakuzō's Critique

On 28 November 1931, as the Wakatsuki cabinet teetered on the brink of collapse, political scientist Yoshino Sakuzō received a request from the leading opinion journal *Chūō kōron* to write an article on the theme of "Nation." Yoshino had once published in almost every issue of the journal, but by this time he had receded from the limelight as a result of changes in the climate of opinion and his own ill health. At first he refused the invitation, citing reasons of health, but in the end he agreed to write the article, which he submitted on 11 December. It was published in the January 1932 issue of the monthly, with the title "Nation, Class, and War."

Yoshino pointed out that although the Manchurian Incident was supposed to have initially been a matter of self-defense, military action had already expanded beyond the Japanese-owned South Manchuria Railway lines and Japan's traditional sphere of influence in Manchuria. Now the complete elimination of Zhang Xueliang and Ma Zhanshan was even being proposed, but this was a broadening of the conflict beyond anything that could be construed as the right of self-defense. This was nothing other than ~~aggression (侵略行動)~~.* Perhaps because of this, in recent days a growing number of commentators were supporting military action not merely on the grounds of self-defense, but as "essential to our existence as a nation." But if this was the case, the true nature of this military action was imperialism. Some were arguing for an international redistribution of resources and territory, but this too was extremely problematic. In any case, while there might be some theoretical grounds for "imperialistic expansion rooted in the imperative of survival as a nation" this argument too had clearly overstepped reasonable bounds. Yoshino wrote that from childhood the Japanese have been taught the adage "even if you feel thirsty, don't drink water from a stolen spring," and so "even if it is said to be for the purpose of asserting demands for legitimate rights, to resort to conducting large-scale ~~military operations (軍事行動)~~* is something about which I cannot help but feel a certain anxiety and regret." Yoshino went on to say that there were two things he found particularly regrettable: first that the newspapers had been unanimous in their praise for the incident; and second that the proletarian political parties had also tended to support it.

It was certainly true that even the "progressive" newspapers such as *Ōsaka asahi shinbun* had been united in support of the incident. There were a variety of reasons for this, but the biggest was probably commercialism. War sells papers. The top newspaper executives may have been concerned about the Manchurian Incident, but the copy desks and the press rooms were abuzz with excitement. As it happened, this was a time at which photojournalism was becoming a major aspect of the news, and the leading papers vied with one another to deliver film from the battlefront to Tokyo as quickly as possible using airplanes.

As far as the proletarian parties were concerned, Yoshino criticized the left wing for silence, the center for its feeble and sporadic opposition, and the right wing for gradually adopting a posture of support for the incident. The proletarian parties were first and foremost class-based, and therefore should have been opposed to a war that forced sacrifices on the part of

---

*Italicized words struck out in this paragraph were suppressed by official censors.

Chūō kōron journal, carrying Yoshino Sakuzō's "Race, Class, and War,"
January 1932 issue

working-class people. But they were being pulled away from their class allegiances by the rhetoric of race and nation.

At this time, Yoshino was fifty-three years old—not yet elderly, but as he would die in 1933 this could be considered an essay of his late period. Yet in it we can also see the vitality and vigor Yoshino commanded in his prime. The number of words deleted by the censors is disconcerting, but overall it is remarkable how outspoken he managed to be in this difficult era.

International Reaction

The Manchurian Incident met with a diversity of international responses. In China, which was most directly affected by the incident, Chiang Kai-shek was personally disinclined to engage in the conflict, and attempted to wage a diplomatic offensive instead. Initially it seemed he might negotiate directly with Japan, but that stance was soon abandoned, and on 21 September 1931 he made an appeal to the League of Nations, and also sought support from the United States.

Great Britain was preoccupied with domestic issues, and was also somewhat sympathetic to Japanese interests in Manchuria, so its response to China's overtures was lukewarm. In the United States, Secretary of State Henry L. Stimson was concerned about how the incident might unfold. Stimson had met with Prime Minister Wakatsuki a number of times during the London Naval Conference of 1930, and thus knew him to be a trustworthy gentleman.

But with the Japanese assault on Jinzhou on 8 October, the posture of the United States began to change, and on 9 October the United States appealed to the League to apply its influence and authority to resolve the conflict. As a result, on 15 October the League invited the United States to participate as an observer. Even so, the US stance was not especially critical of Japan. But it began to harden as the 16 November deadline for withdrawal of Japanese forces mandated by the executive council of the League on 24 October drew closer.

In a press conference on 27 November, Stimson said that if Japan carried out an assault on Jinzhou, the patience of the US government would come to an end, which inflamed public opinion in Japan. After Jinzhou came under Japanese control on 3 January 1932, Stimson issued a statement on 7 January warning Japan that the United States would not recognize any arrangements "brought about by means contrary to the covenants and obligations of the Pact of Paris"—in other words, by acts of aggression contravening the Kellogg-Briand Pact and the Nine-Power Treaty signed at the Washington Conference of 1921–1922.

This policy of nonrecognition came to be known as the Stimson Doctrine. US diplomat George Kennan was critical, writing that this approach offered only general criticisms and failed to resolve the problem because it did not address specific issues, and as a result it served only to complicate relations with Japan. The Stimson Doctrine had its origins in the note issued by US secretary of state William Jennings Bryan in 1915 in response to Japan's "Twenty-One Demands" against China, which stated that the United States would not accept any infringements upon American interests.

Among the great powers, perhaps the most noteworthy response to the Manchurian Incident came from the Soviet Union. Aside from China itself, the Soviet Union was the country whose interests were most directly affected by the Japanese incursion into northern Manchuria. Yet on 29 October the Soviets announced a policy of nonintervention into the Manchurian situation, and on 31 December approached Japanese Ambassador to France Yoshizawa Kenkichi, who was returning to Japan from Europe to assume his new post as foreign minister, with a proposal for the conclusion of a nonaggression pact between the Soviet Union and Japan. In short, the Soviet Union had adopted an extremely cautious posture of appeasement toward Japan.

The Shanghai Incident and
Establishment of Manchukuo

As we have seen, international opinion was not particularly hostile to Japan's behavior. But this would change with the outbreak of the Shanghai Incident.

As of January 1932, there were some 25,000 Japanese residents in Shanghai. On 18 January, a procession of Nichiren-sect monks and lay followers were making their way through the International Settlement in Shanghai when they were attacked by a Chinese mob. One Japanese person was killed and three others sustained serious injuries. But this incident was actually a plot engineered by Tanaka Ryūkichi, military attaché at the Japanese legation in Shanghai, for the purpose of diverting the attention of the foreign powers away from Japan's establishment of the puppet state of Manchukuo. The situation was exacerbated by the feelings of rivalry the Japanese navy harbored for the glorious achievements of the army in Manchuria.

In the resulting clash between Imperial Japanese Navy marines and Chinese forces, the Japanese suffered from a distinct numerical disadvantage. The Inukai cabinet soon decided to send regular army troops as reinforcements, and heavy combat ensued. Despite the vastly larger geographical scale of operations, the Manchurian Incident resulted in only about 1,200 casualties; but in only a month of fighting in and around Shanghai, more than 3,000 people were killed or wounded.

The fierce combat had a significant impact on foreign residents of Shanghai. One of the reasons the international reaction to the Manchurian Incident had been relatively cool was that Manchuria was a rather remote area of China that for many years Japan had claimed as a sphere of influence. But Shanghai was different. An incident in Shanghai was one that took place under the very eyes of the Western powers. Japanese journalist Kiyosawa Kiyoshi, who was traveling in the United States at this time, wrote that in the wake of the Shanghai Incident, US perception of Japan rapidly hardened.

British attitudes, which had been relatively calm, also changed dramatically with the Shanghai Incident. On 7 March 1932, British foreign secretary John Simon introduced before the League of Nations a proposal stating that "it is incumbent upon the members of the League of Nations not to recognize any situation, treaty, or agreement which may be brought about by means contrary to the Covenant of the League of Nations or to the Pact of Paris." This was adopted as a resolution of the General Assembly of the League on 11 March.

Meanwhile, the Kwantung Army was moving to install Puyi, who as a child had briefly reigned as the last emperor (Xuantong) of the Qing dynasty, as the ruler of a new state in Manchuria. Puyi had been living in Tianjin, where he had been under strict surveillance by the Japanese.

Minister of Foreign Affairs Shidehara feared that the army might try to set up Puyi as a figurehead, and was wary. The Kwantung Army sent its most renowned China hand, Colonel Doihara Kenji, to recruit Puyi. Doihara instigated rioting in Tianjin that provided cover for Puyi's "escape" from the city on 8 November 1931.

After debating a number of different proposals, in February 1932 the Kwantung Army decided to establish the state of Manchukuo as a nominally democratic republic, with Puyi as chief executive (he would be declared emperor in 1934) and its capital in Changchun. Officially inaugurated as a state on 1 March, Manchukuo had a population of 34 million, and a total area of 1.15 million square kilometers (about three times the size of present-day Japan). Although it was founded under the slogan "Unity of the Five Races" (Han Chinese, Manchurian, Mongolian, Korean, and Japanese), Manchukuo was a puppet state ruled by Japan. In fact, Japan is said to have invented the very concept of the puppet state—something that should not be considered an honor.

The Inukai Cabinet

The focus of the Inukai cabinet, which was formed in December 1931, was the relation with the military. Initially, the appointment of an officer of the Ugaki faction as army minister was contemplated. But as we have seen, Minister of Army Minami and Chief of Staff Kanaya, both close to Ugaki, had failed in their attempts to confine the Manchurian Incident to a line drawn east of Jinzhou and south of Harbin. This made selecting another officer from the Ugaki camp problematic. The hopes of mid-level officers were pinned on General Araki. In a letter to Seiyūkai leader Ogawa Heikichi, Colonel Nagata Tetsuzan wrote that while Abe Nobuyuki of the Ugaki faction was a strong candidate, "at present, when we are confronted by both the Manchuria-Mongolia issue and the movement for internal reform of the Army, he is definitely not an appropriate choice. I hope you will take this into consideration. Lieutenant General Araki or Lieutenant General Hayashi [Senjūrō] would be safer bets in terms of winning public confidence and support. Mori Tsutomu [chief cabinet secretary with strong connections with the Army] is also well aware of the situation in this regard" (Ogawa Heikichi Monjo Kenkyūkai, ed., *Ogawa Heikichi kankei monjo* [Papers of Ogawa Heikichi]). Araki, a leader of the Kōdōha (Imperial Way faction) within the army, would eventually come into bitter conflict with Nagata, but at this juncture he had the latter's support.

But the first real work of the Inukai cabinet was dealing with the trouble after Japan's return to the gold standard. To this end, Takahashi Korekiyo was appointed finance minister, and immediately placed an

Imperial Japanese Navy marines in the Shanghai Incident
Above, *Japanese forces in a defensive position. Photo courtesy of Kyodo News Images Inc.* Below, *marines preparing for an attack.*

embargo on the export of gold once again. The Inukai cabinet then dissolved the Diet, and general elections were held in February 1932. The Seiyūkai positioned itself as the party of economic prosperity versus the recessionary policies of the Minseitō, and won a massive victory at the polls. When the Diet was dissolved, in the lower house the Seiyūkai held 171 seats, the Minseitō 247, the Adachi faction 11, Kokumin Dōshikai 6, and the proletarian parties a total of 5. After the election, these numbers

Emperor of Manchukuo, Kangde (Puyi, 1906–1967)
Puyi was enthroned at the age of three after the death of Emperor Guangxu; he was forced to abdicate following the Revolution of 1911, becoming the last emperor of the Qing dynasty. In 1924, when the warlord Feng Yuxiang seized Beijing, Puyi took refuge in the Japanese legation, and later came under the protection of the Kwantung Army. In 1932 he returned to his ancestral homeland as the chief executive of the state of Manchukuo, and in 1934 was enthroned as its emperor. Photo courtesy of Kyodo News Images Inc.

were: Seiyūkai 303, Minseitō 144, Adachi faction 5, Shakai Minshūtō 3. This was the largest number of seats ever won by the Seiyūkai before the war. The total number of votes won by the party was 5.68 million, up 1.74 million over the previous election; the Minseitō had only 3.39 million votes, down by 2.08 million.

Immediately before the election, the Minseitō suffered a shocking loss when former finance minister Inoue Junnosuke was assassinated on 9 February 1932 by a right-wing terrorist in what came to be known as the Ketsumeidan (League of Blood) Incident. Inoue was a likely candidate to become the next leader of the party. But more than anything else, the landslide loss of the Minseitō was due to the abysmal economic situation. And public support for expansion in Manchuria was surprisingly strong. A Minseitō defeat was inevitable.

On the other hand, Inukai had been involved in Japan's relations with China throughout much of his long career, and had his own ideas about how to resolve the incident, which was why he appointed his son-in-law Yoshizawa Kenkichi as foreign minister. Inukai proposed a pullback of troops along the border between Manchuria and China proper to create a 20-kilometer-wide neutral zone. And he said he also had a plan for withdrawal of Japanese forces—which may have involved securing a direct imperial order for such action. Inukai was aiming at an autonomous Manchuria under Chinese sovereignty, with economic development of the region as a Japanese-Chinese joint venture. In other words, Inukai was opposed to the establishment of Manchukuo, and was groping for a solution that could somehow coexist with the established international order.

To this end, the question of how to control the army was of crucial importance. On 15 February 1932, Inukai sent a letter to an old friend, Field Marshal Uehara Yūsaku, requesting his assistance in dealing with the culture of insubordination (*gekokujō*) infecting the army. And just before the May Fifteenth Incident, Inukai remarked to Yoshizawa that "the reason the Manchurian Incident has developed into such a major issue for our country

Inukai Tsuyoshi (1855–1932)
(Photo courtesy of the National Diet Library website)

is because the young officers of the army have meddled in political issues beyond their station and disrupted the chain of command. To correct this, I want to dismiss about thirty of these young officers. I want to have an audience with Prince Kan'in, and after gaining his approval, petition the emperor in this regard." It is difficult to say whether Inukai, had he lived longer, would have retained or forfeited his reputation as a China expert. But it is clear that his idea of how to deal with the situation was very different from the one prevailing in the army. On 15 May 1932, a group of eleven young naval officers entered the prime minister's residence and confronted Inukai at his desk. His famous last words were: "If I talk, you will understand." The young assassins told him that dialogue was useless and shot him.

Newspaper special edition reporting Inukai's death in the
May Fifteenth Incident
(Tōkyō nichi nichi shinbun *[Tokyo Daily News], 16 May 1932)*

The Saitō Cabinet

Saitō Makoto Receives the Imperial Appointment

Saito Makoto was named as the successor following the assassination of Prime Minister Inukai. Prince Saionji had considerable difficulty making this selection. Up to this point, Saionji's policy had been to avoid having terrorist incidents or other unanticipated events affect a transfer of power from one party to the other. If Saionji had followed his rule, Inukai's successor should have come from the Seiyūkai.

Anticipating this, the Seiyūkai moved quickly to replace Inukai as leader of the party. On the evening of the incident, 15 May 1932, there was a proposal to install Takahashi Korekiyo as provisional president of the party, but in the confusion of the moment this did not come fruition. On 16 May, the succession developed into a struggle between Suzuki Kisaburō and Tokonami Takejirō, with Tokonami eventually conceding to Suzuki, who was appointed party president. Had things gone according to plan, the next cabinet would have been a Seiyūkai cabinet under Suzuki's leadership.

But Saionji felt profoundly uneasy about the policies Suzuki might implement—especially with regard to foreign affairs. Saionji was convinced that Japan's foreign policy should be a moderate one centered on cooperation with the Anglo-American powers, and Suzuki did not appear to be particularly friendly to Britain or the United States. Moreover, Suzuki was an exponent of direct rule by the emperor. From Saionji's perspective, this was a dangerous ideology. Direct rule was an ideal people could talk about, but it should never be put into practice. To do so would threaten the stability of the emperor system. In almost every respect, a Suzuki cabinet seemed undesirable.

As I have remarked earlier, Saionji was a conditional proponent of "normal constitutional government"—the conditions being, first of all, cooperation with Britain and United States, and second, the capacity to rule in a manner that upheld the constitution. Suzuki clearly did not fulfill either of these conditions, and so Saionji had strong doubts. In this we can perhaps see his attachment to the concept of party cabinets.

Saitō Makoto, who eventually received the imperial order to form a new cabinet, was born in the city of Mizusawa in what is now Iwate prefecture in 1858, and showed outstanding ability as a naval officer. In 1906 he was appointed minister of the navy in the first Saionji cabinet, and would serve in that post until 1914 in the second Katsura Tarō cabinet, the second Saionji cabinet, the third Katsura cabinet, and the first Yamamoto Gonnohyōe cabinet, working assiduously to expand the strength of the navy.

In 1914 he became embroiled in the Siemens bribery scandal, and was placed on the reserve list, but in 1919 he was appointed governor-general of

Korea by the Hara Takashi cabinet, a post he would hold until 1927. Saitō took up the post in Korea immediately after the March First Movement of protest by Koreans against Japanese rule. Saitō was expected to shift away from the hard-line policies and police repression of the previous governors-general, Terauchi Masatake and Hasegawa Yoshimichi, and adopt what was termed a more "culturally sensitive" approach. And in fact, it was Prince Saionji who toasted Saitō at the farewell banquet before his departure for Korea, saying: "Your Excellency, we hope you will bring enlightened rule." Saitō lifted earlier bans on the publication of newspapers and magazines in Korean, and altered other policies, so that while this was still colonial rule, it was also a period in which Korean culture flourished. After this, Saitō was a Japanese representative at the naval arms limitation conference in Geneva in 1927, and served once again as governor-general of Korea from 1929 to 1931. With regard to the Siemens incident, Hiranuma Kiichirō, then public prosecutor-general, later remarked in his memoirs that while there had been sufficient evidence to convict Saitō, he decided not to pursue the case because Saitō showed such promise as a political figure. Hiranuma, who had already been spoken of as a possible candidate for the prime ministership himself, discovered that Saitō, whose potential legal troubles he had deliberately overlooked, blocked his path to that office on several occasions, including this one. Nor did Saitō harbor any particular goodwill toward Hiranuma, who after all had brought down the Yamamoto cabinet and forced Saitō himself to be placed on the navy reserve list.

The Saitō cabinet was the first nonparty cabinet for some time. Yet from the Seiyūkai, Takahashi Korekiyo was named finance minister, Mitsuchi Chūzō minister of railways, and Hatoyama Ichirō minister of education, while Minister of Home Affairs Yamamoto Tatsuo and Minister of Colonial Affairs Nagai Ryūtarō were from the Minseitō. Thus the cabinet could hardly be said to have ignored the parties. Of course the Seiyūkai, having just won an absolute majority in the Diet, were disgruntled, but there was nothing to be done—except, as before when there had been a series of neutral cabinets, to bide time until the next party cabinet could be formed. Saionji, too, likely felt that it was best to give the political situation some time to settle down.

Takahashi's Fiscal Policies

In domestic policy, the Saitō cabinet put its greatest energy into recovery from the global depression, and particularly relief for agricultural villages. In the sixty-third extraordinary session of the Diet, convened in August 1932, the cabinet proposed an emergency supplement to the budget of ¥170 million, the bulk of which was ¥86 million in emergency public works proj-

Inauguration of the Saitō cabinet (26 May 1932–8 July 1934)
When Prime Minister Inukai was assassinated, Saitō Makoto (1858–1936) (standing at the center of the first row) was chosen as his successor. That it took twelve days before this selection was made is indicative of the gravity of the incident. Prince Saionji was impressed by the fact that Saitō had studied abroad in the United States, and had served as navy minister for a total of eight years in five successive cabinets (two of them headed by Saionji himself). Saitō's cabinet was organized as a government of national unity in a time of crisis. Inukai's death heralded the end of party cabinets in prewar Japan. (From Asahi nenkan *[Asahi Almanac], 1933)*

ects for rural villages and an allocation of ¥56 million for subsidies to local governments, for a total of ¥140 million. This would fund civil-engineering work on rivers, ports and harbors, roads, irrigation, and drainage and sewerage, and would also give assistance to maintenance of mulberry fields (necessary for silk production) and the establishment of storehouses for rice and other grains—aiming at increasing the cash income of farm families and restoring rural prosperity. Overall, the rural relief plan was to invest ¥400 million in government funds over a three-year period, supplemented by an additional ¥400 million in low-interest loans from the Nippon Kangyō Bank (Japan Industrial Bank) and other lenders, pumping a total of ¥800 million into reviving rural communities.

Policies for rural recovery aimed at encouraging rural communities to help themselves through organized distribution of land, more effective use of labor, regulation of agricultural production, marketing of agricultural produce, improving supplies of fertilizers and other necessities of agricultural production, improvement of agricultural management techniques, better access to credit, debt reduction, and the like. This was largely a morale-boosting movement, but it did have the effect of shifting the initiative in the villages away from the large landholders and toward the mid-level independent farmers who owned and worked their own land. It also aimed at economic reform centered around agricultural cooperatives that could resist the established power of the fertilizer and grain merchants.

This would eventually lead to the agricultural cooperatives of postwar Japan. In addition to finance minister Takahashi, a central figure in these efforts was Gotō Fumio, minister of agriculture. Gotō is often seen as a representative example of the "new bureaucrats" who positioned themselves against party politics during this period. Displaying considerable power in this cabinet, he in fact pursued a policy line quite different from that of the established parties, which generally spoke for the large landlords.

How should these emergency expenditures be evaluated? A number of the public works projects were poorly planned and slipshod—such as farm roads leading to nowhere. As a result, the spending was slow to take effect, but it is said that by around 1935 they began to have an impact. If the 1920s had been an era of investment in urban infrastructure, in the 1930s the countryside had its turn.

These rural relief programs contributed to an expansion of the national budget from ¥1.48 billion in fiscal year 1931 to ¥1.95 billion in fiscal year 1932. Of this, ¥278 million was for expenditure related to the Manchurian Incident (14 percent), and ¥163 million (8 percent) went to rural relief programs. In fiscal year 1933 the budget swelled to ¥2.25 billion, with ¥196 million (9 percent) going to Manchuria and ¥213 million (9 percent) for emergency relief expenditures, with another ¥240 million (11 percent) earmarked for improvement of military equipment. Thus if we set a base of 100 for fiscal 1931, the budget had swelled to 132 in fiscal year 1932 and 153 in fiscal year 1933. But Takahashi saw this as a temporary and extraordinary measure, and did not intend to continue this trend. And in fact, the budgets for fiscal years 1934 and 1935 both stabilized at around ¥2.2 billion.

Recognition of Manchukuo

Another important policy decision confronting the Saitō cabinet was how to deal with the Manchurian Incident. As already noted, the Inukai cabinet had not extended diplomatic recognition to the state of Manchukuo, founded on 1 March 1932. What type of relationship to establish with Manchukuo—and what effect this would have on Japan's relations with China and the great powers—was the first major foreign policy issue facing the Saitō cabinet.

The League of Nations had dispatched the Lytton Commission to Japan and China to investigate and report on the Manchurian issue. The members of the commission arrived in Tokyo on 29 February 1932, where they met with Prime Minister Inukai, Minister of Foreign Affairs Yoshizawa, Minister of Army Araki, and other Japanese officials before departing for Shanghai on 11 March. They returned to Japan on 4 July to meet with Prime Minister Saitō and Minister of Foreign Affairs Uchida, and then went back to China to draft their report, which was delivered to the League of Nations on 22 September and made public on 2 October 1932.

Meanwhile, however, the Saitō cabinet had decided to recognize the state of Manchukuo. Amid the public mood following the May Fifteenth Incident, the June session of the Diet passed a unanimous resolution favoring recognition. Then, on 6 July, Uchida Kōsai was named foreign minister (up to that time the post had been held concurrently by Prime Minister Saitō), and the government solidified behind the policy, publicly announcing recognition on 12 July. It was decided that Japan would station an ambassador plenipotentiary in Manchukuo who would serve concurrently as the commander-in-chief of the Kwantung Army and governor-general of the Kwantung leased territory. This meant that the ambassador would of necessity be a high-ranking army officer. On 8 August, General Mutō Nobuyoshi was named as the first official to concurrently hold these three offices.

Minister of Foreign Affairs Uchida was enthusiastic about the recognition of Manchukuo. His manner when meeting the members of the Lytton Commission in July had been frosty. And in August, Uchida startled advocates of international cooperation with a fiery speech in which he asserted that the fruits of the Manchurian Incident should be defended "even if it means reducing our country to scorched earth."

And this was not some young hothead talking—Uchida was a highly experienced veteran diplomat. Born in 1865, he was a member of the second Saionji, Hara, Takahashi, and Katō Tomosaburō cabinets, and in the wake of Hara's assassination served briefly as interim prime minister. Thus Uchida had been foreign minister during the establishment of the Versailles and Washington treaty systems, and had been Japan's representative at the signing of the Kellogg-Briand Pact, even resigning from his post as privy councilor to affirm the validity of the pact in the face of the Tanaka cabinet's attempts to meddle with the clause containing the phrase "in the names of their respective peoples" (for details, see "The Kellogg-Briand Pact and International Cooperation" section in Chapter 2). In short, Uchida had been one of the standard-bearers of the cooperative international order of the 1920s.

But during this period neither his speech nor his behavior reflected this. The depth of his commitment to Japan's interests in Manchuria is difficult to dismiss as merely that of an accommodating personality who had been swayed into cooperating with the military. Instead, it is more logical to think that Uchida's cooperative stance on foreign relations had always been predicated on the securing of Japan's special interests in Manchuria.

On 9 September 1932, Japan embarked on the recognition of Manchukuo. On 15 September, the Japan-Manchukuo Protocol was signed by Mutō Nobuyoshi and Zheng Xiaoxu, prime minister of Manchukuo, in the city of Changchun, which was renamed Xinjing (New Capital). The protocol affirmed Manchukuo's intent to abide by all existing international agreements—perhaps the most important of which was the letter dated 10 March 1932 in which Puyi, as chief executive of Manchukuo, requested that Japan undertake the national defense and maintenance of order within the new country and stipulated that Japanese nationals might serve as officials in all branches of the government of Manchukuo, with their appointment and replacement subject to the recommendation and approval of the commander-in-chief of the Kwantung Army. On this basis, Japan was able to send Japanese officials to staff and control the government of Manchukuo—a practice that was known as "internal guidance" (*naimen shidō*). Next in importance was an agreement dated 7 August that entrusted management of all of Manchukuo's railways, ports and harbors, waterways, and airline routes to the commander-in-chief of the Kwantung Army.

The recognition of Manchukuo was tantamount to a deliberate act of defiance against the Lytton Commission, which was then in the final stages of compiling its report. Yet it should also be noted that when the report was released on 2 October 1932, its content was not totally unfavorable to Japan. While it denied the claim that Japan had acted in self-defense and did not agree that the formation of the state of Manchukuo was the result of a genuine and spontaneous independence movement, it also recognized that special circumstances pertained in Manchuria and that a return to the status quo of 18 September 1931 was impractical. Instead, the report proposed the establishment of an autonomous local government in the three northeastern provinces (Manchuria), though one was still nominally part of the Republic of China.

According to diplomatic correspondent Kiyosawa Kiyoshi, when the contents of the report were released in advance to reporters, almost all were impressed with the way that the commission had, under such time pressure, managed to sort out such a complex set of problems and propose a solution. Yet when the newspapers appeared the next day, they were full of heated rhetoric irresponsibly accusing the commission and its report of completely failing to understand Japan's position. Kiyosawa expressed astonishment at the starkness of this contrast, but this divide between truth and pretense remains one of the abuses of the mass media up to the present.

Japan Withdraws from the League of Nations

The issuing of the Lytton Report was followed by the deliberations of the League of Nations. On 11 October, Minister of Foreign Affairs Uchida appointed Matsuoka Yōsuke as Japan's representative to the League Assembly. Matsuoka had emigrated to the United States as a youth, and had worked his way through college, graduating from the University of Oregon. Returning to Japan, he joined the foreign service, involved himself in politics, and became a vice president of the South Manchuria Railway. He was flamboyant in speech and behavior, eloquent and pugnacious, but not the type to finalize or drive a complex issue to a consensus. Even though he did not initially plan to withdraw Japan from the League, he intended to use diplomatic brinksmanship to deflect criticism from Japan while retaining membership in the League of Nations.

In the League, the smaller nations were sympathetic to China, while the major powers wished to avoid conflict with Japan and sought some form of accommodation. But the Japanese government seemed uninterested in accommodation, and instead decided to launch its offensive in Jehol (Rehe) on 17 February 1933. Then on 24 February, the report and recommendations of the Committee of Nineteen, the League's organization for examining the Sino-Japanese disputes, were brought before the Assembly and adopted by a vote of forty-two to one (with one abstention). Matsuoka declared the report and recommendations unacceptable, and led the Japanese delegation from the hall in protest. The single abstention was Siam (now Thailand), which feared conflict with Japan and whose delegation claimed to be awaiting instructions from the home country.

Matsuoka felt he had failed in his mission and, depressed, decided to spend time in the United States before returning. But in Japan, Matsuoka's performance in Geneva had won widespread acclaim. Learning of this, Matsuoka's spirits were suddenly restored and he set out for home, arriving in Japan on 27 April.

It was Kiyosawa Kiyoshi who waged a campaign of criticism against the actions of Minister of Foreign Affairs Uchida and Matsuoka. On 7 February, just at the time that the deliberations at the League reached their climax, Kiyosawa wrote an article that was published in the March 1933 opinion journal *Chūō kōron,* titled "Questions for Foreign Minister Uchida." Kiyosawa wrote:

> You have spoken of defending Japan's interests in Manchuria even if it means reducing our country to scorched earth—but that is the job of the military. Isn't it the job of a diplomat is to prevent such ruin? By deciding to plunge ahead with the recognition of Manchukuo immediately prior to the submission of the Lytton Commission report has immobilized Japanese diplomacy. You frequently use words such as "absolutely" and "always," but I believe it is a taboo for a diplomat to use expressions which hurry a conclusion. You shouldn't use strong language which ensnares the country into a predicament from which it cannot extricate itself.

Kiyosawa went on to observe that the appointment of Matsuoka as chief of the Japanese delegation was also problematic. What was needed here was a harmonious and uninhibited effort at peaceful diplomacy. But Matsuoka merely reiterated rigid demands and presented only obstructions and threats. He objected to allowing the members of the Lytton Commission to participate in the Assembly, opposed inviting the United States and the Soviet Union to participate as observers, and when conflict arose was quick to threaten a Japanese withdrawal. If he was so convinced of the justice of his cause, why would he oppose such things? This type of diplomacy is not intended to persuade, but to play to allies sitting in the bleachers. It may delight family and relatives in the spectators' seats, but it does not convince the judges.

Thus Kiyosawa was essentially saying that Uchida had no foreign policy. An additional problem was the fact that for more than a year after it had been proposed, Uchida had done nothing about signing a nonaggression pact with the Soviet Union, and then, in December 1932, he gave a trivial excuse for not signing a pact. Kiyosawa saw this as leading China and the Soviet Union, two erstwhile adversaries, to come together against Japan (the two countries established diplomatic relations in December 1932). Kiyosawa predicted that cooperation between the United States and the Soviet Union would come next. "With these moves, Uchida has succeeded in completely isolating Japan," he wrote, and called upon Uchida to either undertake a major shift in foreign policy or resign.

A second article by Kiyosawa, "To Plenipotentiary Matsuoka," was written just before Matsuoka's return to Japan and published in the May 1933 issue of *Chūō kōron*. In it, he predicted that Matsuoka would face a storm of adulation when he returned home, a contrast with the one encountered by Komura Jutarō upon his return from the Portsmouth Conference in 1905. Komura had signed an unpopular treaty, convinced it was necessary for his country, and was greeted by rock-throwing mobs. Matsuoka was likely to be met with cheers—but which of these two men had really benefited Japan?

But Kiyosawa did not end merely with criticism. He proposed a series of urgent tasks for Japan: first, to ensure peaceful relations with the United States; second, to sign a nonaggression pact with the Soviet Union; and third, after a cooling-off period, to work toward improving relations with China. He then quoted the imperial rescript issued on 27 March 1933 confirming Japan's withdrawal from the League of Nations. "However, the advancement of international peace is what, as evermore, We desire, and Our attitude toward enterprises of peace shall sustain no change. By quitting the League and embarking on a course of its own, Our Empire does not mean that it will stand aloof in the Extreme Orient, nor that it will isolate itself thereby from the fraternity of nations. It is Our desire to promote mutual confidence between Our Empire and all the other Powers and to make known the justice of its cause throughout the world." By quoting the imperial rescript, Kiyosawa was enlisting the emperor's words to stress the need to rebuild Japan's international relations and argue that it should not attempt to embark on the dangerous course of going it alone in Asia.

These articles by Kiyosawa were both courageous statements and acute analyses of Japan's situation and the direction it should take moving forward. The articles elicited strong support from readers, but the overall tenor of opinion among intellectuals at the time was much more hawkish, and few if any opinion leaders took a stance similar to his.

In April 1933, the month following Japan's withdrawal from the League of Nations, the Kwantung Army crossed south of the Great Wall, invading northern China. The intent was to decisively sever Manchukuo from China proper. This campaign continued through May, and on 31 May 1933 the Tanggu Truce was signed between Japan and the Republic of China, establishing an international border between China and Manchukuo. With this, the Manchurian Incident was concluded and a comparatively peaceful "phony war" period commenced. International relations stabilized, and there appeared the potential for a return to normalcy.

Matsuoka speaking at the League of Nations Assembly in Geneva, rejecting the resolution concerning Japan
Minister of Foreign Affairs Uchida had recognized the state of Manchukuo, boasting that Japan would "not give up our assertion, even if it means reducing our country to scorched earth," and leaving it no path other than international isolation. (Kokkai Shūgiin and Kokkai Sangiin, eds., Me de miru gikai seiji hyakunenshi *[Visual history of a century of parliamentary politics])*

Hirota Diplomacy

A few months later, on 14 September 1933, Minister of Foreign Affairs Uchida resigned and was replaced by Hirota Kōki. Hirota was born in 1878 in Fukuoka prefecture, making him thirteen years younger than Uchida.

Hopes for Hirota were high. From September 1933 through May 1938, Hirota served as foreign minister in the cabinets of Saitō and Okada, then formed his own cabinet as prime minister, and returned again as foreign minister in the first Konoe cabinet and, after leaving office for only four months during the cabinet of Hayashi Senjurō, returned to serve in the reconstructed Konoe cabinet. This was an extraordinary example of political longevity; therefore, his diplomatic record should be given adequate attention.

Soon after Hirota's appointment as foreign minister, the Five Ministers Conference (attended by the prime minister and the ministers of foreign affairs, finance, the army, and the navy) was established to coordinate foreign, defense, and fiscal policies. In October, this conference articulated a foreign policy program that called for "the achievement of solidarity and mutual assistance among the three nations of Japan, Manchukuo, and China under the guidance of our empire, using this to secure an enduring peace in East Asia, and by extension contributing to the advancement of peace throughout the world." It should be noted that this took the concept of a Japanese-Manchurian bloc that had existed before the Manchurian Incident one step further, proposing the creation of a Japanese-Manchurian-Chinese bloc. This is significant because China was opposed to this idea of tripartite cooperation, given that it conflicted with the open-door policy that had become a dominant paradigm in the relationship of the foreign powers to China. This shift may not have been a particularly conscious one. And it is likely that no one at the time felt it to be an especially major departure.

In a speech before the Diet in January 1934, Minister of Foreign Affairs Hirota declared that Japan would bear complete responsibility for the maintenance of peace in East Asia. This was of immense significance, but attracted little attention either at home or abroad.

In April 1934, the so-called Amō Declaration became an issue. In an informal press briefing on China policy, the foreign ministry's chief information officer, Amō Eiji, stated that "Japan is resolved to fulfill its mission to maintain peace and order in East Asia," saying that the collaborative overtures of the Western powers toward China, whether in the form of financial aid or technical assistance, necessarily took on a political coloration, and that Japan was opposed to this in principle—opposed not only to joint assistance, but also individual assistance, in cases in which it might disturb the peace and order of East Asia (Gaimushō, ed., *Nihon gaikō nenpyō narabi ni shuyō bunsho, jō* [Chronological table and key documents relating to Japanese diplomacy], vol. 1). This elicited a major response overseas, where it was seen as the declaration of an Asian Monroe Doctrine. But Amō himself was startled by this response, since he saw his remarks as little more than an amplification of the policy announced by the Five Ministers Conference the previous year and expressed by Minister of Foreign Affairs Hirota in his January 1934 speech. In other words, without being aware of it, Japan had begun to limit its diplomatic vision to Asia and shift its foreign policy toward a pan-Asianism that sought to exclude Europe and the United States from involvement in Asian affairs. This was exactly what Kiyosawa had feared.

Hirota's stance was labeled in certain quarters as one of "cooperative diplomacy." And in fact it displayed elements of moderation. The gregarious Saitō Hiroshi, perhaps the most skillful English-speaker in the foreign ministry, was chosen at an unprecedentedly young age to serve as ambassador to the United States, and his direct appeal to President Roosevelt for an improvement in United States–Japan relations was welcomed with goodwill. But a direct appeal to the head of state is not always effective; it can sometimes harden opposition from lower levels of the bureaucracy. That

Hirota Kōki (1878–1948)
Hirota was a career diplomat who entered the foreign ministry the same year as Yoshida Shigeru. A year ahead of him was Saburi Sadao, close adviser to Shidehara Kijūrō; two years ahead was Matsuoka Yōsuke; Shidehara himself had entered the foreign service eleven years ahead of Hirota. The Saitō cabinet gave Hirota his first ministerial appointment. Photo courtesy of Kyodo News Images Inc.

was not true in this case, but it is also questionable how clearly Saitō perceived that Roosevelt himself was a hardliner on Japan.

Another point in Hirota's favor was his active engagement in the successful negotiations for the purchase of the Chinese Eastern Railway (North Manchuria Railway). Moreover, in 1935, the status of diplomatic relations between Japan and China was upgraded from an exchange of ministers to that of ambassadors. At the time, this was received very favorably in China. But beneath these relatively superficial postures of amity lay a nearly unacknowledged pan-Asianism that posed an even greater challenge to the Washington Treaty system than Japan realized. This might be considered to be the reason that Hirota was able to occupy the office of foreign minister for as long as he did without a head-on collision with the military. We shall soon touch on the significance that this pan-Asianist or Asian Monroe Doctrine bias had at specific historical junctures.

The Transformation of Foreign Trade

This was a period in which Japan's foreign trade was in flux. After removing Japan from the gold standard by restoring the embargo on gold, Minister of Finance Takahashi allowed the exchange rate to go into free fall. As a result, the earlier prevailing rate of approximately ¥100 = $50 plunged to approximately ¥100 = $20. This triggered inflation of commodity prices, but it bolstered the competitiveness of Japanese goods overseas, which allowed Japanese exports to recover from the global depression earlier than those of other countries.

If we establish 1926 as an index of 100, global exports dropped to 94 in 1929, 75 in 1930, 54 in 1932, and 32 in 1934 before beginning to trend upward once more to 35 in 1936 and 44 in 1937. In contrast, Japanese exports increased from 100 in 1926 to 103 in 1929, then fell to 76 in 1930, hit bottom at 41 in 1932, and then commenced a recovery to 66 in 1934, 71 in 1936, and 97 in 1937. The reason for this, more than anything else, was the depreciation in the value of the yen (Ikeda Michiko, *Tai-Nichi keizai fūsa* [The economic encirclement of Japan]).

However, the countries to which Japan was exporting changed dramatically. First, Japanese exports to the United States fell off dramatically. With a base of 100 in 1926, they went from 104 in 1929 to 31 in 1932, 28 in 1934, and 26 in 1936. These calculations are based on dollar valuations, and are not as dramatic if calculated on a yen basis, but this is still a swift decline. The reasons for this included the drop in US purchasing power as a result of the depression and the inroads made by the synthetic fiber rayon into the market for Japanese silk fiber exports, which did not decrease in volume but fell sharply in price, to disastrous effect. On the other hand,

Japanese industrial products began to make advances into other regions of the world at this time, but the high US tariffs and other barriers prevented a comparable entry into the US market.

Second, exports to China proper also declined sharply. With 1926 as an index of 100, they fell to 80 in 1929, 18 in 1932, and 17 in 1934, and rose slightly to 26 in 1937. The major cause of this was Chinese boycotts of Japanese goods. Conversely, as seen in Table 3.1, Japan's exports grew in the Kwantung leased territory, Manchukuo, India, and the Dutch East Indies (now Indonesia).

To oversimplify, Japan had lost big in the United States and China and made significant gains in the regions just mentioned. But exports to Manchukuo and Kwantung were in what was known as the yen bloc, and did not generate foreign currency. Moreover, the sudden increase in Japanese exports to India and the Dutch East Indies invited conflict with the British and Dutch. The negative reaction to Japanese policies that began with the Manchurian Incident were beginning to have an impact. Kiyosawa had anticipated this situation. In the past he had criticized those who argued that Manchuria was Japan's lifeline, and after Japan's hard-line policies in Manchuria invited boycotts in China proper and the deterioration of relations with the United States, he suggested that China and the United States were actually more of a lifeline for Japan than Manchuria.

Fall of the Saitō Cabinet

Under the Saitō cabinet, a number of important shifts in policy had begun: Japan had recognized the state of Manchukuo, withdrawn from the League of Nations, and turned in the direction of a pan-Asian ideology. This despite the attempts of the cabinet to avoid radical change and maintain the status quo.

A powerful force harboring strong discontent with Saitō's government was the Seiyūkai, which at the time held an absolute majority in the House of Representatives. From within the Seiyūkai a variety of efforts arose to unseat the Saitō cabinet by linking up with other opposition forces.

Table 3.1 Share of Japanese Export Trade (%)

	1926 Taishō 15	1929 Shōwa 4	1932 Shōwa 7	1934 Shōwa 9	1937 Shōwa 12
Kwantung Leased Territory	–	5	9	13	12
Manchukuo	–	–	9	13	12
India	7	9	14	11	9
Dutch East Indies	3	4	7	7	6

One of these efforts was a campaign that commenced around February 1934 against Nakajima Kumakichi, minister of commerce and industry. More than a decade before taking office, Nakajima had written an essay that praised Ashikaga Takauji, founder of the fourteenth-century Ashikaga shogunate, who had also played a major role in initiating a lengthy imperial succession dispute between the Northern and Southern Courts. Using this article as leverage, forces in the rightist movement and the House of Peers began a barrage of criticism against Nakajima, saying that anyone who could praise a traitor like Takauji had no right to be a minister of state.

From today's perspective—and even at the time—this was clearly nothing more than a tactical maneuver directed at Nakajima because he had been one of the more vocal advocates of cooperation between the Seiyūkai and Minseitō, and thus was seen by diehard proponents of a Seiyūkai-only government as someone to attack.

About the same time, news of the Teijin scandal was breaking. Mutō Sanji, former president of Kanegafuchi Spinning Company (later Kanebo), had founded the Jitsugyō Dōshikai (Businessmen's Association) with an appeal to break the deadlock of dominance by the established parties, and was now owner and manager of the newspaper *Jiji shinpō*, which between 17 January and 13 March 1934 published a series of fifty-six articles exposing what it claimed was a scandal involving stock in Teijin Limited, a rayon manufacturer. The articles exposed how a group of investors known as the Banchōkai, led by the industrialist Gō Seinosuke, had used the collusion between the worlds of politics and high finance for illicit ends. The criticism focused specifically on manipulation of Teijin stock.

Teijin (Teikoku Jinzō Kenshi [Imperial Artificial Silk]) had been a subsidiary of the trading company Suzuki Shōten, but when Suzuki went bankrupt, Teijin came under the control of the Bank of Taiwan. Artificial silk (i.e., rayon) was a sensational new product, and the core of the scandal was the accusation that the members of the Banchōkai had been able to buy up large amounts of Teijin stock at unfairly low prices.

In February and March the scandal exploded, and was taken up in debate in the Diet. In April, after the Diet session closed, the prosecutors went to work, arresting individuals associated with Teijin and the Bank of Taiwan. In May, Kuroda Hideo, a vice minister of finance, was arraigned and indicted, and the responsibility of the minister of finance himself was criticized. The scope of the investigation would soon extend to Hatoyama Ichirō (former minister of education), Mitsuchi Chūzō (railway minister), and Nakajima Kumakichi (former minister of commerce and industry). All of this led the Saitō cabinet to resign en masse on 3 July.

However, when the case was later tried in 1937, the verdict found all the accused innocent. And this was not a judgment of not guilty by reason of insufficient evidence; the judges made it clear they found the entire case to be baseless and without merit. This was completely unprecedented.

All of those charged had been supporters of the Saitō cabinet and bureaucrats aligned with the politicians advocating cooperation between the Seiyūkai and Minseitō. Behind this investigation was the figure of Kuhara Fusanosuke who was critical of the Seiyūkai-Minseitō cooperation and was willing to bring down the Saitō cabinet. And it was widely rumored that if the Saitō cabinet were toppled, the most likely candidate would be Hiranuma Kiichirō. It is highly likely that the prosecutors under Hiranuma's influence had blatantly pursued the case with political intentions. Needless to say, Kuhara and Hiranuma were close to each other.

The Imperial Court and Hiranuma

One power center that supported the Saitō cabinet was the imperial court. Lord Keeper of the Privy Seal Makino Nobuaki, Imperial Household Minister Ichiki Kitokurō, and the elder statesman Saionji Kinmochi were at the center of palace politics. The Privy Council, though constituting part of the imperial court, as an advisory body to the emperor, occupied a completely different position, and Hiranuma was the de facto power in that body in his capacity as vice president.

Hiranuma was born in 1867 in Okayama prefecture, and became an influential figure in legal circles after entering the Ministry of Justice and serving as chief public prosecutor and chief justice of the Great Court of Cassation, the prewar equivalent of the Supreme Court. In the late Meiji period, the Ministry of Justice was rarely in the public eye. But in 1909, a number of politicians associated with the rising power of the Seiyūkai were arraigned in the Nittō scandal, a bribery incident involving the tariff on sugar imports. Then, in 1914, the Siemens scandal put the spotlight on the Japanese navy. This was followed in 1915 by yet another bribery scandal that led to the downfall of Yamagata Aritomo's trusted associate Ōura Kanetake. Hiranuma was involved in prosecuting all these incidents, and they propelled him to stardom in the legal world.

In 1923, Hiranuma was named minister of justice in the Yamamoto cabinet. In 1924 he was appointed to the Privy Council, and became its vice president in 1926. Meanwhile, he founded the Kokuhonsha (National Foundation Society) in 1924 and became its president. This was occasioned by the Toranomon Incident (the assassination attempt against the regent that occurred during Hiranuma's tenure as minister of justice), which also spurred him to publish the magazine *Kokuhon* and establish himself as one of the most powerful figures in right-wing politics.

Saionji did not like Hiranuma. He was sharply critical of the way the latter had politicized the Privy Council—which he felt should be moderate and steady in its influence—and had brandished the imperial prerogative to gain political advantage. Saionji frequently remarked that fascism was completely unacceptable, and when he did, it was a critique of Hiranuma. For this alone, Hiranuma was keen to topple the Saitō cabinet, which enjoyed strong support from Saionji.

In May 1934, Kuratomi Yūzaburō retired as president of the Privy Council, and as vice president Hiranuma was next in line to succeed him, but Saionji broke with precedent and worked to have Ichiki Kitokurō appointed instead.

Ichiki was born in 1867 in Shizuoka prefecture and became a professor of constitutional and administrative law at the University of Tokyo, where Minobe Tatsukichi was one of his outstanding students. Ichiki served as minister of education in the second Ōkuma Shigenobu cabinet, then served as home minister, and followed Makino Nobuaki as imperial household minister, a post he held from March 1925 to February 1928. In short, Ichiki was a proponent of the emperor-as-organ theory, a member of the so-called senior statesmen bloc within the palace, and had the confidence of Saionji. Prior to his appointment as imperial household minister, Ichiki had also been a member of the Privy Council, serving for a time as vice president. Leveraging this résumé, he was then installed as president of the council.

Under fire from the Seiyūkai and allied forces seeking a change in government, who used the Teijin scandal and whatever else they could find to critique it for collusion with the world of high finance and to attack the influence of the senior statesmen of the palace, the Saitō cabinet collapsed. But its defenders did not give up easily, and succeeded in having Ichiki appointed as president of the Privy Council. This was a political struggle, but it was also a profound ideological battle.

The Okada Cabinet

Retreat of the Political Parties

After Saitō, a new process, different from the past, was used for recommending the prime minister to the emperor. Instead of Prince Saionji being summoned as the sole surviving genrō to offer his opinion to the emperor, on this occasion former prime ministers, the president of the Privy Council, and lord keeper of the privy seal were also called in for consultation.

On 3 July 1934, the day after the resignation of the Saitō cabinet, Prince Saionji, former prime ministers Takahashi, Kiyoura, Wakatsuki, and Saitō,

Privy Council president Ichiki, and Lord Keeper of the Privy Seal Makino assembled at the imperial palace and recommended Okada Keisuke, minister of the navy, as the next prime minister. In response to a query from Prince Saionji, Wakatsuki, president of the Minseitō, promised to support an Okada government. The consensus around the nomination had emerged relatively naturally in preliminary discussions among those involved, and there were a few in the mass media who had anticipated Okada's appointment. There were important political figures such as Prince Konoe Fumimaro who were fiercely opposed to an Okada cabinet (Matsumoto Shigeharu and Rōyama Yoshirō, eds., *Konoe jidai, jō* [The Konoe era, vol. 1]).

Like Saitō, Okada was a moderate internationalist, and a key figure in the successful negotiation of the London Naval Treaty in 1930. But there was a major difference in the careers of Saitō and Okada. Saitō had served as navy minister for eight years and three months, from 1906, the year after the end of the Russo-Japanese War, to the eve of World War I in 1914. After Saitō, Katō Tomosaburō became the standard-bearer for the navy. Katō was appointed navy minister in the second Ōkuma cabinet, formed in 1915, and was retained in that position by the three subsequent cabinets of Terauchi, Hara, and Takahashi. He was also Japan's commissioner plenipotentiary to the Washington Conference, and made a major contribution to its success. As described earlier, when the Takahashi cabinet collapsed, Katō was appointed to form a cabinet of his own as prime minister, but became ill and died in August 1923.

Katō was only three years younger and one class behind Saitō at the Naval Academy. But his career progressed much more slowly, and his appointment as navy minister came nine years later that of Saitō. In contrast, Saitō's career had been extraordinary. Okada was junior to both of these men. Born in 1868, he was ten years younger than Saitō, seven years younger than Katō, and a graduate of the fifteenth class at the Naval Academy, nine classes behind Saitō and eight classes behind Katō. He did not become navy minister until 1927, in the Tanaka cabinet—twenty-one years after Saitō and twelve years after Katō. One major organizational difference between the navy and the army was the power of their respective ministers: the army minister did not necessarily hold absolute power within the army as a whole, while the power of the navy minister remained unchallenged. This is demonstrated by the fact that a handful of individuals had managed to hold on to the post of navy minister over long periods of time. Yamamoto Gonnohyōe, Saitō Makoto, and Katō Tomosaburō each monopolized the post of navy minister for seven or eight years in succession. Okada Keisuke was not regarded as being of quite the same stature as that of his predecessors.

The Okada cabinet, like the Saitō cabinet before it, sought the cooperation of both the major political parties, and a total of five of its ministers were party politicians. But then the Seiyūkai suddenly refused to participate in the cabinet formation, so communications minister Tokonami Takejirō, agriculture minister Yamazaki Tatsunosuke, and railway minister Uchida Nobuya were expelled from the party. The Minseitō provided two cabinet members, commerce and industry minister Machida Chūji and education minister Matsuda Genji. When finance minister Fujii Sadanobu resigned due to illness four months later, Takahashi Korekiyo returned to the post, and the cabinet came to resemble the Saitō cabinet to an even greater extent. But compared to the period when the Saitō cabinet was formed, the cabinet members drawn from the political parties occupied some of the less important ministerial posts, and relations with the Seiyūkai had deteriorated. The power of the parties was clearly waning.

The Okada Keisuke cabinet (8 July 1934–9 March 1936)
Okada was a moderate with a background as a career naval officer, and invited Minister of Foreign Affairs Hirota Kōki, Minister of Army Hayashi Senjūrō, and Minister of Navy Ōsumi Mineo to remain in the posts they held in the Saitō cabinet. In addition to five cabinet members appointed from the political parties, he drew Minister of Home Affairs Gotō Fumio from the House of Peers and elevated Minister of Finance Fujii Sadanobu from his post as a career bureaucrat and vice minister. Other career bureaucrats joining the cabinet were Chief Cabinet Secretary Kawada Isao, who had been a vice minister in the Ministry of Colonial Affairs; Minister of Justice Ohara Naoshi, who had been chief of the Tokyo Appellate Court; and as director-general of the Cabinet Legislation Bureau, Kanamori Tokujirō, who had been head of the bureau's first department.

Advance of the Bureaucrats

As the parties waned, it was career bureaucrats who advanced. Gotō Fumio, who went from minister of agriculture in the Saitō cabinet to home minister under Okada, was regarded as a leading representative of these "new bureaucrats." Although he served only briefly before resigning, Minister of Finance Fujii Sadanobu was another.

Moreover, in May 1935, the cabinet moved to strengthen its own position with the creation of the Cabinet Deliberative Council (Naikaku Shingikai) and the Cabinet Research Bureau (Naikaku Chōsakyoku). The Cabinet Deliberative Council was a body made up of fifteen or fewer eminent figures drawn from the political parties, the military, the bureaucracy, and the world of finance, and given the task of determining the course of fundamental national policies. In fact, its deliberations were infrequent, and it was largely a formality. It served mainly to bolster the cabinet's political base by providing an image of national unity and enlisting powerful figures as allies.

On the other hand, the Cabinet Research Bureau was charged with research concerning important policies, specifically evaluation of key policy proposals ordered by the prime minister, as well as providing administrative support for the Cabinet Deliberative Council. It assembled a group of powerful mid-ranking bureaucrats from each of the government ministries. The director of the bureau was one of the leaders of the new bureaucrats, a career official in the home ministry named Yoshida Shigeru (not to be confused with the individual of the same name who later became prime minister), and among the researchers were those who came to be known as "reform bureaucrats," such as Suzuki Teiichi (an army colonel), Okumura Kiwao (communications ministry), Wada Hiroo (agriculture and forestry ministry), and others.

Their principal function, as things turned out, was the development of the institutions and policies that laid the foundation for a controlled economy and total national mobilization. Policy proposals and legislation considered by the Cabinet Research Bureau included reform of the House of Peers, nationalization of electrical power, a local allocation tax, the creation of a welfare ministry, reform of the educational system, administrative reform, an industrial organization law, a law regulating income, creation of patriotic labor service corps, rural land reform, and even proposals for population planning and social insurance. Among these, nationalization of electric power, creation of the welfare ministry, and implementation of a local allocation tax were all successfully achieved later on the basis of plans drafted by the Cabinet Research Bureau.

The director of the Cabinet Research Bureau, the chief cabinet secretary, along with the director of the Cabinet Legislation Bureau came to be known as the "Three Chiefs" of the cabinet. The first director of the Cabinet Research

Bureau, Yoshida Shigeru, had left the office of chief cabinet secretary to take up this new post, which as a result came to be regarded as more important.

It is certainly true that the men chosen to fill this post during the era of party rule—Egi Tasuku in the Katō Takaaki cabinet; Hatoyama Ichirō in the Tanaka cabinet; Suzuki Fujiya in the Hamaguchi cabinet; Kawasaki Taku-kichi in the second Wakatsuki cabinet; and Mori Tsutomu in the Inukai cab-inet—were all capable young politicians seen as the next generation of party leadership, and played a vital role in maintaining the unity and order of the cabinet. In contrast, the roles of Saitō cabinet's Shibata Zenzaburō and Horikiri Zenjirō, and Kawada Isao, Yoshida Shigeru, and Shirane Take-suke of the Okada cabinet, were almost purely administrative. This was only natural, as during the era of party rule the chief cabinet secretary had worked directly under the prime minister's supervision to engage in the kind of political activities and inter-ministry coordination that the cabinet ministers themselves could not undertake. But in the Saitō and Okada cab-inets, this sort of work ceased being the job of the chief cabinet secretary. Without the common basis of political party affiliation the role of the chief cabinet secretary lost its political focus.

Similarly, during the era of party rule, the Cabinet Legislation Bureau had mobilized young and promising politicians such as Maeda Yonezō in the Tanaka cabinet, and Shimada Toshio in the Inukai cabinet, or, a bit fur-

Yoshida Shigeru when he worked as a chief cabinet secretary

ther back, Yokota Sennosuke, who was director of the bureau in the cabinet of Hara Takashi. The Minseitō cabinets had also placed young stars in this post, such as Kawasaki Takukichi in the Hamaguchi cabinet and Saitō Takao in the second Wakatsuki cabinet. But with the advent of more bureaucratically dominated cabinets, the director of the Cabinet Legislation Bureau became a completely administrative post.

In contrast, the directorship of the Cabinet Research Bureau was administrative in nature, but the duties with which it was tasked were vast—and included a fundamental reassessment of the current situation coupled with long-range planning. Yoshida Shigeru, who had been rather clerkish and unprepossessing as chief cabinet secretary, increased significantly in stature when he took over the Cabinet Research Bureau.

Another agency that began to make its presence felt at this time was the Resources Bureau (Shigenkyoku). Created in May 1927, the bureau was given jurisdiction over matters relevant to the control and management of human and material resources, and the research and facilities necessary to the establishment and implementation of related planning. Active-duty military officers were included in its staff, and their relative weight increased as the wartime economy gained momentum and plans for total national mobilization began to be advanced. Matsui Haruo, who had been an architect of the Cabinet Research Bureau, was appointed director of the Resources Bureau in 1936.

In the wake of the February Twenty-Sixth Incident of 1936 the system of total national mobilization began to be implemented, and in May 1937 the Resources Bureau and the Cabinet Research Bureau were merged to form the Planning Agency (Kikakuchō), renamed the Cabinet Planning Board (Kikakuin) in October of that year. The regulations governing the organization of the Cabinet Planning Board stipulated that in both peace and wartime, it was responsible for drafting proposals concerning expansion and management of the overall "national power" and to submit them, with accompanying explanation, to the prime minister, and in addition, comment on the proposals and budgets submitted by each of the cabinet ministers concerning the management of said "national power" in both peace and war, aiming at integration and unification of the work of all government agencies related to the establishment and implementation of the plan for total national mobilization. It was the Cabinet Planning Board that became the nerve center of the wartime planned economy, and its origins are to be found in the Okada cabinet.

The End of Naval Arms Limitation

Foreign relations were a crucial challenge for the Okada cabinet. A major issue was naval arms limitation. Beginning in the autumn of 1933, public opinion was agitated by talk of a 1935–1936 crisis. As noted previously, one of the major points of contention at the time of the London Naval Treaty was the ratio of heavy cruisers: Japan had wanted a seven-to-ten ratio versus the United States, and secured only a six-to-ten ratio. In return, a compromise was reached in which the United States agreed to delay new construction, so that while it would eventually be able to maintain a fleet of eighteen heavy cruisers, it promised not to build the sixteenth, seventeenth, and eighteenth vessels until 1936, 1937, and 1938 respectively—in the meantime allowing Japan to maintain an actual ratio versus the United States of better than seven to ten. However, both the Washington and London naval arms limitation treaties were due to expire at the end of 1936, at which time the United States would have completed its sixteenth cruiser and would be nearing completion of the seventeenth—degrading Japan's ratio versus the United States and causing anxiety about its national defense.

In addition, although Japan had already withdrawn from the League of Nations, the effects would not really begin to be felt until 1935. Meanwhile, the Soviet Union was scheduled to complete its second five-year plan in 1936, which was creating concern over defense issues within the Imperial Japanese Army.

The result was that in December 1934 the Okada cabinet announced that it was abrogating the Washington Treaty, and in January 1936 it withdrew from the second London Naval Conference, which meant that by the end of 1936 Japan had entered into an era unbound by any arms limitation treaties. The concept of the so-called 1935–1936 crisis was naive: it held that since Japan was likely to be disadvantaged by the treaty system, it should simply withdraw. In fact, by abrogating the treaties and engaging in free competition, Japan might possibly be placing itself at even greater disadvantage—and in fact, this was why the moderates within the Imperial Japanese Navy had decided to sign the Washington and London treaties in the first place. But by the time of the Saitō and Okada cabinets, nobody was making this argument any longer. And the commencement of a new round of naval arms expansion came to place a considerable burden on the Japanese economy as a whole.

Hirota's "Cooperative" Diplomacy

China policy was an even more important issue. From the time of the Tanggu Truce in 1933, relations with China had entered a period of relative calm, but as noted earlier, the pan-Asianist undertones of Hirota's diplomacy had made relations with the Western nations more problematic.

In 1934, not long after the establishment of the Okada cabinet, Britain approached Japan with the idea of concluding an Anglo-Japanese nonaggression pact. In addition, a mission headed by prominent British industrialist Lord Barnby visited Tokyo en route to an inspection of economic conditions in Manchuria. In short, Britain was searching for a way to stabilize the situation in East Asia. But Hirota's attitude toward these overtures was cool. He did not express a strong interest in reviving and strengthening cooperation with Great Britain.

Yet subjectively, Hirota was passionate about improving relations with China. On 22 January 1935, Hirota spoke in the Diet advocating Sino-Japanese amity, and on 25 January declared there would be no war on his watch. In May, he agreed with China to elevate the status of their ministers to ambassadorships. Meanwhile, in December 1934, a customs agreement was reached between China and Manchukuo, representing a de facto improvement at the administrative level. In February 1935, China showed signs of a more conciliatory posture toward Japan by cracking down on anti-Japanese agitation.

The background to this was a changing situation in China from the autumn of 1934 onward. On October 15, the Red Army of the Chinese Communist Party commenced its Long March, retreating from its former stronghold of Ruijin in Jiangxi province. By 10 November, Kuomintang forces occupied Ruijin, and in December, Chiang Kai-shek declared victory in the Fifth Encirclement Campaign against the Communists.

It was at this point that Chiang appears to have begun to seriously reconsider his policies toward Japan. In December, under an assumed name, Chiang published an article in *Waijiao pinglun* (Foreign affairs review) titled "Enemy or Friend? Reevaluating Sino-Japanese Relations." This met with sharp criticism from progressive writer Lu Xun, who wrote in a letter to one of his friends that the very title was an odd one, as Japan had proven itself to be an enemy by its theft of northeastern China (Manchuria), and suggested that the title of the next article might be "Friend or Master?"

Clearly, given the circumstances, even to raise this question of Sino-Japanese relations required considerable resolve. In his article, Chiang proposed several bold arguments concerning developments since the Manchurian Incident. For example, he suggested that it might have been better if, in the immediate aftermath of the Liutiaohu railway bombing, China had entered into direct negotiations with Japan, cooperated with Japanese moderates to prevent the widening of the incident, and admitted that it (China) had expected too much from the League of Nations. He said that Japan bore chief responsibility for the deterioration of matters into their present state, but that China also bore partial responsibility. He stated that to break the diplomatic impasse, a Japanese promise that the four northeastern provinces were to be returned to China was a prerequisite. Certainly there was no way China could simply accept the loss of the northeast. Yet it also appears that Chiang was thinking of ways to achieve compromise under this prerequisite, by a tacit recognition of Manchukuo (Nomura Kōichi, *Shō Kaiseki to Mō Takutō* [Chiang Kai-shek and Mao Zedong]).

The North China Autonomy Campaign

The Japanese army, however, took an increasingly hard-line stance, exemplified by efforts to engineer a North China autonomy movement that became increasingly obvious in June 1935. The motive force behind this was the Tianjin Army (also known as the China Garrison Army). This was a Japanese army stationed in the northern Chinese port city of Tianjin as a result of the Boxer Protocol, which ended the 1900 Boxer Rebellion in China. It was a force of only 2,100 men, but it had been strongly stimulated by the success of the Kwantung Army's exploits in Manchuria. A sense of rivalry with these comrades in arms was one of the factors driving the North China autonomy effort.

In 1934 there was civil unrest in the demilitarized zone established by the Tanggu Truce and an incident in which two pro-Japanese newspaper editors in the city of Tianjin were murdered. Colonel Sakai Takashi, chief of staff of the Tianjin Army, strongly protested to the Hebei provincial chairman, General Yu Xuezhong, that to ignore these incidents would constitute a violation of the Tanggu Truce.

As a result of this, Lieutenant-General Umezu Yoshijirō, commander in chief of the Tianjin Army, signed a pact with Kuomintang general He Yingqin, head of the Beiping National Military Council, on 10 June 1935 that came to be known as the He-Umezu Agreement. Its severe terms included the withdrawal of all central government military forces, Kuomintang organs, and anti-Japanese groups from Hebei, and the dismissal of Yu Xuezhong as provincial chairman. The Tanggu Truce had already mandated the withdrawal of these organizations from specific and limited areas of Hebei, but the He-Umezu Agreement extended this to the entire province.

On 27 June 1935, Major-General Doihara Kenji, director of the military intelligence bureau of the Kwantung Army, based in Fengtian, signed a similar agreement with General Qin Dechun, deputy chairman of Chahar province. The Doihara-Qin Agreement had used a minor confrontation in Jehol (Rehe) and Chahar between the Kwantung Army and the forces of Chinese general Song Zheyuan as a pretext for demanding the withdrawal of the latter from Chahar. Song withdrew into Hebei. Thus the Kwantung and Tianjin Armies aimed at neutralizing north China and aligning it with Japan.

The Possibility of Sino-Japanese Rapprochement

Despite these developments, the Chinese did not abandon hope for improving relations with Japan, proposing in September through its new ambassador to Japan, Jiang Zuobin, the following three principles: mutual respect for each other's independence, maintenance of sincere friendship between the two countries, and resolution by peaceful means of all incidents between the two countries. This can be interpreted, along with the raising of the status of China's diplomatic representative from minister to ambassador, as an expression of Chiang Kai-shek's new policies of conciliation with Japan.

In response, on 4 October 1935, Minister of Foreign Affairs Hirota articulated three principles of his own: China must suppress anti-Japanese agitation; China must extend de facto recognition to the state of Manchukuo; and China and Japan must cooperate to prevent the spread of communism. "Sino-Japanese friendship" became the watchword of the day.

Responding to this, Hu Shih, a Nationalist diplomat and scholar, contributed an essay titled "An Appeal to the Japanese People" to the November 1935 issue of the opinion journal *Nihon hyōron*. He began the essay by asking the Japanese people to stop using the phrase "Sino-Japanese friendship," and continued to the following effect:

Whenever I hear it, I feel an almost unbearable heaviness of heart, similar to that which I feel when I hear Japanese military men speak of "the kingly way" (*ōdō*). To be quite honest, I find this difficult to understand. Japan pays lip service to the kingly way, while what it practices is tyranny; it speaks of cooperation and friendship while sowing the seeds of enmity and resentment. If the Japanese people have any feelings or common sense, they should realize that proclaiming Sino-Japanese friendship in these troubled times is completely meaningless.

What is it that has been created over the last four years—friendship or hatred? In June of this year, the Japanese government demanded that the Chinese government issue a "Good Neighbor Ordinance" prohibiting expressions of anti-Japanese sentiment. This will do nothing to calm the anti-Japanese feelings and thoughts of the Chinese people. Instead, it will deepen them. So first of all, please stop talking of Sino-Japanese friendship—because our task at present must be how to eliminate Sino-Japanese enmity.

And secondly, I ask the Japanese people not to take these sentiments of enmity lightly. For a number of years the Chinese government and people have continually made concessions to Japan. But they have come to realize that the desires of Japan's military are limitless. Manchuria is not enough for them; now they must have Jehol; then that is insufficient, and they want eastern Chahar. Making a demilitarized buffer zone in North China is inadequate; they now want to separate the five northern provinces (Hebei, Chahar, Suiyuan, Shandong, and Shanxi) from China. There are limits to the patience of the Chinese people. Piling enmity upon enmity, humiliation upon humiliation. . . . [I]n the end, the day will come when the entire country will rise up in defiance. China will confront Japan's scorched-earth policy with a scorched-earth policy of its own.

Third, I have been amazed and inspired by the past sixty years of splendid Japanese history. Japan should have a boundless future. Yet in recent years, Japan's democratic and constitutional tendencies are shifting towards militaristic despotism; and the discipline that is one of the most

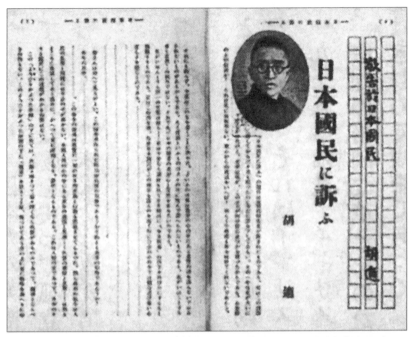

The November 1935 issue of *Nihon hyōron,* carrying Hu Shih's "Appeal to the Japanese People"
The editorial page of the journal expressed the conviction that "Japan has sufficient open-mindedness to lend an ear to the intellectual representative of a neighboring land." But did it?

beautiful virtues of the Japanese is collapsing. A nation to be envied is becoming a nation to be feared; losing friends throughout the world, it is finding itself isolated. The Japanese people must treasure their glorious heritage—but also be careful stewards of their future.

This was the heart of Hu Shih's appeal to the people of Japan.

Currency Reform

Yet the three principles of Jiang Zuobin and the three principles of Hirota Kōki were not necessarily irreconcilable—as the British pointed out. On 10 September 1935, Sir Frederick Leith-Ross, economic adviser to the British government, was sent on a special mission to China, stopping in Japan on the way to consult with relevant parties on his primary objective: reform of the Chinese currency system and the possibility of a joint Anglo-Japanese loan to China for that purpose. The Chinese currency system was extraordinarily complex and viewed as one of the largest obstacles to China's development. Leith-Ross had brought with him an intriguing proposal. In talks on 10 September with Minister of Foreign Affairs Hirota, he spoke of the possibilities of Chinese currency reform, and touched on the problem of Manchukuo, asking if Japan had a mind to "liquidate" that issue. Even when Hirota responded in the negative, Leith-Ross pressed onward, saying: "The independence of Manchukuo has drastically reduced China's revenues. So if at this time Japan might induce Manchukuo to assume a portion of China's debts, and China might be induced in turn to formally recognize Manchukuo, this might prove to be a marvelous resolution of the problem" (Gaimushō, ed., *Nihon gaikō nenpyō narabi ni shuyō bunsho, ge* [Chronological table and key documents relating to Japanese diplomacy, vol. 2]).

Hirota's response to this was brusque. He said that Chiang Kai-shek and his subordinates secretly understood that recognition of Manchukuo was inevitable but were unable to immediately implement it. Thus they were already extending what was tantamount to de facto recognition, and there was no particular need for action on the part of Japan.

Yet Chinese currency reform proceeded, even without Japanese cooperation. The British consulted with T. V. Soong, president of the Bank of China, and H. H. Kung, the minister of finance, and agreed to extend a 10-million-pound loan to China in conjunction with a proposal for currency reform. Using a run on the banks occasioned by an assassination attempt on Premier Wang Jingwei on 1 November as a pretext, the Nationalist government issued an emergency ordinance on currency reform on 3 November, abandoning the silver standard and shifting to a managed currency system. Beginning on 4 November, banknotes issued by the Central Bank, the Bank of China, and the Bank of Communications were mandated as legal tender, and all future payments were required to be conducted in this official currency. The value of this official currency was linked to the British pound, and transactions in silver specie were outlawed, with the government agreeing to buy up silver reserves with the new currency. Britain immediately expressed its support for this move, while Japan vehemently opposed it.

The Second North China Autonomy Campaign

These were the circumstances in which the Kwantung and Tianjin Armies joined forces to mount a second campaign for North China autonomy. In the autumn of 1935, the two armies used Chinese sympathizers to initiate agitation for local autonomy. Then, on 25 November, they set up Yin Rugeng as head of an organization that would soon become the East Hebei Anti-Communist Autonomous Government in Tongzhou. Japanese military intelligence had also approached General Song Zheyuan, but the Chinese government beat them to the punch, installing Song on 18 December as the chairman of a Hebei-Chahar Political Council, based in Beiping and given some degree of actual autonomy. These organizations effectively served as implicit buffers between the Nanjing government and the Japanese forces.

These developments also had significance in opposition to the currency reform that was being implemented in the autumn of 1935. The currency reform begun at the initiative of the British would naturally accelerate the centralization of power in China, something the local Japanese forces adamantly opposed. Moreover, these units were conducting smuggling operations in eastern Hebei in an attempt to undermine Chinese customs administration, and thereby inhibit political centralization in China.

General Minami Jirō, commander-in-chief of the Kwantung Army and concurrently Japanese ambassador to Manchukuo, wrote a letter to Minister of Foreign Affairs Hirota on 13 November 1935 in which he described in the following manner these efforts to break off the northern Chinese provinces:

> To begin with, the recent actions by the Nanjing government are the result of years of misrule that have put Chiang Kai-shek's faction and the Zhejiang financial clique in a precarious situation; in order to extract themselves from this crisis they have resorted to this outrageous action, ignoring the interests of their 400 million people. Especially since lurking behind this is the diabolical support of the British, the result will not simply end in threatening the livelihood of the Chinese people, it will also place the entirety of China under the financial domination of Great Britain. Thus, if we allow this to stand, we face a crisis that will shake the very foundations of our Empire's solemn commitment to establish peace in the Orient under the leadership of Japan. In other words, with this behavior the Nanjing government has clearly abandoned the hypocritical attitude of friendship it has shown to Japan and has once again returned to blatantly anti-Japanese policies. For this reason, our Empire must work to prevent their realization using all legal and appropriate methods at our disposal (Gaimushō, ed. *Nihon gaikō nenpyō narabi ni shuyō bunsho, ge* [Chronological table and key documents relating to Japanese diplomacy, vol. 2]).

In short, the Kwantung Army perceived the currency reform as a threat to Japan, and Minami was arguing for the need to prevent it. And if this was the case, the British were strong-willed, and diplomacy alone might prove insufficient; other methods must be considered: "By this I mean nothing other than seizing upon this opportunity to swiftly and resolutely engage in operations in North China." Minami continued: "The ultimate goal of such operations would be to completely sever the northern provinces from the Nanjing government politically and economically and render them independent; yet at the same time respecting territorial rights and of course refraining from violating them." (It should be noted in passing that it is difficult to see how the complete political and economic separation of North

China from the rest of the country could be accomplished without violating China's territorial integrity.)

By severing the northern Chinese provinces from central government control, the Nanjing government would be denied approximately half of the customs revenues and railway profits that were necessary to secure its loans from the British; it would thereby become unable to buy up the silver in circulation, and as a result the conditions necessary for the currency reform would collapse, and Minami argued that the Nanjing government would be forced in the end to give up on the idea. The vehemence of Minami's argument gives us a clear view of the enormous impact of the British proposal for Chinese currency reform.

To my mind, Hirota's cooperative diplomacy was actually quite weak. In response to Chiang Kai-shek's concessions, Hirota took a hard line; the rest was for show, like the raising of the status of ministers to ambassadors, with little actual content. If he had wanted to seriously grapple with the issue of recognition or tacit acceptance of Manchukuo, then Leith-Ross's plan was one deserving serious consideration. Hirota had strong pan-Asianist tendencies, and frequently took a reactive stance against perceived Western interference. Around this time there was much talk of Sino-Japanese friendship as Hu Shih

The East Hebei Anti-Communist Autonomous Government
East Hebei was declared a neutral zone in the Tanggu Truce of 1933, and became an entrepôt for Japanese illicit trade with China. The autonomous government permitted this trade to continue, with the result that high-tariff items such as rayon and sugar entered China through this region, significantly depressing Chinese customs revenues.

pointed out, and comparisons were made to Shidehara's diplomacy of the 1920s, but Shidehara himself said the superficial resemblance was "a case of mistaken identity"—fundamentally the two approaches were completely different. He was right. Moreover, the Kwantung and Tianjin Armies were at work, and as 1935 drew to a close, Japan had crossed over from Manchukuo to involve itself ever more deeply in North China.

The Imperial Court as a Political Force

Behind the Saitō and Okada cabinets had stood the power of the imperial court as seen in Table 3.2, which I would now like to consider in greater detail. So let's have a look at the principal posts in the imperial palace organization, from the time of Crown Prince Hirohito's appointment as regent for his ailing father in November 1921 to the outbreak of war with the United States in December 1941.

Those associated with the palace possessed several significant characteristics. First, many were from the navy. Saitō had a long career as a naval officer and bureaucrat, and the majority of the grand chamberlains, during this period and in general, came from the navy, although the chief aides-de-camp were from the army. Lord Keeper of the Privy Seal Makino Nobuaki was originally from Satsuma, and thus had many friends and acquaintances in the navy, which had traditionally been dominated by men from the Satsuma domain as the army had been by men from Chōshū. Second, there were numerous veterans of the foreign ministry within the palace—including Makino and Matsudaira Tsuneo, head of the Ministry of Imperial Household from 1936 to 1945. Third, veterans of the Ministry of Home Affairs, such as Yuasa Kurahei and Kido Kōichi, who each served for a time as lord keeper of the privy seal, and in other palace posts, were also highly regarded. In any country one of the greatest bulwarks against a military coup d'état is the police, and the appointment of home ministry officials to palace posts probably had something to do with keeping a channel open for information regarding internal security. Fourth, in terms of experience and mentality, the palace had many internationalists and friends of Great Britain and the United States—as veterans of both the foreign ministry and the navy tended to be. And fifth, it should be pointed out that the majority of palace officials came from distinguished families. Makino was the second son of Ōkubo Toshimichi and Kido was the adopted son of Kido Takayoshi, both heroes of the Meiji Restoration, while Matsudaira was the son of Matsudaira Katamori of the Aizu domain and thus a scion of the Tokugawa family, whose daughter was the wife of Prince Chichibu, a younger brother of Emperor Shōwa. With such pedigrees, they felt a sense of familial identification with the survival of the modern state created during the Meiji era. They were literally, as the old expression had it, "bulwarks of the throne" (*hanpei*). It was these men who would strive to defend the Meiji state during its final crisis.

The Emperor-as-Organ Theory Incident

The Emperor-as-Organ Theory Incident dealt a decisive blow to the Japanese state as conceived by the architects of Meiji Japan. The key figure in the incident, Minobe Tatsukichi, was a former professor of law at the University of Tokyo, and a member of the House of Peers. His theory of the emperor as an organ of the Japanese state had become widely accepted during the Taishō period, though it might actually be more accurate to call it a theory of the state as a juridical person. In short, he argued that the state is a legal entity whose highest institution is the emperor.

This was attacked by right-wing activists as a violation of Japan's national polity (*kokutai*), but their outrage did not gain much traction until 18 February 1935, when Kikuchi Takeo made a complaint on the floor of the House of Peers. Criticism in the House of Representatives followed, causing the situation to escalate. The epicenter of this political earthquake was the army and the Seiyūkai. The Seiyūkai was trying to unseat the Okada cabinet, and seized on this issue as a handy tool for the job.

The issue was not simply one of whether the emperor was an organ or institution of the state. The Meiji Constitution embodied two contradictory elements that supported two conflicting interpretations. The first interpretation was that the emperor would, of his own will, determine all the executive, legislative, and juridical functions of the government, including the power to declare war, make peace, and conclude treaties. The fatal flaw of this interpretation was the question of whether this was actually possible— and if it were, the risk that a major failure of direct imperial rule would endanger the emperor himself and the continuity of the imperial house.

The second interpretation held that while the emperor might appear to make all the decisions, this process was not arbitrary, but rather determined in consultation with a variety of relevant aides and advisers. The emperor himself adopted this interpretation, and saw exercise of his personal will to determine policy as something confined to unusual circumstances. This interpretation was accepted by the majority of those actively involved in the practical conduct of government.

The flaw in this interpretation involved what was to happen in cases in which the opinions of the various institutions advising the emperor came into conflict with one another. The genrō had played the role of sorting out these differences of opinion, and as they faded from the scene the political parties became the principal force in forming unified national opinion. One of the characteristics of Minobe's constitutional theory was its recognition

Table 3.2   Appointed Officials of the Imperial Court

Lord Keeper of the Privy Seal

	Date of Appointment	Prior Offices
Matsukata Masayoshi	2 May 1917	Genrō
Hirata Tōsuke	18 Sept. 1922	Minister of agriculture and commerce, minister of home affairs
Makino Nobuaki	30 Mar. 1925	Imperial household minister
Saitō Makoto	26 Dec. 1935	Prime minister
Yuasa Kurahei	6 Mar. 1936	Imperial household minister
Kido Kōichi	1 June 1940 (served through 24 Nov. 1945)	Minister of welfare

Imperial Household Minister

	Date of Appointment	Prior Offices
Makino Nobuaki	19 Feb. 1921	Minister of education, foreign minister
Ichiki Kitokurō	30 Mar. 1925	Vice president of the Privy Council
Yuasa Kurahei	14 Feb. 1933	Superintendent-general of Tokyo Metropolitan Police, vice minister of home affairs
Matsudaira Tsuneo	6 Mar. 1936 (served through 4 June 1945)	Ambassador to United States, ambassador to Great Britain

President and Vice President of the Privy Council

President	Date of Appointment	Vice President	Date of Appointment
Yamagata Aritomo	17 Nov. 1909	Kiyoura Keigo	20 Mar. 1917
Kiyoura Keigo	8 Feb. 1922	Hamao Arata	15 Feb. 1922
Hamao Arata	13 Jan. 1924	Ichiki Kitokurō	14 Jan. 1924
		Hozumi Nobushige	30 Mar. 1925
Hozumi Nobushige	1 Oct. 1925	Okano Keijirō	1 Oct. 1925
		Kuratomi Yūzaburō	28 Dec. 1925
Kuratomi Yūzaburō	12 Apr. 1926	Hiranuma Kiichirō	12 Apr. 1926
Ichiki Kitokurō	3 May 1934		
Hiranuma Kiichirō	13 Mar. 1936	Arai Kentarō	13 Mar. 1936
Konoe Fumimaro	5 Jan. 1939	Hara Yoshimichi	3 Feb. 1938
Hara Yoshimichi	24 June 1940 (served through 7 Aug. 1944)	Suzuki Kantarō	24 June 1940 (served through 10 Aug. 1944)

Grand Chamberlain

	Date of Appointment
Suzuki Kantarō	22 Jan. 1929
Hyakutake Saburō	20 Nov. 1936 (served through 29 Aug. 1944)

of the superior position of the Diet, and particularly the House of Representatives, among the various institutions advising the emperor. The reason: its members were chosen by the people. This was not an interpretation inherent in the constitution so much as one born of the historical tendencies associated with the rise of the political parties since the late Meiji period.

One target of the critics of the emperor-as-organ theory and their movement for "clarification of the national polity" (*kokutai meichō undō*) was the president of the Privy Council, Ichiki Kitokurō. Ichiki was Minobe's mentor, and Minobe's constitutional theories were a development of Ichiki's previous work. Lord Keeper of the Privy Seal Makino and Prince Saionji were close to Ichiki, both personally and ideologically. Saionji said frequently that people with fascist tendencies must not be tolerated, and when he did, he specifically meant Hiranuma Kiichirō and others preaching imperial absolutism. These men believed that the "evil advisers surrounding the throne" must be eliminated so that the will of the emperor could be freely expressed, and that it was the arbitrary meddling in politics on the part of palace officials that was endangering the imperial house.

Saionji, on the other hand, believed that the national will should be determined in a process that centered on the prime minister, mediated among the relevant advisory institutions, and did not require personal decisions on the part of the emperor. Article 4 of the constitution read: "The Emperor is the head of the Empire, combining in Himself the rights of sovereignty, and exercises them, according to the provisions of the present Constitution." When Emperor Shōwa and Prince Saionji spoke, as they often did, of the need to respect the constitution, they meant this injunction regarding constitutional rule, and the absolute necessity of avoiding the sort of naked display of sovereign power that was advocated by proponents of direct imperial rule.

Prime Minister Okada initially said that he did not think Minobe's theories were mistaken, but he gradually retreated from this position. Phrases such as "the imperial prerogative" and "direct imperial rule" had a certain popular appeal—grand ideals that were difficult to explicitly oppose. The Emperor Shōwa said the emperor-as-organ theory seemed fine to him, and he liked Minobe. Despite this, the movement for clarification of the national polity raged on, and Minobe and other proponents of the emperor-as-organ theory were forced to take cover. Historian Mitani Taichirō has quite appropriately described this furor as a bloodless revolution.

The Ascendancy of the Kōdōha

So what was happening with the army at this point? Let's back up a bit for an overview. As noted previously, in December 1931, General Araki Sadao entered the Inukai cabinet as army minister, with nearly universal support among mid-level officers. Yet Araki's administration of the army rapidly displayed two significant defects. The first was bias in personnel policies. During Araki's tenure, key posts were filled with large numbers of officers affiliated with the Araki-Masaki faction. They were known as the Kōdōha (Imperial Way Faction) because Araki was fond of using the phrase "imperial way" and had begun to refer to the "imperial army" (*kōgun*) rather than the "national army" (*kokugun*).

One of Araki's first moves, in January 1932, was to appoint his ally Masaki Jinzaburō as vice chief of the Army General Staff. Prince Kan'in Kotohito had been invited to serve as chief of staff, so this meant that Masaki was effectively in charge (or presumed to be). In this manner the Araki-Masaki faction established its grip over both the Ministry of Army and the Army General Staff.

Then, in the personnel assignments of February 1932, Yamaoka Shigeatsu was appointed chief of the Military Affairs Bureau, Matsuura Junrokurō was named chief of the Personnel Bureau, and Hata Shinji was named commander of the Kenpeitai (Military Police Corps). In April, Yamashita Tomoyuki was made chief of the Army Affairs Section, Obata Toshishirō was named head of Third Bureau (Transport and Communications) of the General Staff, and Suzuki Yorimichi became head of the Operations and War Plans Section of the General Staff. All of these men were selected on the basis of close ties to Araki and Masaki, and were unorthodox choices for their assignments. For example, Yamaoka was named head of the Military Affairs Bureau without any previous experience in that organization, and the installation of Hata as head of the Kenpeitai was a clearly political move. Obata had been appointed to a second term as head of the Operations and War Plans Section of the General Staff, but after only two months was replaced by Suzuki, another Kōdōha member, and assigned to head the Third Bureau of the General Staff. These machinations are said to have been for the purpose of pushing Imamura Hitoshi out of the leadership of the Operations and War Plans Section, but in any case they were a strangely heavy-handed politicization of staffing to serve the agenda of the Kōdōha.

The assassination of Prime Minister Inukai—the May Fifteenth Incident—took place not long after Araki took office as army minister. As someone who spoke so incessantly of honor and duty, it would not have been at all unusual for Araki to resign, but that would have been a major blow to the Kōdōha. So instead, Araki expressed his intention to resign, inviting Hayashi Senjūrō, commander-in-chief of Japan's Korea Army, to be considered as a possible successor, but ended up remaining in his post. Hayashi was rewarded when Mutō Nobuyoshi was induced to resign as inspector-general of military training, thereby giving that post to Hayashi. The discrepancy between what Araki had long preached and what he was now practicing by his behavior in this crisis shook the confidence many had placed in him. And Hayashi, up to this point seen as inseparable from Araki and Masaki, began to distance himself from them as a result of this incident.

In the personnel transfers of August 1932, Araki removed Koiso Kuni-aki, of the Ugaki faction, from the post of army vice minister, replacing him with Yanagawa Heisuke, an officer with very little experience of military administration. He also installed Mutō Nobuyoshi as commander-in-chief of the Kwantung Army, which was rapidly becoming a key post, and since it was a field command in the midst of an ongoing military intervention, it offered the possibility of its holder being promoted to the rank of field marshal. Promotion to this rank was predicated upon outstanding achievement on the battlefield, which was why other prominent military men such as Katsura Tarō, Tanaka Giichi, and Ugaki Katsushige did not attain it (though personal disinclination to pursue the rank may have played a part as well). With the rank of field marshal came lifetime active-duty status, and at this time (aside from members of the imperial family), only one man, Uehara Yūsaku, held it, and he was at the end of his life. Thus, if Mutō managed to become a field marshal, it would be a powerful addition to the faction controlled by Araki and Masaki.

Honjō Shigeru, previous commander of the Kwantung Army, returned to Japan to become a military councilor, and then chief aide-de-camp to

Masaki Jinzaburō *(left, 1876–1956)* and Araki Sadao *(right, 1877–1966)*
Araki won support from young officers with his idealistic and "spiritual" rhetoric and behavior, becoming with Masaki a central figure in the Imperial Way Faction. Both of these generals were taken off the active-duty list as a result of the February Twenty-Sixth Incident. In addition to senior officers such as Obata Toshishirō and Yanagawa Heisuke, support for the Kōdōha came mainly from mid-level or junior officers assigned to regiments. Photo of Araki Sadao courtesy of Kyodo News Images Inc.

Emperor Shōwa in April 1933. Preceding him in this post was Nara Takeji, who had served the emperor in this capacity since 1922 and gained his trust. Honjō was a member of the Kōdōha, but I will touch on his relationship with the emperor a bit later, in discussing the February Twenty-Sixth Incident.

Kōdōha Policies

Araki's regime had another major problem aside from personnel issues, and that was its failure to make progress with expansion of military preparedness. Despite the Manchurian Incident, there was little strengthening of the army. Troop strength in Manchuria was increased from one to three divisions (provided by rotation of standing units from Japan). But there was no actual expansion of forces, aside from the addition of a single heavy field artillery regiment and the reorganization of the two existing tank battalions into a single tank regiment in 1933. An additional infantry regiment was finally organized in 1934, followed by two more in 1935 and 1936. But the first was an independent regiment that remained unintegrated into a division, and the latter two were independent regiments organized to reinforce the Tianjin Army—hardly a large-scale buildup of troops.

Large-scale reorganization and creation of new units would not take place until after the Kōdōha era came to an end in 1936, when in Manchuria two independent field artillery regiments and an independent mountain artillery regiment were created, and a heavy field artillery regiment, two anti-aircraft regiments, and a balloon regiment were reorganized from existing units. In addition, an existing engineer battalion and transport battalion were reorganized and expanded into regiments. This expansion of artillery firepower and divisional support services was clearly intended as preparation for combat with the Soviets, and is a sign of the rise of the Tōseiha (Control Faction) within the army.

In any case, during the Araki years Japanese military expansion was sluggish, while the Soviet military buildup in the Far East was dramatic. Airfields near the border were pulled back to the interior, a series of heavily fortified zones were constructed, and submarines were introduced to Far Eastern waters—these were large-scale undertakings. Around 1934, the inferiority of Japanese forces in the region, particularly in terms of airpower, became difficult to conceal—and even for the Imperial Way Faction to deny (Kitaoka Shinichi, "Rikugun habatsu tairitsu [1931–35 nen] no saikentō" [A reevaluation of army factional conflict, 1931–35]).

Why was there no military buildup during the Araki era? The most salient reason was Araki's embrace of what was known military circles as "idealism." During his tenure as army minister, Araki had occasion to meet George Bernard Shaw, who was visiting Japan. The general mystified the playwright by boasting that the bravery of the Japanese soldier was due to the frequency of earthquakes in the country; repeated experience of the uncertainty of the ground beneath a soldier's feet honed his courage. He went on to startle Shaw by arguing that warfare with bamboo spears would be the most economical.

In other words, Araki had a very pronounced tendency to emphasize the elements of psychology and morale in military preparedness. At the end of 1933, the two big issues facing the country were military expansion and economic relief for farm communities. Rural poverty at the time was atrocious, as noted earlier, with large numbers of families selling their daughters into prostitution in order to survive. Araki believed that this would eventually destroy the foundations of military morale. So in the final stages of the budget negotiations, Araki conceded to the priorities of the Ministry of Agriculture—because Araki himself believed this to be the correct choice.

It is fairly easy to see from the encounter with Shaw why Araki was a popular figure. If he had been simply a straight-laced and humorless military man, it is doubtful that he would have met with Shaw, the notoriously acerbic ironist, or that any magazine would have set up such a meeting.

According to contemporary journalist Takamiya Taihei, an expert on military affairs, Araki once addressed a meeting of army bureau chiefs, saying:

> Today's young officers are like the young activists (*shishi*) around the time of the Meiji Restoration. They are low in rank but the intensity of their love for their country brings tears to my eyes. In contrast, the senior officers of high command are like the domain elders back then; they understand the need to protect their house, but they are lukewarm in their love and concern for the country as a whole. And because of this, they cannot provide leadership for the young officers.

From this perspective, Araki valued the young officers. But from another point of view, one could also say he both flattered and incited them.

Takamiya provides us with an additional anecdote:

> At New Year's or other holidays, groups of drunken young lieutenants would barge into the entryway of the army minister's official residence with muddy boots, bellowing "Is Araki here?" without using an honorific. Araki would welcome them, saying "You young lads are certainly full of spirit, aren't you!" and then it was "Your Excellency, Your Excellency," from them. This was certainly a strange phenomenon. Is there any other country in which young soldiers—drunk or otherwise—would think they could call out the minister of the army in such an insulting manner? (Takamiya Tahei, *Gunkoku taiheiki* [A chronicle of militarism])

From the perspective of those impatient to expand the country's military forces, Araki was seen as a popular figure, good at flattering his subordinates and prized as a member of the cabinet, but unable to deliver when it came to the budget. In other words, he was an ambitious man with a gift for gab, but an incompetent general who was blind to the real interests of the military or the needs of the nation.

The Fall of the Kōdōha

All of this set the stage for disaffection in the middle ranks of the army bureaucracy, and the beginning of the demise of the Kōdōha. In June 1933, Masaki Jinzaburō was promoted to the rank of full general, and appointed to the Conference of Military Councilors. He resisted this, since his position as vice chief of general staff was more powerful, but it was a post normally occupied by a lieutenant-general (the rank from which he had just been pro-moted) and he was also disliked by Prince Kan'in, the chief of staff, so he reluctantly became a military councilor. Prince Kan'in had been a cavalry-man, and got on well with Minami Jirō, also a former cavalry officer—and Minami was an ally of Ugaki.

In January 1934, Araki resigned as army minister due to illness. His successor was Hayashi Senjūrō. Hayashi was a figure like Araki and Masaki who enjoyed the support of mid-ranking army bureaucrats, and the Kōdōha felt that it would be possible to control him to a certain extent. Meanwhile, Masaki was appointed inspector-general of military training, so the Kōdōha held on to at least one of the "Three Chiefs" (army minister, chief of general staff, and inspector-general of military education).

In fact, however, there was considerable distance in the relationship between Hayashi and the Araki-Masaki duo. In the March personnel reas-signments, Hayashi appointed Nagata Tetsuzan as chief of the Military Affairs Bureau. Hayashi wanted powerful support, and Nagata hoped, by serving under Hayashi, to initiate a reform of the army. Masaki was strongly opposed to this appointment, but Hayashi forced it through anyway.

The August 1934 personnel lists revealed the extent to which the Kōdōha had lost its grip. Hata Shinji, head of the Kenpeitai, was trans-ferred, and Yamashita Tomoyuki, chief of the Army Affairs Section, was reassigned to other work in the Ministry of Army. Then, in July 1935, Hayashi and Nagata relieved Masaki of his position as inspector-general of military training.

Masaki kept a journal. I had an opportunity to see it for the first time more than twenty years ago. From the time of the fateful "Three Chiefs" personnel conference on 15 July 1935 that resulted in Masaki's dismissal as inspector-general, Masaki never again referred to Hayashi in the journal by his name or title, instead using epithets such as "spider" or "demon spider" (*tsuchigumo*). "Demon Spider looked straight at me and said he would accept any and all of my other demands but pleaded that I must concede my own case." "As usual, the Spider evaded the point by blathering on with an endless flow of words." "In the end, the Spider offered two or three lame excuses." The preceding quotations are all from his entry for 15 July, and he continued in this vein on 16 July: "Private Secretary Arisue [Arisue Seizō, private secretary to the army minister] came calling at 8:30 A.M. to convey to me Demon Spider's troubled mind. Could it be that even spiders have some kind of conscience?"

When I read these lines they send a chill down my spine. "Hayashi" is a common surname, and simple enough to write in kanji. But Masaki went out of his way, repeatedly, to write the complicated kanji for Demon Spider to express the depth of his contempt—an extraordinary degree of resentment. It seems to me that a man like Masaki, plunged into the rough and tumble of the political world, and possessed of such extremely unbalanced views, must be particularly prone to factional intrigue.

Masaki's dismissal as inspector-general of military training was followed by Lieutenant-Colonel Aizawa Saburō's assassination of Nagata Tetsuzan, chief of the Military Affairs Bureau. The February Twenty-Sixth Incident occurred after Aizawa's trial.

The February Twenty-Sixth Incident

Terrorism and Coup d'État

In 1930, Prime Minister Hamaguchi Osachi was shot; in 1931 there were plots for two military coups, in March and October; in 1932, Inoue Junnosuke and Dan Takuma were assassinated in the Ketsumeidan (League of Blood) Incident and then Prime Minister Inukai was assassinated in the May Fifteenth Incident. This series of bloody incidents was followed by three years of relative peace. But 1935 was marked by the Aizawa Incident,[1] and 1936 by the February Twenty-Sixth Incident. Of these events, the March and October Incidents in 1931 and the February Twenty-Sixth Incident in 1936 can be classified as coups or attempted coups, while the shooting of Hamaguchi, the Ketsumeidan Incident, and the May Fifteenth Incident can be described as terrorism.

Terrorism and coups d'état are different in nature. Terrorism generally aims at taking the life of an individual or a small number of people, while coups d'état are intended to seize governmental power. Coups thus require a significantly larger scale of planning and careful preparation. Yet terrorism and coups are similar in that they are a resort to violence for the purpose of toppling political enemies. And terrorism can create an atmosphere in which the use of violence to effect political change becomes normal, laying the groundwork for a coup d'état. And the individuals involved in terrorism and in coups are often connected with one another in some way. The terrorism and coups of Shōwa Japan can, to a remarkable degree, be traced to the actions of a small minority. And if it had been possible to stifle the nucleus of such activity, it might also have been possible to prevent violence as the agent of political change.

The March and October Incidents

The first coup attempt was the March Incident of 1931. It centered on Lieutenant-Colonel Hashimoto Kingorō, Chō Isamu, and other members of the Sakura-kai, and the civilian right-wing activist Ōkawa Shūmei and his followers. Indignant over the corruption of the political parties, they resolved to take direct action to overthrow the government and install a new regime with General Ugaki Kazushige as its leader. They did not have particularly close contact with Ugaki, but at the time he seemed an obvious choice to head an army-led government.

It is rumored that key figures in the army—Tatekawa Yoshitsugu, head of the Second Bureau (Intelligence) of the Army General Staff, and Koiso Kuniaki, chief of the Military Affairs Bureau—expressed their approval for the plot. They were members of Ugaki's inner circle, and some sources suggest that Ugaki also gave his assent.

The specifics of the plot called for a mob of civilians mobilized by Ōkawa and his activists to surround the Diet. The army would then be called out to defend the Diet from this disturbance, and martial law would be declared. Troops would enter the Diet and demand the resignation of Shidehara Kijūrō, the acting prime minister. Meanwhile, negotiations with the imperial palace would result in an imperial order for Ugaki to form a new cabinet. Planning had reached the stage that operating funds and explosives to create an air of emergency were being procured. The plot was to be put into action on either 17 or 18 March. But about a week prior to this, Ugaki had a change of heart, and the plot was canceled. This is what many sources refer to as the March Incident.

But I believe the reality of the March Incident has been exaggerated. The timing is convincing—Prime Minister Hamaguchi had been gravely wounded and was unable to attend the Diet, and the Seiyūkai was mounting a vigorous attack on his cabinet, plunging the assembly into extreme disorder. But the plot itself was absurd. It was quite unlikely that Ōkawa and his associates had the capacity to assemble a mob large enough to surround and threaten the Diet, and it had yet to be determined which army units and their commanders might participate in the action. Even if things had proceeded to that point, it is questionable that Shidehara would have simply thrown in the towel and resigned, and even more unlikely that an imperial order to form a new cabinet would be bestowed upon Ugaki in such circumstances. With these issues unaddressed, there was no way that a coup d'état could be executed a week later. In his memoirs, Koiso called the plot "a childish game" and said there was no way he would have involved himself in it. This is probably an evasion of responsibility on his part, but the plot was certainly a slipshod affair.

Yet the fact that a coup had been contemplated, even for a brief period, was a serious problem. And this was why Ugaki would be the object of criticism for years to come—as would Nagata Tetsuzan, said to have drafted a plan for execution of the coup at the order of Koiso, despite his personal opposition to the idea. In the end, the significance of the March Incident may have been its usefulness, amid the army's factional conflicts, as a tool for criticizing Ugaki.

Compared to this, the October Incident was a somewhat more serious matter. At its nucleus were Hashimoto, Chō, and other members of the Sakura-kai, while the right-wing thinkers Ōkawa, Nishida Mitsugi, and Kita Ikki were also involved. The purpose was to carry out a radical domestic restructuring in response to the Manchurian Incident: attacking the cabinet while in session to assassinate all members, occupying police headquarters, surrounding the Ministry of Army and General Staff Office, and sending Admiral of the Fleet Tōgō Heihachirō to the palace to encourage the emperor to name General Araki Sadao to form a new cabinet. The date was set for 21 October. The projected cabinet lineup was to be Araki as prime minister, Hashimoto as home minister, Tatekawa (who had been transferred as chief of the Second Bureau [Intelligence] to chief of the First Bureau [Operations] in August) as foreign minister, Ōkawa as finance minister, and Chō as superintendent-general of police. However, Hashimoto and his associates styled themselves after the "men of high purpose" of the Restoration years—including their habits of enjoying the pleasures of restaurants and geisha houses—and word of the plot leaked out, resulting in arrests on 17 October by the Kenpeitai.

To my mind, the October Incident was similar to the March Incident in its sloppiness. Even a few days before the anticipated date, no concrete proposals had been made concerning which army units would be involved, security was extremely lax, and the idea that Admiral Tōgō would agree to go to the palace to persuade the emperor to make Araki prime minister was laughably childish.

Yet because this plot was uncovered in the midst of the Manchurian Incident, it caused quite a shock. The existence of such unrest within the military was even utilized as the rationale by those wanting to put an end to the Wakatsuki cabinet. Moreover, after the plot was uncovered the only punishment given its ringleaders was twenty days' house arrest for Hashimoto and ten days for Chō. This was altogether too lenient, considering the significance of the plot in the context of the Manchurian Incident, and signaled that even attempted coups would be met with negligible punishment.

The Ketsumeidan and the May Fifteenth Incident

Four months later, on 9 February 1932, former finance minister and influential Minseitō politician Inoue Junnosuke was shot to death on the way to a campaign rally at an elementary school in Tokyo. Then, on 5 March, Dan Takuma, director-general of holding company of the Mitsui zaibatsu, was gunned down as he emerged from the headquarters of Mitsui Bank. The assassins were two young men from farm villages in Ibaraki prefecture—Konuma Tadashi in the former case and Hishinuma Gorō in the latter. The plight of rural villages at this time has already been described. Inoue was responsible for reimposing the gold standard, while Mitsui had been heavily criticized for selling massive quantities of yen when Britain went off the gold standard on 21 September 1931. This was a natural economic response to the scarcity of gold, but was widely construed as unpatriotic. The headquarters of Mitsui Bank was an impressive building immediately next door to the Bank of Japan, neighbored by the Yokohama Specie Bank and Mitsukoshi Department Store. It is not difficult to imagine why the assassins saw this as symbolic of the way the zaibatsu and political parties seemed to be prospering on the backs of Japan's impoverished rural villages.

These assassinations later came to be known collectively as the Ketsumeidan (League of Blood) Incident, and were the work of three groups: naval air cadets from a training facility at Kasumigaura; young farmers (including Konuma and Hishinuma) who assembled at the Gokokudō, a temple headed by the Nichiren-sect priest Inoue Nisshō at Ōarai on the coast of Ibaraki prefecture; and right-wing university students led by Yotsumoto Yoshitaka (four from the University of Tokyo, three from Kyoto University). Twelve of the members of these groups were arrested; Inoue and the two assassins were sentenced to life imprisonment, while the others were given lighter prison terms.

Not long afterward, the May Fifteenth Incident occurred. Naval officers led by Koga Kiyoshi and Mikami Taku, joined by a number of army officer cadets, forced their way into the prime minister's residence, demanding to see Prime Minister Inukai, whom they shot. Before losing consciousness, the wounded Inukai lit a cigarette with a trembling hand and told aides to call the young men back in and he would persuade them to give up the plot. Hand grenades were tossed into the residence of the home minister, and the headquarters of the Seiyūkai, Mitsubishi Bank, was also attacked, along with six electrical power substations, but damage was minimal and those responsible either gave themselves up to police or were arrested.

The May Fifteenth Incident was the work of young navy officers, army officer cadets, and students at Tachibana Kōzaburō's Aikyōjuku, a right-wing academy. The linkup between very junior naval officers and young civilian right-wingers resembled the Ketsumeidan Incident, and drew from similar sources. Rather than having any clear plan for national renovation, they had united behind a romantic promise of direct action to eliminate evil forces in society.

The March and October Incidents galvanized the young officers of the military, but the response of their superiors to these incidents disappointed them utterly. They also wanted to avoid directly involving military units in a coup, which is why they chose to act as individuals in league with the civilian right wing. This is also related to the fact that while there were coup-like elements in their planning, such as the assaults on banks and electrical substations, the results were more like isolated terrorist incidents than a full-fledged coup d'état.

The May Fifteenth trial was deluged by public demands for clemency for the defendants, and partly as a result of such pressure the sentencing was much more lenient than what was asked for by the prosecutors. As with the March and October Incidents, this was tantamount to approval of such behavior. After all, these men had actually assassinated the prime minister—making this a far more dangerous precedent than either of the two earlier cases, which had been thwarted before any harm had been done.

The Ketsumeidan Incident and the May Fifteenth Incident had two other important consequences. One was that they drew attention to the plight of rural villages. That at least one of their motives had been relief for rural Japan may be said to be a factor in the bold policies subsequently adopted by the Saitō Makoto cabinet. The second was a change of political course on the part of the zaibatsu, which grew increasingly nervous about right-wing criticism of their deep ties to the mainstream political parties. The zaibatsu pulled back from leadership of their enterprise groups and, ironically, began to establish conduits to the right wing. For example, right-wing ideologue Kita Ikki received quite substantial funding from Mitsui, in return providing the combine with a flow of various intelligence.

The Young Officers' Movement and the Kōdōha

For some time after the May Fifteenth Incident, terrorism and coup attempts receded from public view. This happened to coincide more or less precisely with the ascendency of the Kōdōha (Imperial Way Faction) within the army. The senior officers aligned with the Kōdōha anticipated reform under the leadership of Araki and Masaki, while the Tōseiha (Control Faction) aimed, as the name implied, at a restoration of order within an army plagued by politically motivated insubordination. The young officers' movement that underlay the drive for reform within the army was also betting on the Kōdōha as the vehicle for change.

The majority of activist junior officers were members of the thirty-seventh through thirty-ninth graduating classes of the Imperial Japanese Army Academy. Ōgishi Yoriyoshi was in the thirty-fifth, Nonaka Shirō in the thirty-sixth, Ōkura Eiichi in the thirty-seventh, Isobe Asaichi in the thirty-eighth, and Suematsu Tahei in the thirty-ninth. Nishida Mitsugi, who retired early from active duty as a result of illness, and then served as an important liaison between the young officers' movement and the civilian right, was in the thirty-fourth class. On the whole, these men were more than a decade younger than the youngest members of the Isseki-kai (which drew its members from the fifteenth to twenty-fifth classes at the Imperial Japanese Army Academy). A member of the thirty-eighth class would have been born in 1905, graduated from the academy in 1926, and been twenty-six years old at the time of the Manchurian Incident and thirty-one at the time of the February Twenty-Sixth Incident. By the time they were assigned to regiments, there was ample evidence of corruption in the political parties and the zaibatsu control of Japan, and it is not surprising that the young officers saw this as the cause of the extreme poverty of the farm villages. Given only a narrow education by the army and still without much life experience, they were easy prey for idealistic rhetoric. It is often said that they came under the influence of Kita Ikki, but how much they actually understood of his revolutionary theory and program—much of which seems quite absurd to me—is questionable. Probably the most important thing they learned from him was simply a negative perspective on the current situation.

For the most part, these young officers did not advance to the Army War College, and resented the daily discrimination they experienced in comparison to the elite graduates of that institution (who were known as the Tenposen-gumi). The army was extremely elitist when it came to academic achievement, and while the War College graduates might sometimes serve with a regiment, for the most part they landed important jobs in the Ministry of Army or the General Staff Office and were rapidly promoted. Others were not so lucky, and found themselves perennially attached to a regiment, on a slow track to any advancement. Let us compare, for example, Aizawa Saburō (who might be seen as a young officer who had hit middle age) and Suzuki Teiichi, the central figure in the Mokuyōkai. Both graduated in 1910, in the twenty-second class of the academy. If we examine their careers up to 1935, when Aizawa assassinated Nagata Tetsuzan, we find that Suzuki served only four years with a regiment immediately after graduation before enrolling in the War College, after which he served either in the high command or overseas. In 1925 he was again assigned to a regiment, but in only eight months was made a company commander, and four months later was posted overseas, after which he returned to posts in high command. In contrast, aside from a total of six years as an instructor at the Toyama Military Academy or attached to the Imperial Japanese Army Academy, Aizawa spent nineteen years assigned to regiments. He was promoted to lieutenant-colonel in 1933; the same year, Suzuki made full colonel.

For young officers who deeply resented the staff officer elite, a figure such as Minister of Army Araki was an encouragement and inspiration. As mentioned earlier, Araki met frequently with junior officers. This had the effect of weakening army discipline, because it was difficult for the immediate superiors to discipline young officers who had a direct connection to the top hierarchy.

Moreover, the official directly responsible for maintaining order within the army during the Araki years was Hata Shinji, commander of the Kenpeitai from February 1932 to August 1934—and Hata was very lenient with regard to the unrest caused by members of the Kōdōha. Araki had himself been commander of the Kenpeitai from January 1924 to May 1925, so he knew the duties of that position well, and had personally selected his friend Hata for the post immediately after assuming office as army minister. Serving directly under Hata as chief of the Tokyo Kenpeitai from June 1932 to March 1935 was Mochinaga Asaji, a protégé of Masaki from Saga and a graduate in the sixteenth class of the academy. And even after Mochinaga left this post, Moriki Gorō (Saga, twenty-fifth class) remained as head of the Police Affairs Section, so the stance of turning a blind eye to the activities of the young officers' movement continued.

The Kenpeitai, of course, were collecting intelligence. A report in August 1933 listed fifty-four army officers who needed watching—including members of the Sakurakai and most of the young officers involved in the incidents to come. The majority were stationed in Tokyo, and the key figures in the February Twenty-Sixth Incident—Kurihara Yasuhide, Kōda Kiyosada, Andō Teruzō, Isobe Asaichi, and Muranaka Takaji—all made the list. A number of other central figures in the young officers' movement who would not participate in the February Twenty-Sixth Incident were also listed: Ōgishi Yoriyoshi, Suematsu Tahei, Ōkura Eiichi, and Aizawa Saburō.

So these young officers were marked as dissident elements. Yet not only was almost nothing done to deal with them, but the majority were stationed in Tokyo, where the danger of a coup was the greatest. And many of them were serving in the First Division, commanded from August 1934 to December 1935 by the Kōdōha general Yanagawa Heisuke.

The Army Academy Incident

The Army Academy Incident of 20 November 1934 (and thus also known as the November Incident) involved the arrest of three young officers and five officer cadets, led by Muranaka Takaji and Isobe Asaichi, on suspicion of plotting a coup d'état. The plot involved two waves of attacks on civilian officials to coincide with the convening of a special session of the Diet on 28 November. The targets of the first wave of attacks were to be former prime minister Saitō Makoto, Lord Keeper of the Privy Seal Makino Nobuaki, Prime Minister Okada Keisuke, Minister of Home Affairs Gotō Fumio, Grand Chamberlain Suzuki Kantarō, Prince Saionji Kinmochi, and the Metropolitan Police headquarters. The second wave was aimed at Ichiki Kitokurō, president of the Privy Council; former finance minister Takahashi Korekiyo; former prime minister Kiyoura Keigo; Izawa Takio, a member of the House of Peers; Minister of Imperial Household Yuasa Kurahei; former navy minister Takarabe Takeshi; and former foreign minister Shidehara Kijūrō. The plotters hoped to establish a military government headed by Araki and Masaki; if that proved impossible, they hoped to install somewhat less senior staff officers such as Suzuki Teiichi or Ishiwara Kanji. In most respects, including the choice of targets, the plot closely resembled that of the February Twenty-Sixth Incident.

The plot was discovered by Tsuji Masanobu (thirty-sixth class), then a company commander of cadets at the Army Academy, who got in touch with Tsukamoto Makoto, a former classmate of his at the academy who was now serving with the Kenpeitai, who reported the information to Vice Minister of Army Hashimoto Toranosuke. A court-martial was convened, but did not indict any of the accused, citing insufficient evidence. Muranaka and Isobe were placed on administrative suspension, and the cadets were expelled from the academy. Meanwhile, Tsuji, who had uncovered the incident, was dismissed from his post as company commander. What was really happening here remains unclear. Members of the Kōdōha claimed that Tsuji had used spies to fabricate the entire affair, and it is true that the manner in which Tsuji made his accusations was somewhat suspicious. But the court-martial was conducted in the First Division, commanded by Kōdōha stalwart Yanagawa Heisuke, making it likely that the verdict was biased to favor the Kōdōha. There was a certain amount of suspicious activity, but the accusations may also have been a bit forced; it is quite possible that both sides were at fault. On 7 February 1935, while still under arrest and awaiting trial, Muranaka, Isobe, and the others accused Tsuji, Tsukamoto, and Major Katakura Tadashi of making false accusations. Their complaint gave detailed accounts of the actions of Katakura and Tsuji that make it difficult to believe it was written in prison; as writer Matsumoto Seichō has suggested, this would have required the assistance of someone on the outside (Matsumoto Seichō. *Shōwa-shi hakkutsu, dai-4 kan* [Unearthing the Shōwa period, vol. 4]). When this was ignored, on 11 May they filed an appeal for expediting their case with the army minister and the presiding officer of the court-martial. Then, on 11 July, they distributed a pamphlet titled "Shukugun ni kansuru ikensho" (Memorandum on the army purge). This was a savage attack on the Tōseiha, and resulted in both men being discharged from military service.

The Dismissal of Masaki

Masaki Jinzaburō was dismissed from his post as inspector-general of military training soon after Muranaka and Isobe were discharged from the army. The circumstances of Masaki's dismissal have already been touched on. The Kōdōha was outraged, and criticized this move as a violation of the tradition that staffing of the "Three Chiefs" should be decided as a consensus among the current holders of those offices. In fact, however, army personnel decisions were the jurisdiction of the army minister and, ultimately, the prerogative of the emperor. The convention of a consensus of the Three Chiefs was merely a convenience—and one that could hardly be expected to apply if one of the chiefs refused to resign and had to be removed. It was the generals of the Kōdōha who blew this up into a major scandal, and the young officers simply believed them.

On 17 July 1934, an unofficial meeting of military councilors was convened at which Masaki was simply supposed to tender his resignation as inspector-general of military training, and his successor, Watanabe Jōtarō, was to accept his new appointment. But Masaki launched into a critique of Minister of Army Hayashi, supported by Araki. In response, Hayashi said that it was Masaki's factionalism that necessitated his replacement. Masaki retorted by asking, if that was the case, why nothing was being done about Nagata Tetsuzan (seen by many as the leader of the rival Tōseiha), bringing up the March Incident and brandishing a copy of a coup d'état plan he claimed was in Nagata's own handwriting. Nagata, who happened to be in the room, acknowledged that he had written the document. But then Watanabe began to pursue the question of how Masaki had come into personal possession of such a document. At this, Araki and Masaki wilted, unable to mount a decisive counterattack. What is remarkable is the openness with which this fierce debate was conducted.

Failing to achieve victory in this venue, the Kōdōha resorted to a campaign of propaganda and anonymous pamphleteering. The Tōseiha was not completely foreign to such tactics, but the Kōdōha did more of it. A favorite theme was Nagata and his purported plots. Some of the printed pamphlets even made it into the bookstores, though a good deal of this went by word of mouth, as rumors. Some pamphlets—such as the "Memorandum on the Army Purge"—contained detailed accounts of the 15 July meeting between Hayashi and Masaki that could have only come from Masaki himself. The factional conflict within the army was intensifying to an explosive level. About this time, the August personnel changes were announced, with a number of major Kōdōha figures slated for transfer. In the midst of all of this, there was a single individual who would trigger a major incident as a result of Masaki's dismissal: Lieutenant-Colonel Aizawa Saburō.

The Aizawa Incident

On the morning of 12 August 1935, Aizawa strode into the Ministry of Army office of Nagata Tetsuzan and cut him down with a sword. Nagata's position as chief of the army's Military Affairs Bureau was arguably the most powerful in the prewar Japanese bureaucracy. And Nagata was seen at the time as a central figure in the army, a present and future leader of the nation. It was an immense shock for a man such as this to be felled by an assassin's sword.

Aizawa was forty-five years old, a master of kendo, and said to be simple and plainspoken, and quite sensitive. When he was stationed in Aomori he met Ōgishi Yoriyoshi, a key figure in the young officers' movement, and came to look upon the younger man with great respect, calling him "sensei" and referring to him as "my mentor." Aizawa had a fanatical aspect to his personality, and came to believe that Nagata Tetsuzan was the root of all the evils afflicting the army. Those around him said that if there was anyone who was likely to cause trouble, it was Aizawa.

In July 1935, Aizawa traveled to Tokyo from his regimental post in Fukuyama. On the way, he stopped to see Ōgishi in Wakayama, and on 19 July he had a meeting with Nagata. He brought with him a short sword that he had recently purchased. It seems he was contemplating murder but had not yet completely planned it out. The two men exchanged words, but Aizawa was certainly not going to best Nagata in a battle of wits, nor was Nagata going to persuade Aizawa. After this, Aizawa called on Nishida and Ōkura, and met with Ōgishi once more on his way back to Fukuyama. Meanwhile, he became even more firmly convinced that Nagata was the source of all evil. After he arrived back at his regiment, Muranaka and Isobe sent him a pamphlet detailing the main points of Masaki's dismissal, and this further cemented Aizawa's views.

In the army personnel transfers of August 1935, Aizawa was slated to be transferred to Taiwan. This would remove him from the possibility of direct action for an indefinite period. So on 10 August he departed once again for Tokyo. This time he carried with him his freshly honed sword, and after stopping on the way to pray at the Grand Shrine of Ise, he arrived in Tokyo on the night of 11 August. He stayed at Nishida's home, and the next morning went to the Ministry of Army. A dangerous dissident had come to the capital after meeting with other dangerous dissidents, and yet he was not being watched.

At the Ministry of Army he met with Yamaoka Shigeatsu, chief of the Economic Mobilization Bureau and a Kōdōha member. Yamaoka thought something was up—Aizawa was wearing his field sword rather than a ceremonial saber, and looked a bit wild-eyed when he said he was going to see Nagata—but did nothing to deter him. This was tantamount to being an accomplice to murder, but this is indicative of how vicious the army's factionalism had become. After killing Nagata, Aizawa said he was heading to his new post in Taiwan. Taken into custody by the Kenpeitai, he complained that he had lost his cap and it would not do to be seen without it. Under investigation he claimed that he had received divine instructions at Ise Shrine to carry out the vengeance of Heaven. In short, he was not in his right mind.

Nagata was assassinated on a Monday. That weekend, he had been relaxing at his second home on the beach in Kurihama, a summer retreat in Kanagawa prefecture. On 11 August, he had been writing a memo to Minister of Army Hayashi concerning the rebuilding of the army. This document, "Gun o kenzen ni akaruku suru tame no iken" (Ideas for rebuilding the army as a clean and healthy organization), contained the following points:

I. Why is control of the army insufficient?

1. [The army] has been flooded with subversive ideology; Central Command has not established a clear mission; pronouncements from Central Command and high officials are incompetent (不謹慎なる言動); officers maintain subversive relationships with outside conspirators.
2. Officers are actively establishing horizontal networks to take insubordinate action.
3. There is a proliferation of pamphleteering and subversive propaganda and leaking of military secrets [to outside groups].
4. [Officers] are colluding with outside groups (especially activists in the political parties).
5. Personnel policies are unfair; unqualified officers are assigned to inappropriate positions; there is an increase in radical, illogical and narrow minded attitudes.
6. Officers do not take experience and ability seriously, they denounce those who disagree with them, and they restrict themselves to those who share their narrow views. They form feudalistic master-follower (*Oyabun-kobun*) relations or family like relationships which result in factionalism. For example, as a result, subordinates do not give support or advice to their immediate superior or superior officers. Instead, they act on the advice of people with whom they have personal ties rather than relying on the counsel of their subordinates. This results in officers operating outside of the chain of command or taking action outside of

their area of responsibility in order to oppose duly constituted authority. Or they consort with a handful of co-conspirators in order to obstruct authority. Officers show extraordinary antipathy toward and attack those who disagree with their views.

II. In order to weed out these problems, we must move forward selflessly and steadfastly with conviction.

1. Unlawful radical thought must be eliminated and the high command must be strengthened. Our empire has been brought to the brink of crisis by incompetent and disloyal leadership.

It may seem to some that salvation is impossible without using the power of the army. However, I firmly believe that, barring an almost unimaginable circumstance, we cannot use the army to accomplish the reformation of society. Reformation must come through more gradual and legal means.

2. We should investigate concrete measures for domestic and foreign policies.

3. The high command must be staffed by officers of integrity and strength who can resist becoming the puppets of factions. We should dismiss officers who cannot wholeheartedly advise and serve the chiefs of the three agencies [the Ministry of Army, the Army General Staff headquarters, and the Inspectorate-General]. It is important to assign appropriate personnel to appropriate posts, and people who create factions should not be employed in high command.

While deleting some sections, I have quoted the majority of Nagata's text, and his views on the factionalism of the Kōdōha are clear. He saw it as circumventing the vertical chain of command of military organization by forming informal horizontal associations, leaking intelligence, making contact with external agents, and failing to support superior officers or listen to the advice of subordinates—and thus paralyzing the high command of the army as a bureaucratic organization. Such a situation is lethal in a bureaucracy, and it is obvious that Nagata was bound and determined to correct it. In fact, he probably thought he was staking his life on it—which unfortunately turned out to be the case.

Yatsugi Kazuo, a politician and conservative intellectual, recalls that among the many military figures he met in his career, Nagata "was rare for the intellect and sharpness of talent he displayed." When Yatsugi related his impressions of a recent trip to China and Manchuria to Nagata, the latter responded by saying the Kwantung Army should stop giving "internal guidance" to the leadership in Manchuria, and he even felt Japan should move in the direction of giving autonomy to Korea except in matters of defense and foreign affairs. He also said that in order to correct the narrow-mindedness and dogmatism prevalent in military men, he wanted to bring them into greater contact with civilians, perhaps by participating as members of organizations like the Kōjunsha (a social club centered on businessmen associated

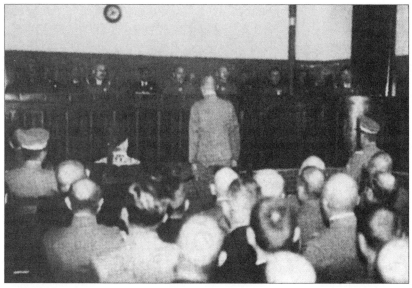

The court-martial of Aizawa Saburō

The court-martial of Aizawa (standing at center, with his back to the camera) was convened at the First Division on 28 January 1936, the year following Nagata's assassination, and on 3 July, Aizawa was executed by firing squad. Aizawa's actions would become an indirect cause of the February Twenty-Sixth Incident.

with Keiō University) or the Kōgyō Kurabu (Industrial Club, another business association). Yatsugi said that talking with Nagata was more like talking to a university professor than a military man (Matsumoto Seichō, *Shōwa-shi hakkutsu, dai-6 kan* [Unearthing the Shōwa period, vol. 6]).

From the Aizawa Incident to the February Twenty-Sixth Incident

How did Nagata's assassination affect the balance of power between the Kōdōha and Tōseiha? It would seem that the Kōdōha would be at a disadvantage because it was responsible for the crime of assassinating Nagata, but in fact the opposite was true. Nagata, the central figure in efforts to purge the Kōdōha from the army, was now dead, and his ally Minister of Army Hayashi was forced to take responsibility for the incident and resign on 5 September 1935. He was replaced by Kawashima Yoshiyuki. Kawashima was a neutral figure in the factional conflict, but he was friends with Masaki, so actually the influence of the Tōseiha declined. Before Hayashi's resignation, he had been considering taking Minami, Araki, and Masaki off the active-duty list in the December personnel assignments, but this never came to pass. Among the top military officials, only Watanabe, inspector-general of military training, seemed interested in clearly pursuing the responsibility of Masaki and others for the recent disturbances.

In the autumn of 1935, the furor over the emperor-as-organ theory was reaching its peak. Prime Minister Okada and Minister of Home Affairs Ohara Naoshi both hoped that Minobe Tatsukichi would voluntarily resign from the House of Peers. Under intense pressure from the right wing, the Ministry of Justice decided that if Minobe would do so, they would defer prosecuting him, on charges of lese majesty, but if he refused they would take him to court. This stance was relayed to Minobe privately by his close friend Matsumoto Jōji (a former University of Tokyo professor and former director-general of the Cabinet Legislation Bureau). On 14 September the Tokyo Criminal District Court's Public Prosecutors Office issued a new summons to Minobe, the first since April. Upon returning home, Minobe immediately sent a letter to the prosecutors expressing his intention to resign, and on 18 September the Ministry of Justice decided to suspend prosecution.

However, that same day Minobe publicly announced that his resignation was intended to calm the turmoil in the House of Peers, but that it was not a repudiation of his constitutional views. This perplexed the Ministry of Justice and also infuriated the hardliners in the army. A resolution was reached amid the complexities of this situation when Minobe issued a second statement retracting his first.

On 3 October, Watanabe, inspector-general of military training, publicly remarked that looking up to the emperor as the highest organ of state did not necessarily imply any disrespect. This enraged the military hardliners. But Watanabe had served as Yamagata Aritomo's aide-de-camp, worshiped the elder statesman, and thus was sympathetic to the emperor-as-organ concept. So even within the army, there were top officials who were not enthusiastic about the conservative campaign against Minobe. But the government bowed to popular criticism and on 15 October found itself forced to issue a second declaration concerning clarification of the national polity.

Yet after the end of October, the uproar quickly died down. If the army wanted to continue to pressure the cabinet, it would probably end in Kawashima resigning as army minister, in which case it was possible that a figure might be appointed who was unacceptable to the Kōdōha; moreover, if the army toppled the cabinet, there was a strong possibility that Ugaki might become prime minister. Particularly with Saitō Makoto's impending appointment as lord keeper of the privy seal, the prospects for an Ugaki cabinet had increased. At the very least, because Saitō, Okada, and Ugaki were both moderates in foreign policy and domestic policy, the next cabinet after Okada would begin to suppress the army radicals. That was why the uproar over clarification of the national polity (*kokutai*) died down. This shows that this movement was more political than ideological.

The Road to the February Twenty-Sixth Incident

The Aizawa Incident had a great impact on the young officers who shared his convictions—instilling in them a desire to emulate his fervor. Preliminary hearings in Aizawa's case ended on 2 November 1935, with public hearings beginning on 28 January 1936. Aizawa's supporters hoped to use this opportunity to propagandize for the Kōdōha ideology and build sympathy for Aizawa. The court-martial was under the jurisdiction of the First Division, in whose district the incident occurred, which meant that Yanagawa, the divisional commander, was able to select the judges. Naturally, he chose a Kōdōha lineup. Things went extremely well from their perspective until 12 February, when Lieutenant-General Hashimoto Toranosuke, commander of the Imperial Guards Division, was called as a witness and refused to testify, citing administrative confidentiality. Hayashi Senjūrō adopted the same stance. It had now become more difficult to utilize the trial for propaganda purposes and steer it in a direction that could be advantageous for the Kōdōha.

Meanwhile, an important decision had been made that would affect the young officers' movement. In December it was announced that the First Division was to be transferred to Manchuria. As previously noted, the dissident young officers were concentrated to an extraordinary degree in the First Division. If they were transferred en masse to Manchuria, it would remove their ability to engage in subversive action. So when the Aizawa court-martial also began go in an unfavorable direction, they decided on an uprising. The date was set only a few days before 26 February.

But preparations were already under way. Certain units even practiced an assault on the prime minister's residence. Ammunition for the uprising had been stockpiled bit by bit as opportunity afforded.

Unlike previous incidents, the February Twenty-Sixth Incident was the work of junior officers—lieutenants and captains—in direct command of troops. What had been absent in previous coup attempts was this direct grasp of military power at the unit level. They had been diligent in training and indoctrinating their soldiers, and had won their strong allegiance. Another distinguishing feature of this incident was that the civilian right wing was almost completely uninvolved.

At the time, relations between the police and the army were antagonistic. The Go-Stop Incident of 1933 is a well-known example—a case in which soldiers ignored a traffic signal and were arrested by police officers, leading to protests by army officials and a major confrontation between the home ministry and the army. In the end, the police had to give up on any investigation of army personnel, and as a result could keep an eye on civilian right-wing activity only. The dissidence within the army itself could only be monitored by the Kenpeitai, but the military police were sympathetic to the Kōdōha. It was because of this conflict between the police and the army that highly inappropriate acts, such as the field exercises for an assault on the prime minister's residence, had been ignored by the police.

The February Twenty-Sixth Incident could have been anticipated. The likely perpetrators were known. It was already rumored in the ranks that something dangerous could happen when Captain Yamaguchi Ichitarō of the First Infantry Regiment and Captain Andō Teruzō of the Third Infantry Regiment were both on weekly duty (Ōtani Keijirō, *Shōwa kenpeishi* [History of the Shōwa military police]). And in fact, the incident took place on their watch.

The February Twenty-Sixth Incident

Early in the morning of 26 February 1936, army units comprising nearly 1,400 troops, commanded by Captain Andō Teruzō, Lieutenant Kurihara Yasuhide, Lieutenant Nakahashi Motoaki, and other young officers, attacked the prime minister's residence and other key locations in central Tokyo, killing Lord Keeper of the Privy Seal Saitō Makoto, Minister of Finance Takahashi Korekiyo, and Inspector-General of Military Training Watanabe Jōtarō, and gravely wounding Grand Chamberlain Suzuki Kantarō. They also murdered the prime minister's personal secretary, as well as several police officers guarding the prime minister's residence, and occupied the Nagatachō district where government offices and official residences were concentrated. (See Table 3.3.) The goal of the uprising was to establish a Kōdōha-led military dictatorship and force a "Shōwa Restoration." They believed that a bloc of elder statesmen and palace officials surrounding the throne was obstructing the genuine expression of the will of the emperor, and aimed at removing these evil advisers in order to bring about direct imperial rule. The path to the restoration of order was not a smooth one, but by 29 February their rebellion was suppressed. There had not been a domestic troop mobilization of this size since the Satsuma Rebellion in 1877.

In the attack on the prime minister's residence, Prime Minister Okada was spared because the rebels mistakenly shot his brother-in-law Matsuo Denzō instead (Matsuo in fact closely resembled the prime minister, and was said to have worked as Okada's personal secretary with the intention of serving as a body double in event of an emergency). The public also believed that the prime minister was dead, and the cabinet resigned, but

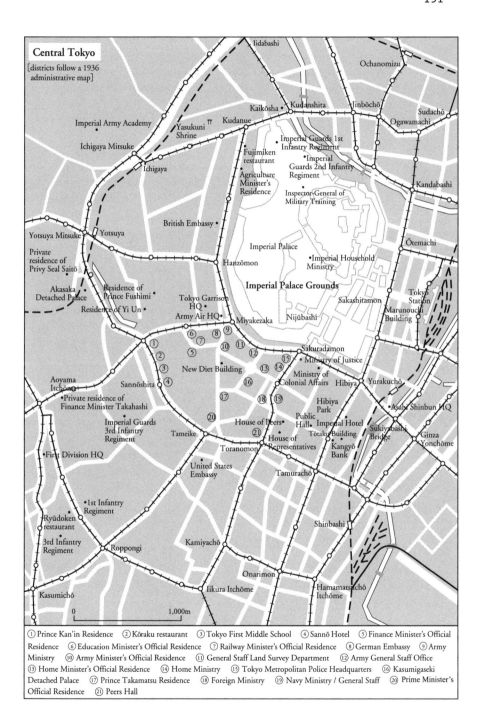

① Prince Kan'in Residence ② Kōraku restaurant ③ Tokyo First Middle School ④ Sannō Hotel ⑤ Finance Minister's Official Residence ⑥ Education Minister's Official Residence ⑦ Railway Minister's Official Residence ⑧ German Embassy ⑨ Army Ministry ⑩ Army Minister's Official Residence ⑪ General Staff Land Survey Department ⑫ Army General Staff Office ⑬ Home Minister's Official Residence ⑭ Home Ministry ⑮ Tokyo Metropolitan Police Headquarters ⑯ Kasumigaseki Detached Palace ⑰ Prince Takamatsu Residence ⑱ Foreign Ministry ⑲ Navy Ministry / General Staff ⑳ Prime Minister's Official Residence ㉑ Peers Hall

Table 3.3   Attacks and Occupations on the Morning of 26 February 1936

Time	Place of Attack	Leaders and Outcomes
Around 5:00 a.m.	Army minister's official residence	150 men under First Lieutenant Nibu
Around 5:00 a.m.	Tokyo Metropolitan Police Headquarters	400 men under Captain Nonaka
5:05	Finance minister's private residence	100 men under First Lieutenant Nakahashi; Finance Minister Takahashi Korekiyo murdered and 1 policeman wounded
Around 5:05	Privy seal's private residence	150 men under First Lieutenant Sakai; Privy Seal Saitō Makoto murdered
5:10	Grand chamberlin's official residence	150 men under Captain Andō; Grand Chamberlin Suzuki Kantarō gravely wounded and 2 policemen wounded
Around 5:10	Prime minister's official residence	300 men under First Lieutenant Kurihara; Prime Minister Okada Keisuke escapes; Colonel Matsuo Denzō murdered and 4 policemen killed
Around 5:40	Itōya Inn	6 men under Captain Kōno; Count Makino Nobuaki escapes; 1 policeman killed and 3 other people wounded
Around 6:00	Private residence of inspector-general of military education	30 men under Second Lieutenant Yasuda; Inspector-General Watanabe Jōtarō murdered
Around 6:35	Home minister's official residence	60 men under Second Lieutenant Suzuki; Home Minister Gotō Fumio not present
Around 8:55	Asahi Shinbun (news media)	60 men under First Lieutenant Kurihara
Around 8:55	Denpō Tsūshin Sha (news media)	60 men under First Lieutenant Kurihara
9:30	Hōchi Shinbun (news media)	60 men under First Lieutenant Kurihara
9:30	Army Ministry	150 men under First Lieutenant Nibu; Major Katakura Tadashi wounded
9:30	Army General Staff Office	150 men under First Lieutenant Nibu
Around 9:35	Nichi-nichi Shinbun (news media)	60 men under First Lieutenant Kurihara
9:40	Kokumin Shinbun (news media)	60 men under First Lieutenant Kurihara
Around 9:50	Jiji Shinpō (news media)	60 men under First Lieutenant Kurihara

Okada had hidden in a maid's closet and escaped on the night of 27 February. Saitō was a former prime minister and now served as lord keeper of the privy seal, and was regarded as one of the chief obstacles to plans for a Shōwa Restoration. Takahashi Korekiyo was a statesman who had won the affection of the public for a lengthy career in which he had demonstrated an indifference to honors and fame. He was targeted because he had been a pillar of both the Saitō and Okada cabinets and had served in both as a brake upon unlimited expansion of military spending. As inspector-general of military training, Watanabe Jōtarō had shown little enthusiasm for the clarification of the national polity movement (and thus was seen as sympathetic to the liberal emperor-as-organ theory); moreover, he had been a strong supporter of Minister of Army Hayashi's decision to dismiss Masaki as inspector-general.

It was Masaki upon whom the young officers of the rebellion pinned their strongest hopes. There is no evidence that there was direct collusion between Masaki and the young officers, but as soon as he learned of the incident, Masaki attempted to make use of it. At about 4:30 A.M., just before the attacks started, Masaki was informed of the rebellion by Kamekawa Tetsuya, a civilian right-winger. Masaki immediately contacted his close friend Navy admiral Katō Kanji, hatching a plan in which Katō would persuade Prince Fushimi Hiroyasu, navy chief of staff, to go to the palace and convince the emperor to appoint a "strong" cabinet (headed by either Masaki or Hiranuma, for example), declare martial law, and issue an imperial rescript declaring a Shōwa Restoration. Having taken this step, Masaki set out for the army minister's residence, where the young rebel officers greeted him expectantly, and he famously said to them, "So you've finally done it! I understand your feelings completely."

The immediate responsibility for restoring order lay with the army minister. But Kawashima was flustered and confused and simply kept repeating an injunction not to fire upon imperial troops. His desire to avoid fratricidal combat between army units was the typical reaction of a bureaucrat. Rather than assigning blame or getting to the root of the problem, he simply wanted to restore peace and order. The second of the "Three Chiefs," Chief of General Staff Prince Kan'in, was convalescing from an illness. And the third, Inspector-General Watanabe, who would certainly have had firm opinions on this crisis, had been murdered. So it was the Conference of Military Councilors that stepped into the breach. As the elders of the army, they felt responsible for the situation and took action to bring it under control. The lineup of military councilors who assembled at the imperial palace included Araki, Masaki, Hayashi, Abe Nobuyuki, Nishi Yoshikazu, Ueda Kenkichi, and Terauchi Hisaichi, with Minister of Army Kawashima and Vice Chief of Staff Sugiyama Hajime also attending. Among these officers, Araki and Masaki were the most senior and experienced.

Former army minister Hayashi, perhaps fearing that he would be targeted for attack, stayed home.

This meeting produced the famous "Minister of War's Proclamation." Issued at 3:30 P.M. on 26 February from the headquarters of the Tokyo Garrison, it read:

1. The purpose of your rising has been reported to His Majesty.
2. We recognize that your actions are based on a sincere desire to clarify the national polity.
3. The current state of the national polity (including its defilement) is a matter of great regret to us.
4. All the military councilors have agreed to unite and move forward in accordance with the principles stated above.
5. Beyond this everything depends upon His Majesty's will.

Several versions of this text exist, with slight differences in phrasing, notably the substitution of "motives" for "actions" in the second item, but is unclear which version was approved by the councilors, or how it came to be altered. In any case, its respectful tone quite obviously expressed sympathy for the rebel forces.

Moreover, the emperor's chief aide-de-camp, serving as liaison between himself and the army, was Honjō Shigeru, who not only was a Kōdōha general, but whose son-in-law, Yamaguchi Ichitarō, was an officer in one of the rebel units. Lieutenant-General Kashii Kōhei, the commander of the Tokyo Garrison, with direct responsibility for restoring order in the capital, was also a Kōdōha man. The rebel units had met with almost perfect conditions. Their coup d'état was on the verge of success.

Fury of the Emperor

However, it was Emperor Shōwa himself who most clearly judged the February Twenty-Sixth Incident to be a rebellion, and insisted on an uncompromising response. Already on 26 February he was referring to them as rebel forces and expressing his desire that they be suppressed. At 1:00 A.M. on 27 February the cabinet voted to resign, and early the next morning formally presented letters of resignation to the emperor. But the emperor asked why it was that the letter of the army minister, who bore the heaviest responsibility for the crisis, was no different from that of the other ministers, and went on to say that at the time of the Toranomon Incident in late 1923 (the assassination attempt against him when he was crown prince), the letter of resignation tendered by Minister of Home Affairs Gotō Shinpei, who had been the chief official responsible for security, had been especially sincere, and compared this unfavorably to the present situation.

The diary of Chief Aide-de-Camp Honjō Shigeru further records the following, which took place on 27 February. Well-known as the most forceful expression of emotion and will on the part of Emperor Shōwa, it is well worth reading:

> Today when I went to see His Majesty, I said that the officers of the active units had willfully mobilized the emperor's troops, a blatant violation of the imperial right of supreme command that was fundamentally impermissible, but that their spirit, which emanated from a deep concern for our imperial land, should not necessarily be faulted. Later, I was summoned to his presence again, and he said "What sympathy should I have for the spirit of officers brutal enough to slaughter my trusted and loyal senior retainers?" Then, somewhat later, he sighed "To cut down my most trusted old advisors in this way is no different from strangling me with a silken cord."
>
> To this I said once more that while that the murder of the emperor's advisors was certainly a most evil act, even if we might attribute it to misguided motives, what had led the officers to do what they had done stemmed from the belief that it was for the good of the nation. But the emperor retorted that all you are saying is that they were not acting out of personal gain or private ambition.
>
> Furthermore, on this day His Majesty expressed considerable irritation that the military authorities were not making any progress in implementing measures to suppress the active units, and declared to the aides-de-camp, "I will personally lead the Imperial Guards Division and put this down myself!" This was mortifying to us all. All we could do was say to him repeatedly that this was a matter about which His Majesty need not concern himself (Honjō Shigeru. *Honjō nikki* [The Honjō diary]).

In other words, Honjō, sympathetic to the Kōdōha and with a son-in-law among the dissident officers, was offering a defense of the "active units" (his use of this euphemism is significant) on the grounds of their sincerity and patriotism, even if the actions themselves were indefensible. But the emperor was having none of this; he was enraged by the loss of close advisers and government ministers to the attacks, feeling them tantamount to an assault on his own person. Moreover, he was deeply frustrated by the failure of the military to put down the revolt, to the point that he was threatening to deal with it personally.

With this clear expression of the emperor's will, many senior officers had a change of heart. If they continued to express sympathy for the dissident units, they might now be seen as allies of a rebel army. From 27 February onward, the situation changed dramatically.

In contrast to the vacillation that had gripped the highest levels of the army, Ishiwara Kanji was firmly in favor of suppressing the revolt. At the time, he was chief of the Operations and War Plans section of the Army General Staff, had experience commanding combat troops in the Manchurian Incident, and was not squeamish about the deaths that might result. Quite the contrary, he saw February Twenty-Sixth Incident as an opportunity to implement plans of his own, which he would advance in the wake of the incident.

The February Twenty-Sixth Incident has been criticized for being a plot to destroy, not to construct. However, though it may be strange to say so, as a destructive plan it was actually well-designed. In fact, I am not exaggerating when I say that it came very close to succeeding. And because of this, the February Twenty-Sixth Incident would have a profound impact on subsequent Japanese politics.

Japan in a "Period of Emergency"

Urban Development

The second chapter of this book has brought us from the Manchurian Incident of 1931 to the February Twenty-Sixth Incident of 1936. At the time, this was frequently referred to as a "period of emergency" (*hijōji*). But what was Japanese society like during this era of crisis?

War was clearly beginning to show its impact. In 1932, the "Three Human Bullets" (or "Three Human Bombs") were taken up by the media as heroes of the Shanghai Incident. Three Japanese soldiers had reportedly run through the barbed wire entanglements of the Chinese defenses by acting as suicide bombers with explosives strapped to their chests. When this story broke (although it is now believed to have been a fabrication) it caused such a sensation that five different film companies produced motion pictures on this theme in March 1932, the month following their deaths. The story swept the other media as well: radio, the theater, and publishing. Children played at being the "Three Human Bullets," and the Takashimaya Department Store in Osaka sold a "Three Human Bombs" lunch, with barricades of ingeniously sliced daikon radish and bombs represented by stalks of butterbur. In the town where the three soldiers had been based, Kurume in Fukuoka prefecture, vendors of sweet bean paste buns and saké adopted "Three Heroes" as a brand name. One wonders what people were thinking when they were eating and drinking such things.

But such fads can also be seen as evidence that warfare had not yet become an oppressive burden. The fad for padded shoulders in men's suits in 1932 is said to have been a military look influenced by the Manchurian Incident, but such fashion statements are a long way from a genuine wartime mentality. Despite the vast geographic scale of the fighting in the Manchurian Incident, Japanese losses were comparatively light: a July 1933 report of the Ministry of Army put them at 2,530 dead and 6,896 wounded.

There was little combat between then and the outbreak of the Sino-Japanese War in 1937,[2] so the impact of warfare on the general population was not that great. The development of urban culture that had been taking place since the beginning of the Shōwa era continued apace.

The cities themselves continued to expand. In October 1932, the municipality of Tokyo absorbed five outlying counties (*gun*) and eighty-two townships and villages, increasing its population to 4.97 million in thirty-five wards and making it the second largest city in the world. The Hattori Clock Tower (now the Wakō Building) in the heart of Ginza was completed that year, and stands to this day as symbol of the district. Also in 1932, Kaō Soap began marketing shampoo for the first time, and "shampoo" as a foreign loanword quickly entered the language. There is something modern and bright in such events, an indication that the depression had not cast a serious pall over all of Japanese society.

Department stores were the emblem of urban culture. In the spring of 1932, the Nankai Takashimaya in Osaka (where the "Three Human Bombs" lunch was sold) drew throngs of customers when it introduced air-conditioning to its ground floor and salon-restaurant, and central air and heat were soon expanded throughout the building. November 1932 saw the first domestic production of department-store mannequins, though they were modeled on foreign body types. In November 1934 the Matsuzakaya in Nagoya installed escalators. Escalators had made their first appearance in the Taishō era, but did not become widespread until this time. We tend to think of things like mannequins, air-conditioning, and escalators as phenomena of the postwar economic boom, but they had already been elements in the prewar department stores.

Tokyo already had a subway line running from Asakusa to Ueno, but it was being extended from Ueno to Shinbashi, and in June 1934 service was completed between Asakusa and Shinbashi. The major department stores of the era—Shirokiya, Takashimaya, Mitsukoshi—all had entrances linking them directly to subway stations. The stores subsidized the construction of such access, and Mitsukoshi, which underwrote the entire cost, had the stop named after it (*Mitsukoshi-mae*).

The Shirokiya Department Store in Nihonbashi (later the Nihonbashi branch of Tōkyū Department Store until it closed in January 1999) caught fire on 16 December 1932, and fourteen people died in the blaze. Among the dead were female clerks in the store who, as they were wearing traditional kimono, were not wearing underwear, and delayed their escape because they were embarrassed at the gaze of onlookers. It is said that this led to a campaign for all women to wear underwear thereafter. This story is now disputed, but it is certainly true that Western-style dress began to become much more prevalent from around this time. In July 1933, Matsuzakaya began requiring

Department store interiors

Department stores symbolized urban consumer culture. The major stores vied with one another to draw customers with a broad selection of clothing, cosmetics, and other goods, and luxurious interior designs not much different from today. (Above, from Kawakami Sumio, Shin Tōkyō hyakkei [New one hundred views of Tokyo]; below, a sales counter at Mitsukoshi in Nihonbashi in the early Shōwa era, photo courtesy of Kyodo News Images Inc.)

all its female employees to wear Western-style uniforms, and Shirokiya offered employees subsidies for purchase of Western-style outfits.

Such developments were connected with the advancement of women in the workplace. In 1932, the Tokyo Metropolitan Police hired three former public health nurses as its first female police officers. The same year, Kyoto registered its first woman taxi driver, which caused quite a stir. Her husband was Ninagawa Torazō, an assistant professor at Kyoto University who would dominate the office of governor of Kyoto for a good part of the postwar era. Women also advanced into specialized professional fields. In May 1933 the Attorney Act was revised, permitting women to practice law for the first time. But the most significant reason for the increased participation of women in the workplace was the fact that they could be paid lower wages. In January 1934, the city of Tokyo advertised for women conductors on public transport—but offered average monthly wages of less than ¥36 at a time when men were averaging ¥95 for the same work. In a Ministry of Home Affairs survey of the wages of working women conducted in June 1935, the highest earners were typists at ¥450 a month, while elevator attendants were paid ¥27 and bus guides ¥46.

Urban Culture

The development of urban culture also continued from the 1920s, despite the effects of the global depression. Motion pictures continued to be immensely popular. Charlie Chaplin arrived in Japan on 14 May 1932 to a prodigious welcome. In September 1933, the American film *King Kong* was screened. The famous final scene, featuring the newly completed Empire State Building, gave an overwhelming impression of the wealth and power of the United States, even in the midst of the Great Depression.

Music also flourished as before. In January 1936, just before the February Twenty-Sixth Incident, the Russian basso profundo Feodor Chaliapin came to Japan for a solo recital. Though somewhat past his prime, he was still a legendary figure, one of the world's greatest singers. He was staying at the Imperial Hotel in Tokyo, and suffering from a toothache, so he asked for something tasty but easy to eat. The head chef pondered this for a while, and came up with a recipe for a tenderized steak marinated in finely grated onion that is still known as a Chaliapin Steak. At the time it cost ¥1.30.

The recording industry was also taking off in Japan. Around 1932, fees for recorded performances ran a wide gamut, from naniwa-bushi singer Suzuki Yonewaka at ¥14,000, and soprano Sekiya Toshiko at ¥9,600, and composer Nakayama Shinpei at ¥9,700, to lower rates for pop singers like Awaya Noriko at ¥2,700 or a newcomer like Fujiyama Ichirō at only ¥15.

The Olympics and Baseball

Sports grew to new heights of popularity. In July 1932, the Summer Olympics were held in Los Angeles. The Japanese contingent performed impressively, with athletes such as Nambu Chūhei, Nishi Takeichi, and Nishida Shūhei winning a total of seven gold medals. Japan took first place in swimming overall, winning more gold, silver, and bronze in those events than any other nation. The games were broadcast over the radio, captivating a large listening audience.

However, here we must attach some caveats. First of all, at the time, NHK (Japan's national broadcasting company) did not offer live coverage of the games, but simulated such coverage afterward in the studio, with announcers reading scripts that made it sound as if they were giving play-by-play for events that had already taken place.

In addition, we must discount something from the success of the Japanese athletes, since this was the first Olympic Games to be held outside Europe for some time, and since it was on the West Coast of the United States, European participation was more limited than usual. For example, Japan's Nishi took gold in the equestrian competition, but it is likely that he would have had difficulty against a stronger European showing.

Nor did the Americans make that much of a fuss about the Olympics. Even today, American football, basketball, and baseball seem to attract a larger following in the United States than the Olympics, and at the time the Olympics were a much smaller affair than they are now, a specialty of a small number of athletes. According to journalist Kiyosawa Kiyoshi, who attended the Los Angeles Games, the stands were empty and the newspaper coverage minimal—quite a contrast from the excitement with which the Olympics were met in Japan that year.

In Japan itself, the biggest sporting event was the annual baseball play-offs among Big Six universities in Tokyo. In October 1933, during the Waseda-Keiō game, Keiō University third baseman Mizuhara Shigeru touched off a riot when he picked up an apple thrown onto the field from the stands and hurled it into the Waseda bleachers. A routine featuring the Waseda-Keiō game by the great prewar standup comedy duo of Yokoyama Entatsu and Hanabishi Achako was also enormously popular. Waseda University's Totsuka Baseball Stadium (later Abe Stadium) was equipped with nighttime illumination in July 1933, another indication of the popularity of university-league baseball in those days.

The National Secondary School Baseball Championship was also quite popular, the precursor of the National High School Baseball Championship held every summer at Kōshien Stadium to this day. The twenty-five-inning shutout game in the semifinals at Kōshien between Chūkyō Shōgyō and Akashi Chūgaku in August 1933 is still discussed by baseball fans.

Japan participates in the Tenth Olympiad in Los Angeles, 1932
Above, *the second group of Japanese athletes returning home from the Olympics bow in front of the imperial palace.* Below, *Japanese athletes disembark from a ship, with runner Oda Mikio as their standard-bearer. Photos by Nihon Denpō Tsūshinsha, courtesy of Kyodo News Images Inc.*

This fascination with baseball eventually produced professional teams. The visit to Japan in November 1934 of an American all-star team headed by Babe Ruth and Lou Gehrig was the catalyst. In December 1934, the Greater Japan Tokyo Baseball Club was launched, later becoming the Tokyo Giants. In January 1936, the second professional baseball team, the Golden Dolphins, was launched in Nagoya, followed by the Osaka Baseball Club (better known as the Osaka Tigers, now the Hanshin Tigers) on 9 March. The Japanese Professional Baseball League was created in February 1936.

In preparation for the 1936 Olympics, Japanese athletes set a number of records. On 9 June 1935, Yoshioka Takanori tied the world record in the 100-meter dash with a time of 10.3 seconds, winning himself the nickname "Dawn Express." On 3 November of the same year, a Korean runner named Sohn Kee-chung (because Korea was a colony, he was considered a Japanese national) set a world's record for the marathon, 2:26:42. In other sports, in July 1934, Miki Ryūki paired with Dorothy Round to win the mixed doubles in tennis at Wimbledon. And on 5 October 1936, a climbing team from Rikkyō University achieved the first successful ascent of Nanda Kot, and the first Japanese summit of a Himalayan peak.

Extravagance and Austerity

The origin of the Shirokiya Department Store fire was believed to have been a display of celluloid toys, and as a result the popularity of such toys plunged dramatically. But this gives us some idea of what children of this era had as playthings.

Some toys were quite expensive. In 1932 the market for high-end electric model railway sets drew attention, with some sets including a locomotive, three passenger cars, and a crossing with signal going for as much as ¥120 or even ¥200. As mentioned earlier, this was a time when the average monthly income of a typical salaryman's household was around ¥100. The Hamaguchi cabinet was vigorously promoting austerity, but there was still considerable extravagance among some consumers.

That said, symbols of diligence and thrift were also popular. In 1932, statues of the Edo-period agrarian philosopher Ninomiya Sontoku in his youth, book in hand as he carried firewood on his back, were selling like hotcakes. Ninomiya had become the symbol of the rural self-help movement, and the virtues of self-discipline, hard work, and idealism. One could also say that such massive sales of rather expensive bronze statues was a sign that at least some rural communities were not as hard-up as is usually assumed. But it is also true that before long many of these statues would be surrendered to the wartime requisitioning of iron and other metals.

One example of extravagance that was much discussed at the time was a wedding in November 1933 between members of the Maeda family of Kaga and the Kuroda family of Fukuoka, both former daimyo houses. The marriage furniture filled fifty large moving trucks and took three days to deliver. Meanwhile, a movement had been under way since February of that year to simplify wedding ceremonies to cut down on expense. It is unclear whether it was the mood of austerity or the increasing extravagance of weddings that inspired the movement, and in any case it gained little traction.

One of the upper-class luxuries of the era was the automobile. The "motorization" of the country that began in the mid-1920s continued. A June 1932 survey put the number of automobiles nationwide at 90,110, with Ford the top brand at 32,122 vehicles and General Motors's Chevrolet in second place with 30,430. Cars were still a luxury item and foreign makes predominated. When Fords first started appearing in Japan, they cost about ¥3,000 each, though this price eventually dropped to around ¥2,000.

The poor state of the roads was one of the biggest problems, but the spread of automobiles began to spur improvements. In July 1932, the resort area of Hakone became home to Japan's first automobile tollway, followed by Nikkō in August of the same year. The inevitable result of the motorization of Japan was an increasing number of traffic accidents. In 1934, the annual number of traffic casualties had reached 53,430. This represented the prewar peak. After this, priority was given to providing vehicles for the military, and the percentage in civilian use declined. The decline in traffic accidents was laudable, but unfortunately it also was an indicator of the rapid militarization of Japanese society that took place after the February Twenty-Sixth Incident.

The Plight of Rural Japan

Meanwhile, the conditions in impoverished regions and among impoverished classes were disastrous. In July 1932, the Ministry of Education announced that there were some 200,000 malnourished children nationwide. A survey of rural villages in Niigata prefecture found that in the first six months of 1932, a total of 4,962 girls had been indentured by their families, winding up as entertainers (1,750), prostitutes (1,502), hostesses (1,630), or something else.

In 1934 there was a major crop failure in the Tōhoku region of northern Japan, and hungry schoolchildren scavenged for the remains of boxed lunches tossed out of train windows. In October of that year a survey in Aomori prefecture found that a total of 7,083 women and girls had left their home villages, 2,129 of them in the preceding year and a half, and that almost all of them had been indentured. A November 1934 survey in Hokkaido found that crop failures had also resulted in the sale of young women and girls: 735 as entertainers or prostitutes, 575 as hostesses, 633 as factory workers, and 813 unclassified.

By the end of 1934 in the Tōhoku region and Hokkaido, it is said that more than 50,000 young women had been sold into some form of servitude. The numbers—and the price of sale—follow. The more onerous the work—in a variety of respects—the higher the price paid:

Maids/nannies	19,244	¥76
Factory workers	17,260	¥76
Hostesses	5,952	¥491
Prostitutes	4,521	¥1,011
Waitresses	3,271	¥83
Geisha	2,196	¥702

In 1935, living conditions for the average Japanese household were as follows: one or two light bulbs per house; drinking water from a well or river stored in large jugs; a wood or charcoal fired cook stove; and a wood-fired bath. Toilets were pit toilets, little more than a hole cut in the floor-boards, and with outhouses in the rural areas. In the cities there were some areas in which the lifestyle was not that different from what the postwar era would bring, but these were limited, and basic infrastructure such as sewers and roads was inadequate. In 1935 the average life expectancy was 44.8 years for men and 46.5 for women. The high rate of infant mortality was partially responsible for these figures, but even before the impact of the war began to be felt demographically, Japanese lives were brief.

So this was the reality of Japan from the perspective of the national average. The urban prosperity and even extravagance to be seen in the midst of this was taken by the right wing and the young officers as evidence of impermissible corruption and indulgence.

The Move Toward Discipline

In around 1934 or 1935 the Japanese people began to lose some of their freedom—less in a material than in a psychological or spiritual sense. In 1934, Mikami Sanji, doyen of the Japanese historical establishment and member of the House of Peers, called for cutting the number of hours devoted to English instruction in the schools, while Minister of Education Matsuda Genji made news by advocating the abandonment of the use of the words "papa" and "mama"—which suggests how prevalent their use had become. Matsuda formerly worked under Hara Takashi, who encouraged his son to use "papa" and "mama," and journalist Kiyosawa Kiyoshi mocked Matsuda for "trivialism" and narrow prejudice, wondering what Hara would think of all this if he were still alive.

In October 1934 the Tokyo Metropolitan Police banned university and secondary school students and other minors from entering cafes or cabarets. However, it was difficult to tell whether students were underage or not, so as long as they did not wear school uniforms, they were largely ignored. Here we might note that it was the norm for students to wear uniforms until the early 1960s. In December 1934, there was a move to bar students from part-time jobs in department stores, on the grounds that too many of them were using such work as an opportunity to date members of the female staff. Such free association between young men and women was frowned upon.

Also, from about 1934 onward, home ministry censorship of the media grew increasingly stringent. Even popular songs were not exempt: "Kohan no yado" (Lakeside inn) was banned for excessive sentimentality, while "Kirameku seiza" (Glittering constellations) had to have its lyrics rewritten because the inclusion of stars—symbol of the army—in a popular song as symbols of love or romance was deemed inappropriate.

In February 1934, the army remodeled the standard-issue military swords carried by officers and noncommissioned officers from Western-style sabers to more traditional Japanese-style swords with gorgeous hilts wrapped with silk cord. These were called Shōwa *shintō* (new swords of Shōwa), and were derided by experts as being difficult to wield. This change was a product of the rise of ultra-nationalism. Historian Alfred Vagts makes an important distinction between a superficial "militaristic way" and a more rationally grounded "military way"; the Shōwa *shintō* are a symbol of the superficiality of Japanese militarism (Alfred Vagts, *A History of Militarism: Civilian and Military*).

Development of the Heavy and Chemical Industries

From 1932 to 1936, the heavy and chemical industrial sectors in Japan underwent rapid development. If we compare average production in various sectors for the period 1935–1937 to a base in the period 1929–1931, electric power grew by 1.75 times, coal by 1.33, steel by 2.43, shipbuilding by 2.02, industrial machinery by 10.36, and electric motors by 2.36.

The major trend in industrial organization during this period was large-scale corporate mergers and the formation of conglomerates and trusts. In the iron and steel industry, the government-operated Yawata plant in Fukuoka merged with Wanishi (Hokkaido), Kamaishi (Iwate), Fuji (Kanagawa), and others to form Japan Iron & Steel (Nihon Seitetsu) in January 1934. In the pulp and paper industry, Ōji Paper absorbed Fuji Paper and Karafuto Industries to conquer a 90 percent share of the market.

One outstanding aspect of the wave of heavy industrial development was the rise of what were called the "New Zaibatsu." Notable examples of these were Aikawa Yoshisuke's Nihon Sangyō (Nissan); Noguchi Shitagau's Nihon Chisso; Mori Nobuteru's Shōwa Fertilizers and Shōwa Denkō; Ōkōchi Masatoshi's Riken; Nakano Tomonori's Nippon Soda; and Nakajima Chikuhei's Nakajima Aircraft. According to economic historian Nakamura Takafusa, all of these corporate founders with the exception of Mori were originally engineers, and this infusion of new technical and entrepreneurial imagination was an immense stimulus to the rapid growth of their ventures. The biggest weakness of the New Zaibatsu was financial, but ballooning government budgets and low interest rates made up for this. In other words, the technological know-how amassed in the early years of the Shōwa era now found the conditions in which it could thrive (Nakamura Takafusa, *Shōwa-shi* [A history of Shōwa Japan, 1926–1989], abridged translation).

Industrial policies that would carry through into the postwar era also began to be hatched in this period. Government subsidies to companies willing to scrap old ships and build new ones began to be implemented in 1932—the beginning of the postwar planned shipbuilding system. In the oil industry, also connected to military affairs, the Petroleum Industry Act of 1934 established a system in which refiners and importers of oil were licensed by the government, which required them to make regular reports and to maintain specified stockpiles.

Domestic Production of Automobiles

Here I would like to touch on the issue of domestic auto production as a link between the phenomena of urbanization and industrialization described earlier. It was also an issue that related to Japan's fundamental diplomatic posture.

As mentioned earlier, American automobiles dominated the prewar Japanese market. Ford was the first to move into Japan, setting up a final assembly plant in 1925. General Motors established a base in Osaka in 1927, and Chrysler came to Japan in 1930. American companies accounted for 97 percent of the manufacturing and production of automobiles in Japan.

The catalyst for diffusion of the automobile was the Great Kantō Earthquake. In order to respond quickly to the destruction of major rail lines, Model T Ford chassis were imported and remodeled into buses. Autos also played a significant role in the Manchurian Incident, especially the campaign in Jehol. Before Jehol, the army had only three motorized transport companies, but in the course of the campaign this number soon swelled to thirteen companies. The principal vehicles were Fords. The rapid success of this campaign in an area that had no rail lines was due to the use of automobiles. One vehicle that departed Chaoyang on 1 March 1933 traveled

2,500 kilometers in twenty-five days, thus averaging 100 kilometers a day—a remarkable record for the time.

By around 1935, the performance of Japanese autos was improving. The army had been quick to appreciate the mobility they afforded, and poured massive amounts of funding into development. But the performance of domestically produced automobiles was still poor. To hold up under brutal battlefield conditions, large numbers of vehicles with completely interchangeable parts were essential. In 1935, expert opinion on the future of the automobile was divided into two camps: those who wanted to keep on using Ford and General Motors, and those who wanted to develop a domestic industry.

The army eventually settled on a strategy of domestic production, and in the Ministry of Commerce and Industry it was Kishi Nobusuke who worked to comply with this plan. Kishi had been appointed chief of the ministry's Industrial Affairs Bureau on 17 April 1935, and he was a fervent believer in domestic auto production. He believed that along with strong military demand, the development of the auto industry, with its multitudinous requirements for parts and components, would prove to be a powerful engine for the growth of Japanese industry as a whole. Up to that point, the Ministry of Commerce and Industry had not become so involved in economic control. In the Okada cabinet, Minister of Commerce and Industry Machida Chūji of the Minseitō had opposed the idea, as had Ogawa Gōtarō, also of the Minseitō, who served as minister in the Hirota cabinet. Even the New Zaibatsu leader Aikawa frequently said joint ventures with foreign firms were fine with him. The main force promoting domestic production was the army and reform bureaucrats like Kishi.

On 4 May 1936, the bill for the Automobile Manufacturing Industry Act was presented to the Diet and enacted and promulgated on 23 May. Article 1 of the act stated: "It is the purpose of this Act to establish automobile manufacturing enterprises in our Empire, for the sake of maintaining our national defense and the development of industry." Article 4 stated that companies eligible for licenses to manufacture automobiles must be incorporated under Japanese law and more than one-half of the shareholders and more than one-half of the voting rights had to be held by Japanese subjects or juridical persons organized under Japanese law. This was the first industrial legislation of this kind ever proposed by the Ministry of Commerce and Industry.

At the time, Ford was shifting its strategy for Japan and the Far Eastern market from knock-down assembly operations where all parts were imported from the United States, to full-scale manufacturing plants in which all the parts would be both manufactured and assembled in Japan. Among the figures who opposed nationalization of the auto industry and welcomed this further commitment by Ford to local production were Akaboshi Shirō, a pioneer in the world of Japanese golf, and Iwasaki Koyata,

scion of the Mitsubishi zaibatsu, both of whom had graduated from the
University of Pennsylvania, and Yoshida Shigeru, at the time Japan's
ambassador to Britain. Yoshida would remain a consistent and strong supporter of keeping the door open to US capital through the postwar era, and
at this point also welcomed Ford's inroads into Japan as a stabilizing influence on Japan–United States relations. But this combination of blue-
blooded sports figures, zaibatsu heirs, and Anglophile diplomats were an
easy target for attack by the army and the reform bureaucrats.

The de facto domestication of the auto industry was a significant victory for the policy of autarky over international cooperation, which was a
victory for the military and reform bureaucrats over the establishment
forces represented by the political parties and the zaibatsu. It is also inter-

Kishi Nobusuke of the Ministry of Commerce and Industry's Bureau of Industrial Affairs inspecting the first Toyoda vehicles
*In 1933, Toyoda Automatic Loom Works set up an automotive division within the
company and began domestic production of trucks, announcing its first Model
G1 Truck in 1935. This was followed by experiments in producing mass-market
passenger cars, and beginning on 14 September 1936 the company sponsored a
three-day exhibition to commemorate the completion of the "Toyoda Domestically Made People's Car" in the Marunouchi district of central Tokyo. The auto
manufacturer would officially change its name to Toyota in 1937. (From Sōzō
kagirinaku: Toyota Jidōsha 50-nen shi [Unlimited creation: a fifty-year history of
Toyota Motor Corporation)*

esting to note that the two most important figures in United States–Japan relations in the postwar period—Yoshida and Kishi—found themselves on completely opposite sides of the fence on this crucial issue of domestic automobile production.

Notes

1. The Aizawa Incident was an attempted coup d'état in which Lieutenant-Colonel Aizawa Saburō murdered General Nagata Testsuzan.

2. The Sino-Japanese War that broke out in 1937 and continued until 1945 is often referred to as the Second Sino-Japanese War after the First Sino-Japanese War of 1894–1895. However, due to their very different nature of both wars, I think the first war should be referred to as the Qing-Japan War or Japan-Qing War and the second war as the Sino-Japanese War. In the period of the first war, China was ruled under the Qing dynasty in which the Manchu ethnic group suppressed the Han Chinese. By the time of the second war, China had become the Republic of China after the revolution of 1911, representing the people of China theoretically. Many Japanese in the 1930s did not understand this key difference between the two wars, a fundamental mistake on Japan's part.

4

Wartime Japan

~

The Cabinet of Hirota Kōki

The selection of a new prime minister in the wake of the February Twenty-Sixth Incident did not go smoothly. Had the incident not occurred, Prince Saionji Kinmochi had intended to recommend Ugaki Kazushige. But given the situation, this would have been too provocative a choice; antipathy to Ugaki among the young officers involved in the rebellion had run so high that they were calling for his arrest if the coup succeeded. But neither did Saionji wish to nominate a figure connected with the Kōdōha (Imperial Way Faction). At a loss, on 4 March 1936 he proposed Konoe Fumimaro, then president of the House of Peers. When Saionji had sounded him out in advance, Konoe had demurred, but Saionji recommended him anyway. Konoe then adamantly refused the selection. Saionji had previously been apprehensive that Konoe was too close to the Imperial Way Faction, but the circumstances were such that he had put aside such reservations. Saionji thought of pressing more forcefully for Konoe to accept the nomination, but Konoe stood firm, saying he would give up his peerage to decline the post, and Saionji had to give up on the idea of a Konoe cabinet.

Saionji was running out of cards to play. On the night of 4 March, Minister of Imperial Household Yuasa Kurahei; Privy Council president Ichiki Kitokurō; Saionji's private secretary Harada Kumao; and Kidō Kōichi, chief secretary to the lord keeper of the privy seal, had a conversation in which Ichiki suddenly suggested Hirota Kōki as a possibility, because he had a favorable impression of Hirota's cooperative diplomacy. This idea was relayed to Prince Saionji, who concurred, and on 5 March he made his official recommendation to the emperor, who immediately issued the order for Hirota to form a cabinet. At the same time, Yuasa was named lord keeper of the privy seal as successor to Saitō Makoto, who had been assassinated in the February Twenty-Sixth Incident, and Matsudaira Tsuneo, in turn, replaced Yuasa as imperial household minister.

The emperor's appointment of Hirota as prime minister was greeted with approval by the general public. Journalist Kiyosawa Kiyoshi commented on the selection as follows: Just as a pregnant woman taking a fall will instinctively protect her womb, people pay the most attention to their vulnerabilities, and in Japan's case, that vulnerability is diplomatic, and thus the choice of Minister of Foreign Affairs Hirota to become prime minister is an interesting one. It is said that Hirota initially resisted the appointment, but Yoshida Shigeru, a colleague who entered the Ministry of Foreign Affairs in the same year as Hirota was sent to persuade him, which he did by saying, "What we need now is someone who looks good in a suit"—rather than a military uniform.

However, the formation of the cabinet did not proceed as anticipated. With Yoshida as his chief strategist, Hirota set about the selection of the other ministers. The overall concept was the same as that of the Saitō and Okada cabinets, with a balance of the principal civilian ministers drawn from both major parties, two from the Seiyūkai and two from the Minseitō. But the army meddled with this plan, rejecting a number of the prospective ministers: Yoshida Shigeru (as foreign minister) because he was the son-in-law of the liberal courtier Makino Nobuaki; Shimomura Hiroshi (as minister of colonial affairs) because he had been an executive at the liberal newspaper *Asahi shinbun*; Kawasaki Takukichi (as home minister) because he was too partisan a member of the Minseitō; and Ohara Naoshi (slated to continue as minister of justice) because he had been too soft on Minobe Tatsukichi during the uproar over the emperor-as-organ theory. Moreover, instead of four representatives of the parties, the army wanted to limit it to two.

Hirota almost gave up on forming a cabinet, but was persuaded by the elder statesmen (genrō and *jūshin*) to persevere. The result was that Yoshida, Ohara, and Shimomura withdrew as candidates and Kawasaki moved from the post of home minister to minister of commerce and industry. But the army's demand that there be only two party-affiliated ministers was rejected and the original goal of four was achieved by promising to adopt certain other policy proposals by the army, and on 9 March the organization of the cabinet was complete:

The Hirota Kōki cabinet (9 March 1936–2 February 1937)
Although Hirota was chosen because he was the man who "looked good in a civilian suit," the army meddled in the formation of the cabinet from the beginning and forced compromises when it was finally launched. Proclaiming "a renovation of policy," the new cabinet aimed at domestic reform, but in economics, Minister of Finance Baba's fiscal policy acquiesced to pressures to expand the military budget and did little more than to shift the economy to a quasi-wartime footing. (© The Mainichi Newspapers)

Prime minister: Hirota Kōki

Minister of foreign affairs: Arita Hachirō (until 2 April, held concurrently by Prime Minister Hirota)

Minister of home affairs: Ushio Shigenosuke (House of Peers, Kenkyūkai)

Minister of finance: Baba Eiichi (House of Peers, Kenkyūkai)

Minister of the army: Terauchi Hisaichi

Minister of the navy: Nagano Osami

Minister of justice: Hayashi Raizaburō

Minister of education: Hirao Hachisaburō (House of Peers; until 25 March held concurrently by Minister of Home Affairs Ushio)

Minister of agriculture and forestry: Shimada Toshio (House of Representatives, Seiyūkai)

Minister of commerce and industry: Kawasaki Takukichi (House of
Peers, Minseitō, Dōwakai; until 27 March, then Ogawa Gōtarō
[House of Representatives, Minseitō])
Minister of communications: Tanomogi Keikichi (House of
Representatives, Minseitō)
Minister of railways: Maeda Yonezō (House of Representatives,
Seiyūkai)
Minister of colonial affairs: Nagata Hidejirō (House of Peers,
Dōwakai)
Chief cabinet secretary: Fujinuma Shōhei (House of Peers,
Kenkyūkai)
Director-general of the Cabinet Legislation Bureau:
Tsugita Daizaburō (House of Peers, Dōseikai)

The military had interfered in cabinet formation in the past, but only
with regard to the posts of army or navy minister. Meddling in the selection
of other ministerial posts was quite unusual.

The Advance of Militarism

In fact, a general election was held on 20 February 1936, immediately
before the February Twenty-Sixth Incident. The result was that the Minseitō
picked up 59 more seats to increase its total to 205. Allied with the Kokumin Dōmei (National Alliance, a party formed by Adachi Kenzō and others
who had left the Minseitō) and the Shōwa Kai (Shōwa Association, led by
Yamazaki Tatsunosuke, who was expelled from the Seiyūkai for joining the
Okada cabinet), it controlled a majority in the lower house. In contrast, the
Seiyūkai suffered a significant defeat, losing 130 seats, including the one
occupied by its president, Suzuki Kisaburō, and holding on to only 171.
This may be interpreted as a vote of confidence by the electorate in the
Okada cabinet's policy of preserving the status quo—in other words, a sign
that the people were not in favor of the militaristic tendencies that had
become increasingly apparent in 1934 and 1935. During the Diet session
that followed the February Twenty-Sixth Incident, on 7 May 1936 the Minseitō representative Saitō Takao gave a famous speech on the necessity of
disciplining the military and sternly criticizing the inappropriateness of military men meddling in politics. This received broad support from the public,
and even Minister of Army Terauchi expressed his agreement.

It is certainly true that after this we see few examples of military men
as individuals engaging in political action. Under the leadership of Minister
of Army Terauchi, those involved in the February Twenty-Sixth Incident
were tried in rigorous courts-martial, and between March and August 1936

large numbers of politically active military figures—primarily associated with the Imperial Way Faction—were forced into the reserves. Among them even officers in the cliques headed by Ugaki Kazushige and Minami Jirō were affected. This was a genuine, concerted effort to completely rid the army of all political activities that cut across organizational structure and the chain of command. However, what replaced this was political pressure brought to bear by the organization of the army as a whole, rather than by insubordinate individuals. This was not something the Hirota cabinet was capable of resisting—or even tried to resist.

Only a month after the cabinet was formed, the army proposed a revival of a regulation that required military ministers in the cabinet to be officers on active duty. The first Yamamoto Gonnohyōe cabinet had done away with this rule in 1913, permitting the appointment of reserve officers of the rank of lieutenant-general or general. (It should be noted, however, that not a single reserve officer had ever been appointed.)

The rationale given for the reintroduction of this system was that it would prevent members of the Imperial Way Faction forced into the reserves as a result of the February Twenty-Sixth Incident (though as we have seen, not all were Imperial Way Faction–affiliated) from regaining influence within the army. It is questionable whether Imperial Way Faction generals like Araki Sadao and Masaki Jinzaburō could have revived their fortunes sufficiently to be considered for the post of army minister—but it was not impossible. Later, as prime minister, Konoe would consider pardons for those involved in the incident, and Araki eventually made a comeback and was appointed minister of education. There was even an effort at one point to make peace between Ugaki and Masaki and have them cooperate in leading a government.

The Hirota cabinet accepted the revival of the active-duty rule without much resistance. It was approved in a cabinet meeting on 24 April, and an imperial ordinance was issued on 18 May. The cabinet probably did not even see it as a significant concession, given the fact that since 1913 no reserve officer had ever been appointed to a ministerial post, nor were they likely to be appointed while the nation was engaged in overseas conflict. But in less than a year's time, this would prove to be a miscalculation.

On 8 June 1936, a revised version of the Imperial Defense Policy was adopted. In the previous version, adopted in 1923, the United States ranked first on the list of Japan's hypothetical enemies, followed by the Soviet Union and China. The revised version placed both the United States and the Soviet Union as primary objectives, with Britain and China as subsidiary concerns. Force levels required for defense were set at twenty standing divisions for the army, to be increased to fifty in time of war; the navy's main battle fleet was to have twelve battleships, twelve aircraft carriers, and twenty-eight cruisers. Both the foreign minister and the prime minister were involved in drafting this ambitious revision.

In addition to the revision of the Imperial Defense Policy, an outline of national policy was drafted that would later be approved by the Five Ministers Conference (prime, foreign, army, navy, and finance) on 7 August 1936 with the title "Fundamental Principles of National Policy." This document contained passages such as the following:

> The keynote of our policies for continental Asia should be to eliminate the threat of the Soviet Union to the north by aiming at the sound development of the state of Manchukuo and solidify the national defenses of Japan and Manchukuo, while at the same time making preparations against Britain and the United States by achieving close cooperation among Japan, Manchuria, and China and planning the further development of our economy. The implementation of these policies will require care in maintaining amicable relations with the other powers.

But was that even possible? This would appear to be an almost random list of mutually incompatible goals. In the past, the policy of the Soviet Union toward Japan had been comparatively cautious. But the situation began to change from around 1933 onward. One reason for the change was the success of the Soviet military buildup. Another was the restoration of diplomatic relations between the United States and the Soviets in 1933. Japan was talking about eliminating the threat of the Soviet Union while at the same time making preparations for battle against Britain and the United States—to accomplish either of these goals would be difficult, and yet conditions were making both of them necessary. Moreover, the "Fundamental Principles of National Policy" heaped additional goals on top of this: "The fundamental policy our Empire must establish is to solidify our national defense, and, while securing our foothold on the Asian continent, to advance into the southern seas." In other words, ambitions to establish spheres of Japanese control not only on the Asian mainland but also in Southeast Asia and the Pacific Islands were clearly articulated in this document.

In order to accomplish this, military readiness for the army was defined as including "augmentation of forces in Manchuria sufficient to oppose the forces the Soviet Union can bring to bear in the Far East, and particularly with the capacity to strike in the early stages of hostilities against forces already stationed there." For the navy, the plan called for "enhancing our forces so that they are sufficient to secure command of the sea in the Western Pacific against the United States Navy." The amount of military funding required for this was, of course, vast. The budget the army came up with in July in response to this was a twelve-year plan, the first half of which alone called for expenditures of ¥3 billion. Prior to the February Twenty-Sixth Incident, Minister of Finance Takahashi Korekiyo had approved the issue of government bonds, but not for military expenditures. But the new finance minister, Baba Eiichi, accepted the fact that government expenditures must increase in support of national policy, hoping to respond to this with a mixture of government bond issues, tax increases, low interest rates, and the encouragement of industrial growth.

In November the cabinet approved a budget for fiscal 1937 of ¥3.04 billion, of which military spending accounted for ¥1.41 billion. This was an increase of ¥730 million (31 percent) over the previous year, funded by a tax hike of ¥420 million and a government bond issue of ¥980 million (an increase of ¥200 million). In addition, the Ministry of Finance promised budgetary support beyond the 1937 fiscal year for a six-year armaments buildup for the army (to cover 41 wartime divisions, 142 air force squadrons, and the requisite operational supplies) and for a third supplementary program for naval armaments (a five-year plan for the construction of 66 warships totaling 270,000 tons and a 14-squadron addition to its land-based air arm). The budget also included funding for construction of the super-battleships *Yamato* and *Musashi*. The result was a massive expansion of military demand, and a rapid increase in imports of raw materials and industrial plant and equipment, producing a sudden worsening of the country's balance of payments. Up to this point, Japan had maintained a fairly even trade balance, but this was because the trade deficit with the dollar bloc had been offset by a trade surplus with the yen bloc (Manchukuo, Kwantung, etc.). But this balance was becoming increasingly difficult to achieve.

The Anti-Comintern Pact with Germany

Another new issue that arose for the Hirota cabinet was relations with Germany, at a time when Japan was growing increasingly nervous about the expanding strength of the Soviet Union. It was in this context that Germany began to make approaches toward Japan. The Nazis came to power in Germany in 1933, two months before Japan withdrew from the League of Nations. Germany followed suit in October of that year. Then, in March 1935, Germany challenged the arms limitations imposed by the Treaty of Versailles by building an army of thirty-six divisions, and in March 1936 moved troops into the demilitarized Rhineland.

In the early summer of 1935, Hitler's foreign policy adviser, Joachim von Ribbentrop, sounded out Ōshima Hiroshi, military attaché to the Japanese embassy in Germany, regarding the possibility of some form of defensive alliance against the Soviet Union. At the time, Germany was friendly with China, and Japan also did not want to alarm the British, so even Ōshima, who would later become something of an agent of Hitler, did not give an immediately positive response. But he was interested, and after receiving a go-ahead from General Staff, he began to pursue this plan.

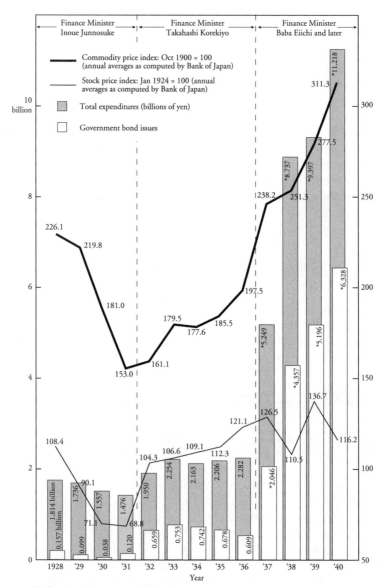

Ballooning Government Spending

Figures for fiscal expenditures are on a general account basis. However, for years in which amounts are marked with an asterisk, extraordinary military expenditures have been added by incorporating the extraordinary military budget approved by the emperor and the amount of government debt and loan diverted (in the total amount of revenue in the extraordinary military budget) into the general account expenditures and the amount of government bond issues, respectively, based on the Finance Ministry's *Shōwa zaisei shi* (Fiscal History of the Shōwa Era), vol. 4.

(Source: Takahashi Kamekichi, *Taishō Shōwa zaikai hendō shi, ge* [A History of Financial Fluctuations in the Taishō and Shōwa Eras, vol. 3], Tōyō Keizai.)

The plan that was presented in November 1935 was conceived as a counter to the popular front against fascism initiated as a critique of Germany, Italy, and Japan at the Seventh World Congress of the Communist International (Comintern), held in July and August 1935. The idea was that it might be possible to form an alliance solely against the Soviet Union that would avoid antagonizing the British. Moreover, since the Soviet Union claimed not to be involved in the Comintern, if the pact were directed solely at the Comintern the Soviet Union should have no grounds for complaint, though of course the Comintern was dominated by the Soviet Union.

The proposed pact with Germany met with little resistance from either the foreign ministry or the navy. Of Japan's top foreign service officers stationed overseas, only Yoshida Shigeru, who became ambassador to Great Britain in 1936, voiced strong objections. The foreign policy guidelines articulated on 7 August 1936 gave the following rationale for advancing

Ōshima Hiroshi and Adolf Hitler
Ōshima (1886–1975) was an army officer, fluent in German, who was appointed as military attaché in Berlin in 1934, and in 1938 became the Japanese ambassador to Germany, all the while promoting a pro-German diplomatic stance. (From Sekai gahō *[World illustrated] magazine, May 1939)*

"Latest Map of the European Continent"
A supplement to the January 1936 issue of King *magazine.*

toward positive collaboration with Germany: "With regard to relations with the Soviet Union, Germany largely shares our interests, and in light of the special relationship between France and the Soviet Union, it is beneficial for Germany to cooperate with us, from both the standpoint of national defense and against the spread of communism." The Anti-Comintern Pact was signed on 25 November 1936. A secret codicil to the pact contained an agreement that if either signatory were attacked by the Soviet Union, the other must refrain from taking actions that would be disadvantageous to the signatory under attack. And in fact, beginning in July 1936, the Spanish civil war was rapidly becoming an international incident, with Germany and Italy taking sides against the Soviet Union and France.

Collapse of the Hirota Cabinet

As militarization proceeded from the summer of 1936 onward, the military began to envisage reforms of the government. In September, Minister of Army Terauchi Hisaichi and Minister of Navy Nagano Osami jointly presented Prime Minister Hirota with an opinion paper on administrative reform. It proposed the creation of an institution incorporating the Cabinet Intelligence

Committee that would report directly to the prime minister and would be in charge of investigation and supervision of all major national affairs and the control and distribution of related budgets. Also proposed was the creation of an agency to reform and control personnel administration, also under direct control of the prime minister. Both of these proposals aimed at strengthening the leadership powers of the prime minister, the first by reorganizing the Cabinet Investigation Bureau, the Ministry of Finance's Budget Bureau, and the Intelligence Committee to integrate them into the new institution, the second by providing him greater control over personnel matters. In both the Imperial Defense Policy and the "Fundamental Principles of National Policy" mentioned earlier, the military was no longer attempting to wrap itself in the emperor's right of supreme command as a defense against interference from other forces within the government. Instead, by giving strong powers to the prime minister—and then by manipulating him—they aimed at constructing a system organized for total mobilization for war.

This proposal sent out major shockwaves, and since it included suggestions for parliamentary reform as well, the political parties reacted with strong opposition. Hamada Kunimatsu's famous "*kappuku* interpellation" in the Diet was connected with this. In the House of Representatives, on 21 January 1937, Representative Hamada spoke regarding proposed reforms of government institutions and the parliamentary system, criticizing the military for its interference in politics. Minister of Army Terauchi responded by claiming that Hamada's remarks had insulted the army. Hamada, a veteran parliamentarian, countered: "I have not insulted the Army. Consult the parliamentary record. If it shows I have made any remarks of that nature, I will apologize by committing suicide (*kappuku*). If it does not, then it is you who should kill yourself to make amends."

Terauchi had miscalculated, thinking he could easily intimidate his opponent, but this backfired on him, and left him in quite a quandary. He was certainly not going to kill himself over this, nor was he going to apologize. So he demanded that the prime minister dissolve the Diet, but the cabinet ministers affiliated with the political parties would not accept this. The government temporarily adjourned the Diet, but the stalemate continued, and on 23 January, Hirota had to resign.

Hamada's speech was certainly courageous. But the political parties were gradually finding themselves in a position in which this was virtually the only form in which they could express their discontent. The presence of four party-affiliated ministers in the cabinet proved to be of little effect in the conflict between the parties and the military.

When the Hirota cabinet was formed on 9 March of the previous year, the emperor had given it three guiding principles: govern in accordance with the provisions of the constitution; with international amity as a keynote, do not overextend yourself in foreign affairs; and avoid radical changes in fiscal or domestic policy. But the Hirota cabinet proved incapable of fulfilling any of these instructions.

The Abortive Ugaki Cabinet

As successor to Hirota, on 24 January 1937 Prince Saionji nominated General Ugaki Kazushige, and on 25 January Ugaki received the imperial order to form a cabinet. Ugaki was one of the remaining aces in Saionji's hand. As noted earlier, both the Saitō and Okada cabinets had been intended as bulwarks to contain the increasingly radical behavior of the military. But what they had lacked was participation by more moderate members of the military establishment.

Opposition to the Ugaki cabinet came from the army itself, and particularly the mid-level staff officers of the Ministry of Army and General Staff. Nakajima Kesago, commander of the Kenpeitai, jumped into the car taking Ugaki to the capital the night he received the imperial order, and urged him not to accept it. Nakajima said the appointment would cause a ripple of shock in the army, which had only recently regained some internal stability. Responding to this, Ugaki asked Nakajima if another February Twenty-Sixth Incident was likely to occur, and Nakajima said no. In other words, there was a threat of terrorism, but not of a coup. Ugaki said he was prepared for that, and rebuffed Nakajima's suggestion.

But the army was uncooperative. A meeting of the "Three Chiefs" (army minister, chief of general staff, inspector-general of military training) was convened to select a new candidate for army minister, but reported to Ugaki that Sugiyama Hajime, Nakamura Kōtarō, and Kazuki Kiyoshi had all declined consideration for the post. Ugaki immediately asked for other recommendations, but Minister of Army Terauchi said there were none. Ugaki made a telephone call to one of his former associates, General Koiso Kuniaki, commander-in-chief of the Korean Army, asking him to take the position, but Koiso also declined. Koiso was quite sensitive to the currents of opinion within the army.

Even so, Ugaki did not give up easily. On 27 January he met with Lord Keeper of the Privy Seal Yuasa Kurahei at the imperial palace and proposed three possible solutions to the dilemma: form a cabinet without an army minister, with Ugaki himself concurrently taking over the duties of army minister; selecting an appropriate candidate from the reserve list and restoring him to active duty to serve as army minister (there were some generals who were sympathetic to Ugaki within the reserve list and Ugaki himself was also a candidate); or selecting an appropriate candidate from the active list and having the emperor issue a personal command to him to cooperate with the new cabinet as army minister. But Yuasa refused on the grounds that any of these alternatives would inconvenience the emperor, and that a cabinet that required such an extraordinary effort to bring into being was not likely to last very long. On 29 January, Ugaki finally found himself having to decline the imperial order. The recently revived active-duty order (the rule that only active-duty generals could occupy the military cabinet posts) had quickly demonstrated its power. It is quite ironic that Ugaki had been one of the most vociferous opponents of the decision by the Yamamoto cabinet back in 1913 to do away with this requirement.

Yet the constitution stated that it was the emperor who appointed all civil and military officials. Procedures for this might include recommendations by the Three Chiefs or other advisory bodies, but now such procedures were actually obstructing the imperial appointment. Such problems are sometimes still seen today. Japanese organizations sometimes set major policy goals, but then they overly refine the tactics for achieving the goals to the point that the tactics subvert the goals themselves.

If, at this time, Yuasa had sensed this was a critical moment, he might have made an emergency decision. But he did not. He was more optimistic, and thought that somehow, before long, things would return to normal.

The Ishiwara Plan

But why was the army opposed to the formation of a cabinet by General Ugaki? First, he is said to have incited resentment for his role in the arms reductions of the 1920s. But personal grudges should not be the rationale for policy. Second was his purported involvement in the March Incident of 1931, but this was peripheral. Third, and probably the most decisive objection, was that it was believed that he would not support the plans for military expansion that were currently being put together by the mid-ranking staff officers of the army—especially plans for enhanced preparedness against the Soviet Union.

At the center of this was Colonel Ishiwara Kanji, who in August 1935 was assigned as chief of the Operations and War Plans Section of the First Bureau (Operations) of the Army General Staff, and in June 1936 was named head of the newly created War Leadership Section, and then in January 1937 became the acting chief of the First Bureau.

Ishiwara was aiming to mechanize Japanese forces in Manchuria and enhance their airpower in order to confront Soviet forces in the Far East that had been strengthened during the Soviet Union's second five-year plan. To facilitate this, he invited Miyazaki Masayoshi of the South Manchuria Railway Company's economic research bureau to form a new Research Institute on Public Finance and Economy in Japan and Manchukuo. The outline of the first report of this organization called for a five-year plan

Ugaki after receiving the imperial order to form a cabinet
With the army repeatedly refusing to provide him with an army minister for five days, Ugaki finally failed to form a new government. The public referred to it as the "miscarriage" of the Ugaki cabinet.

from fiscal years 1937 to 1941 that would increase steel production capacity by 2.6 times to 13 million tons annually; pig iron by 3.7 times to 11.5 million tons; electric power by 1.7 times to 12.57 million kilowatts; shipbuilding by 1.9 times; weapons production by 2.1 times to ¥940 million; and aircraft production to 10,000 units. The required investment would be ¥8.5 billion, shared between Japan and Manchukuo.

It is highly unlikely that Ugaki would have accepted such a proposal. Ugaki took Japan's relations with the United States and Great Britain very seriously, and he had amicable relations with the political parties. Free markets were integral to close relations with the Anglo-American powers. The zaibatsu and major corporations wanted trade, and they were the sponsors of the political parties. This situation was not one that would allow for a sudden military buildup. In short, the radical military expansion of the sort advocated by Ishiwara would be achieved only with a tightly controlled economy and political system. This was something that neither the established political parties nor the zaibatsu would accept, and it was also the reason why the army rejected Ugaki as prime minister.

The Short-Lived Hayashi Cabinet

In the wake of Ugaki's failure to form a cabinet, on 29 January Prince Saionji was asked once again by the emperor to provide recommendations for a new prime minister. His first choice was Hiranuma Kiichirō; his second, Hayashi Senjūrō. In the past, Saionji had been antipathetic toward Hiranuma, but now saw him as better than a military man, while on the other hand Hayashi was at least a comparative moderate among army figures. Hiranuma declined the offer, and the imperial order went to Hayashi.

Hayashi's brain trust in forming the new cabinet was Sogō Shinji and Asahara Kenzō. Both were figures close to Ishiwara, and it was Ishiwara who was pulling the strings. Ishiwara hoped to see Itagaki Seishirō as army minister and Suetsugu Nobumasa as navy minister—but this clashed with the opinion of the senior figures in both the army and navy. The military's elders were not necessarily ready to line up behind Ishiwara's idiosyncratic and forceful national defense policies. When Hayashi dumped Asahara and Sogō from his transition team, it also terminated his relationship with Ishiwara.

The Hayashi cabinet formed on 2 February 1937 was as follows.

Prime minister and minister of education: Hayashi Senjūrō
Minister of foreign affairs: Satō Naotake (until 3 March held
    concurrently by Prime Minister Hayashi)
Minister of home affairs: Kawarada Kakichi
Minister of finance / Minister of colonial affairs: Yūki Toyotarō
Minister of the army: Nakamura Kōtarō (resigned 9 February
    due to illness); Sugiyama Hajime
Minister of the navy: Yonai Mitsumasa
Minister of justice: Shiono Suehiko
Minister of agriculture and forestry: Yamazaki Tatsunosuke
    (House of Representatives, Shōwakai)
Minister of commerce and industry / Minister of railways:
    Godō Takuo
Minister of communications: Kodama Hideo (House of Peers,
    Kenkyūkai; until 10 February held concurrently by Minister
    of Agriculture Yamazaki)
Chief cabinet secretary: Ōhashi Hachirō (House of Peers, Kenkyūkai)
Director-general of the Cabinet Legislation Bureau: Kawagoe Takeo

Only one minister in the cabinet was drawn from the political parties. This was a considerable drop from the four party ministers in the Hirota cabinet, and relations between the new government and the parties turned worse. Moreover, while the cabinet proclaimed "the unity of religion and government" (*saisei itchi*) and had a strongly reactionary flavor that made it unsympathetic to the sort of total national mobilization concept promoted by Ishiwara, it in fact possessed neither the power nor the will to derail these plans.

When the Diet reconvened on 15 February 1937, there was a forceful backlash from the political parties. The Hayashi cabinet managed to push its budget through, after which it dissolved the House of Representatives on 31 March. Dubbed the "dine and dash dissolution," this further infuriated the Minseitō and Seiyūkai, which voiced unified opposition to the cabinet. In the general election on 30 April, the Minseitō took 179 seats (down 26) and the Seiyūkai 175 (up 4). Between them, the two parties controlled three-quarters of the seats in the lower house—leaving the Hayashi cabinet no choice but to resign. It had been one of the most insignificant cabinets in the history of Japan.

If the Hayashi cabinet produced anything noteworthy, it was the appointment of the pro-Anglo-American Satō Naotake as foreign minister. Japan's ambassador to Great Britain, Yoshida Shigeru, was also a staunch advocate of cooperation with the Anglo-American powers, and under the influence of Ishiwara Kanji the army for the time being adopted a policy of deferring any further action in China in order to prepare itself against the Soviet Union. This resulted, for the first time in a while, in a policy orientation that did not favor further expansion into China.

On 16 April, a meeting of the foreign, finance, army, and navy ministers produced two documents: "Action Policies on China" and "Policy Guidelines for North China." The first urged an avoidance of aggressive or provocative policies, stating that "we adopt an impartial stance to the Nanjing government and the movement for the unification of China that it is leading" and that "we should have consideration for the pride of that government and avoid measures that will provoke expressions of anti-Japanese sentiment among its people."

The "Policy Guidelines for North China" rejected further plotting to expand Japanese interests in North China, saying that with regard to the East Hebei Autonomous Council and the Hebei-Chahar Political Council, "we must adopt as impartial an attitude as possible, avoiding political machinations that might unnecessarily stir up popular sentiment, or which might threaten to provide the Chinese with a pretext for anti-Japanese agitation." It prioritized economic development, and stated that rather than trying to force third-party nations to acknowledge Japan's position in North China, Japan should protect third-party interests: "In other words, we should seek opportunities for cooperation and mutual assistance with third-party states, especially Great Britain and the United States, sharing facilities, engaging in joint ventures, and utilizing their capital and materials when possible." But this slight shift in policy would soon be blown to pieces by the full-fledged Sino-Japanese War that would soon occur.

The Konoe Cabinet and the Second Sino-Japanese War

Establishment of the Konoe Cabinet

When the Minseitō and Seiyūkai combined into a victorious opposition force in the election of 30 April 1937, it was inevitable that the Hayashi cabinet would soon step down. Well before this, Prince Saionji had already declared that due to his advanced age he would prefer not to be called upon by the emperor to nominate a candidate for the next prime minister. As a result, this established practice was abandoned, and instead the lord keeper of the privy seal took responsibility for sounding out the opinions of the elder statesmen and reporting personally to the emperor. A proposal was finalized on 26 April.

There were advocates in a number of quarters for the choice of Prince Konoe Fumimaro as successor to Hayashi, but there was also a proposal to have Minister of Army Sugiyama Hajime form a cabinet while still serving on active duty as an army general. On 31 May, when the Hayashi cabinet decided to resign, Saionji voiced strong opposition to a cabinet headed by a military officer, and backed Konoe as an alternative. On 1 June, the imperial order was given to Konoe to form a cabinet, which was completed on 4 June. The lineup was as follows:

Prime minister: Konoe Fumimaro (House of Peers, Kayōkai)
Minister of foreign affairs: Hirota Kōki (House of Peers)
Minister of home affairs: Baba Eiichi (House of Peers, Kenkyūkai)
Minister of finance: Kaya Okinori
Minister of the army: Sugiyama Hajime (held over)
Minister of the navy: Yonai Mitsumasa (held over)
Minister of justice: Shiono Suehiko (held over)
Minister of education: Yasui Eiji (through 22 October);
    Kido Kōichi (House of Peers, Kayōkai)
Minister of agriculture and forestry: Arima Yoriyasu
    (House of Peers, Kenkyūkai)
Minister of commerce and industry: Yoshino Shinji
Minister of communications: Nagai Ryūtarō (House of
    Representatives, Minseitō)
Minister of railways: Nakajima Chikuhei (House of
    Representatives, Seiyūkai)
Minister of colonial affairs: Ōtani Son'yū (House of Peers,
    Kenkyūkai)
Chief cabinet secretary: Kazami Akira (House of Representatives)
Director-general of the Cabinet Legislation Bureau: Taki Masao
    (House of Representatives)

Konoe Fumimaro was born in 1891 as the eldest son of Konoe Atsumaro. The Konoe family was the foremost of the Gosekke, the five houses of the Northern Branch (Hokke) of the Fujiwara clan of the imperial court nobility that had traditionally been eligible to occupy the two highest court offices, those of regent (*sesshō*) and chief councilor (*kanpaku*). Tracing its lineage back to Fujiwara no Kamatari, the Konoe were the second most prestigious family in Japan after the imperial house itself. Fumimaro's father, Atsumaro, had been regarded as one of the brightest and most capable members of the peerage, had a deep interest in the issue of Japan's relations with continental Asia, and was thought of as one of the country's future leaders.

But Atsumaro died in 1904 at the age of forty. His premature death left the family without supporters and saddled with debts, so Fumimaro's youth was somewhat troubled and unhappy, and he developed a rebellious streak. A flirtation with socialist thought left him feeling guilty about his noble birth, and he had little interest in studying law, politics, or economics. He advanced from the First Higher School to the Faculty of Letters at the University of Tokyo, but after half a year there transferred to the Faculty of Law at Kyoto University.

At Kyoto he had a happy student life with friends such as Kido Kōichi (who later served as a cabinet minister and lord keeper of the privy seal) and Harada Kumao (who would later serve as secretary to Prince Saionji). He was a frequent visitor to the home of Kawakami Hajime, the Marxist economist and Kyoto University professor. Once, he decided to drop in unexpectedly on Prince Saionji, who gave him the seat of honor in the reception room and addressed him as "your lordship." Konoe was still a student; Saionji was an elder statesman. It must have been a quite uncomfortable situation. Such discomfort haunted Konoe throughout his life.

Konoe graduated from university in 1917, the year before World War I ended. In 1919, he accompanied Prince Saionji to the Paris Peace Conference. Just prior to their departure, Konoe wrote an article titled "Eibei hon'i no heiwa shugi o haisu" (A rejection of Anglo-centric pacifism) that was published in the November 1918 issue of the leading nationalist journal *Nihon oyobi Nihonjin* (Japan and the Japanese). The gist of his argument was that while Britain and the United States proclaimed the beautiful rhetoric of pacifism, the contemporary world was one in which they enjoyed unquestionable supremacy, and in which that pacifism was actually nothing more than a defense of their own vested interests. Saionji found this disturbing. He believed that Japan's position as a world leader derived from its cooperation with the Anglo-American powers, and that there was nothing to be gained from antagonizing them.

Before long, Konoe came to be regarded as the shining star of the peerage. Intelligent, and a good listener, he left people who met him excited by the sense that their opinions were being heard. That this also signified that Konoe had no firm convictions of his own was something still not widely understood.

At the time he formed his cabinet, Konoe was immensely popular— scion of a noble family second only to the imperial house, young at age forty-five, intelligent, tall, aristocratic. As noted earlier, the cabinet included two party members: Nagai Ryūtarō of the Minseitō, and Nakajima Chikuhei of the Seiyūkai. But in the past, such involvement by party politicians had usually been the result of consultation with party officials, though on occasion a party member joined a cabinet despite the objections of his party. But in this case, the cabinet appointments were made without even speaking to the parties, and the individuals involved jumped over several levels of more senior party politicians who would have been regarded as more obvious choices for cabinet-level posts. Both Nagai and Nakajima were politicians who were attempting to change the status quo in the political parties—what historian Itō Takashi has called "the reformists" (*kakushin-ha*) (Itō Takashi, *Konoe Shintaisei* [Konoe's New Order]). And they would long occupy a position in Konoe's inner circle.

Konoe Fumimaro (1891–1945)
From "Portraits of Modern Japanese Historical Figures," the National Diet Library website.

The first Konoe cabinet (4 June 1937–5 January 1939)

The Situation in China

The Konoe cabinet would face its first major test soon after its formation—the Marco Polo Bridge (Lugouqiao) Incident. But before discussing this, we should review the situation in China leading up to it.

The East Hebei Autonomous Council was conducting what was referred to as "special trade." Earlier, the Chinese government had enforced high tariffs that had hurt Japanese businesses, especially vendors of sundries in the Osaka area. Countering this, the East Hebei government lowered its import tariffs to one-fourth of those charged by the Nationalist government. As a result, Japanese goods flooded into East Hebei, and from there into the rest of China. This produced a major increase in East Hebei customs revenues, and a correspondingly steep decline in those going to the Nationalist government. A portion of the East Hebei customs revenues were said to have been fed into the Kwantung Army to fund campaigns in Inner Mongolia.

In the latter half of 1936 there were a number of incidents in various parts of China involving attacks on Japanese nationals or Chinese sympathetic to Japan. Japanese ambassador Kawagoe Shigeru and Zhang Qun, the Nationalist foreign minister, met repeatedly to discuss this issue. But with the Suiyuan Incident of November 1936, talks were broken off in December.

The Suiyuan Incident was a skirmish in which an Inner Mongolian army led by De Wang (Prince Demchugdongrub) attacked Chinese Nationalist forces, but eventually withdrew in defeat. From the time of its establishment in 1934, the Inner Mongolian Administrative Committee, led by De Wang, was accorded broad powers of self-government. Beginning around 1935, De Wang began to make overtures to the Kwantung Army, and with its support advanced into the eastern part of Suiyuan province in November 1936, but was repulsed by the forces of Fu Zuoyi. In China this was reported as a victory over the Kwantung Army and greatly boosted nationalist sentiment.

Then, in December 1936 the Xi'an Incident occurred. Beginning in 1935, the Chinese Communist Party had appealed to the Kuomintang for the formation of a united front against Japan, but Chiang Kai-shek would not alter his policy of prioritizing KMT efforts to eliminate the Communists. He pushed Zhang Xueliang, who had been driven from Manchuria, and Feng Yuxiang to use their forces in an effort to envelop the Communists, but the two warlords were unenthusiastic about this campaign. They urged Chiang to shift his priority to resisting the Japanese, but he did not listen. So on 12 December, when Chiang arrived on a visit to encourage these forces in their mission against the Communists, Zhang Xueliang placed Chiang under house arrest. One of the famous sights of Xi'an is the Huaqing Hot Springs, where the Tang-dynasty emperor Xuanzong dallied with his consort Yang Guifei. Chiang was staying there when seized by Zhang's men.

The news shook the world. Zhou Enlai of the CCP mediated between Chiang and Zhang, and an agreement was reached based on a suspension of hostilities in the Chinese civil war. Chiang soon returned to Nanjing, and the fighting stopped. In April 1937, further talks between Chiang and Zhou resulted in a more formal accord that called for a suspension of internal fighting, a united front to resist Japan and save China, freedom of speech, and a reorganization of the Red Army.

Beginning in 1937, the Chinese posture toward Japan noticeably hardened. When Suma Yakichirō, newly appointed Japanese consul-general in Nanjing, paid his initial visit to Minister of Foreign Affairs Zhang Qun, the latter requested that Japan dissolve the East Hebei government. H. H. Kung, vice president of the Executive Yuan and sympathetic to Britain and the United States, brought up the issue of Manchuria for the first time in several years, proposing that Japan return Manchuria to Chinese sovereignty, after which it would be granted the right to autonomous rule.

In short, in a climate characterized by rising nationalistic sentiment and a sense after the failed Suiyuan Incident that Japan was less fearsome than it seemed, a truce took effect between Nationalist and Communist forces, as China was in the process of unifying to resist Japan. These were the developments on the Chinese side leading up to the Sino-Japanese War.

Outbreak and Expansion of the Sino-Japanese War

The Lugouqiao Incident occurred when Japan, under the Hayashi cabinet, adopted a moderate policy toward China, but the Chinese, after 1936, adopted a more hardened policy against Japan. Lugouqiao was a historic bridge, known in the West as the Marco Polo Bridge, located about 20 kilometers southwest of Beijing. On the night of 7 July 1937, elements of Japan's Tianjin Army, stationed nearby, were conducting field exercises in the vicinity of the bridge when they were fired upon with several live rounds. One of the Japanese soldiers went missing (although later found), and the situation grew tense. The next day, 8 July, a Japanese counterattack was met with disorganized return fire from the Chinese. Sporadic fighting ensued, but on 9 July the two sides reached a mutual agreement to withdraw. At this point the toll was eleven dead and thirty-six wounded on the Japanese side, and approximately a hundred Chinese dead. But conditions for a truce were being worked out, including an apology from the Chinese.

In Tokyo, many people, including Prime Minister Konoe himself, suspected that this was another army plot. But on 8 July, the Army General Staff ordered no further use of force, hoping to prevent an expansion of the conflict. The forces really eager for a fight were the Kwantung Army and the Chinese Communist Party.

In a cabinet meeting on 9 July, Minister of Army Sugiyama proposed sending three divisions from Japan to the continent. But Minister of Navy Yonai opposed this idea, arguing for nonexpansion and a local settlement. Prime Minister Konoe also expressed opposition to the dispatch of troops, and Sugiyama withdrew his proposal.

However, on 10 July, the Army General Staff decided on a new plan for dispatching reinforcements: one division each from Japan's Korean Army and the Kwantung Army, and three divisions from Japan. The real center of power in the General Staff at that time was Ishiwara Kanji, as chief of the First Bureau (Operations). The chief of staff was a member of the imperial family, and Vice Chief of Staff Imai Kiyoshi and Watari Hisao, chief of the Second Bureau (Intelligence), were on sick leave. This meant that it was essentially up to Ishiwara to determine the stance the General Staff would take. Ishiwara opposed the dispatch of troops to China, because his priority was a military buildup against the Soviet Union. Kawabe Torashirō, chief of the War Leadership Section of the First Bureau, shared this view. But Mutō Akira, chief of the Operations Section of the First Bureau, was in favor of sending more troops to the continent. The Imperial Japanese Army had only about 5,000 troops around Beiping, while there were close to 400,000 Chinese troops in North China. Moreover, reports had come in that the Nationalist government had decided to send four divisions of its army northward. This threatened the possibility of an encirclement and complete destruction of the numerically inferior Japanese forces—as well as a grave threat to the security of the 12,000 or so Japanese civilians resident in the region.

Kawabe and others were of the opinion that in order to achieve a local resolution of the conflict it would be better not to send in reinforcements, especially troops sent directly from Japan. But Ishiwara had become worried by the potential for a local bloodbath, and he made the decision to commit more troops. On the evening of 10 July, Minister of Army Sugiyama contacted the chief cabinet secretary and that requested a cabinet meeting be held the next day, a Sunday, to approve a decision to send in more troops. Receiving this communication, Prime Minister Konoe contacted the other cabinet ministers—at about 3:00 A.M.—to tell them a cabinet meeting would be convened.

However, on the morning of 11 July, Ishiwara called on Konoe at his private residence and requested that the prime minister reject the army's plan for dispatching troops. Perhaps he regretted having failed to override the opinions of his subordinates, but he pleaded with the prime minister to reject a plan that Ishiwara himself had approved only hours before, which was highly unusual behavior. There were similar efforts afoot in the Ministry of Army. The East Asian Bureau of the Ministry of Foreign Affairs had a communication from the Military Affairs Section of the Ministry of Army that Ushiroku Jun, chief of the Military Affairs Bureau, had signed off on the plan to commit more troops because of internal pressure within the Ministry of Army, but the Military Affairs Section asked that the foreign minister do what he could to stall approval of the plan. This was probably at the behest of Shibayama Kenshirō, chief of the Military Affairs Section, who was among those opposed to an expansion of the conflict. So that morning, Ishii Itarō, chief of the East Asian Bureau, went to Tokyo Station to meet Minister of Foreign Affairs Hirota, returning from a weekend vacation trip, to urge him to block the army plan—and tell him that the Military Affairs Bureau of the Ministry of Army was of the same mind.

At 11:30 A.M. the Five Ministers Conference was convened, and the troop plan was debated. Ministry of Army Sugiyama argued for sending troops, saying that Japan could not abandon its Tianjin Army nor the Japanese residents in the Beiping and Tianjin region, and that there was a good chance that the Chinese would back down simply at the announcement of Japanese reinforcements. Minister of Navy Yonai countered by saying that dispatch of more troops would escalate the incident, and within a month or two fighting would expand into central China. In the end, a decision to dispatch troops was made, but with two conditions: stress was to be placed on nonexpansion and local resolution of the incident, and that even after mobilization, if the dispatch of troops proved to be unnecessary, it was to be immediately suspended. The emperor was not enthusiastic about this decision, but in the end indicated his approval. Konoe approved the dispatch of troops because he believed that if he did not, the army minister would resign, forcing the resignation of the entire cabinet, and if this should occur, there would be no one with the capacity to rein in the army—an explanation that the emperor also accepted.

At 6:24 P.M. that evening, the government announced the dispatch of troops. In addition, beginning at 9:00 P.M., Prime Minister Konoe assembled nearly a hundred leading figures from the media, political, and financial worlds and met with them in three separate groups, seeking their support for this dispatch of troops to urge the Chinese to reconsider their actions.

Meanwhile, also on 11 July, efforts to arrive at a local settlement began to make progress. Around noon, discussions were under way concerning the terms of a ceasefire agreement. But when the announcement of the dispatch of Japanese troops arrived, the attitude of the Chinese negotiators, understandably, started to harden. Even so, by 8:00 P.M. that evening, an agreement was reached. When this news reached Japan, mobilization of home divisions was suspended, but reinforcements from the Korean and Kwantung Armies were already arriving on the scene.

In response, the Nationalist army began to move northward, and on 17 July, Chiang Kai-shek gave a speech titled "The Limit of China's Endurance," in which he said that while his country would continue its efforts for peace, if these efforts should fail, "once that stage is reached, we can only sacrifice and fight to the bitter end." Meanwhile, in Tokyo the cabinet decided on 20 July to mobilize three more divisions, though they were not to be immediately dispatched. But on 25 July new fighting broke out in the vicinity of Beiping and Tianjin, and on 27 July it was decided to send the three divisions as reinforcements. On 28 July, Japanese forces commenced an all-out attack, and the situation developed into a full-fledged war.

Principal responsibility for the expansion of the conflict probably rests in the Ministry of Army, and particularly with Minister of Army Sugiyama. Prime Minister Konoe and Minister of Foreign Affairs Hirota were also heavily at fault. At the time, the army itself was divided between General Staff, which wanted to keep the situation from getting out of hand, and the Ministry of Army, which hoped for a quick and decisive victory. It should have been possible to intervene between them, but neither Konoe nor Hirota seized the opportunity to stop the aggression.

On the other hand, the locus of nonexpansionist sentiment in the army was in the General Staff, centering on Ishiwara Kanji. But when he tried to talk down those favoring an expansion of hostilities, they rebutted him by saying they were only following the model he had established in the Manchurian Incident, which left him at a loss for words. Ishiwara is frequently spoken of as a tragic figure. But I think this is an over-assessment of Ishiwara. First of all, the Manchurian Incident that Ishiwara engineered destroyed the integrity of Japan's supreme command. It created a dangerous

Lugouqiao, the Marco Polo Bridge
This stone bridge, spanning the Yongding River about some 600 meters west of the walled city of Wanping and about 20 kilometers from the outskirts of Beijing, was completed in 1189 during the Jin dynasty. The locale was an important crossroads for traffic headed south of Beijing, with an important rail line running nearby. (From Nakatogawa Yōkō (Tenshin), Shina jihen shussei kinen shashin chō [A commemorative photo album of the China expedition])

precedent in which unauthorized mobilization of troops could be justified by the results. Ishiwara is the figure most responsible for the incidents of insubordination that would follow. Second, Ishiwara did not think that the resources of Manchuria alone would be sufficient for Japan's needs, and wanted, if possible, to gain control of China proper—which made it difficult for him to commit absolutely to a nonexpansion policy, as Suzuki Teiichi later observed. And third, Ishiwara should have been able to rebuff the expansionists by saying that the present international situation was completely different from that at the time of the Manchurian Incident—but he did not, or could not, and this failure lessens his stature considerably. I do not see the Sino-Japanese War as part of the tragedy of Ishiwara. Rather, a figure like Ishiwara was a tragedy for Japan.

From Shanghai to Nanjing

The flames of war had finally reached central China. On 9 August 1937, Ōyama Isao, a lieutenant in the Japanese Special Naval Landing Forces, and his driver were shot in an altercation with members of the Chinese Peace

Preservation Corps. On 13 August this incident led to combat between units of the Japanese Special Naval Landing Forces and Chinese forces, and the Konoe cabinet decided to send additional troops to Shanghai. On 15 August, the Japanese government issued a statement that it would take disciplinary action against the Nanjing government and commenced long-range bombing raids against Nanjing, which was the headquarters of the Chinese air force. Total war had begun—and would continue for the next eight years.

It was in part a Chinese decision to turn central China into a battlefield (Nomura Kōichi, *Shō Kaiseki to Mō Takutō* [Chiang Kai-shek and Mao Zedong]). Part of it was a natural desire, if a fight was necessary, to fight on advantageous ground. As noted earlier, following World War I, China forged a close relationship with Germany. When the first United Front between the Kuomintang and the Chinese Communist Party fell apart and the Soviet Union withdrew its military advisers, China became dependent upon a team of German military experts. With German assistance, Chiang believed he had prepared his troops to defend Nanjing and Shanghai. As the war expanded into central China, what had been dubbed in Japan as the North China Incident (as of 11 July) began to be called simply the China Incident (as of 2 September). War was not officially declared, primarily because to do so would engage the US Neutrality Acts and make it more difficult to import US goods and materials.

In the Shanghai region the Japanese forces had a hard fight. Chiang Kai-shek made it into a key battleground, bringing in the cream of the Nationalist army, along with supporting forces from central and southern China, totaling some 300,000 troops. Against this, Japan kept pumping in reinforcements from the home islands, and was also forced to transfer existing forces from North China. But on 26 October, Dachang-zhen, one of the last strongholds on the outskirts of the city, fell to the Japanese. Then on 5 November, the Tenth Army made a surprise landing on the northern shore of Hangzhou Bay, hitting the Chinese army from the rear. The Chinese forces collapsed, and by 11 November, Japanese forces were in control of Shanghai. The leader of the Tenth Army was Kōdōha general Yanagawa Heisuke, who had been taken off the active-duty list in 1936, and at the time his identity was concealed—he was known as "the masked general." Japan had committed a total of nine divisions to the fighting in the Shanghai region, more than the seven it had in North China. In the Shanghai fighting alone, more than 9,000 Japanese were killed and 31,000 wounded, while casualties on the Chinese side are said to have been more than 83,000 (Bōeichō bōeikenshūjo senshishitsu, *Shina jihen rikugun sakusen* [Army operations in the China Incident], vol. 1). China paid an enormous price, but also succeeded in winning the sympathy of the Western powers. On the other hand, Japan failed in its goal of delivering a quick, decisive blow that would break China's war morale. It can only be called a pointless war.

The ravages of warfare in Shanghai:
Oriental Library of the Commercial Press
In the battle for Shanghai, the most intense fighting is said to have taken place in the Zhabei district, a dense urban environment with many multistory buildings that served as the setting for bitter street fighting. The photo is of the Oriental Library, affiliated with the publisher Commercial Press, the former being used as a headquarters by the Chinese forces. The scars of artillery bombardment are plain to see. (From Sanekisha, Chūshi no tenbō *[Perspectives on central China])*

With Shanghai under Japanese control, Nanjing emerged as the next objective. But there was strong opposition to this idea. Nanjing was more than 300 kilometers from Shanghai, Japan had little military force to spare, and capturing the city was seen as a difficult proposition. At the time, the Imperial Japanese Army consisted of twenty-four divisions—seventeen regular and seven newly created—of which sixteen had already been sent to China, six were stationed in Manchuria, and one was in Korea, leaving only a single division in the home islands. It was also questionable whether taking Nanjing would even be significant; on 20 November 1937, Chiang Kai-shek announced his intention to move the Nationalist capital to Chongqing.

But on 15 November, the Tenth Army made its own decision to set out for Nanjing, and the Shanghai Expeditionary Army also began to move. Their commander, General Matsui Iwane, had been a vocal advocate of seizing Nanjing. Vice Chief of General Staff Tada Hayao attempted to stifle these developments, but failed, and on 28 November the assault on Nanjing was approved by the General Staff.

The Japanese forces advanced at a savage pace over the 300 kilometers between Shanghai and Nanjing. They had just been liberated from the intense fighting of the Shanghai campaign but were also in a vengeful mood; they were engaged in a forced march with completely inadequate lines of supply; and they were hopeful that once Nanjing fell the war would be over and they could go home. All of these psychological factors combined to impel Japanese troops toward looting and unnecessary violence. Thus the stage was set for the Nanjing Incident.

The Nanjing Incident

What is called the Nanjing Incident (*jihen*) in Japan is often called the Nanjing Massacre, or the Rape of Nanjing, elsewhere. It refers to the actions of the Japanese forces in December 1937 after they entered the city of Nanjing, where in the course of battle they killed a large number of Chinese soldiers, civilians, and prisoners of war. Historians often call this the "second Nanjing incident," to distinguish it from the incident in 1927, when Chinese forces (both KMT and Communist troops) went on a rampage against foreign residents and consulates in Nanjing, killing a number of British, Americans, and Japanese. Official Chinese sources put the number of dead in the second Nanjing incident at around 300,000. This incident has been examined and written about by many Japanese scholars, most of whom are highly critical of the Japanese military, with accounts of the number killed ranging from 40,000 to as many as 200,000. Even the lower number would amount to a massacre by any standard. While this incident has been studied and written about by many Japanese scholars over the decades, it was largely forgotten in post-revolution China, even in the city of Nanjing, until an American Chinese author named Iris Chang revived the memories of the tragic incident in her 1997 bestseller *The Rape of Nanking*. Partly because of Chang's book, this tragedy once again entered the narrative of this period.

It is impossible to deny that this tragic massacre occurred. Chang's book was criticized for some inaccuracies, but she also succeeded in introducing important firsthand accounts, particularly by third-party nationals who were in Nanjing. Though reliable accounts are scarce, there is ample evidence to prove the lack of discipline of Japanese soldiers and the ignorance of international law in the Japanese army of that time, including the failure to prepare for humane treatment of prisoners of war, the brutal execution of large numbers of prisoners of war, and the murder, rape, and robbery of a large number of civilians.

The tragedy of Nanjing is due not only to problems in the Japanese military, but also to tactical problems on the Chinese side. It was obvious to all that the Japanese would attempt to capture Nanjing after the battle of

Nanjing after the fall
On the left is Zhonghua Road, one of the main streets of the city, lined with major stores and corporate offices. At right is Dama Road in Xiaguan, with civilians making their way through the rubble left by artillery bombardment. (From Sanekisha, Chūshi no tenbō *[Perspectives on central China])*

Shanghai, because it was the Nationalist capital at the time. In planning their defense against this attack, Chiang Kai-shek's generals and advisers held heated debates over three possible alternatives, including defending Nanjing to the end, abandoning Nanjing and retreating to Wuhan for the next battle, or capitulating to the Japanese and thereby saving Nanjing by surrendering. Chiang Kai-shek vacillated among these alternatives, and in the end he chose a combination that proved tragically fatal. Before the Japanese arrived, Chiang Kai-shek and many of his generals left Nanjing. They took many of the troops with them, and before they left they ordered key buildings to be torched so they could not be occupied by the Japanese. General Tang Shengshi, an advocate for defending Nanjing to the death, was ordered to remain as commander of the defending forces. On December 11, Tang refused an order from General Matsui Iwane to surrender, but then on December 12, when the Japanese troops had surrounded the city, Tang received orders from Chiang Kai-shek to retreat, and he suddenly ordered his troops to break through the lines of Japanese soldiers and escape. The result was chaos, because the Chinese troops by that time could organize neither an orderly retreat nor an orderly defense. Many Chinese soldiers tried to disguise themselves as civilians, which meant that all Chinese, whether in uniform or not, became targets of the Japanese. The Japanese, many of whom believed that the capture of Nanjing would end the war, went after the disorganized Chinese army and the city with vengeance and brutality.

The Reaction of International Society

Let's examine the international reaction to the ongoing situation in China. China first appealed to the Soviet Union for help. After initial overtures in late July, on 21 August 1937 a nonaggression treaty was signed between the Republic of China and the Soviet Union. Then, in response to a Chinese request, on 27 August the Soviet Union agreed to provide military assistance to China, and began supplying bombers, fighter planes, tanks, anti-tank guns, anti-aircraft guns, and other weaponry. The first shipment of aircraft arrived in November. Between 1937 and 1941, in addition to 1,250 airplanes, the Soviet Union provided China with $250 million in assistance in the form of tanks, artillery, vehicles, and the construction of armament factories; 700 Soviet pilots were sent as combatants, and groups of military advisers were attached to Chinese forces. Moreover, in light of the difficulty in arranging cash payment, Stalin agreed to accept compensation in the form of mining and agricultural products (Nomura Kōichi, *Shō Kaiseki to Mō Takutō* [Chiang Kai-shek and Mao Zedong]). But the Soviet Union refused to enter the war on the Chinese side, as Chiang Kai-shek had hoped. It was preoccupied with preparing itself against Germany.

China also appealed to the League of Nations to condemn Japan's actions as violations of the League Covenant, the Kellogg-Briand Pact, and the Nine-Power Treaty. The General Assembly of the League adopted a resolution on 28 September condemning Japan for indiscriminate bombing, and a second on 6 October that declared Japan's actions to be in violation of the Kellogg-Briand Pact and the Nine-Power Treaty.

In the United States, President Franklin D. Roosevelt gave a speech in Chicago on 5 October in which he said that just as when an epidemic breaks out in a community, a quarantine must be imposed on the patients in order to prevent the spread of the disease, and international society must act to quarantine the lawless nations in its midst. Though he did not specifically name them, this was clearly a critique of Japan, Germany, and Italy. The United States had still not recovered from the wounds of the Great Depression, and isolationist sentiment was strong among the public. Roosevelt knew his administration was not, at this point, capable of much action in the realm of foreign policy, but he wanted to turn the attention of the public in that direction. And he was meeting great resistance in trying to do so.

On 3 November 1937 the Nine-Power Conference convened in Brussels to address Japanese violations of international law. But both the United States and Britain were reluctant to intervene in the problems between Japan and China, which is one reason why the meeting was convened in Brussels. Japan claimed that this was an issue better settled bilaterally, and therefore it did not attend the conference. And in the middle of the conference, Italy announced that it was joining the Anti-Comintern Pact, which had already been established between Japan and Germany. So the Nine-Power Conference produced almost no significant results—except to encourage the Japanese military to have a low opinion of the international community.

Japan's actions were largely indifferent to foreign relations. On 26 August, the British ambassador to China, Sir Hughe Montgomery Knatchbull-Hugessen, was en route from Nanjing to Shanghai when his car was machine-gunned by a Japanese fighter plane and he was gravely wounded. The Japanese resisted accepting responsibility for the incident but, concerned with diplomatic image, finally admitted the high probability that it was a mistaken attack by Japanese forces, and to defuse the incident they sent Vice Minister of Navy Yamamoto Isoroku to convey official regrets. But on 12 December, during the Japanese assault on Nanjing, Japanese navy aircraft bombed and sunk the US naval gunboat *Panay* on the Yangtze River, and the Japanese army shelled the British vessel HMS *Ladybird*. It is likely that these attacks were intentional. Even if they were in error, this was clearly a major breach of military discipline. Saitō Hiroshi, Japanese ambassador to the United States, immediately made a radio broadcast expressing regret for the incidents. The Japanese government immediately apologized to both the United States and Britain, and this quickly defused the matter.

But these incidents also unquestionably hardened Anglo-American public opinion toward Japan. And it is also impossible to ignore the fact that they also gave rise to a mistakenly contemptuous impression on the part of the Japanese that Britain and the United States were incapable of effective action, even when their warships were attacked.

The Trautmann Mediation

One person who was concerned about the expansion of the Sino-Japanese War was Adolf Hitler. Germany had friendly relations with both China and Japan. The most desirable situation for Germany would be if Japan and China teamed up to threaten the Soviet Union from the east; conflict between Japan and China was the worst possible combination for Hitler. So it was only natural that Germany would attempt to broker a peace between the two countries.

On 21 October 1937, Minister of Foreign Affairs Hirota invited the German ambassador to Japan, Herbert von Dirksen, to engage in an effort at mediation. On 2 November, Hirota gave him a list of Japanese conditions that included: establishment of an autonomous government in Inner Mongolia; creation of a demilitarized zone from the Manchukuo border to the Tianjin-Beiping area; expansion of the demilitarized zone around Shanghai; abandonment of anti-Japanese policies; cooperative action against the Communists; reduction in tariffs on Japanese imports; and respect for rights and interests of foreigners in China. All of these were aimed at resolving exist-ing disputes between China and Japan in a manner favorable to the Japan-ese; there was nothing particularly new in these demands.

On 5 November, Oskar P. Trautmann, the German ambassador to China. conveyed Japan's demands to the Chinese, and on 7 December, Dirksen relayed to the Japanese that China was prepared to enter negotiations based on the conditions Japan had proposed. When Hirota told Prime Minister Konoe and Minister of Army Sugiyama about this, they both agreed, but the next day Sugiyama suddenly said that he wanted to reject the German mediation.

When Hirota had first approached Dirksen, the Japanese army was not doing well in the battles in Shanghai. But by the beginning of November, the front line of the Chinese forces had collapsed. This changed the army's attitude toward Trautmann's mediation. The army thought it would be bet-ter to continue fighting. Their reasoning was that once Nanjing fell, the Chinese would probably surrender, and there would be no need to negotiate a conditional peace.

Meanwhile, on 20 November 1937, a new Imperial General Headquar-ters had been created, along with a liaison conference of that headquarters and the Japanese government for coordination and consultation between the military and government. On 14 December, the latter body deliberated on conditions for a peace if Germany were invited to mediate. The foreign ministry and the navy supported a proposal that added an indemnity (to be paid by the Chinese for deliberate damage inflicted upon Japan) to the other conditions articulated on 2 November, but the army wanted to append even harsher conditions. The capital of Nanjing had fallen the day before, and the Nationalist government had withdrawn to Hankou, on its way to Chongqing, and Japan's North China Area Army had already established in Beiping a puppet government called the Provisional Government of the Republic of China. Hardliners within the army were arguing that the Nationalist government was now no more than a regional government, and one with which Japan no longer needed to negotiate.

What the army proposed was making all of North China into a special zone; declaring a demilitarized zone in "occupied areas of Central China"; indemnification of Japanese war expenditures; conclusion of a ceasefire agreement following an agreement on the terms of the peace; the dispatch of a Chinese peace delegation to Japan; and a response from China before the end of the year. Although this audacious proposal did not include explicit cession of Chinese territory to Japan, it was tantamount to a call for an immediate and unconditional surrender because of the extremely limited time the Japanese gave the Chinese to reply and the threat that combat would continue until a peace agreement was reached. It appears that the army underestimated the likelihood of China accepting these conditions—or perhaps they did not care whether China accepted them or not.

With some alterations, this proposal was adopted as a cabinet resolution on 21 December. Then, on 24 December, the government decided upon an outline of measures for the China Incident in which it was proposed that rather than negotiating solely with the Nationalist government, a new regime should be established in North China. Matters were moving in the direction of making all of China into a puppet state like Manchukuo.

On 21 December, Hirota conveyed the cabinet's decision to Dirksen, and Trautmann brought it to the Nationalist government. Dirksen believed it was unlikely that the Chinese would accept it, but he passed it along anyway. As expected, the Nationalist government was not quick to reply. In Japan, the Army General Staff took a positive view of the Trautmann mediation, but in contrast the Ministry of Army and Prime Minister Konoe were cool to the idea.

On 14 January 1938, Ambassador Dirksen delivered a message from the Nationalist government that since the Japanese conditions were vague, it wanted more concrete proposals. The Japanese saw this as an insincere play for time on the part of the Nationalist government. It is significant to note that Tada Hayao, vice chief of the Army General Staff, argued for giving the Chinese a bit more time to respond, but the cabinet rejected this idea. The General Staff was concerned that if the war with China dragged on, preparations against the Soviet Union might be adversely affected. The Army General Staff were the professional warriors, and they were positively inclined toward peace, while Prime Minister Konoe and Minister of Foreign Affairs Hirota were unable to seize this opportunity and move toward a peaceful resolution of the conflict. It was doubtful whether the Chinese actually intended to accept the Trautmann mediation, and the likelihood that they were simply stalling was high. In that sense, the remarks of Konoe and others that Chiang Kai-shek was insincere were probably correct. But sincerity was not the issue: the issue was ending the war, and on what conditions.

On 16 January 1938, Konoe announced that the imperial government would henceforth "no longer deal with" (*aite to sezu*) the Nationalist government. This was amplified by a supplementary statement issued on 18 January explaining that the statement to no longer deal with meant "non-recognition" (*hinin*) and that Japan intended to "ignore" (*massatsu*) the Nationalists. With this, Japan's diplomatic relations with China were broken off.

It should be noted that during Japan's war with the Qing dynasty of 1894–1895, Prime Minister Itō Hirobumi insisted, as the nation's supreme political official, on participating in the deliberations of the Imperial General Headquarters, and when this was accepted, he played an active role in influencing the conduct of the war. Particularly in its latter stages, when a campaign to seize Beijing was being considered, he was vehemently opposed, arguing that without a counterpart government a peace could not be negotiated. This attitude is diametrically opposed to Konoe's "*aite to sezu.*" Moreover, Konoe was not permitted to attend meetings of the Imperial General Headquarters, and received information only in the liaison conference. In any case, the "*aite to sezu*" declaration was one of the most monumentally stupid acts in the political history of the Shōwa era.

Toward a Controlled Economy

A war of this magnitude naturally required immense expenditure. It was clear that normal economic management would not suffice. In the 1937 fiscal year, emergency military funding amounting to ¥2.5 billion was appropriated: a ¥500 million supplement passed in a special Diet session in July 1937; and in an extraordinary session in September, ¥2 billion more. As the entire budget for fiscal 1937 had been a little over ¥2.8 billion (cut from the cabinet proposal of ¥3.04 billion in November 1936), an amount almost equivalent to that of Japan's entire annual budget had been added for the military.

This gave the army and the navy an embarrassment of riches, and new budget requests poured in from all reaches of the military establishment. For example, this struck the Imperial Japanese Army's band, which had up to this point used only brass and woodwinds, to seek appropriations so that it could expand into a full-fledged orchestra, with a string section (Nakamura Takafusa, *Shōwa-shi* [A history of Shōwa Japan, 1926–1989], abridged translation).

The September Diet session also enacted three important pieces of legislation: the Temporary Funds Adjustment Act, the Temporary Act to Regulate Imports and Exports, and the Act Concerning the Application of the Military Industry Mobilization Act. The first of these aimed at controlling the flow of funding by classifying Japanese industries into three categories: A, to be actively encouraged with prioritized funding; B, investment in plant and equipment by the government and Bank of Japan to be determined on a case-by-case basis; and C, expansion of facilities to be discouraged. Class A industries were related to military demand, and included iron and steel, shipbuilding, and aircraft and machinery manufacture; Class C included textiles, paper, and commerce. In short, private-sector demand was suppressed, and military-related investment prioritized.

The Temporary Act to Regulate Imports and Exports provided for orders to be given in the form of ministerial ordinances or bureau-level directives concerning the production, processing, distribution, storage, and consumption of import- or export-related goods. The Act Concerning the Application of the Military Industry Mobilization Act specified procedures for the management, use, and expropriation of factories by the army and navy pursuant to the 1918 Military Industry Mobilization Act, and provided for army and navy supervisors to be assigned to oversee factories producing for military consumption.

According to economic historian Nakamura Takafusa, the reason for this type of control may have been wartime necessity, but at the same time it is important to note that many academics, journalists, bureaucrats, and military men had come to believe that economic liberalism was the source of a many social problems, and therefore they supported a controlled or planned economy (Nakamura Takafusa, *Shōwa-shi* [A history of Shōwa Japan, 1926–1989], abridged translation).

In October 1937, the Cabinet Planning Board was created and set to work on material mobilization plans. The first product of its work was a plan covering the period from October to December 1937, which projected the types and quantities of imported materials anticipated for that period, the scope of goods that could be produced with them, and the way they should be allocated among the army, navy, and civilian sector. Beginning in 1938, this continued as an annual plan.

But planning centered on military demand was difficult to achieve given Japan's balance of payments. The 1938 Material Mobilization Plan estimated a potential import total of ¥3 billion—a significant reduction from the ¥3.8 billion of 1937. A major reason for this was a decline in civilian imports of materials as a result of the prioritization of imports of military raw materials. For example, raw cotton imports had declined and production of cotton textiles had fallen off, depressing exports and making it more difficult to earn foreign currency. Prioritizing the military was suppressing civilian demand, weakening export performance, and inviting economic stagnation.

The National Mobilization Act and Nationalization of Electric Power

In February 1938, the cabinet presented a draft of the National Mobilization Act to the Diet. It defined national mobilization as "the control and management of human and material resources in order to demonstrate optimum effectiveness of our country's power in order to achieve our national defense objectives in time of war (including incidents tantamount to war)." Here it is worth examining in detail the sweeping powers that were to be given to the state in order to achieve these ends:

- Civilian conscription (Article 4)
- Directives to civilians to cooperate with mobilization activities (Article 5)
- Directives concerning working conditions including employment and labor (Article 6)
- Directives regarding production, repair, rationing, disposal, use, consumption, ownership, and transfer of goods (Article 8)

- Regulation or prohibition of trade; imposition, increase, or decrease of tariffs (Article 9)
- Utilization and expropriation of vital materials (Article 10)
- Regulation or prohibition of the establishment of corporations, increase in capital, merger, and other acts of corporations; directives concerning disposition of profits and accounting; directives concerning funds of financial institutions (Article 11)
- Management, utilization, and expropriation of vital facilities including factories, places of business, and shipyards (Article 13)
- Regulation, prohibition, or directives for construction, expansion, or improvements of plants and equipment (Article 16)
- Control of cartels (Article 17)
- Directives for the establishment of associations for the control of enterprises and for mandatory participation in such organizations (Article 18)
- Directives concerning prices, transport and storage fees, and insurance rates (Article 19)
- Power to regulate or prohibit publications, and to prohibit sale or distribution of published material (Article 20)
- Power to order its subjects or those who employ them to report vocational skills of their own or their employees (Article 21)

The detailed implementation of all of this was left to imperial ordinances (*chokurei*), which placed enormous power in the hands of the government. Naturally, there was sharp dissent from industrial circles, and fierce resistance from the political parties. But in the end, the National Mobilization Act was enacted on 20 March 1938. At the time, Konoe was riding a wave of immense popularity, making it quite difficult to oppose him directly.

Another major issue that came before the Diet in 1938 was the nationalization of electric power. This was something the Cabinet Research Bureau had already drafted at the end of 1935. It was proposed as legislation by the Hirota cabinet, but the cabinet fell before it could be enacted, so the Konoe cabinet submitted a new proposal to the Diet.

Electrical power in Japan had developed initially through thermal power generation, and then switched to a model centered on hydroelectric generation. In 1938, the electric power sector had a total capitalization of ¥4.9 billion—accounting for more than 25 percent of the capitalization of all Japanese industry. But there were also 830 enterprises involved in this sector; it was a disorganized jumble of relatively small firms, without unified standards. There was competition among them: Company A might be expensive but provide quality service (stable power, few outages), while Company B might be cheaper but offer inferior service. Such competition seemed unnecessary and wasteful. The goal of nationalization was to provide cheap and plentiful power to all.

In 1938, the nationalization plan created under Minister of Communications Nagai Ryūtarō exempted hydroelectric generation, but all thermoelectric power plants and electrical transmission equipment were to be unified into Nippon Hassōden K.K. (Japan Electric Generation and Transmission Company), a semipublic "national policy company" (*kokusaku-gaisha*).

Many of the existing private electric companies had close ties to party politicians, and there was considerable opposition to this plan in the Diet. It was criticized as "Red legislation" because of the level of state control. But this was a wartime Diet, and neither the Seiyūkai nor the Minseitō had the courage to engage in all-out resistance. The result was the establishment, in April 1939, of Nippon Hassōden. Capitalized at little over ¥700 million, it was the largest of Japan's national policy companies. In 1941, hydroelectric power would also be absorbed into it. Electrical power distribution was organized according to nine regions nationally—the forerunners of the nine electric power companies of postwar Japan.

This Diet session also saw the enactment of legislation establishing the national health insurance system. At first this was aimed at people employed in agriculture and fisheries and the self-employed, but along with bringing modern medical care to rural villages, it supported the wartime policy of "healthy people, healthy soldiers" and enrollment was eventually made mandatory.

In January 1938, the Ministry of Health and Welfare was created as an agency independent of the Ministry of Home Affairs (its first minister was Kido Kōichi, already minister of education, who initially held the post concurrently and then solely). It was tasked with social welfare, social insurance, improvement and promotion of public health, and labor administration. Under the wartime regime and its "healthy people, healthy soldiers" policy, it also was responsible for promoting hygiene and physical fitness in support of the war effort and securing, mobilizing, and assigning a labor force for war-related industries.

In the midst of the Diet deliberations on the National Mobilization Act, Satō Kenryō of the Military Affairs Department of the Ministry of Army was involved in an especially lengthy explanation of some point in the proposal and was heckled by some of the Diet members. Satō yelled "Shut up!" at the hecklers, and was roundly criticized for doing so. He said that his outburst had actually been directed at an acquaintance of his, Miyawaki Chōkichi, who was one of the members causing the disturbance, and that he had meant to say, "Shut up, Chōkichi!" In any case, he went unpunished for this indiscretion—an episode that gives a sense of the atmosphere of the Diet at that time.

If anything, it was the proletarian parties who favored this series of legislation. The Shakai Taishūtō (Socialist Mass Party) was an enthusiastic supporter of the Konoe cabinet. One of its Diet members, Nishio Suehiro, cheered Konoe on by saying on 16 March, "Great! You must boldly execute radical reforms like Hitler, Mussolini, and Stalin!" This landed him in trouble with the Diet's Disciplinary Committee, which took him to task for speaking favorably of Stalin. But this was more than squeamishness concerning comparisons with Stalin; it also represented resistance within the Diet to the idea of the Shakai Taishūtō supporting the Konoe cabinet. Yet the right-wing Tōhōkai, led by Nakano Seigō, was opposed to expelling Nishio from the Diet. Left and right had their differences, but they were united in rejecting liberalism and supporting greater economic and social control—and they were sharply in conflict with the established political parties like the Minseitō and Seiyūkai.

Foreign Minister Ugaki

At the time these historic pieces of legislation were being enacted by the Diet, the military situation in China was relatively quiet. On 16 February 1938, Imperial General Headquarters held a conference in the presence of the emperor (*gozen kaigi*) that agreed on a policy of not pursuing further campaigns and working to maintain the status quo for the time being. Within the Army General Staff, there was a vocal element calling for placing top priority on bolstering the nation's economic and military power. However, in April the local field army launched a campaign to seize Xuzhou, with the aim of opening the rail line between Tianjin and Pukuo (on the opposite bank of the Yangtze from Nanjing), and on 19 May Japanese forces occupied Xuzhou. Then, on 18 June, a campaign to take Hankou was initiated.

Chiang Kai-shek abandoned Xuzhou, foiling the Japanese strategy of trapping and eliminating Nationalist forces there. But in order to halt the advance of Japanese armies moving southward to attack Hankou, Chiang blew up the Yellow River dikes in Henan province. The muddy waters of the Yellow River inundated forty-four counties in three provinces, leaving 4.8 million people homeless or worse. The mechanized units of the Japanese army were immobilized, and the Japanese lost the opportunity for a blitzkrieg offensive against Hankou, having instead to advance westward through central China along the Yangtze River.

Immediately after the completion of the Xuzhou campaign, on 26 May, Konoe undertook a major reshuffle of his cabinet. Ugaki Kazushige was appointed foreign minister; top Mitsui executive Ikeda Shigeaki was assigned concurrently to head the Ministries of Finance and Commerce and Industry; Araki Sadao was picked as minister of education; and several days later, on 3 June, Itagaki Seishirō was named minister of the army. Ugaki and Ikeda were known as being friendly to the United States and Britain, while Itagaki had worked with Ishiwara to engineer the Manchurian Incident, and it was believed that, like Ishiwara, he was against expanding the war in China. On the other hand, having a Kōdōha general like Araki in the cabinet was supposed to serve as a check on the Tōseiha. Konoe had realized that his non-recognition policy toward Nationalist China had failed, and had launched this bold cabinet reorganization in an effort to effect a change in course.

Of particular importance was the installation of Ugaki as foreign minister. To fill this post with someone who had not come up through the ranks of the foreign ministry was rare in prewar Japan. In fact, the only previous examples were Prime Minister Tanaka's concurrent holding of the office of foreign minister, and Gotō Shinpei in the Taishō period. Ugaki's condition for accepting the post was a retraction of Konoe's *"aite to sezu"* declaration on China, and Konoe accepted this.

In fact, Ugaki's plan was precisely to reengage the Nationalist government as a negotiating partner. There seemed to be no other way to bring the war to an end. When Ugaki received his appointment as foreign minister, his old acquaintance Zhang Qun, an adviser of Chiang Kai-shek's, sent him a congratulatory telegram. Encouraged by this, Ugaki reached out to H. H. Kung, president of the Executive Yuan (essentially Nationalist China's prime minister), and on 23 June, top secret talks were initiated in Hong Kong between Kung's private secretary Qiao Fusan and Japanese consul-general Nakamura Toyoichi. These continued for some time, but Kung was essentially offering the following responses to earlier Japanese demands: implicit recognition by China of the state of Manchukuo in the form of a tripartite alliance between China, Japan, and Manchukuo; acceptance of the autonomy of Inner Mongolia; acceptance by Japan that it was difficult to convert North China into a special zone; recognition from Japan of demilitarized zones; the Nationalists would abrogate their relationship with the Chinese Communists; and acceptance that China would not be able to pay indemnities. In addition, Kung offered his own resignation in place of that of Chiang Kai-shek, which had been a consistent Japanese demand.

What followed was an intricate series of negotiations between the two countries. The Chinese sought a termination of the Hankou campaign by the Japanese, while the Japanese pressed on with the campaign in order to pressure the Chinese into further concessions. Even for Ugaki, it proved very difficult to rein in the army because it felt it was on the eve of victory in Hankou. This was one of the reasons why Ugaki was so insistent upon Chiang Kai-shek's resignation. On the other hand, Chiang's own position was founded upon his role as supreme commander in the war against Japan, so retirement was not an acceptable option for him. In light of these conflicts, negotiations reached a stalemate around the end of August 1938.

Meanwhile, Ugaki was engaged in talks with Robert Craigie, British ambassador to Japan. Prior to this, the British had repeatedly protested that their trade and economic activity in China was being obstructed and discriminated against by Japan. On 26 July, Ugaki began discussions intended to address Craigie's concerns, and they touched upon topics such as restoration of the status quo ante in the areas to the north of Shanghai, opening of the Yangtze River to transport, and the reopening of British textile factories in the city. But a statement in Parliament by Prime Minister Neville Chamberlain concerning the need to restrain Japan inflamed Japanese public opinion and prevented the second session of these talks from being held until 17 August. The gap between the two sides was large, and progress elusive.

About this time a group emerged within the foreign ministry that was sympathetic to the Axis powers, Germany and Italy. They called themselves "reformists" and pressed Ugaki not to negotiate with the British. Ushiba Nobuhiko, who in the postwar era was active as a pro-American diplomat, was serving as vice foreign minister and ambassador to the United States, and was one of this group who petitioned Ugaki in protest. If this was the atmosphere inside the foreign ministry at that time, it is small wonder that the talks went nowhere.

Another problem that Ugaki had to deal with was the Changkufeng (Lake Khasan) Incident. In July 1938 there was a dispute over the eastern border of the Soviet Union and Manchukuo on the lower reaches of the Tumen River as Japan attempted to redefine the boundaries and the Soviet Union resisted this, resulting in skirmishes between border guards on both sides. On 29 July, Japanese forces invaded Soviet territory to attack elements of the Soviet army. The Soviets counterattacked, and on 7 August retook Changkufeng from the Japanese. Negotiations between the two powers proceeded, and the Japanese, at a military disadvantage, withdrew their demands on the Soviet Union and accepted the established border demarcation. The Japanese had suffered a stinging military defeat, but the Soviets had no inclination to escalate the dispute, so the matter was quickly resolved. Even so, Ugaki's calm and skillful administration of the affair was noteworthy.

Ugaki's diplomacy may not have achieved impressive results, but it was rational and orthodox. Diplomatic commentator Kiyosawa Kiyoshi wrote that it had been a long time since Japan actually had a foreign policy, and praised Ugaki, especially since he was not a professional diplomat.

That Ugaki's diplomacy did not achieve greater results was in part due, as mentioned earlier, to organized opposition within the foreign ministry itself. Another factor was that rather than supporting Ugaki's diplomatic efforts, Prime Minister Konoe acted to frustrate them. Konoe had a jealous and suspicious nature often seen in members of the nobility, and feared his own position might be threatened if Ugaki was too successful.

One specific issue that arose involved the creation of a central agency for dealing with China. The concept behind this was to establish a new cabinet-level agency headed by the prime minister that would serve to unify all political, economic, and cultural policy planning and execution related to China, and coordinate all China operations of the various ministries. This had the potential for giving the prime minister greater capacity to restrain the military, but it also threatened to strip the foreign ministry of much of its powers, so Ugaki was staunchly opposed to the idea. On 29 September, when Konoe would not support Ugaki's position, Ugaki resigned. The foreign policy shift headed by Ugaki had failed after only four months. Establishment of a central agency for China affairs was approved on 1 October, and realized in December 1938 with the creation of the Asia Development Board (Kōain).

A New Order in East Asia

But on 6 October 1938, Joseph Clark Grew, US ambassador to Japan, delivered a lengthy letter of protest to the Japanese government that enumerated various specific examples of actions by Japan that had failed to uphold the principles of the Open Door and equality of opportunity and had damaged legitimate US interests in China.

At this time, Japan was engaged in two military offensives. The first was the campaign to seize Hankou that commenced on 22 August and was completed on 27 October. The second was a campaign against Guangdong (Canton), initiated on 19 September and ending on 21 October. Both were extremely important strategic objectives: Hankou had been the Nationalist stronghold, and Guangdong was a major import trade entrepôt for all of southern China.

In part because these two military campaigns were still in progress, Japan delayed responding to the US protest until 18 November, when Minister of Foreign Affairs Arita Hachirō (appointed to succeed Ugaki on 29 October) sent a written reply. In it, after a detailed rebuttal of the US complaints, Arita wrote:

> At present, Imperial Japan, devoting its entire energy to the establishment of a new order based on genuine international justice throughout East Asia, is making rapid strides toward the attainment of its objective. The successful accomplishment of this purpose is not only indispensable to the existence of Japan, but also constitutes the very foundation of the enduring peace and stability of East Asia.
>
> It is the firm conviction of the Japanese Government that now, as new conditions continue to develop in East Asia, an attempt to apply to present and future conditions without any changes *concepts and principles which were applicable to conditions prevailing before the present incident* does not in any way contribute to the solution of immediate issues and further does not in the least promote the firm establishment of enduring peace in East Asia. (Office of the Historian, "The Japanese Minister for Foreign Affairs [Arita] to the American Ambassador in Japan [Grew]" November 18, 1938, https://history.state.gov/historicaldocuments/frus1931-41v01/d608; emphasis added by the author of this book)

In other words, Arita was not only seeking acceptance of the violation of US interests resulting from the war in China, but also stating that the Open Door was no longer a guiding principle for Japanese policy. Up to this point, Japan had accepted the Open Door policy, with minor adjustments. But this heralded a major shift in policy: a point-blank rejection of the Open Door. Kiyosawa Kiyoshi described this as the most significant document in the period after the Manchurian Incident, and while this may be a bit of an exaggeration, it demonstrated his understanding of the importance of the principles of the Open Door and equality of opportunity—something that Arita and Konoe seem to have failed to appreciate.

Previous to this, on 3 November 1938, Konoe had released a second statement declaring: "What Japan seeks is the establishment of a New Order which will insure the permanent stability of East Asia. In this lies the ultimate purpose of our present military campaign." He went on to say: "Even the participation of the Kuomintang government would not be rejected, if, repudiating the policy which had guided it in the past and remolding its personnel, so as to translate its rebirth into fact, it were to come forward to join in the establishment of the New Order." Exactly what was meant by a "New Order" in East Asia is unclear from this statement, but what is certain is that Konoe and his government no longer had in mind principles such as the Open Door, equality of opportunity, and the equality of sovereign states.

This declaration served as a corrective to Konoe's previous "*aite to sezu*" declaration of nonrecognition, but what was envisaged was a merging of elements of the Nationalist party with the puppet governments that Japan had already set up in various parts of China. The key to this plan lay in overtures to Wang Jingwei. In February 1938, the Army General Staff had initiated secret contacts with the Kuomintang.

Involved in this were Dong Daoning, chief of the Japan section of the Nationalist foreign ministry; Gao Zongwu, head of the Asia Bureau; and Zhou Fohai, vice chief of the office of aide-de-camp to Chiang Kai-shek. On the Japanese side participants included Kagesa Sadaaki, head of the Stratagem Section of the Army General Staff; Imai Takeo, head of the China group; and Vice Chief of General Staff Tada Hayao. Their objective was to extricate Wang Jingwei, the number two man in the Nationalist regime, and its number one political officer, from Chongqing.

On 20 November in Shanghai, Kagesa, Imai, Gao, and Wang's associate Mei Siping negotiated an agreement that contained the following objectives: signing of an anti-Comintern pact between Japan and China; recognition of Manchukuo; freedom of residence and trade for Japanese nationals in China, with Japan agreeing to consider abolition of extraterritoriality and the return of its concessions in China; economic joint ventures, with special consideration given to Japanese access to the resources of North China; indemnities

Wang Jingwei (1883–1944)

Wang joined Sun Yat-sen's Tongmenghui (United League) while studying abroad in Japan. After Sun's death, he engaged in a series of conflicts and compromises with Chiang Kai-shek. After the outbreak of the Second Sino-Japanese War, he defected from the Nationalist government in Chongqing, and became head of state in the Reorganized National Government of China, a puppet regime of the Japanese based in Nanjing. He tried but failed to broker a peace between Chiang and the Japanese, dying in Japan before the war's end. Photo courtesy of Kyodo News Images Inc.

for damages to Japanese residents in China; and a withdrawal of Japanese troops, except for the areas designated in the agreement, within two years. (This agreement would later be gutted by Japanese hardliners.)

Wang Jingwei is today regarded as a traitor and sell-out, but his actions are understandable. Chiang Kai-shek was pursuing a total war of resistance that was bringing immense suffering to the Chinese people. Wang wanted more than anything to restore peace and save the people from this plight.

In Japan, on 30 November, an imperial conference (*gozen kaigi*) approved a plan for a new adjustment of Sino-Japanese relations. It proclaimed three major priorities—first, amity among neighbors; second, cooperative defense against communism; and third, economic cooperation—and as specific "good neighbor" policies proposed recognition of Manchukuo; the establishment of Mongolia-Xinjiang (the Chahar-Suiyuan region) as an "enhanced anti-communist autonomous region"; and Japanese consideration of the return of its concessions in China. These were all items corresponding to proposals worked out by Gao Zongwu and Imai Takeo in their Shanghai agreement. But it is notable that there was absolutely no mention of the withdrawal of Japanese troops.

Wang Jingwei fled Chongqing on 18 December 1938, slightly later than anticipated, reaching Hanoi on 20 December. This defection of the number two man in the Nationalist government shocked the world. As if awaiting this news, Prime Minister Konoe issued his third declaration. It incorporated the plan for a new adjustment of Sino-Japanese relations, with its appeal for amity, cooperative anticommunism, and economic cooperation as well as recognition of Manchukuo and the conversion of North China and Inner Mongolia into a special zone. At the same time, it announced that Japan would not annex new territory, nor seek indemnities, and that it would consider letting go of extraterritoriality and returning its concessions in China.

If anything, the result of this policy line was to antagonize the United States, since it was a frontal assault on the principle of the Open Door. On 30 December the United States vehemently criticized the statement of Minister of Foreign Affairs Arita of 18 November, declaring that there was no basis for any power to prescribe terms and conditions of a "New Order" in areas not under its sovereignty to another sovereign state. Not long before this, the United States extended a $25 million loan to China. Up to this point, despite proclamations of a "moral embargo" on export of war-related materials, the United States had done nothing to impose sanctions on Japan. The isolationism of the American people was still too strong. Now the United States changed its stance and decided to extend the loan to China, and Britain immediately followed suit. In light of the declarations of a New Order in East Asia in November and December 1938, and the back-and-forth between Minister of Foreign Affairs Arita and the United States, it would be no exaggeration to say that the war between Japan and the United States had already begun on the ideological level.

World War II

The Hiranuma Cabinet

On 4 January 1939, Konoe Fumimaro resigned as prime minister, and was succeeded by Hiranuma Kiichirō, president of the Privy Council. Konoe, in turn, took Hiranuma's position as president of the Privy Council. Organization of the new cabinet was completed on 5 January, but it consisted largely of holdovers from the Konoe cabinet: Itagaki Seishirō as army minister, Yonai Mitsumasa as navy minister, Arita Hachirō as foreign minister, Araki Sadao as minister of education, and Shiono Suehiko as minister of justice. Kido Kōichi shifted from welfare minister to home minister, and Konoe remained a member of the cabinet as a minister without portfolio while simultaneously heading the Privy Council.

Kiyosawa Kiyoshi wrote of this with characteristic irony, saying that cabinet changes were usually the result of one of three factors: illness of the prime minister, deadlock in policy, or mere whim. But since Konoe was remaining in the cabinet as a minister without portfolio, it would appear that he was not sick. And since his policies looked like they were going to be inherited, a policy deadlock did not seem to be the problem. So mere whim seemed to be the only remaining reason for this change in government. The basic framework of policy in a cabinet system is usually the budget, and so it was certainly unusual for Konoe to resign after his budget was approved, meaning this resignation was another indication of Konoe's irresponsible character.

As noted previously, Prince Saionji detested Hiranuma. Yet at the end of December, when he was consulted about the choice of Hiranuma as successor to Konoe, Saionji assented, on the sole condition that Hiranuma prioritize relations with Britain and the United States in foreign policy. Hiranuma accepted this condition, and was given the prime ministership. This was not so much an opportunistic shift on Hiranuma's part as it was a consequence of his idealistic conservatism: he disliked communism more than he disliked the Anglo-American powers, and he was not much inclined toward totalitarianism. With the brand of totalitarianism represented by the army's Tōseiha in the ascendancy, even Saionji seemed to think that Hiranuma might serve as bulwark against this tendency. This was the context in which Hiranuma rose, first to president of the Privy Council, and then to the office of prime minister.

Strengthening the Anti-Comintern Pact

The Hiranuma cabinet was kept busy with a series of important diplomatic items. The Sino-Japanese War was now a year and a half old and bogging down; international criticism, which had been silent during the initial fighting, was now beginning to emerge, and in Japan as well a variety of political movements were now afoot to try to break the stalemate. And the international situation had begun to revolve around Germany.

The biggest issue that the Hiranuma cabinet had inherited from Konoe was whether to strengthen Japan's commitment to the Anti-Comintern Pact. Germany had begun sounding out the Japanese in this regard in January

1938, and in August, Major-General Kasahara Yukio, who had been stationed in Germany, returned home with a German proposal for a tripartite alliance that would obligate the signatories to provide mutual military assistance to one another in the event that any of them were attacked by a third party. A Five Ministers Conference on 26 August 1938 produced a weaker alternative proposal, which was that a revised pact should, as an extension of the Anti-Comintern Pact, be explicitly premised as having the Soviet Union as its object, not the Anglo-American powers, and that military assistance should be subject to consultation rather than being mandatory. The army was favorable toward the German plan, but the navy was against strengthening Japan's ties to Germany, which made it difficult to reach a consensus.

The vanguard of opposition to an enhanced Anti-Comintern Pact was Minister of Navy Yonai, who stated quite explicitly that the Japanese navy was not prepared to fight against the United States and Britain, and that if it had to, it had no chance of victory. But this was not the opinion of everyone within the navy. There were those who for reasons of institutional advantage welcomed a more aggressive stance toward the United States and Britain, since a concentration on the Soviet Union as the chief theoretical opponent would mean a national defense centered on the army and render the navy relatively unimportant. If the United States and Britain were seen as more of a threat, the navy would do better in budget negotiations and other matters.

On 6 January 1939, immediately after the formation of the Hiranuma cabinet, Germany made a formal proposal for an alliance. Hiranuma opposed drawing closer to Germany, and believed the Anti-Comintern Pact should have defense against the Soviet Union as its sole object. Arita Hachirō was appointed foreign minister with the understanding that he affirmed this position. However, as a compromise with the German proposal and pressure from the army, he proposed that Britain and France be added to the Soviet Union as objects of the pact, but that with regard to conflict with these nations, mutual assistance would be political and economic only, with military assistance to be determined according to circumstances. In a Five Ministers Conference on 19 January, these were agreed upon as confidential conditions for acceptance.

However, Japan's ambassador to Germany (and former military attaché), Ōshima Hiroshi, and Shiratori Toshio, ambassador to Italy, were unhappy with these terms and refused to convey them to the respective governments, jointly signing a communication on 4 March proposing that the confidential conditions be eliminated. In a Five Ministers Conference on 22 March, further concessions were made to the army: it was agreed that if the 19 January proposal were rejected by Germany, Japan would agree in principle to the use of force against nations other than the Soviet Union.

Concerned by this state of affairs, the emperor questioned whether there would be any other alterations to the terms of the pact, and what was to be done if Ambassadors Ōshima and Shiratori once again failed to follow

Hitler Youth marching
20 April 1939 was Hitler's fiftieth birthday. Enormous celebrations were held that day in Berlin, serving as a demonstration of the power of Nazi Germany. (From a special issue on Germany of Sekai gahō *[World illustrated] magazine, June 1939)*

instructions. In response, Hiranuma said that any further requests for alteration of the terms would result in a termination of the negotiations and that Ōshima and Shiratori would be recalled from their posts. An unprecedented written memorandum by the Five Ministers to this effect was submitted.

But when this policy was cabled to Ōshima and Shiratori on 25 March, the ambassadors did not convey the original Japanese proposal of 19 January but rather the compromise proposal of 22 March. When Italian foreign minister Galeazzo Ciano asked Ambassador Shiratori whether Japan would enter a war in Europe on the side of Italy and Germany, he was given a definite affirmative, as was German foreign minister Joachim von Ribbentrop when he asked the same question of Ambassador Ōshima.

This completely blindsided Minister of Foreign Affairs Arita, and the emperor himself questioned whether this was not a violation of the imperial prerogative. In a Five Ministers Conference on 8 April, Arita attempted to have these actions revoked, but failed in the face of resistance from the army minister; vague instructions for an indirect retraction were all that

Mussolini and Hitler
On 16 March 1935, Hitler unilaterally broke with the terms of the Treaty of Versailles and officially began to rearm Germany. Mussolini founded the Fascist Party in 1921, putting pressure on the king to appoint him prime minister and paving the way to a dictatorial regime. Photo courtesy of Album, Science Source, Omikron, and Kyodo News Images Inc.

was forthcoming. In another meeting on 18 April, Arita proposed breaking off negotiations, but this failed because of opposition from the army minister. Dismissal of the ambassadors also proved impossible. By this time, the army's pro-German stance had advanced to the point that it was drastically distorting the normal channels of government. But after this, little progress was made on the revision of the Anti-Comintern Pact.

Ugaki had been the architect of the August 1938 proposal. He thought the insubordinate ambassadors should be fired, and he had no desire to see Japan ally itself to Germany and Italy with conditions disadvantageous to its own interests: "Rather than deciding which of two masters to serve, it is essential to preserve a free hand in today's conflicted world and maintain a stance that allows us to lead the world political situation. . . . There is nothing to prevent us distancing ourselves from Germany and Italy if we choose. Of course this would require giving a good deal of attention to fixing things up with Britain and the US" (Tsunoda Jun, ed., *Ugaki Kazushige nikki* [Diary of Ugaki Kazushige], 20 April 1939).

When Germany and Italy entered into a military alliance on 22 May, there were those in Japan who lamented being left out of the deal, but Ugaki was unfazed by this. Rather, he was concerned that becoming entangled in the issue of revising the Anti-Comintern Pact would lead Japan into abandoning the more important issue of resolving the Sino-Japanese War (*Ugaki Kazushige nikki*, 2 June 1939).

Wang Jingwei

In order to break the deadlock in Sino-Japanese relations, the Hiranuma cabinet sought to utilize Wang Jingwei. By the end of 1938 it was becoming increasingly clear that a military solution to the Sino-Japanese War was impossible, and that it was time to seek a political solution instead. The idea was to create a new center of political power in China, headed by Wang Jingwei, one of the most prominent of the Kuomintang leaders, and then make peace with this new group.

As mentioned previously, Wang Jingwei fled Chongqing on 18 December 1938, arriving in Hanoi on 20 December. On 17 April 1939, Wang disappeared from Hanoi and reappeared in the French concession in Shanghai on 8 May. Then on 31 May, he made a secret visit to Tokyo. Wang offered three proposals to the Japanese: if Japan wished to reach a compromise with the Chongqing government, he would mediate; if Japan wanted to create a new government out of a merger of the various pro-Japanese political groups that had been established in different parts of China, he would support this from outside the government; or if Japan wanted to establish a new government to be headed by Wang himself, he would be willing to accept the role. What Wang's second and third proposals signified was that he would not accept being treated at the same level as the regional puppet regimes Japan had been setting up, such as the Provisional Government of the Republic of China in Beiping, headed by Wang Kemin, or the Reformed Government of the Republic of China in Nanjing, led by Liang Hongzhi.

In Japan, on 6 June 1939, a Five Ministers Conference agreed upon a policy to establish a new central government in China, defining this new government in the following terms:

1. It would include Wang Jingwei, Wu Peifu, other existing regimes, and "a reoriented and reorganized Chongqing regime."
2. It would work to harmonize Sino-Japanese diplomacy in accordance with the fundamental principle of a new readjustment of relations between the two countries.

3. [omitted by author]
4. Its political structure would be one of "decentralized collaboration, in accord with China's history and present situation," but North China, and Mongolia-Xinjiang in particular, would, for reasons of both national defense and economics, be treated as a high-level anti-Comintern autonomous zone. The lower Yangtze River basin would also be treated separately as "a special zone of advance Sino-Japanese unity in the economic realm," and "a special zone would also be established among specific islands off the South China coast." Aside from these special areas, the rest of the country would be left to the Chinese to govern.
5. Japan had no problem with the continued existence of the Kuomintang and its "Three People's Principles," as long as it abandoned its policies of tolerating communism and opposing Japan, and shifted to amity with Japan and Manchukuo and anticommunism.
6. The Chongqing government could make itself eligible to become an element in the new central government if it would abandon its toleration of communism and anti-Japanese stance and undertook a restructuring of its personnel.

This policy document was not shared with Wang Jingwei, and if it had been, it is likely Wang would have found being lumped together with old-school Japanese collaborators like Wu Peifu difficult to accept.

Wang Jingwei presented his own wish list to Japan on 15 June. In it, he said that while Japan had repeatedly announced its respect for China's sovereignty, this was still not widely understood, and therefore, first, China must act to control anti-Japanese public opinion, but Japan should also control opinion that was aggressive and disrespectful toward China; second, in order to avoid the misperception that Japan was interfering in China's internal affairs, the Japanese should not assume the position of political consultants, advisers, and the like in the new central government, and all negotiations should be handled through the Chinese ambassador in Japan; and third, employment of Japanese personnel in Chinese administrative institutions should be limited to strictly technical roles.

With regard to military affairs, Wang proposed the creation of an advisory group that would include German and Italian advisers in addition to Japanese at a ratio of one to one to two, respectively. Economically, Wang asked for the speedy restitution of places and property occupied or expropriated by Japanese institutions or individuals during the period of conflict; a revaluation according to objective standards of public and private joint ventures in operation; and that the share of Japanese capital in joint ventures be limited to no more than 49 percent.

Clearly, no government could be created in China without the support of the Chinese people, so it was absolutely imperative that Japanese pressure had to be drastically reduced. But it is equally clear that Wang's proposals were difficult to accept, particularly by the Japanese military, given all that had transpired between Japan and China. So in this sense, Wang's proposals were very difficult.

Trouble with Britain

The question of how to handle relations with the Anglo-American powers was a crucial one, whether in relation to the strengthening of the Anti-Comintern Pact or to the negotiations with Wang Jingwei. And in this regard, one of the biggest problems that arose during the tenure of the Hiranuma cabinet was the blockade of the foreign concessions in Tianjin.

From the time of their creation, the British and French concessions in Tianjin limited Chinese sovereignty within their boundaries, and when North China fell under Japanese control, the concessions similarly constrained the authority of Japanese forces. Because of this, the concessions became the location of frequent anti-Japanese agitation. They were also zones in which the Chinese currency called fabi circulated, and where foreign banks kept reserves of silver. Japan's North China Area Army was attempting to confiscate these silver reserves. The Japanese army also ordered Japanese banks and trading companies to leave the British and French concessions, with the goal of isolating the area. In 1938, Japanese forces established checkpoints for a time to inspect persons entering and leaving the concessions.

Then, on 9 April 1939, a newly appointed pro-Japanese inspector of customs, Cheng Xigeng, was murdered in Tianjin. The Japanese claimed the perpetrators had taken refuge inside the British concession, and demanded that they be handed over. But the British ambassador to China, Sir Archibald Clark Kerr, refused to do so on the grounds of insufficient evidence, and the British foreign secretary, Lord Halifax, backed him up. In response, on 14 June, Japan's Army announced that "in order to stifle the activities of anti-Japanese elements infesting the British and French concessions," it was implementing a blockade of the concessions and establishing checkpoints where persons entering and leaving and their belongings would be subject to search. Britain immediately protested this action, but the British ambassador to Japan, Sir Robert Leslie Craigie, argued that as a practical matter it would be best to move the venue of negotiations to either London or Tokyo, and as a result it was decided to open talks between Ambassador Craigie and Minister of Foreign Affairs Arita Hachirō in Tokyo.

Down with Britain!
This was the protest message delivered to the Ministry of Army on 16 August 1939. The first character was embroidered by 3,000 Japanese women using black silk thread; the remaining three characters were formed by the personal seals and thumbprints of 7,000 Japanese men, in an expression of popular antipathy toward Great Britain.

In the first meeting, on 15 July, Arita presented Craigie with the Japanese position, asking that

the British Government fully recognize the actual situation in China, where hostilities on a large scale are in progress and note that, as long as that state of affairs continues to exist, the Japanese forces in China have special requirements for the purpose of safeguarding their own security and maintaining public order in the regions under their control, and they have to take the necessary steps in order to suppress or remove any such acts or causes as will obstruct them or benefit their enemy. The British Government, therefore, will refrain from all acts and measures which will interfere with the Japanese forces in attaining their above mentioned objects.

The British essentially accepted this formula, though insisting on somewhat softer language, saying that "His Majesty's Government has no intention of countenancing any act or measures prejudicial to attainment of the above-mentioned objects by Japanese forces and they will take this opportunity to confirm their policy in this respect by making it plain to British authorities and British nationals in China that they should refrain from such acts and measures." (Antony Best, *Britain, Japan, and Pearl Harbour: Avoiding War in East Asia, 1936–1941*, 1995)

As a result of this accommodating attitude on the part of the British, and particularly Ambassador Craigie, this Arita-Craigie agreement was concluded on 24 July.

The opposition to this came from the United States. On 26 July 1939, the United States gave notice of termination of the United States–Japan Treaty of Commerce and Navigation, an action it had been contemplating for some time. This inspired a change in the British stance as well, and the British broke off talks with Japan, saying they would discuss security issues but not issues of economics. They also minimized the significance of the agreement just concluded, arguing that it was merely an acknowledgment of the realities of the situation. Britain was already being placed in an increasingly difficult position in Europe, but it did not intend to make any further concessions.

In a letter to Hatoyama Ichirō (a Seiyūkai Diet member whose father, Kazuo, was a Yale graduate), Asakawa Kan'ichi, then a professor at Yale, wrote that he had heard that "in Tianjin, Englishmen were being strip-searched [by Japanese troops], and even women were being made to remove their slips" (Itō Takashi and Suetake Yoshiya, eds., *Hatoyama Ichirō, Kaoru nikki* [Diaries of Hatoyama Ichirō and Kaoru], vol. 1, 19 August 1939). Whether or not this was true, such rumors were afoot in the United States, and it is not difficult to imagine the impact they must have had on public opinion.

Failure to Separate the Anglo-American Powers

The confrontation between Japan and Great Britain in Tianjin provoked a wave of anti-British agitation throughout Japan. Kiyosawa Kiyoshi wrote that such a broad and explicit movement directed against a single country was unprecedented. On the other hand, Japan was seeking to improve its relations with the United States. In short, there were hopes that the Anglo-American powers might be dealt with separately.

When Saitō Hiroshi, Japanese ambassador to the United States, died of disease on 26 February 1939, in Washington, D.C., the US government dispatched the cruiser *Astoria* to carry the ambassador's ashes home to Japan, which arrived there on 17 April. This was received as a token of US friendship toward Japan, giving rise to a pro-American public mood.

The government as well had no desire to make enemies of the Americans, and on 28 May, Prime Minister Hiranuma had a confidential meeting with Eugene H. Dooman, US embassy counselor and chargé d'affaires, in which he proposed cooperative efforts to forestall war in Europe. But the US response to this was cool: on 8 July, Secretary of State Cordell Hull suggested that the first order of business should be to put things in order in East Asia.

Since about 1938, the United States had been considering sanctions against Japan, but it was clear that one of the obstacles to such action was the free-trade provisions of the United States–Japan Treaty of Commerce and Navigation. On 18 July 1939, amid the Anglo-Japanese tensions surrounding the blockade of the British concession in Tianjin, matters had progressed to the point that a resolution was introduced into the US Senate to abrogate the treaty. Then, on 26 July, the US government went ahead to announce its intention to terminate the treaty. Historically, Matthew Perry and Townsend Harris had come to Japan in the cause of free trade. Now the United States was choosing to move in the direction of shutting it down.

In a diary entry of 30 July 1939, Ugaki wrote: "There have always been many in our country who argue an anti-British and pro-American stance. And for many years I have felt that while that might be desirable, it was virtually impossible. Even if attempted, it would probably not work, because when it comes down to it, blood is thicker than water, and in a pinch the Anglo-Saxons will act in concert" (Tsunoda Jun, ed., *Ugaki Kazushige nikki* [Diary of Ugaki Kazushige]).

Ugaki was especially critical of those who were overly quick to interpret the sympathy the United States showed for Ambassador Saitō as general US goodwill toward Japan. He saw them as unable to distinguish between diplomatic etiquette and international politics. Ugaki also was skeptical of the argument that since the United States did not have particularly large interests and concessions in China, there was little reason for conflict with Japan, saying that this was a self-serving analysis that failed to understand "that the atmosphere towards Japan in the US derives from emotions and rhetoric, and has little to do with logic or interests." He wrote:

> The pro-American fever seems to be reaching a peak, but as I've said many times before, it is terribly difficult to be anti-British and pro-American. . . . The loan [from America] that some people talk about is still a dream, and it is nothing more than an illusion, I think that the recent unexpected announcement of the termination of the US-Japan treaty should have awakened people from these fantasies in a flash. (*Ugaki Kazushige nikki*, 30 July 1939)

Ugaki was addressing those who were preaching the idea that the United States and Britain could be treated separately and were boasting that the US abrogation of the commerce treaty was merely for domestic political consumption, or that the United States would really be the one to suffer from the impact of this move.

The Nomonhan Incident

During the period of the Hiranuma cabinet, Japan was beset by yet another serious foreign policy issue: the Nomonhan Incident, which erupted at the end of May 1939 on the border between Manchukuo and Mongolia. The western border of Manchukuo, where it met Mongolia, had never been very clearly defined. On 11 May, Mongolian forces crossed over a borderline that was claimed by Japan, and were repulsed by elements of the Kwantung Army. The following day other "border crossings" were observed, but by the time the Japanese Twenty-third Division, stationed in Hailar, was mobilized, Mongolian forces had already withdrawn. Repeated "border crossings" followed, and on 21 May the commander of the Twenty-third Division ordered an offensive by a task force under the command of Colonel Yamagata Takemitsu.

Yamagata's force, which had initiated action on 27 May, encountered a mechanized Soviet division with far superior firepower. According to the terms of a treaty of mutual assistance between the Soviet Union and Mongolia, the Soviets were committed to the defense of Mongolia. The Japanese force was defeated, sustaining casualties of 159 dead, 119 wounded, and 12 missing, and was forced to withdraw on 31 May.

It would have been well had the matter ended there. But the Kwantung Army wanted to recover its prestige by striking a blow at the Soviet army. On the other hand, the Soviets knew that Japan was preoccupied with the war in China and could not commit its full strength to fight the Soviet Union, and thought this might be an opportunity to hit the Japanese. From 2 to 5 July, the Japanese mounted a major offensive, but were defeated by Soviet mechanized units. At the end of July, the Japanese had begun preparing for another major assault. But on 20 August the Soviet army unleashed a ferocious bombing raid using 150 planes, followed by an attack with ground forces. Japanese forces fled beyond the border claimed by Mongolia. Of the 15,000 Japanese troops committed by the Twenty-third Division, a third were killed and another third wounded. In the end, 8,400 Japanese were killed at Nomonhan, and 8,800 were wounded. The normal ratio of dead to wounded in combat was one to three; the high proportion of deaths shows how futile the Japanese operations had been. Imperial General Headquarters ordered the Kwantung Army to suspend operations on 3 September, and a truce agreement was signed in Moscow on 15 September.

Since the time of the Manchurian Incident, the Soviet Union had been steadily building up its military forces in the surrounding region. This was the situation that had been predicted in Japan during the crisis of 1935–1936. Ugaki, who at the time had been promoting the mechanization of the Japanese army, later wrote of the Nomonhan Incident as follows, in his inimitable style:

> In years past, when I was minister of the army, I reduced the army by four divisions in an attempt to divert the operating budget to mechanize and modernize the forces as a first step towards great reforms to revitalize the Army, but among my successors was a gang who boasted of bamboo-spear tactics, not only frustrating the reforms but painting me as some sort of disarmament fanatic, which had a chilling effect on morale within the ranks. I thought this propaganda was a deliberate and malicious slander directed against me, which was a bitter pill to swallow, but since the autumn of last year I began to wonder if this might not be a misperception on my part. In light of the shock these military men displayed at the Nomonhan disaster and the present capabilities of the German armies, I now realize that this crew really believed that their priority in improving and expanding the Army was simply to increase the number of divisions, and that this conviction meant they sincerely thought of my efforts to trade divisions for mechanization and modernization was a form of disarmament. While we should be grateful for the exposure at Nomonhan of the Army's lack of preparedness and the recent activities of the German armies, the fact that these military men are so astonished at these developments is an indication of the poverty of their judgment concerning technology, and it is men possessed of such poor judgment who have currently embroiled us in a protracted war. If, as I have been saying for years, we had taken the spirit of Genghis Khan's tactics and put it to work in modern mechanized warfare, then we could have driven Chiang and his gang out of China long ago, and that would have been the end of it. There's not much to be done about it now, which is extremely regrettable. (*Ugaki Kazushige nikki*, 30 May 1940)

World War II Begins

Even as it was concluding a military alliance with Italy, Germany also began a rapprochement with the Soviet Union. The Soviet Union, encountering difficulties in its negotiations with Britain and France, was receptive to these overtures. On 21 August 1939, Germany informed Japan that it planned to conclude a nonaggression pact with the Soviet Union, which was signed, along with a secret protocol, on 23 August. This news shocked the world, but was particularly shocking to the Hiranuma cabinet, which was still wrestling with the issue of what to do about the Anti-Comintern Pact. The stinging defeat Japan had suffered at Nomonhan, and the fact that it was still bogged down in the war with China, only deepened the dismay. On 25 August the cabinet informed Germany that it was breaking off negotiations regarding the revision of the Anti-Comintern Pact, and on 28 August the cabinet resigned en masse, issuing a famous statement expressing its astonishment at the "complex and bizarre events arising in the realm of Europe."

When the nonaggression pact between Germany and the Soviet Union was signed, Ugaki criticized the Japanese authorities in his diary, remarking that since foreign papers had been writing for some time about the increasing similarity of German and Soviet interests and the fact that Hitler had suddenly stopped his verbal attacks on communism since the preceding year, this situation was something that could have been predicted.

Journalist (and later politician) Ishibashi Tanzan saw this turn of events as shameful for Japan, but also perhaps a blessing in disguise, as it might provide a turning point for Japanese diplomacy. Ugaki shared this view.

Having signed the nonaggression pact with the Soviet Union, Germany invaded Poland on 1 September 1939. Britain and France, which had mutual

The German-Soviet Non-Aggression Pact

On 23 August 1939, German foreign minister Joachim von Ribbentrop and Soviet minister of foreign affairs Vyacheslav Molotov signed an agreement pledging mutual nonaggression between their two countries. In this photo, Joseph Stalin, general secretary of the Communist Party of the Soviet Union (middle right) *stands next to Ribbentrop* (middle left) *while Molotov signs the pact. Photo courtesy of Album, Fine Art Images, and Kyodo News Images Inc.*

security treaties with Poland, declared war on Germany. World War II had begun. Within two weeks the blitzkrieg campaign of the German army, with heavy deployment of its armored divisions, destroyed the Polish military.

The Abe Cabinet

Around 22 August, the day after the news of the German-Soviet nonaggression pact reached Japan, the search for a new prime minister was begun by the associates of Lord Keeper of the Privy Seal Yuasa and Prince Saionji. Konoe envisaged a cabinet headed by Kōdōha general Araki Sadao, and Prince Saionji was briefly sympathetic to this idea, but soon changed his mind. Konoe relented, and for a time Hirota Kōki became the prime candidate. But Hirota was neither ready nor determined to take up the post. The next names that arose for consideration were Ikeda Shigeaki and Ugaki Kazushige.

Saionji was prepared to go with the unconventional choice of Ikeda, a central figure in the Mitsui zaibatsu who had served as Konoe's finance minister, but on the condition that Konoe would claim this choice as his own idea. This was to pin Konoe down, since he was prone to be irresponsible and noncommittal. Konoe would not rise to the occasion, however, and the Ikeda plan was dropped.

Certainly, with the conclusion of the German-Soviet nonaggression pact, the policy line of pursuing closer relations with Germany was in retreat. So it seemed to be the turn of those who wanted to improve relations with the United States and Britain. This was the principal reason that Ikeda had emerged as a candidate. But there was a problem with a major shift in this direction, and that was whether the army would be willing to go along with it.

As a result, in the end, the imperial order to form a cabinet went to the army's recommendation, to General Abe Nobuyuki. To his credit, Abe, who had occupied a number of important posts in the General Staff and the Ministry of Army, had not previously been an adherent of the pro-German line. This gave the army no choice but to accept a retreat from its pro-German position; on the other hand, it was promoting a candidate who was neither pro-British nor pro-American. The order was handed down on 28 August.

Emperor Shōwa himself was a major influence on the formation of this cabinet. Abe had no prior experience at the ministerial level, and if there had been vocal opposition from any quarter, he might not have been given the job, but the emperor had fond memories of Abe as his tutor in military affairs, and this sealed the selection (it also helped that Kido Kōichi's eldest daughter was married to Abe's eldest son). The emperor also, and quite unusually, made several requests with regard to the formation of the cabinet: that either Hata Shunroku or Umezu Yoshijirō be considered for army minister; that priority be placed on cooperation with Britain and the United States; and that particular care be exercised in the selection of the justice and home ministers. The instruction to cooperate with the Anglo-American powers was something the emperor had said on a number of prior occasions, but the other two admonitions were unprecedented—especially the first. This is an indication of how displeased the emperor had been with the behavior of the army during the whole business of the revision of the Anti-Comintern Pact. The emperor obviously hoped that the by-the-book Hata or Umezu (he was especially well-disposed to Hata, who had served as his chief aide-de-camp) would work to rein in such tendencies. The third point was an expression of his dissatisfaction with Minister of Justice Shiono, a member of the Hiranuma clique, as well as with Minister of Home Affairs Kido for failing to contain the anti-British agitation.

The lineup of the Abe cabinet was Ohara Naoshi as home minister, Aoki Kazuo as finance minister, Hata Shunroku as army minister, and Yoshida Zengo as navy minister. Party-affiliated ministers were limited to Nagai Ryūtarō (Minseitō) holding concurrent posts as communications and railways ministers; Kanemitsu Tsuneo (Seiyūkai) as minister of colonial affairs; and Akita Kiyoshi, who had already left the Seiyūkai, as welfare minister (replacing Ohara, who held the post concurrently with that of home minister until 29 November).

Not long after the cabinet was formed, Nomura Kichisaburō of the navy was appointed foreign minister (replacing Prime Minister Abe, who had held the post concurrently until that time). Nomura's deep experience with the United States was expected to prove useful in mending Japan's relations with that country. Reviewing the appointments of foreign ministers, we see that after a period of pan-Asianist policies after the Saitō and Okada cabinets' choice of Hirota as foreign minister and the Hirota cabinet's appointment of Arita Hachirō, the Hayashi cabinet selected the pro-Anglo-American Satō Naotake as foreign minister. Then after Hirota returned to the post, he was followed by the pro-Anglo-American Ugaki, who was succeeded by the pan-Asianist Arita, with Nomura next in line. This apparent inconsistency actually represents a recurring series of swings between right and left, in the midst of which the pro-Anglo-American forces had been gradually weakening overall. But with the outbreak of war preoccupying the European powers, the choice of the new foreign minister reflected a concern for Japan's relations with the United States—something Ugaki also welcomed.

At the time, the most urgent task was to forestall the termination of the United States–Japan Treaty of Commerce and Navigation. After a period of home leave, Ambassador Grew had returned to Japan, and on 19 October gave a famous speech sternly admonishing Japan regarding its policies in China. In response to this, Ugaki noted that abrogation of the treaty by the

United States had been a nonverbal critique of Japan's attitude in an attempt to induce Japan to reconsider its policies; next came Ambassador Grew's speech as a verbal attempt to get Japan to reconsider. Next, he observed, "This was another way to wake Japan up, when facts were not enough." This was a keen insight into the overall situation of the times.

One important issue regarding the termination of the United States–Japan Treaty of Commerce and Navigation was the reopening of the Yangtze River to international navigation. Since the siege of Nanjing, the fate of shipping on the Yangtze, the major transportation artery to Nanjing, had become a major concern. Even after the fall of Nanjing, Japan had prohibited international shipping traffic on the river. This action was protested by a number of countries that found it especially reprehensible that Japanese military vessels were engaging in commercial trade. In other words, Japan was trading while at the same time blocking other nations from doing so. A meeting of the Asia Development Board (Kōain) decided on 8 December that beginning in February 1940, the stretch of the Yangtze below Nanjing should be opened to international shipping. Japan thought this move might appease the United States and avoid the termination of the commerce and navigation treaty, but such hopes were in vain.

Confusion in China

Meanwhile, the political and military situation in China had descended into chaos. Wang Jingwei, who had visited Tokyo at the end of May 1939, returned to China on 18 June to prepare for the establishment of a new government, and at the end of September convened the sixth national congress of the Kuomintang in Shanghai in an effort to assert the legitimacy of his new government as a continuation of the former Nationalist government. But this congress failed, forcing Wang Jingwei into negotiations with Wang Kemin of the Provisional Government of the Republic of China in Beiping, and Liang Hongzhi of the Reformed Government of the Republic of China in Nanjing.

When Wang Jingwei reengaged negotiations with the Japanese on 1 November 1939, he found that the conditions presented by the Japanese had changed significantly, with backpedaling from what they had decided upon in the agreement signed on 20 November 1938. Mongolia-Xinjiang was marked as a special anti-Comintern autonomous zone, and the boundaries of that zone had been expanded; other special zones were to be established in North China, the lower Yangtze, and South China; and timing of Japanese troop withdrawals was left deliberately vague. This was a major disappointment for Wang. These contradictions began with the deliberations at the Imperial Conference of 30 November 1938 and were confirmed in the Five Ministers Conference of May 1939, but the content of these decisions had never been fully conveyed to Wang. Wang insisted on the conditions set forth in the transcript of the talks that had taken place a year before, but Kagesa Sadaaki, the army intelligence officer who had been one of the principal negotiators of the original agreement, countered this by claiming that Wang had not established the power base (especially military forces) that he had promised, and negotiations bogged down.

However, with concessions by Wang, a new agreement was finally put together on 30 December 1939. This comprised an outline, basic principles, specific principles, and sets of both confidential and top secret items of agreement. The only portion of the document to be released to the public was the portion concerning basic principles. But on 4 January 1940, Wang's close associates Gao Zongwu and Tao Xisheng, who had worked in concert with him up to this point, defected and fled to Hong Kong. Then, on 21 January, the content of the 30 December agreement was exposed in the newspapers. Wang claimed that what was printed was only a partial draft, and that there had been later amendments, but this was undeniably a major shock. Wang would eventually establish his new government on 30 March 1940 (by this time the Yonai cabinet had taken power in Japan), but given the circumstances related earlier, it was hopeless that it could become a viable replacement for the Chongqing regime.

The military situation in China was similarly confused. Japanese armies confronted a major Nationalist force in the vicinity of Hankou and Jiujiang, while working elsewhere to stabilize and secure occupied areas. Lieutenant-General Okamura Yasuji, commander of the frontline Eleventh Army, insisted in November 1939 that the objective should be to destroy the forces under the direct command of Chiang Kai-shek. Okamura argued that the core of China's war-making capacity was not its 400 million people, nor the rabble of warlord armies, but the officer crops trained at the Whampoa Military Academy. There was some truth to this assessment. Though Okamura's advice was not accepted, a Chinese counterattack soon ensued—an attempt, commencing around 12 December, to retake the city of Hankou. Until the end of January 1940, some seventy Chinese divisions (though their unit strength was smaller than a corresponding Japanese division) hurled themselves against the Japanese Eleventh Army, forcing a bitter defense. The Eleventh Army repulsed the attack, and the Chinese left 50,000 dead on the battlefield, while the Japanese suffered 2,100 dead and 6,200 wounded.

From the Abe to the Yonai Cabinet

On 20 October 1939, the Abe cabinet made a decision to freeze all commodity prices at the level of 18 September of that year. Coupled with domestic factors, the outbreak of the war in Europe had produced inflation.

Accompanying the price freeze was a freeze on wages. The National Mobilization Act, which up to this point had scarcely been utilized, was now put into full effect: provisions for management, utilization, and expropriation of factories, places of business, and materials were invoked, and controls on corporate profits were initiated. Controls even extended to the rural landholding system, with the 1938 Agricultural Land Adjustment Act supplemented on 11 December by an ordinance for the control of rents paid by tenant farmers.

Meanwhile, this year saw droughts in western Japan and Korea, with crop failures in Korea, which had a particularly heavy impact because it had become a major supplier of rice to the home islands of Japan. Severe drought also put the squeeze on hydroelectric power, crippling not only civilian but also military-related industries. In the midst of all this, on 20 December the army minister and chief of general staff presented the emperor with a four-year plan for military expansion, aiming at a force of 65 divisions and 160 air squadrons by fiscal year 1943. Truly, it seemed the sky was the limit.

In these circumstances, when the Diet session opened, there was a movement afoot to present the Abe cabinet with a vote of no confidence. To head this off, Abe considered dissolving the Diet and holding a general election. But the army was afraid that holding an election might encourage the spread of antiwar opinion. Nor had the army been that keen on Abe in the first place. This put Abe in a position in which he was unable to dissolve the Diet, and instead his cabinet resigned.

It was Yonai Mitsumasa, who had been serving as navy minister, who received the imperial order to form the next cabinet. Initially, either Sugiyama Hajime or Konoe Fumimaro had been favored as the most likely candidates, with Minister of Army Hata Shunroku also a strong possibility. But it was Yonai—who had staunchly opposed the strengthening of the Anti-Comintern Pact—who was selected. This was because the officials of the imperial palace did not want to see Japan drawing closer to Germany. The emperor was delighted by the choice, to the point that he did not deliver his usual admonishment concerning the importance of cooperation with Britain and the United States. With Yonai, this went without saying. The Yonai cabinet was formed 16 January 1940, with two cabinet members from the Minseitō, including Sakurauchi Yukio as finance minister, and two from the Seiyūkai, Shimada Toshio (agriculture and forestry) and Matsuno Tsuruhei (railways)—a cabinet composition that recalled the days of the Saitō and Okada cabinets.

Ugaki Kazushige's take on this change in government was interesting. Ugaki had been quite favorably disposed toward the Abe cabinet. During the period when Araki and Masaki had been riding high, Abe had distanced himself from Ugaki, and Ugaki had not forgotten this. He did not see Abe as an especially logical or coherent individual, but still had hopes for him as prime minister. However, three months into the new cabinet, Ugaki was already criticizing Abe for what he said might be politely termed "inconsistency" and in more vulgar terms "bullshit." And when Abe resigned, Ugaki wrote: "He swallowed whole the scenario written for him by the men of the Army, but danced ineptly to their tune, and now they have thrown him aside. It's almost unbearably pathetic and at the same time I am dumfounded by the heartlessness of the Army" (*Ugaki Kazushige nikki* [Diary of Ugaki Kazushige], 10 January 1940).

Around this time, Ugaki came to be openly critical of the army. On 8 October 1939 he had written: "The people have given the Army exactly the budget it wanted for the last two or three years. Yet in the public announcements it has made regarding what happened at Nomonhan, the Army seems to be complaining that it didn't have adequate armaments or the best troops—but at this point it is in no position to make such claims." This was followed by an entry on 4 December: "There are a lot of politicians who seem to think that the theme of politics these days is working to accommodate to the tyranny of the military. But what concerns me is how best to correct this military tyranny." This was a fundamental difference.

From this point of view, the next cabinet had to be one that was not under the thumb of the army. An army cabinet was being advocated in certain quarters, but as far as Ugaki was concerned, this was unacceptable: a government headed by the same crew that had already proven incapable of keeping their subordinates in line would be "an indulgent gamble." For this reason, when the order to form the cabinet was given unexpectedly to Admiral Yonai, Ugaki said it was a choice superior to all the other names that had been mentioned to date (*Ugaki Kazushige nikki* [Diary of Ugaki Kazushige], 14 January 1940).

The Expulsion of Saitō Takao

Soon after the formation of the Yonai cabinet, on 1 February the Diet began its next session. The first item on the agenda was the adoption of the budget that had been submitted by the Abe cabinet. This was an unprecedentedly massive budget, totaling ¥10.3 billion, of which ¥4.5 billion was earmarked for extraordinary military spending.

This provided the context for a famous incident: Saitō Takao's speech in the Diet opposing the military. On 2 February 1940, Saitō, a member of the Minseitō, held the floor of the Diet for two hours with a speech addressing the government's plan for management of the Sino-Japanese War. Saitō was a hardcore liberal known for making a number of major speeches in the past, and this time he took up the subject of the war and asked what were the conditions for its resolution. If the conditions were those set forth in the Konoe Statement, then how was respect for the independence of China to be reconciled with the construction of a New Order in East Asia? How was refraining from infringement on the rights of foreign powers to be reconciled with the liberation of China from Western exploitation? If Japan was not after territory or indemnities, then where were the funds for the war and reconstruction to come from? And what precisely was this "New Order" in East Asia anyway? Was there anything more to it than good-neighbor relations, anticommunism, and economic cooperation? Saitō pressed sternly onward. He demanded to know when and how the war could be brought to an end, and he was critical of branding this as a "holy war" (*seisen*) so that it could command unlimited sacrifice on the part of the Japanese people—something he dismissed as empty rhetoric and hypocrisy.

When Saitō ended his speech there were applause and cheers, and many of the Diet members praised Saitō for his characteristic eloquence. The war was becoming a stalemate, and Saitō had pinpointed this. The speech is usually called an "anti-military speech," but in fact it was not. Saitō acknowledged that wars were sometimes necessary, and his basic tone

Saitō Takao (1870–1949)
Saitō graduated from Waseda University, became a lawyer, and studied at Yale Law School. He was elected to the House of Representatives thirteen times, beginning in 1912. In the sixty-ninth special session of the Diet in 1936, he delivered a speech calling for disciplining the army in the wake of the February Twenty-Sixth Incident, and in 1940 was expelled from the Diet for another speech critical of the military— evidence of the extent to which the political parties were collapsing from within. Photo courtesy of Kyodo News Images Inc.

was realistic. He criticized the government's policies, not with empty rhetoric but with a tough and logical realism, in one of the most eloquent addresses the Japanese parliamentary system ever produced. However, Saitō's speech was soon under attack as blasphemy against Japan's holy war, and there were enough opportunistic politicians among the ranks of the Diet that Saitō was eventually expelled from the House of Representatives, in the most shameful event in the history of that institution.

Yet there was also strong opposition to Saitō's expulsion. A portion of the Minseitō, the Hatoyama faction of the Seiyūkai, and part of the Shakai Taishūtō stood with him. But a number of these individuals were in turn expelled from or disciplined by their parties—who were afraid of the military. On 25 March 1940, certain members of the House of Representatives formed a League of Diet Members Supporting the Prosecution of the Holy War, in direct opposition to what Saitō had enunciated in his speech. They upheld the Konoe Statement and New Order in East Asia, criticized the free-market economy, and attacked the Yonai cabinet. It goes without saying that the army was behind their activities.

The Widening War

In Europe, England and France had declared war on Germany in September 1939 after the invasion of Poland, but combat had not yet begun. All was still quiet on the Western Front. But on 9 April 1940, Germany staged a blitzkrieg invasion of Denmark and Norway. Then, on 10 May, German armies invaded northern France, the Netherlands, Belgium, and Luxembourg. In France, they broke through the vaunted Maginot Line, dealing a decisive blow to the French and British defenders. The British forces in France were pushed to the coast and withdrew through Dunkirk. In Britain, Neville Chamberlain's cabinet collapsed; and on 14 June the German forces bloodlessly occupied Paris. On 10 June, Italy entered the war on the side of Germany. There were those who predicted that Britain would stubbornly continue to fight, but the vast majority believed that the British, too, would soon capitulate to German military superiority.

With the surrender of the Netherlands and France, the Dutch East Indies (now Indonesia) and French Indochina (now Vietnam, Laos, and Cambodia) emerged as a power vacuum. This happened to come at a time when Japanese tensions with the United States were finally reaching a critical point, and Japan was beginning to suffer from deficiencies in natural resources. Germany's impressive string of victories also contributed to a powerful revival of sentiment favoring closer German ties.

In response to Japanese demands, on 17 June 1940 the authorities in French Indochina cut off supplies of weapons, ammunition, trucks, and gasoline that had been reaching Chiang Kai-shek's government in Chongqing via Indochina. Additional pressure persuaded French Indochina to accept the dispatch of Japanese military specialists to monitor compliance with this ban, effectively eliminating French Indochina as a source of supply for Nationalist China. On 24 June 1940, Japan took advantage of Britain's difficulties to demand a similar suspension of the transport of military supplies through Burma, and Britain agreed to close the Burma route for three months.

But the Yonai cabinet was cautious. Minister of Foreign Affairs Arita Hachirō gave a radio broadcast on 29 June but did not even mention joining the Axis powers. The military police suspected foreign ministry information officer Suma Yakichirō of deliberately deleting this from Arita's broadcast speech, and interrogated him on this subject. The tyranny of the army was now extending even to senior foreign ministry officials engaged in the performance of their duties.

On 3 July, a meeting of top army officials of both the ministry and General Staff approved a plan for military expansion into Southeast Asia. Then, the key personnel of the General Staff, in the name of its chief, presented Minister of Army Hata with a request for the exercise of his good offices in bringing about a "strong national unity cabinet"—in other words, they were asking him to topple the current cabinet. On 16 July, Minister of Army Hata resigned from the cabinet. When Prime Minister Yonai asked the army to nominate a replacement, it refused, and Yonai's cabinet was forced to resign en masse.

Ugaki and the Yonai Cabinet

After resigning as foreign minister in the Konoe cabinet, Ugaki Kazushige frequently made insightful observations on political affairs. Of the preceding four cabinets—Konoe, Hiranuma, Abe, and Yonai—Ugaki was unquestionably strongest in his support for Yonai. He was also moved by Saitō Takao's Diet speech. In a diary entry for 5 April 1940, Ugaki wrote as follows of the role of the Diet:

> We must wipe away the outdated and pernicious notion that politics is something that should be left entirely to professional politicians, military men, and bureaucrats. We must eliminate the deplorable situation in which a refusal to cut even a few dollars and cents from the military budget is seen as an expression of national unity and the key to prosecution of the war. We must throw open the door widely to frank and forthright deliberations on the fiscal policy of our nation, at least to the extent that they do not reveal military secrets. The bureaucrats, the military, and the people must all give this serious consideration! (*Ugaki Kazushige nikki* [Diary of Ugaki Kazushige])

Perhaps it was the fact that he was not currently in a responsible official position that allowed Ugaki to make such observations. But most military men would not have been thinking in this manner, regardless of status. Ugaki really understood the role of the Diet and the political parties, and this was one of the reasons he was rejected by the army.

Ugaki also had interesting things to say about Germany's initial string of victories in Europe. Tactically, it was brilliant. But if one examined the bigger strategic picture, it was doubtful that this was all to Germany's advantage. Germany's methods meant that neutral countries would not be able to maintain their independence unless they were strong enough to defend themselves or blessed by an advantageous geographical position. "International treaties and international morality have been trampled on by the strong, losing the sympathy and trust of the nations of the world. Just how far the train of absolute power can run will truly be something to see," he wrote (*Ugaki Kazushige nikki* [Diary of Ugaki Kazushige] 10 April 1940). Ugaki believed that even if Germany was able to seize Denmark and Norway, this would be of little value, and the risk of loss from this action might far outweigh the gains. These observations were written prior to Germany's conquest of France, but display an insight Ugaki attained only through participating in government during the previous era of international cooperation.

Konoe's New Party Movement

Behind the Yonai cabinet's collapse was a movement to create a new political party led by Konoe Fumimaro. Konoe's attempt to form a new political party had first surfaced as early as 1938. In February 1938, as the Sino-Japanese War intensified, some 600 khaki-uniformed members of a group calling themselves the Anti-Communist National Defense League (Bōkyō Gokokudan) attempted to invade the headquarters of the Minseitō and Seiyūkai, calling for the dissolution of the established parties. The Minseitō successfully staved off this assault, but Seiyūkai headquarters was temporarily occupied by the demonstrators. In February and March of that year the passage of the legislation related to national mobilization and the expulsion of Nishio Suehiro from the Diet demonstrated a rising tide of sentiment for dissolving the existing parties. Around August of that year, Konoe himself showed active interest in the creation of a new political party, but by the end of October he seemed to have cooled on the idea. The resignation of Ugaki as foreign minister, the success of the Hankou offensive, and the developing negotiations with Wang Jingwei had emboldened Konoe, but the difficulties surrounding the strengthening of the Anti-Comintern Pact soon had him ready to throw in the towel on his cabinet, and as a result the movement toward a new party fizzled out.

However, it should be noted that there were a number of different movements afoot for the creation of a Konoe-led new party—from plans centering on progressive forces to ones almost diametrically opposed, in which the established parties saw support for Konoe as a way to restore their own power. In other words, while everyone seemed to want Konoe as a leader, there was considerable vagueness on what this new party might look like or what its orientation might be.

Here a review of developments within the parties prior to this is useful. Wakatsuki Reijirō resigned the presidency of the Minseitō on 1 November 1934, and Machida Chūji was nominated to succeed him, but initially refused, becoming chairman of the party's executive council. Machida was eventually appointed president on 20 January 1935, but the party never again displayed the unity it had during the era led by Katō, Wakatsuki, and Hamaguchi. As for the Seiyūkai, Suzuki Kisaburō lost the 1936 general election and resigned as party president on 28 February 1937, after which an acting presidential committee of Hatoyama Ichirō, Maeda Yonezō, Shimada Toshio, and Nakajima Chikuhei led the party. However, on 30 April 1939, the Nakajima faction forced an extraordinary meeting of the party general assembly and made Nakajima president. In response to this, the Hatoyama faction and the rest of the party's mainstream held a second extraordinary general assembly on 20 May, and elected as president Kuhara Fusanosuke, who had been indicted in relation to the February Twenty-Sixth Incident but found innocent. This move split the Seiyūkai in half. The Nakajima faction was cooperative with the army, while the mainstream faction was itself divided, with Kuhara supportive of establishing a new political order, and Hatoyama unenthusiastic. Meanwhile, on 9 February 1939, the Shakai Taishūtō (chaired by Abe Isoo) and the Tōhōkai (Far East Society, chaired by Nakano Seigō) convened a meeting for the formation of a new party and issued a joint declaration, but a dispute emerged over who should lead the new organization, and on 22 February these plans were canceled.

The next effort at a Konoe-led new party would begin in 1940, triggered by the expulsion of Saitō Takao from the Diet. As mentioned earlier, a group in favor of his expulsion, called the League of Diet Members Supporting the Prosecution of the Holy War, formed in March 1940. They looked to Konoe for leadership. Beginning in about April, Konoe, Kido Kōichi, and Arima Yoriyasu began discussions regarding the formation of a new party. Developments in the war in Europe were also a significant catalyst.

On 26 May, these three men arrived at the following agreement:

1. No active moves toward formation of a new party should be undertaken prior to receiving the imperial order to form a cabinet. However, if there is spontaneous activity in that direction on the part of the political parties, and momentum for establishing a party develops, this should be considered.

2. Items to be considered in the event that the imperial order is received:
    a. A Supreme National Defense Council should be created, comprising the chiefs of the Army and Navy General Staffs, the prime minister, and the army and navy ministers
    b. The army and navy should be consulted on their wishes with regard to national defense, foreign policy, and fiscal administration
    c. The intention of forming a new party should be announced and existing parties requested to disband themselves
3. A cabinet should be formed with only the prime minister and the army and navy ministers, with other cabinet posts to be held by them concurrently; though depending upon the situation, two or three of the other ministerial posts (for example, foreign minister) might also be filled.
4. As soon as the new party is formed, the rest of the cabinet posts should be filled with talented individuals selected from among its members. Any cabinet members appointed before the formation of the new party must enroll in it.

On 1 June 1940, Yuasa Kurahei resigned as lord keeper of the privy seal and was replaced by Kido Kōichi. Other candidates for the post had been Wakatsuki, Konoe, and Hiranuma. But there was opposition to Wakatsuki because he was tainted as a party politician and had been a target of right-wing criticism since the days of the London Naval Treaty; Prince Saionji was against Hiranuma; and Konoe was being held in reserve as the leading candidate for prime minister—so Kido was appointed privy seal. Saionji had suggested Ichiki Kitokurō or Okada Keisuke as other possibilities, but this went nowhere.

The forces working to destabilize the Yonai cabinet were the army on the one hand and Prince Konoe on the other. Konoe frequently said, and has been frequently quoted as saying, that he was not keen on founding a new party and that he had no desire to be manipulated by the army, but actually he was quite willing. When he was speaking with Harada Kumao, Saionji's secretary, he often concealed his real feelings so as not to arouse Saionji's antipathy, and this should be kept in mind when reading Harada's diary, in many respects one of the most valuable sources for this period.

On 1 June 1940, Konoe met with Yabe Teiji, a political scientist and key figure in Konoe's brain trust, and spoke of his intention to found a new party, composed of about 40 percent members of existing parties and 60 percent new political forces. On 18 June, he notified the government of his intention to step down as president of the Privy Council, which was officially accepted on 24 June. In the announcement of his resignation, Konoe stated: "The necessity of establishing a strong and unified national political structure to deal with the unprecedented foreign and domestic developments of our changing times is recognized by everyone. I am resigning my position as president of the Privy Council at this time so that I may devote all of my energies to the establishment of this new political order."

Following this, Nakano Seigō's Tōhōkai disbanded on 19 June, followed by the Shakai Taishūtō on 6 July. On 16 July, the Kuhara faction of the Seiyūkai dissolved. Then, subsequent to the inauguration of the Konoe cabinet, Nagai Ryūtarō's group defected from the Minseitō on 25 July, calling for the dissolution of the party. On 26 July, Adachi Kenzō's Kokumin Dōmei disbanded, on 30 July the Nakajima faction of the Seiyūkai followed suit, and finally, on 15 August the Minseitō—the standard bearer for party politics and international cooperation from the 1920s onward—was the last of the political parties to dissolve itself.

Kido Kōichi (1889–1977)

Eldest son of Kido Takamasa, Kido Kōichi was the adopted son and heir of Kido Takayoshi, one of the key figures of the Meiji Restoration. Appointed chief secretary to Lord Keeper of the Privy Seal Makino Nobuaki in 1930, he became acquainted with Saionji Kinmochi, Konoe Fumimaro, and Suzuki Teiichi, and participated in Konoe's movement to found a new party. In the 1930s and 1940s, the lord keeper of the privy seal, heading an informal advisory council of former prime ministers and other senior statesmen, gradually supplanted the power of the genrō to play the central role in the selection of candidates for prime minister. Kido, who was appointed as privy seal in June 1940, pushed strongly for the selection of Minister of Army Tōjō Hideki as prime minister in October 1941, following the demise of the third Konoe cabinet. He was given a life sentence at the International Tribunal for the Far East but was released on parole due to illness, living out the rest of his life in retirement. Photo courtesy of Kyodo News Images Inc.

The Second Konoe Cabinet

After the collapse of the Yonai cabinet, the successor was chosen by a *jūshin kaigi*, an informal council of senior statesmen meeting on 17 July 1940. Presided over by Kido Kōichi, lord keeper of the privy seal, the council consisted of Hara Yoshimichi, president of the Privy Council (Konoe's successor in that post), and former prime ministers Wakatsuki, Hirota, Hayashi, Konoe, and Hiranuma. Their choice for the new prime minister was Konoe. Konoe initially declined, but when Kido said that the heads of the military were insisting on a Konoe cabinet, Konoe was nominated. Prince Saionji was not happy with this decision, but did not actively oppose it.

Konoe was immediately given the order to form a cabinet. Minister of Army Hata recommended as his own successor General Tōjō Hideki. On 18 July, the navy indicated that it would be satisfied with the retention of Yoshida Zengo as navy minister, and Konoe selected Matsuoka Yōsuke as foreign minister. On 19 July, Konoe invited these candidates for the top three cabinet posts to Tekigaisō, his private residence in Ogikubo, to discuss fundamental policy—a meeting that later came to be known as the Ogikubo Conference. This was the first meeting of the three men who would play the leading roles in bringing Japan into the Pacific War.

At this conference, it was agreed that "in response to the rapidly changing world situation and in order to swiftly build a New Order in East Asia, we will work to strengthen the Tokyo-Berlin-Rome Axis and cooperate, East and West, to implement a range of important policies." Additional policy guidelines decided upon at this meeting were, first, to sign a boundary agreement and nonaggression pact with the Soviet Union concerning its borders with Japan, Manchuria, and Mongolia, while at the same time building an invincible military power for dealing with the Soviet Union; second, to implement positive measures to incorporate British, French, Dutch, and Portuguese colonial possessions in East Asia and the neighboring islands into the New Order in East Asia; and third, to avoid confrontation with the United States, but to resolutely reject any attempts by it to forcibly interfere with the construction of the New Order in East Asia. Here we see incorporated all of the key policies of the second Konoe cabinet: the Triple Alliance, Japan's expansion into Southeast Asia and the Pacific, and the Soviet-Japanese Neutrality Pact.

The second Konoe cabinet was officially formed on 22 July 1940. The lineup was as follows:

Prime minister: Konoe Fumimaro
Minister of foreign affairs: Matsuoka Yōsuke
Minister of home affairs: Yasui Eiji (House of Peers)
Minister of finance: Kawada Isao (House of Peers, Kōseikai)

Minister of the army: Tōjō Hideki
Minister of the navy: Yoshida Zengo
Minister of justice: Kazami Akira (House of Representatives)
Minister of education: Hashida Kunihiko
Minister of agriculture and forestry: Ishiguro Tadaatsu
    (held concurrently by Prime Minister Konoe until 24 July)
Minister of commerce and industry: Kobayashi Ichizō
Minister of communications: Murata Shōzō
    (House of Peers, Dōwakai)
Minister of railways: Ogawa Gotarō (House of Representatives)
    (held concurrently by Minister of Communications Murata until
    28 September)
Minister of colonial affairs: Akita Kiyoshi (House of Representatives)
    (held concurrently by Minister of Foreign Affairs Matsuoka until
    28 September)
Minister of welfare: Kanemitsu Tsuneo (House of Representatives) (held
    concurrently by Minister of Home Affairs Yasui until 28 September)
President of the Cabinet Planning Board: Hoshino Naoki
Chief cabinet secretary: Tomita Kenji
Director-general of the Cabinet Legislation Bureau: Murase Naoki

Ordinarily when a new cabinet was being formed, the emperor would offer instructions to observe the articles of the constitution, to avoid giving any shocks to the financial system, and to cooperate with the Anglo-American powers. Konoe of course knew this, and also knew that his policy program deviated from it significantly. If he was given such admonishments, he could not readily accept the order to form a cabinet. Konoe argued that the interpretation of the constitution evolved with the changing times, and that relations with Britain and the United States were also changing. To a certain extent, strengthening cooperation with Germany and Italy was unavoidable. Konoe's assertiveness on these points persuaded the emperor to alter his traditional instructions to the new prime minister.

The choice of Yasui Eiji as home minister made the emperor uneasy. During the first Konoe cabinet, Yasui had been a strong advocate of imperial pardons for individuals involved in the February Twenty-Sixth Incident. And Minister of Justice Kazami Akira had been widely rumored to be one of the most fascistic members of the home ministry. Konoe thought he could use the right wing to control the right wing. Konoe's thinking on all of these points prevented the emperor from carrying through his usual policy.

The cabinet meeting of 26 July approved an "Outline of Fundamental National Policy." In terms of foreign policy, it essentially followed the points agreed upon at the Ogikubo Conference. In addition, however, it addressed domestic policy with an item that called for "aiming at a comprehensive unification of national politics through the creation of a powerful new order," whose details included the following three points: "(a) the establishment of a new popular organization whose keynote shall be cooperation and unity between government officials and the people, with each individual contributing to serve the state in accordance with his profession; (b) reform of the parliamentary system to make it responsive to the new political order; and (c) a new orientation in government offices, aiming at unity and efficiency through a fundamental reform of administrative management." This was leading in the direction of the Imperial Rule Assistance Association.

Then, on 27 July, the Liaison Conference approved a document titled "Outline for Measures to Deal with Current Situation in Accordance with World Developments." It acknowledged that a Japanese southward advance was possible even if the Sino-Japanese War remained unresolved, and made the following provisions regarding the possible use of force. If the "China Incident" was resolved, then Japan should seize the opportunity for the exercise of military force in order to solve the issues of southern areas. While the war in China remained unresolved, Japan should avoid actions that might lead to war with third-party nations, but in certain circumstances should not abstain from the use of military force. In such a case, efforts would be made to confine the object of hostilities to Great Britain, "but since it is possible that conflict with the United States might also become unavoidable, we must thoroughly prepare for such a possibility." In other words, at the highest levels of the Japanese government, decisions had come to reflect a level of resignation to war with the United States.

The Tripartite Pact and Stationing of Japanese Troops in Northern French Indochina

The central pillar of the foreign policy of the Konoe cabinet was strengthening Japan's cooperative ties with Germany. On 1 August 1940, Minister of Foreign Affairs Matsuoka sounded out German ambassador Eugen Ott regarding the possibilities of a triple alliance of Japan, Germany, and Italy, and on 23 August, Ott informed Matsuoka that German foreign minister Joachim von Ribbentrop was sending one of his trusted advisers, Heinrich Georg Stahmer, as a special envoy to Japan. Minister of Navy Yoshida Zengo was unenthusiastic about the conclusion of such an alliance, but his objections were overcome. Okada and other senior figures in the navy had supported Yoshida, but there were others in the navy who agreed with the concept of the alliance. On 5 September, Yoshida resigned, claiming illness, and was replaced by Oikawa Koshirō.

Stahmer arrived from Germany on 7 September. Just before this, beginning in late August, Germany had begun a fierce aerial bombardment of

London, which grew even fiercer after the night of 8 September. Stahmer's goal was to use Japan as a check upon the United States entering the war against Germany. His proposal was an agreement in which the signatories "promised to assist and aid one another, using any and all political, economic, and military means, in circumstances in which any one of the three nations was attacked by any nation not presently participating in the war in Europe or the Sino-Japanese War." The nation not currently involved in either the war in Europe or the Sino-Japanese War that had the capacity to attack either Germany or Japan was of course the United States.

On 12 September, a Four Ministers Conference (prime, foreign, army, and navy) was convened, and Minister of Navy Oikawa joined the others in assenting to this tripartite alliance, after receiving assurances that it was intended as a deterrent and that it did not mandate an automatic commitment to declare war. This decision was in turn adopted by the cabinet on 16 September and approved in an Imperial Conference on 19 September. Concern was expressed over the effect this might have in terms of worsening relations with the United States and making access to essential raw materials more difficult, but in the end the cabinet's assurances were accepted. After a bit of further negotiation with the Germans, the Privy Council gave its approval on 26 September, and the following day, September 27, the Tripartite Pact was signed in Berlin by Japanese ambassador Kurusu Saburō, German foreign minister von Ribbentrop, and Italian foreign minister Galeazzo Ciano.

In 1939, during the Hiranuma cabinet, the army had promoted a strengthening of Japan's ties with Germany but had been blocked by the opposition of the foreign ministry and the navy. But this time, Minister of Foreign Affairs Matsuoka was pushing for the alliance, and so was Prime Minister Konoe. In such circumstances, it was difficult for the navy to maintain its opposition. It is also unclear how committed Konoe himself was, and why. But this issue had been a source of anxiety for the three preceding governments of Hiranuma, Abe, and Yonai. Konoe appears to have decided that since the army was pushing for a strengthening of ties with the Axis, and the political situation could not be stabilized without the cooperation of the army, there was no choice but to accept the Tripartite Pact. In other words, his decision was grounded in his judgment of domestic politics rather than on foreign policy.

The Axis alliance and Japan's movement into French Indochina were closely linked. Already, from 17 to 20 June, the authorities in French Indochina had agreed to a blockade of the route providing war materials to Chiang Kai-shek and accepted the dispatch of a Japanese force to monitor this. Then beginning on 1 August, talks were held concerning French rights and concessions in the Far East and Japan's special interests in French Indochina. An agreement was reached on 30 August that would permit Japan to use a number of air bases in French Indochina and gave it the right

Popular rallies celebrating the Tripartite Alliance
On 13 October 1940, large rallies were held at six different Tokyo locations, including Hibiya Park, Shiba Park, and the Outer Gardens of Meiji Shrine. (From Gahō yakushin no Nihon *[Illustrated journal of Japan's advance], December 1940)*

to station troops there. There were difficulties in working out the particulars, and conflict arose—but on 22 September, Japan began stationing troops in northern Indochina. In response to this, US secretary of state Cordell Hull declared on 23 September that the United States would not accept such a coercive disruption of the status quo. Then, on 28 September, the United States implemented a total embargo on export of scrap metal to Japan, and provided Chiang Kai-shek with a $25 million loan. Secretary of the Treasury Henry Morgenthau Jr. and Secretary of War Henry L. Stimson argued for an embargo on oil as well, but Hull urged caution, and this was held in abeyance.

Prince Saionji was strongly opposed to the Axis alliance. Knowing this, Kido did not keep Saionji informed regarding the Tripartite Pact. Harada Kumao remarked at one point to Saionji, "Some people think Matsuoka might be a bit crazy." From Saionji's reply, we may sense the depth of his concern: "Being a bit crazy is not so bad. What bothers me is this might be what he's like when he's in his right mind." Yet public opinion welcomed the Tripartite Pact. The Tokyo newspaper *Asahi shinbun* praised it in an editorial, saying on 28 September 1940 "we truly cannot contain our joy at this epochal event in the history of international relations."

Early in this book, we noted that Saionji's guiding principle was a priority on foreign policy, and an emphasis on cooperation with the United States and Britain. And now, suddenly, Japan had concluded an alliance that assumed the Anglo-American powers as the hypothetical enemy. This was a fatal blow to the elderly Saionji. He died at the age of ninety on 24 November 1940, and was given a state funeral. Writer Nagai Kafū observed: "What is strange is that our present military government did not treat the prince's passing as ridding them of a nuisance, but instead expressed sorrow and are treating him to the great honor of a state funeral. All one can say is that they must think the people are very stupid indeed" (Nagai Kafū, *Danchōtei nichijō* [The diary of Nagai Kafū], 27 November 1940). In other words, Kafū sharply highlighted the hypocrisy of those who would honor Saionji in death while trampling upon everything he believed in while still living.

The Imperial Rule Assistance Association

A variety of hopes and expectations swirled around the Konoe cabinet with regard to domestic policy, among them the concept of a new economic order. On 28 September, the Cabinet Planning Board (Kikakuin) formulated an "Outline for the Establishment of a New Economic Order" that called for establishing the spirit of a national defense economy, reforming the liberal economic order, organizing the national economy into a comprehensively planned production cooperative, and at the same time creating a framework of national incentives to compensate work defined as national service. This was an overtly totalitarian plan to turn the entire nation into a production collective in which freedom of business activity would be limited and placed under government direction. One key to this was the separation of capital from management. The business community was naturally opposed to this, and it was attacked from the traditional right wing as "Red." As a result, the totalitarian orientation was watered down, the explicit reference to separating capital and management was eliminated, and in December the document was passed as a cabinet resolution. The arrest of bureaucrats Wada Hiroo and Katsumata Seiichi for suspected communist affiliations in the Cabinet Planning Board Incident of April 1941 was one expression of a backlash against this. The minister of commerce and industry, Kobayashi Ichizō, was an entrepreneur who had made his mark in a free economy, and it was about this time (January 1941) that he clashed with the vice minister of commerce and industry, Kishi Nobusuke, a model reform bureaucrat, and had Kishi dismissed.

The Imperial Rule Assistance Association
*The leaders of the association, with Prime Minister Konoe front and center, outside
the prime minister's official residence. Photo courtesy of Kyodo News Images Inc.*

Konoe's efforts to form a new party also ran into difficulties. After all,
parties are an association of individuals sharing similar goals and aspira-
tions, founded on the principle of voluntary association. And because of
this, ordinarily several or more can be formed. On the other hand, there is a
different vision of the political party as an organization of activists formed
to rule the nation—the vanguard party of Lenin, or the totalitarian system
envisioned by the Nazis. Among those promoting Konoe's new party were
fundamental differences of opinion concerning whether the party should be
a powerful new party of ideologically united activists or a looser and more
inclusive association that was open to virtually anyone to join.

In the end, Konoe shifted toward the latter, more inclusive model. He
feared criticism from the traditional right for creating something akin to the
Tokugawa shogunate—in other words, that by establishing a one-party state
under dictatorial leadership, he would be infringing on the imperial prerogative. Konoe himself was strongly influenced by the traditional right, and did
not really feel the urgent necessity for totalitarian control. In his address to
the inaugural meeting of the Imperial Rule Assistance Association (IRAA;
Taisei Yokusankai) on 12 October 1940, he said: "The fundamental principles
of the IRAA are contained in two phrases: assisting the imperial rule and

288

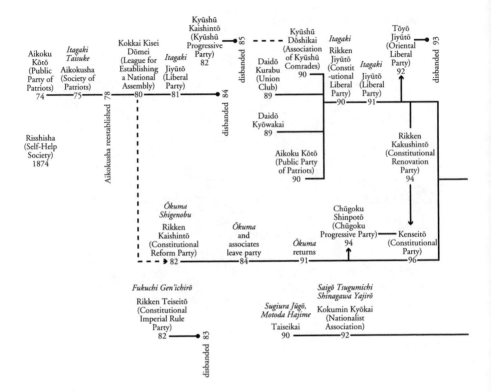

Japan's Political Parties and Factions, 1874–1945

Personal names are those of party leaders

—————— Direct organizational connection

- - - - - - Historical affiliation

84 etc: Numbers represent year of founding

Source: *Nihonshi kōjiten* (Dictionary of Japanese History), Yamakawa Shuppansha.

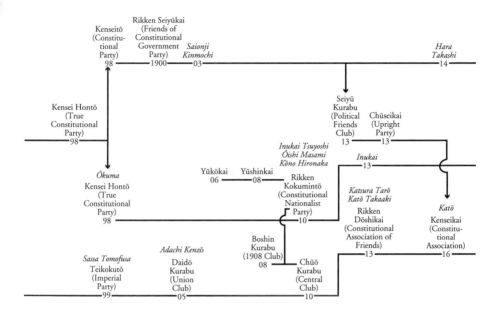

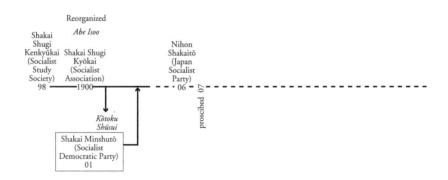

(continues)

Japan's Political Parties and Factions, 1874–1945, *continued*

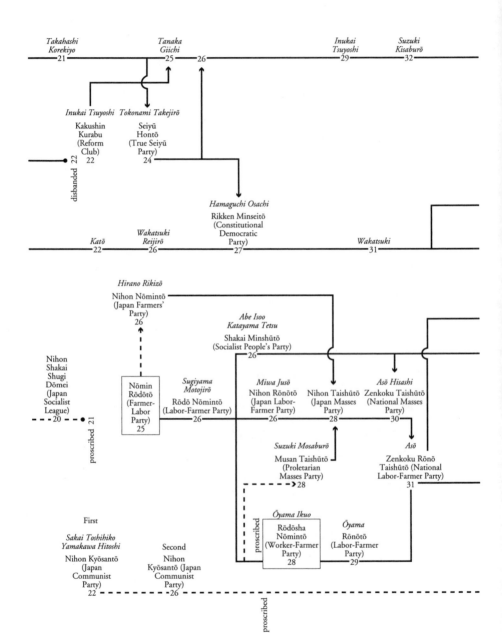

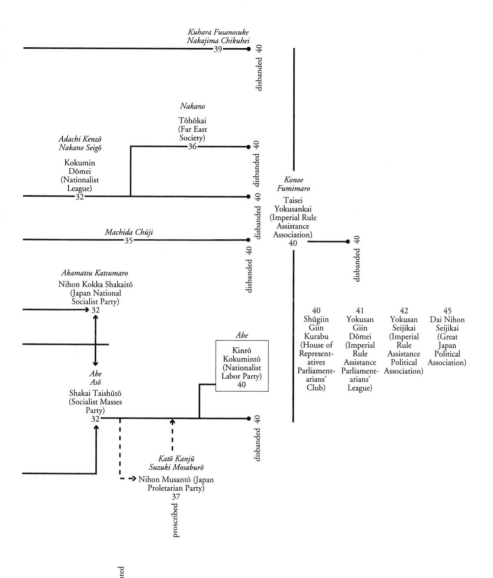

Kuhara Fusanosuke
Nakajima Chikuhei
39

Nakano

Tōhōkai
(Far East
Society)
36

Adachi Kenzō
Nakano Seigō

Kokumin
Dōmei
(Nationalist
League)
32

Machida Chūji
35

Akamatsu Katsumaro

Nihon Kokka Shakaitō
(Japan National
Socialist Party)
32

Abe

Kinrō
Kokumintō
(Nationalist
Labor Party)
40

Abe
Asō

Shakai Taishūtō
(Socialist Masses
Party)
32

Katō Kanjū
Suzuki Mosaburō

Nihon Musantō (Japan
Proletarian Party)
37

Konoe
Fumimaro

Taisei
Yokusankai
(Imperial Rule
Assistance
Association)
40

disbanded 40

40
Shūgiin
Giin
Kurabu
(House of
Representatives
Parliament-
arians'
Club)

41
Yokusan
Giin
Dōmei
(Imperial
Rule
Assistance
Parliament-
arians'
League)

42
Yokusan
Seijikai
(Imperial
Rule
Assistance
Political
Association)

45
Dai Nihon
Seijikai
(Great
Japan
Political
Association)

disbanded 40

proscribed

eliminated

practicing the way of the loyal subject. Aside from these, I believe there is no need for other platforms and pronouncements, but only for each and every one of our people to sincerely serve the common good at all times in all their walks of life." This statement dumbfounded those of a more totalitarian bent, and delighted the traditional right wing. Just before the opening of the Diet session at the end of 1940, Konoe reshuffled his cabinet, adding Hiranuma as a minister without portfolio, replacing Kazami Akira as minister of justice with Kōdōha general Yanagawa Heisuke, and then dismissing Yasui Eiji from his post as home minister and shifting Hiranuma into that post. All of these personnel changes represented advances for the traditional right.

In the Diet, the IRAA came under heavy fire from former members of the established political parties, who criticized it as unconstitutional and communistic. Minister of Home Affairs Hiranuma defended the organization, saying it was not a political association but a public service association, like a public health cooperative. It was certainly not a political party; it was an administrative organization. It became an organ for the dissemination of government policy to the people, and for mobilizing them to support it.

Already, on 1 August, the National Spiritual Mobilization Headquarters had erected 1,500 billboards throughout Tokyo proclaiming "Luxury is the Enemy!" (*Zeitaku wa teki da!*). Leaders of organizations such as the Greater Japan Women's National Defense Association, civil defense units, and veterans associations were beginning to interfere in private life, calling for restraint in everyday dress, abandonment of jewelry, and so forth. In September, the home ministry announced a policy for strengthening and enhancing the role of village councils (*burakukai*), block associations (*chō-naikai*), and neighborhood groups (*tonarigumi*) as the grassroots organizations of the new political order.

The neighborhood groups of five to ten households became the lowest-level building blocks of government administration, shouldering the tasks of allocating rationed goods, collecting savings, distributing government bonds, sending off troops, and collecting scrap metal for wartime industry. The neighborhood and block associations' chairmen became the noncommissioned officers of the nation-state, and the IRAA functioned as the organization representing this system.

The Soviet-Japanese Neutrality Pact

Having concluded the Tripartite Pact, Minister of Foreign Affairs Matsuoka's next goal was a neutrality agreement with the Soviet Union. The German-Soviet Non-Aggression Pact of August 1939 had spurred a reevaluation of Japan's relations with the Soviet Union. At that time, Germany was enthusiastic about cooperative ties among Germany, Italy, the Soviet Union, and Japan, and there were Japanese who were responsive to this idea, such as Shiratori Toshio, former ambassador to Italy. In addition, there was also a proposal that a linkup with the Soviet Union might induce the Soviets to cut off aid to Chiang Kai-shek. And with the outbreak of war on the Western Front, an agreement with the Soviet Union might facilitate Japan's southward advance. In the final days of the Yonai cabinet in July 1940, Tōgō Shigenori, ambassador to the Soviet Union, proposed a neutrality pact to Soviet foreign minister Vyacheslav Molotov. The Soviets agreed to this in principle, but demanded the Japanese give up their coal and oil concessions on northern Sakhalin.

Minister of Foreign Affairs Matsuoka incorporated this idea into a much grander scheme. First, by solidifying the Axis alliance with the Tripartite Pact, Japan could bring Germany's influence to bear on the Soviet Union to create a four-nation entente. Strengthened by this, Japan could then engage in negotiations to resolve its issues with the United States, induce the Americans to pull back from Asia and Europe, and contribute to the restoration of peace. At the beginning of October a plan was drafted for the adjustment of relations with the Soviet Union that called for accommodating the Soviets to a certain degree on the return of the northern-Sakhalin concessions and proposing an agreement defining spheres of influence for Japan in Manchukuo and Inner Mongolia, North China, and Southeast Asia, and for the Soviet Union in Mongolia, Xinjiang, and the Middle and Near East. But the Soviets responded to this by demanding the return of the northern-Sakhalin concessions. In November, there were talks in Berlin between Germany and the Soviet Union concerning the issue of Eastern Europe, and the concept of a four-nation entente entered the discussion, but the Soviets were unenthusiastic. Moreover, in the course of these negotiations, Hitler saw how difficult it would be to reach a compromise with the Soviets, and would arrive at the decision to launch Operation Barbarossa—Germany's surprise attack on the Soviet Union.

In February 1941, the Liaison Conference approved a European trip by Minister of Foreign Affairs Matsuoka to negotiate a four-nation entente. Matsuoka departed for Europe on 12 March, armed with a plan for talks with Germany, Italy, and the Soviet Union. In the prewar era, it was quite unusual for a foreign minister to travel abroad on such a mission. But when Matsuoka spoke with the Germans at the end of March, they expressed no interest in the entente, and instead requested a Japanese attack on Singapore. A frustrated Matsuoka then headed for Moscow, where he dropped the idea of the entente and proposed a nonaggression pact instead. But when he saw that the concession issue was impeding progress of the talks, he began to push for a neutrality pact. Progress continued to be elusive until he met with Stalin on 12 April, which turned the tide and resulted in an agreement.[1]

In addition to the Soviet-Japanese Neutrality Pact, there was a joint declaration to the effect that in order to ensure peace and amicable relations between the two countries, Japan would agree to honor the territorial integrity and inviolability of Mongolia, and the Soviet Union would do the same for Manchukuo. This was a vestige of the earlier idea of a mutual recognition of spheres of influence. The declaration also violated the spirit of the Sino-Soviet Non-Aggression Pact of 1937, and had the effect of driving a wedge between China and the Soviet Union, since it seriously damaged China's claims to sovereignty over Mongolia. With the conclusion of this pact, one more constraint on Japan's southward expansion had been removed. And as far as the Soviet Union was concerned, this also relieved, if only temporarily, the threat posed to it by Japan.

On 22 April, Matsuoka returned to Japan like a conquering hero—just as he had eight years before after Japan's withdrawal from the League of Nations. He now planned to enter into negotiations with the United States. Meanwhile, however, there were two significant developments Matsuoka did not anticipate. The first was Germany's preparations for its invasion of

Konoe greets Matsuoka on his return from Europe
Matsuoka landed at Tachikawa Airfield on the outskirts of Tokyo after signing the Soviet-Japanese Neutrality Pact in Moscow. (From Shashin shūhō *[Weekly photographic journal] no. 166, 1941)*

the Soviet Union. The second was that talks aimed at improving relations with the United States had already commenced in his absence.

Japan at War

The Berlin Olympics

The Berlin Olympics were held in August 1936, and recorded in Leni Riefenstahl's famous documentary film *Olympia* (in two parts, *Festival of Nations* and *Festival of Beauty*). Riefenstahl was accused of being a Nazi collaborator and even rumored to have been Hitler's lover, and for a long time after the war was ostracized from public life. Today she is admired for her cinematography, which was advanced for her time, but her legacy still evokes controversy as an artist who used her talents to support an evil regime.

I have had the opportunity to visit the former Olympic stadium in Berlin, and it is still a forceful and imposing work of architecture. And the polo stadium next to it, with its gigantic statue of horses, also has an uncanny power. The Olympic swimming pool stands quietly to one side. When you think that only a little more than eighty years ago, Hitler stood here and was welcomed by the cheers of the German people, it makes one question how much progress humanity has actually made in the intervening years. It is as if one can still hear the reverberations of those cheering crowds.

Japanese athletes were active in the Berlin Olympics, taking home gold in the triple jump (Tajima Naoto) and marathon (Sohn Kee-chung, Korea) in track and field events; and in swimming, the women's 200-meter breaststroke (Maehata Hideko) and the men's 200-meter breaststroke (Hamuro Tetsuo), the 1,500-meter freestyle (Terada Noboru), and the 800-meter relay. The names of these Japanese are engraved with those of the other medal winners, on the wall of the marathon gate. Germany made the strongest showing, but the United States was second overall in terms of medals won. This was the Olympiad in which Jesse Owens, known in the press as the "Brown Bullet," had such stunning victories. Various other northern European nations also did well. As the title *Festival of Nations* suggests, this was a showcase of national strength and pride.

The Los Angeles Olympics had drawn few European participants, and so it was the 1936 Berlin Games that became the first with truly global competition. Growing interest in sports coincided with a rising tide of nationalism to excite the people of many countries, including Japan. Four years later, the next Olympic Games were scheduled to be held in Tokyo. But the outbreak of the Sino-Japanese War in 1937 led Japan to officially forfeit hosting the Games in July 1938.

Everyday Life in 1937

Despite the fiscal policies initiated in 1936 by Minister of Finance Baba, which featured an enormous expansion of military spending coupled with tax increases, 1937 probably represented the peak for the prewar standard of living. In January 1937, the Rokku entertainment district of Asakusa in Tokyo was the busiest it had been since the end of World War I, with over 300,000 visitors a day. The Imperial Diet Building (which still houses today's Diet) was completed in 1936. At the time, it was the tallest building in the country.

In 1937, the monthly salary of a department head at a major company was about ¥400, and he might receive an annual bonus of ¥3,000 to ¥5,000. A section chief might make ¥100 a month, with a bonus of ¥600 to ¥1,000, while an ordinary full-time employee would make ¥60 per month, with a bonus of ¥150 to ¥200. In the city of Kawasaki, midway between Tokyo and Yokohama, a house on 50 *tsubo* of land (about 160 square meters or 1,800 square feet), with five rooms on two stories, an entry gate, privacy hedge, garden, and running water, would cost about ¥3,650. This meant that someone in the department-head class could buy with cash, and a section chief could manage with a loan. But buying a house would be difficult for an ordinary company employee, who might use an annual bonus to purchase a console radio or the like for ¥140. And since the radio was an effective tool for the government's drive to unify the people, radio broadcasting developed rapidly and spread quickly. The inequality of income distribution continued as before.

In 1937, before the Sino-Japanese War began, the US firm General Electric did a survey of the diffusion of electrical appliances in Japan. It found that there were 12,215 refrigerators nationwide (4,700 in the Tokyo area), 3,917 washing machines (1,190 in Tokyo), and 6,610 vacuum cleaners (3,000 in Tokyo). The survey predicted that if July 1937 was set as a distribution index of 100, four years later refrigerators would be at 285, washing machines at 490, vacuum cleaners at 470, electric well-pumps at 120, electric irons at 150, clocks at 340, commercial refrigeration units at 240, and air conditioners at 926. If the 1940 Tokyo Olympics had been held, and large numbers of foreign tourists had visited Japan for that event, it is likely that the Westernization of daily life would have proceeded at an even faster rate (Kusayanagi Daizō, *Shōwa tennō to sanma* [Emperor Shōwa and sauries]).

In short, the trends toward urbanization, electrification, and Americanization of the Japanese lifestyle that emerged in the 1920s continued unabated in Japan during the "period of crisis." But when Japan plunged into the Sino-Japanese War in July 1937, the same month as the General Electric survey, everything would begin to change.

The Pressures of War

The Sino-Japanese War had its most immediate impact in the large number of soldiers mobilized and the large number of casualties suffered. On 1 October 1937, it became customary to mark the entrances of homes in Tokyo that had sent a soldier off to the war. On 29 December, the Ministry of Railways placed the words "fallen heroes" (*eirei*) on the destination boards and windows of trains transporting the remains of soldiers who had been killed in combat, and decorated the interior of the cars with black bunting. The large number of men mobilized, as well as the significant number of dead and wounded, were facts that could not be concealed.

The authorities were acutely concerned with how to mitigate this situation. The mobilization was so large that it could not be restricted to single men in their twenties; many married men in their thirties with families were being called up as well. Deaths or injuries of such men were even more tragic in their effect. The 101st Division, with many conscripts from working-class neighborhoods in Tokyo, was deployed in the attack on Shanghai and suffered massive casualties. Surviving families were so enraged by the barrage of telegrams reporting battlefield deaths that armed guards were assigned to one regimental commander's residence to defend it in his absence, while another commander's wife was so distraught by the numbers of dead and wounded that she killed herself (Hata Ikuhiko, *Nankin jiken* [The Nanjing Incident]).

In 1937, a patriotic version of the *Ogura hyakunin isshu*, a popular card game based on an anthology of classical poetry that even today is played at New Year celebrations, was released but had tepid sales—quite the opposite reaction to the boom surrounding the Three Human Bullets at the time of the Shanghai Incident. This was no doubt because the casualty rate in the Sino-Japanese War was so much higher than it had been during the Manchurian Incident and related combat. At this point, the public was in the midst of a mah-jongg boom—seeking momentary escape from the stresses of everyday life.

Troop strength had begun to be a problem even before the outbreak of the Sino-Japanese War. As of January 1936 the number of young men ranked in Class A (suitable for active service) in the physical examinations for conscription declined, and the number of Class C (unsuitable for active service) increased. Because of this, on 19 February 1937, the Enforcement Order of the Military Service Act lowered the standards for passing the conscription exams. The minimum height requirement was lowered by 5 centimeters, and requirements for vision and hearing were relaxed. The army needed able-bodied men so badly that it had proved necessary to redefine what was meant by "able."

The large number of men being called to military service and the boom in war-related industry began to create severe labor shortages. In 1937, there were reports that employment of physically handicapped workers, previously an issue, was making progress. And in September 1937, with wartime industry running full tilt, house rents in industrial areas also rose rapidly. One solution to the shortage of labor was to mobilize women workers. In January 1939, Mitsui Bank began hiring female secondary school graduates as clerical staff, and Mitsubishi Bank soon followed suit. This began to be reflected in educational opportunities for women, and in February 1939, Waseda University enrolled women in its standard undergraduate program for the first time.

Pressure on Everyday Life

The war also brought abrupt shortages of materials. Military demand was prioritized, and civilian demand severely regulated. One commodity that soon became scarce was leather goods. The war in China meant that large numbers of soldiers were on the march in leather boots. In December 1937, leather goods began to be rationed, and a movement encouraging people to wear wooden clogs (*geta*) was promoted. This did little to eliminate the shortages, however, and in June 1938 prices for leather items skyrocketed.

In July 1938, the Tokyo municipal bus system debuted charcoal-burning buses. What had been a steadily growing consumer market for automobiles now clearly began to fall off. In August, production of passenger vehicles was effectively halted. All automotive production capacity was now devoted to military purposes.

Regulation extended to nonmilitary goods as well. Beginning 1 March 1938, cotton cloth was subject to rationing. Then, on 29 June, the production and sale of cotton textiles was restricted. As a result, shortages arose, and the word *yami* ("black market") entered the vocabulary. The era of synthetic-cotton blends also commenced. On 12 August, newsprint began to be restricted, cutting that available to newspapers by 12 percent. Newspapers actually hit their peak physical volume in 1936, with Tokyo papers running eighteen to twenty pages (counting both morning and evening editions) daily from January 1936 through the autumn. Beginning in 1938, the number of pages they were printing began to fall off precipitously.

Of all commodities, metals were the most thoroughly prioritized for military use. In 1938, ceramic cookware, bamboo spoons, and wooden buckets began to replace their metal counterparts. Then, in February 1939, drives to recover iron and steel from existing products began. Post boxes, benches, streetlamps, advertising hoardings, ashtrays, and other items were recycled. Even nails and other hardware used by carpenters were rationed. In June, mandatory recycling of metal goods began. Learning of this, writer Nagai Kafū stripped the 18-carat gold fittings from his tobacco pouch and tossed them from the Azuma Bridge into the Asakusa River. "I'd rather get rid of it altogether than make a piddling amount of money by simply handing it over to some bureaucrat," he wrote (*Danchōtei nichijō* [Diary of Nagai Kafū], 1 July 1939). It was also during 1939 that bamboo-reinforced concrete appeared as a replacement for steel-reinforced concrete.

Regulation extended into the service industries as well. With the implementation of the Shop Act on 1 October 1938, retail businesses (with the exception of eating and drinking establishments) were forbidden to operate after 10:00 P.M. In October 1939, a directive was issued officially freezing prices and wages at the levels pertaining on 18 September of that year. The directive covered prices of 40,000 items nationwide and 430,000 regionally, while wage controls regulated everything from starting wages for recent graduates and seniority-based annual raises to familial and housing allowances.

The government did what it could to hold down general commodity prices, but in order to fund the war it also implemented price hikes on certain goods. In November 1936, the price of cigarettes was raised for the first time in eleven years; Golden Bat went from 7 sen to 8 sen (1 sen was equal to one-hundreth of 1 yen), Cherry from 10 to 12 sen, Asahi from 15 to 17 sen, and Shikishima, the luxury brand, from 18 to 20 sen. A little more than a year later, on 31 January 1938, there was another price hike, and Asahi went to 18 sen and Shikishima to 22 sen. This was a blatant effort by the fiscal authorities to increase revenue, and by the time of the outbreak of the Pacific War the price of Shikishima had risen to 35 sen a pack.

Postal rates went up as well. In April 1937, postcards rose from 1 sen 5 rin to 2 sen, and regular mail from 3 sen to 4 sen, in the first rate increases since 1889. In August 1940, lottery-prize New Year postcards were invented as a source of additional revenue.

A new method of tax collection was also introduced in this period: withholding at source from salary or wages. Implemented as a way of expanding the tax base to fund the war effort, this system was initiated in March 1940. From a monthly salary of ¥100, the standard deduction was ¥60, while the remaining taxable income was subject to a 6 percent rate, so the tax withheld amounted to ¥2.40. If the worker was married, an additional ¥1 deduction would be allowed, leaving the tax payment at ¥1.40.

By 1940, the impact of war on the economics of everyday life was beginning to be keenly felt. There were serious shortages of electric power. In January 1940, use of heaters, refrigerators, and other electrical appliances was prohibited. It is the custom during the Setsubun festival in February to scatter beans to celebrate the beginning of spring, and then gather them up again to eat, with the number of beans eaten correspond to the age of the person; by 1940 people were also collecting them to put into care packages for soldiers at the front. In April 1940 it was decided to place rice, miso, soy sauce, salt, matches, charcoal, sugar, and other basic commodities on a ration ticket system, which was implemented in November. The sugar ration was 300 grams a month; five matches were allotted per day. In December, cotton and gauze were also rationed.

In 1941, government regulations grew even more detailed and intrusive. In January, hotcakes and roasted apples were defined as confections and assigned an official price. In February, towels became a rationed item—one to every eight people, at a cost of 24 sen. In July, the Ministry of Commerce and Industry prohibited buying up and hoarding of goods—but such practices were the result of fundamental commodity shortages. By July 1941 there were even shortages of vegetables, and lines at the greengrocers. In November 1940 a khaki-colored national civilian uniform for men, modeled on military dress, was introduced by government order. One of these outfits cost ¥40 at the official price, and ¥80 on the black market, in December 1941. A year later the black-market price would rise to ¥150.

Spiritual Mobilization

A variety of "spiritual mobilization" movements were initiated to promote and smooth the way for the unnatural demands being placed on the populace by the war effort, and to control the psychology of the people with a rhetoric of frugality, patriotism, and public service.

We have already touched on some of the ultra-nationalist tendencies that had been apparent even before the war. Soon after the February Twenty-Sixth Incident, on 18 April 1936 the foreign ministry announced that the nation would henceforth be known officially as the Greater Japanese Empire (Dai Nippon Teikoku), and the emperor would be known not as Emperor of Japan but as Emperor of the Greater Japanese Empire—in a rather smug and senseless appeal to ultra-nationalism.

In July 1937, the city of Yokohama prohibited the use of pancake makeup, eyebrow pencils, and eyeshadow by female municipal employees. In January 1938 the Tokyo Metropolitan Police declared hair-permanents to be an affront to good morals and manners, and prohibited new construction or changes in location of shops offering them. In October 1938 the city of Nagoya ordered all of its male employees to get military-style buzz cuts. With the government beginning to meddle with men and women's hairstyles, Nagai Kafū observed: "Some people are laughing at what they might do about the suspicious facial hair of the likes of [Generals] Hayashi and Araki" (*Danchōtei nichijō* [Diary of Nagai Kafū], 21 June 1939).

On 7 July 1938, the first anniversary of the Sino-Japanese War, the government proclaimed a "one soup and one side" movement for frugality in eating. This provoked a backlash, with opponents arguing that working women needed better nutrition if goals of the government's

Good morals and manners
The government wanted the people to simplify their lives. Under the pressure of spiritual mobilization campaigns, luxury items that brought enjoyment to everyday life began to disappear into the monotony of wartime regulation.

other campaigns—"Healthy People, Healthy Soldiers" and "Bear Children, Increase the Population!"—were to be met. The limitations of propaganda and spiritual mobilization were already becoming apparent.

In 1939, the "Rising Sun" lunch became popular—a box of cooked rice with a single red pickled plum at the center, reminiscent of the national flag. This idea had debuted in 1937, but had not caught on until connected with the rising tide of austerity and nationalism. Ironically, however, the white rice that served as the background for the red plum was beginning to be in short supply. In November 1939, sale of fully milled white rice was prohibited, and only 70 percent–polished rice was sold. By October 1939, locusts were being promoted as a food source—boiled in soy sauce and sugar as *tsukudani* or made into croquettes.

The major targets of the spiritual mobilization movement were luxury and entertainment. In September 1938, the seeking of autographs of movie stars and other entertainers was prohibited. On 1 October 1939, the Motion Picture Act was enforced, with entry to theaters barred to children under fourteen years of age. Import of foreign films was limited to fifty per annum (up to this point it had been about a hundred), scripts had to be approved in advance by censors, and directors and actors had to be registered with the government. The provisions of this law were simultaneously a form of thought control, an attack on Western culture, and a means to conserve foreign currency reserves.

On 31 October 1940, the dance halls of Tokyo were closed. On that last night, they were packed. When this closure was being rumored, Nagai Kafū wrote, "Next they will be prohibiting cafés, and after that it will be novels" (*Danchōtei nichijō* [Diary of Nagai Kafū], 29 December 1937).

He continued: "What is really striking these days is how sneaky the faces of Japanese [men] under the age of 40 are beginning to look, and the increasing insolence of their attitude. Dressed in cheap western suits with fedoras pushed down low over their eyes, they look like a bunch of detectives. . . . The beautiful manners and customs of Tokyo began to decline year by year after the earthquake in Taishō 12 [1923], to the point that now not even a shadow remains."

As noted earlier, 1,500 billboards emblazoned with the slogan "Luxury is the Enemy!" appeared in the streets of Tokyo on 1 August 1940. But at the same time, regular advertising billboards and neon signs fell victim to restrictions on the use of electric power, and use of vivid colors in advertisements was forbidden. Commercial ads were being replaced by what were probably even more annoying government exhortations to be on the lookout for spies, conserve rice, and save money. In September of that year, village councils (*burakukai*), block associations (*chōnaikai*), and neighborhood groups (*tonarigumi* or *rinpo*) were formalized into an administrative system, as discussed earlier. At the lowest level, the neighborhood groups might comprise as few as five to ten households, and were promoted under the slogans of family values, solidarity, and local self-government, but were in fact operated as the most basic administrative units for enforcing mobilization, requisitioning, rationing, and air-raid drills.

The 1940 Tokyo Olympics were canceled, but in their place a celebration of 2,600 years of imperial rule was staged on 11 November. Just before this, in October, the cigarette brands Golden Bat and Cherry (named in English) were renamed Kinshi and Sakura. Ultra-nationalism had come to the world of brand management. Entertainers who had been going by stylish foreign names—Miss Wakana and Dick Mine, for example—were also forced in this year to revert to their Japanese names: Tamamatsu Wakana and Mine Kōichi. In April 1941, blond and blue-eyed department store mannequins were repainted to a more native brown and black. And then, the day before the attack on Pearl Harbor, actors were forbidden to use stage names, with the famous Ōkōchi Denjirō becoming Ōbe Masao, and Bandō Tamasaburō becoming Tamura Denkichi.

Culture and Sports

Even so, the Japanese infatuation with Western culture did not wane. In December 1937, the film *One Hundred Men and a Girl*, featuring the famous conductor Leopold Stokowski, was a hit in Japanese theaters. The year 1938 saw the importation of other prewar classics such as *Modern Times* and *Life Dances On*. Nagai Kafū's only opera libretto, *Katsushika jōwa*, was performed at the Asakusa Opera from 17 to 26 May 1938, to music composed by Sugahara Meirō. As a young man, Kafū had fallen in love with opera in New York and Lyon, and had visited the Metropolitan Opera night after night to hear Enrico Caruso and other famous singers. He was the forerunner of the serious opera aficionados of Japan, and dreamed of writing an opera of his own. Despite this—or perhaps because of it—he ignored the Asakusa Opera, which enjoyed immense popularity in the Taishō period. But two years into the Sino-Japanese War, he completed the libretto for *Katsushika jōwa* and saw it performed. Revived in July 1999 after sixty-one years, it is a wonderfully lyrical minor work with a simple and romantic story line serving as a beautiful framework for melodies drawn from the Noh drama, *jōruri* narrative chant, and other traditional sources. During its original run the opera was performed three times each day, and celebratory red beans and rice were served to full houses.

There were stunning developments in science and technology, out of which emerged weapons such as the Zero fighter plane (developed for use on aircraft carriers) and the battleships *Yamato* and *Musashi*. But such technology did not lead to development of products for civilian use. Aircraft development made great strides, but it was all geared to the military. On 6 April 1937 an air-plane named *Kamikaze* (Divine Wind) owned by the *Asahi shinbun* newspaper company, took off from Tachikawa airfield outside Tokyo and landed in London on 9 April. The flight time was 94 hours, 17 minutes, and 56 seconds, a new world's record for air travel between Asia and Europe. On August 26 1939, the *Nippon,* an aircraft sponsored by *Ōsaka mainichi shinbun* and *Tōkyō nichi nichi shinbun* newspaper companies, departed Haneda airfield in Tokyo for an around-the-world voyage, flying to Los Angeles, Washington, D.C., Buenos Aires, Rome, Calcutta, and Taipei before returning to Japan on 20 October. With a crew of five, it recorded a flight time of 194 hours. Both of these airplanes had originally been developed for military use.

The sports touched on at the beginning of this section continued to be popular into the war years. As noted in Chapter 2, the Japanese Professional Baseball League was launched in February 1936 with seven teams: the Tokyo Kyojin (Giants), Team Greater Tokyo, Tokyo Senators, Nagoya Golden Dolphins, Osaka Tigers, Team Hankyū, and Team Nagoya. In 1937 two new baseball stadiums were completed: one in May at Nishinomiya (between Osaka and Kobe), and the Kōrakuen stadium in Tokyo in September. In June

1939 the first professional baseball tournament between teams from eastern and western Japan was held, with attendance—at 28,000 people—rivaling that of the big Waseda-Keiō university baseball game being played the same day. This is said to be the point at which professional baseball began to overtake the university league in popularity. In a November 1940 game between the Tokyo Kyojin and Hanshin (renamed from the Osaka Tigers in October 1940 to avoid the use of English), a hit by Kawakami Tetsuharu of the Tokyo Kyojin was described as a "bullet line drive" by one announcer, and the term has remained in baseball vocabulary to this day. Baseball, as before, continued to be a much-loved sport.

Sumo gained popularity with the rise of militarism. The great string of victories by wrestler Futabayama began on the seventh day of the spring tournament of 1936. Starting out as a third-ranked east *maegashira* (rank-and-file wrestler in the highest division), he advanced to *ōzeki* (second highest rank) in the spring tournament of 1937, and after the summer tournament in May 1937 was promoted to *yokozuna* (grand champion). On 15 January 1939, on the fourth day of the spring tournament, he was toppled by third-ranked west *maegashira* Akinoumi, bringing to an end an unbroken streak of sixty-nine victories. Special editions of the papers were put out with this electrifying news, which had the entire country in an uproar.

Yamaguchi Yoshiko (Ri Kōran) in 1941

In February 1941, the actress Ri Kōran (or Li Xianglan in modern Pinyun) made her first appearance at the Nichigeki Theater in Tokyo. It caused quite a sensation, and theatergoers turned out in droves. Ri Kōran, whose original name was Yamaguchi Yoshiko, was born in Manchuria in 1920 to Japanese parents. From childhood she was taught to speak Chinese by her father, who was committed to an ideal of Sino-Japanese friendship and cooperation. She was informally adopted by a friend of her father's, a pro-Japanese businessman and former warlord named Li Jichun, and given the Chinese name Li Xianglan (Ri Kōran). From that time onward she was educated in Beijing as a Chinese. In Beijing she lived in the home of another pro-Japanese politician named Pan Yugui, which was frequented by warlords such as Wu Peifu, Song Zheyuan, and Wang Kemin. In 1938, Ri Kōran was scouted by the Manchukuo Film Association (Man'ei; also known as Manchuria Film Production) and almost immediately became a star. The chairman of Man'ei was Amakasu Masahiko, known for the incident involving the murder of the anarchist Ōsugi Sakae following the Great Kantō Earthquake of 1923. Amakasu also organized the Shinkyō (Xinjing) Symphony Orchestra and invited renowned guest performers such as the conductor Asahina Takashi and the violinist Tsuji Hisako to play in the capital of Manchukuo.

Songs sung by Ri Kōran—"When Will You Return?" (*Heri jun zailai*) (this one was banned by Japanese censors for disturbing public morals), "China Nights," "Suzhou Serenade," and others—were huge hits, and the beautiful "Chinese" singer Ri Kōran became the symbol of "friendship between Japan and Manchukuo" and "Sino-Japanese amity." She came to Japan promoted as "the singing ambassador of friendly relations between Japan and Manchukuo" and gave a special concert, "Ri Kōran Sings!" celebrating Japan's National Foundation Day, Kigensetsu). On the day of the concert, the line of waiting fans encircled the theater seven and a half times, and pandemonium ensued. On the bill were her hits, such as "Suzhou Serenade" and "China Nights," as well as "Speak to Me of Love" and "Brindisi," the drinking song from the opera *La Traviata*.

Film critic Iwasaki Akira first heard Ri Kōran on the radio singing "Suzhou Serenade" while imprisoned as a Marxist activist. He later wrote of this experience:

> One early evening, a song managed to waft its way into our prison cell; it must have come from a radio in a house somewhere. . . . The tempo was quite slow, so much so that if it had become any slower, the singing would likely have gotten out of tune. The voice belonged to that of a young woman, and it was the first time I heard the song. A hushed silence quickly fell upon the entire cell as I listened to it intently. The intonation in her voice and the way she carried the melody suggested a Chinese flavor as the singing became more and more alluring along with her long drawn-out notes. Violent and vulgar men though they were, prisoners with stubbly faces all listened with their eyes closed; one could even see tears streaming down some of their faces. . . . Something strange had happened to all those intimidating and filthy characters. Meanwhile, we were all dreaming of a world far away as our bygone memories began to stir up bittersweet emotions within us. Even after the song ended, for a while no one spoke a word. (Iwasaki Akira, as quoted in Yamaguchi Yoshiko and Fujiwara Sakuya, *Ri Kōran* [Fragrant orchard])

The crowds that lined up outside the Nichigeki Theater were not there for the cause of Japan-Manchukuo friendship or because it was National Foundation Day. What the spectators were after, what they were seeking in Ri Kōran's songs, was an escape from reality into a distant world, into forgotten memories. And they wanted to hear love songs. France had fallen, so French songs could be sung. Italy was an ally, so its opera could be heard. And for the listeners of the time, I believe that was good.

Ri Kōran's popularity continued right up to the end of the war. "Evening Primrose" (*Ye lai xiang*), recorded in 1944, was a major hit. The composer, Hattori Ryōichi, made a Gershwin-style arrangement of it inspired by "Rhapsody in Blue" that was given the suitably Japanese title "Ie rai shan gensōkyoku" but that he privately referred to as "Ie rai shan

Ri Kōran (1920–2014)
Original name, Yamaguchi Yoshiko. (© The Mainichi Newspapers)

Rhapsody" or "Ie rai shan Fantasy." This was an immense success as the featured piece in a recital Ri Kōran gave, backed by the Shanghai Symphony Orchestra, at the Shanghai Grand Theatre in May 1945. The shadow of defeat was already falling heavily over Japan, but she was enthusiastically welcomed by Chinese audiences. An encore recital was held at the Shanghai International Racecourse on 9 August—the day before Japan agreed to accept the terms of the Potsdam Declaration.

Yamaguchi Yoshiko (1920–2014) attempted a music and acting career in the United States under the stage name Shirley Yamaguchi and was even named as one of two future hopefuls one year. However, after meeting her rival Julie Andrews, she became overwhelmed and gave up on her dream of becoming a US star. She went on to marry the famous Japanese-American sculptor Isamu Noguchi but later divorced and remarried a Japanese diplomat. In 1958 she retired from the world of film but came back ten years later in 1968 to appear on TV. In 1974, two years after the normalization between Japan and China, she was elected to the House of Councillors and served until 1992, working mainly on issues concerning diplomacy and the environment. She became a symbol of the complex relationship between Japan and China in the twentieth century.

Japan–United States Diplomacy

The Draft Understanding Between Japan and the United States

In April 1941, when Matsuoka Yōsuke returned to Japan, flushed with victory, from signing the Soviet-Japanese Neutrality Pact in Moscow, movement was already afoot to try to break the deadlock in Japan–United States relations. On 29 November 1940, Bishop James E. Walsh and Father James M. Drought of the Catholic Maryknoll Society used an introduction from Lewis L. Strauss, a partner in the New York investment bank Kuhn, Loeb & Company (which had assisted Japan in securing foreign loans at the time of the Russo-Japanese War) to call on Ikawa Tadao, a director of the Central Bank for Industrial Cooperatives in Tokyo. They said that they wanted to discuss possible methods for breaking out of the impasse in Japan–United States relations, and Ikawa relayed this information to Prime Minister Konoe and also consulted with Mutō Akira, head of the army's Military Affairs Bureau, and Iwakuro Hideo, chief of the Army Affairs Section, before agreeing to continuing talks with Walsh and Drought as a private individual.

On 14 December, Walsh and Drought presented a basic plan for an accord that they said had been drafted from the Japanese standpoint, and even the army seemed to have hopes for this proposal. Ikawa introduced the two priests to Minister of Foreign Affairs Matsuoka and Vice Minister of Foreign Affairs Ōhashi Chūichi, but Matsuoka displayed no interest. The Maryknoll Society was anticommunist, anti-British, and isolationist—reflecting fairly strong currents of opinion in the United States generally.

Walsh and Drought returned to the United States on 28 December, and reported back to Japan on the encouraging reactions of the US government. On 13 February 1941, Ikawa visited the United States and met with Postmaster-General Frank C. Walker, who was a major supporter of Walsh and Drought's efforts. Toward the end of February, Walker urged President Roosevelt to come to an agreement with the Japanese, contingent upon Japan's withdrawal from the Tripartite Pact. In March, Iwakuro also came to the United States, and joined Iwata and Drought's work in drafting a proposal. Meanwhile, on 11 February, Reserve Admiral Nomura Kichisaburō, who would eventually play an important role in these negotiations, arrived in Washington, D.C., to take up his duties as Japanese ambassador.

After numerous revisions, the text of the proposal, which we now know as the "Draft Understanding Between Japan and the United States," was completed on 16 April. Let's review its main points. First, in order to initiate and conclude "a general agreement disposing the resumption of our traditional friendly relations," Japan and the United States were to avoid debating the origins of their recent estrangement from each other, and instead make a joint effort to prevent the recurrence of incidents that had damaged these relations of friendship.

The draft proposal identified seven sources of conflict between Japan and the United States: (1) concepts of international relations and the character of nations; (2) attitudes on the part of the two governments toward the war in Europe; (3) attitudes of the two governments toward the China Incident; (4) naval forces in the Pacific; (5) bilateral trade and financial ties; (6) bilateral economic activity in the southwestern Pacific; and (7) policies of both nations concerning political stability in the Pacific.

With regard to the second point, the document stated that Japan saw the Axis alliance as purely defensive, and that "the Government of Japan, with no intention of evading its existing treaty obligation, desires to declare that its military obligation under the Axis Alliance comes into force only when one of the parties of the Alliance is aggressively attacked by a power not at present involved in the European War." In other words, the draft proposal interpreted Japan's military commitment to the Axis alliance in extremely limited terms.

With regard to the third point, the document called for the US president to urge Chiang Kai-shek to make peace with Japan, if the United States could "approve" and the Japanese "guarantee" the following eight items: (a) the independence of China; (b) withdrawal of Japanese troops from Chinese territory on the basis of a bilateral agreement; (c) no acquisition of Chinese territory by Japan; (d) no imposition of indemnities; (e) resumption of the Open Door principle (with interpretation and application of it to be the subject of future discussions between Japan and the United States); (f) a merger of the governments of Chiang Kai-shek and Wang Jingwei; (g) no large-scale or concentrated immigration of Japanese into Chinese territory; and (h) recognition of Manchukuo. Then, if Chiang Kai-shek's government responded to the US recommendations, Japan would enter into peace negotiations with a new central government or other new regime. Of these above terms, the sixth (f) and eighth (h) were items that the United States had never accepted previously.

Concerning the fifth point of the overall draft proposal, Japan and the United States would agree to provide each other with essential commodities, and in order to bolster economic cooperation between the two countries, the United States would provide gold credits to Japan. Regarding the sixth point, on the basis of a guarantee by Japan that its activities in the southwestern Pacific would be carried out by peaceful means, the United States would provide cooperation and support in procurement of natural resources from that region, such as oil, rubber, tin, and nickel. The draft proposal was clearly specifying significant US cooperation toward Japan after the agreement was signed. And with regard to seventh point, Japan was to guarantee the independence of the Philippines, while the United States was to end discrimination against Japanese immigration. The draft proposal closed with a recommendation that Roosevelt and Konoe convene a summit conference in Honolulu and that each nation limit its delegation to five members or less.

The final text of the draft proposal was delivered to Japan between 17 and 18 April. Vice Minister of Foreign Affairs Ōhashi read it and was so startled by the advantages it offered to Japan that he had Prime Minister Konoe called out of a cabinet meeting to inform him of the contents, which Konoe presented that day to the Liaison Conference. The conference was an unusually relaxed and cheerful affair, and some of those present suggested a wire should be sent immediately to accept the draft proposal, but a decision was made to wait until Minister of Foreign Affairs Matsuoka returned from Moscow. The emperor himself remarked: "It comes as something of a surprise that the American president has come so directly to the point, but depending on how one looks at it, the fact that things have taken this turn might be said to be a result of our alliance with Germany and Italy. All things come to he who waits" (Kido Nikki Kenkyūkai, *Kido Kōichi nikki, gekan* [Diary of Kido Kōichi, vol. 2] 21 April 1941). But this was an ephemeral hope, based upon a misunderstanding.

Problems with the Draft Proposal

If the Japanese genuinely believed without question that the draft proposal was one by the US government, then all one can say is that this demonstrates remarkable ignorance on the part of the United States. Looked at from the US side, the only real concessions from Japan included in the document were the statement of a policy of withdrawing troops from China (with no specified timeframe) and a limitation on Japan's military obligations to the Axis alliance. Conversely, the United States was expected not only to adopt concessions it would have absolutely rejected previously— such as the recognition of Manchukuo and at least partial recognition of the Wang Jingwei regime—but also to provide Japan with material aid and financial assistance.

It is well known that this document was in fact a private draft authored by individuals who were not official representatives of the United States, and though Secretary of State Cordell Hull was aware of its contents, he had not approved or agreed to them. Hull had four principles of his own that he wished to be conveyed to the Japanese government along with this document, to seek assurance that Japan was willing and able to go forward in that spirit: (1) respect for the territorial integrity and the sovereignty of each and all nations; (2) noninterference in the internal affairs of other countries; (3) the principle of equality, including equality of commercial opportunity; and

(4) nondisturbance of the status quo in the Pacific except as it might be altered by peaceful means. If we read these carefully, the first and second might be said to signify a rejection of the machinations surrounding the Wang Jingwei regime, and the fourth a rejection of Japan's use of military force in its southern advance. And in fact, if the Japanese were willing to use the draft agreement as a point of departure for negotiations, then Hull had no problem with continuing talks on that basis (thus the United States referred to what was happening between the two countries as a "conversation" rather than a "negotiation"). He also wanted to give the Japanese hope for a negotiated settlement and avoid further conflict, at least for a time. Hull had an aspect of inscrutability about himself as well. And though he spoke gently, he also stuck stubbornly to the principles he had enunciated.

But Ambassador Nomura Kichisaburō conveyed the nature of the draft proposal to his government in highly ambiguous terms that could be taken to indicate an official commitment to it on the part of the US government, and he did not accompany it with a transmission of Hull's four principles. Iwakuro went even further, conveying the impression that Roosevelt himself had agreed to the plan. This was a technical mistake on the part of Nomura, who was not a career diplomat, and is an example of a blunder stemming from his eagerness to achieve a negotiated settlement.

In more normal circumstances, there might have been cooler heads in Tokyo that would have been more careful in considering the nature of the draft proposal and its implications. But such a possibility was blown apart by Matsuoka Yōsuke's emotionally charged response.

Matsuoka returned from Moscow on 22 April in high spirits, but plunged into a foul mood upon learning of the draft proposal. Just as he was about to launch his own negotiations with the United States based on the pressure of a four-nation entente among the Axis powers and the Soviet Union, he was confronted with a different approach that seemed close to fruition, which wounded his pride. He voiced objections to the draft, and, misinterpreting it as an official US plan, on 12 May sent a counterproposal. From the US perspective, this was Japan's first response. Matsuoka had eliminated all concessions on the part of Japan regarding the Axis alliance, arbitration of the Sino-Japanese conflict, and Japan's southern advance, and had even struck mention of the proposed bilateral summit in Hawaii. On 31 May the United States delivered a preliminary response to Ambassador Nomura, followed by a formal response on 21 June. This was accompanied by an "oral statement" from Hull that, while not naming Matsuoka, suggested that as long as the "foreign minister" was in office, it would be difficult to reach a negotiated settlement. This enraged Matsuoka, who made a show of refusing to accept the document. All the while, the unprofessional Ambassador Nomura managed to confuse the situation further by delaying cables and using ambiguous and misleading language.

The Third Konoe Cabinet

It was at this juncture that Germany suddenly invaded the Soviet Union with a 3 million–man army on 22 June. Matsuoka's vision of a four-nation bloc with which to confront the United States immediately collapsed. More than a few people had predicted war between Germany and the Soviet Union, but Matsuoka had not wanted to believe them. Wishful thinking can be dangerous.

In any case, Matsuoka's prestige was greatly damaged. He became almost incoherent, arguing for entering the war against the Soviet Union in direct contravention of the neutrality pact he had just signed and saying that Japan should not be afraid to risk war with the United States either. Konoe, who still had hopes for the talks with the United States, had his cabinet resign en masse on 16 July in order to remove Matsuoka as foreign minister. Sure enough, on 17 July the imperial order to form a new cabinet was once again given to Konoe, who named Toyoda Teijirō, a navy admiral on the reserve list, as the new foreign minister. This was an unexpected choice, but a good transition, especially in light of Toyoda's friendly relations with US ambassador Joseph C. Grew. Ironically, the US suggestion regarding the removal of Matsuoka had come to pass. Yet from this time forward, the United States showed little enthusiasm for negotiations with Japan. With the commencement of war between Germany and the Soviet Union, the gravest crisis—the plight of Britain—had been dispelled. And as we shall see, the policies adopted by Konoe were not an especially rational approach to avoiding war with the United States.

Japan's southward advance had, by September 1940, extended to northern French Indochina. Following this, the important issue became that of oil imports from the Dutch East Indies. From September 1940 to June 1941, this was the subject of sporadic but inconclusive discussions between Japanese representatives (Kobayashi Ichizō until November 1940, Yoshizawa Kenkichi afterward) and the Dutch governor-general, Alidius Tjarda van Starkenborgh Stachouwer.

On 25 June 1941, the Liaison Conference decided to move troops into southern Indochina, in order to establish what it termed a comprehensive military relationship with French Indochina for the stability and security of East Asia. Japan's occupation of northern Indochina had been justified as a means for cutting off supply routes supporting the Chiang Kai-shek regime, but the occupation of southern Indochina was clearly a threat to the Dutch East Indies. An Imperial Conference convened on 2 July approved a document outlining the policy response of the Japanese empire to the changing international situation, which stated that Japan would for the time being refrain from intervention in the war between Germany and the Soviet Union and instead concentrate on "strengthening our preparations for the southern advance," concluding that "to achieve this objective, our empire must be ready to risk war with the Britain and the US."

On 14 July, Japan demanded of the Vichy government in France that Japanese forces be allowed to enter southern Indochina, and on 21 July, France capitulated to this demand. Specifics were worked out locally on 23 July, and Japanese troops began landing in southern Indochina on 28 July. The US reaction to this was swift: on 25 July the US government froze all Japanese assets in the United States. This was a sanction one step short of war. Britain and the Dutch East Indies followed suit. On 1 August, the United States prohibited all exports, including petroleum, to Japan, with the exception of cotton and foodstuffs. The United States had summoned the will to go to war with Japan.

The developments just mentioned were completely in line with the decision of the Imperial Conference of 2 July. Yet it is questionable whether Japan was truly resigned to war with the United States and Britain at this point. But the United States took this action by Japan quite seriously. Japan's Achilles' heel was oil, and if it could not import it from the United States, it would have to get it from the Dutch East Indies. Japan's pressure on the Dutch East Indies and preparations for aggressive action seemed to spell war to the United States. In Japan, one person who understood this quite well was Shidehara Kijūrō. When he was informed by Konoe that the occupation of southern Indochina was under way, Shidehara said that would mean war with the United States, and asked if it were possible to get the emperor to issue a decree and have the troopships turned back. Hearing this, Konoe responded sheepishly, merely stating that they had already sailed.

When he received the news of the tough US sanctions against Japan, Konoe used the Liaison Conference of 4 August to prepare a new proposal to present to the United States, but it amounted to little more than a declaration that Japan would move no further southward, and would guarantee the neutrality of the Philippines. When this was delivered to Secretary Hull by Ambassador Nomura, Hull's reaction was quite cold. On 4 August, Konoe tried to resolve all outstanding issues in a single leap by holding a summit conference with Roosevelt, and sounded out the army and navy ministers on this idea. The emperor was delighted by this show of resolve by Konoe. On 7 August, a proposal for the summit was conveyed to the United States. Hull's response was noncommittal, but when Ambassador Nomura met with Roosevelt himself on 17 August, the president spoke positively, though he said Hawaii might be difficult and wondered if Alaska might be a possible venue instead. These contacts emboldened the Japanese to begin selecting a distinguished entourage to accompany Konoe: the foreign ministry would provide Shigemitsu Mamoru as its chief delegate, with Vice Minister Amō Eiji as chief secretary; the army would send General Doihara Kenji as lead delegate, accompanied by Mutō Akira, chief of the Military Affairs Bureau of the army ministry, and Tsukuda Osamu, vice chief of the Army General

Staff; the navy would send Admiral Yoshida Zengo as lead delegate, accompanied by Oka Takazumi, chief of the Military Affairs Bureau of the navy ministry, and Kondō Nobutake, vice chief of Navy General Staff. But it is entirely unclear what sort of concessions Konoe might have been contemplating. According to Sudō Shinji, he had no concrete proposals for the withdrawal of Japanese troops from China, nor clearly defined limitations on the Axis alliance. It is questionable whether anything would have come of what he would be bringing to the table.

In a Liaison Conference on 26 August, a personal message from Konoe to President Roosevelt was approved, and the summit plan became official. The president's response seemed positive, but Secretary Hull expressed the opinion that it would be necessary to get the talking points worked out in advance. Learning of these reactions, Konoe was pleased though somewhat apprehensive, and set about making preparations. However, on 3 September, Roosevelt said that preliminary talks would be needed to address the fundamental issues. A disappointed Konoe brought another proposal for the United States to a Liaison Conference on 4 September, which approved it. This hinted at Japan moving toward withdrawal from the Axis alliance. But there was no response to this overture from the United States.

The Imperial Conference of 6 September

With the implementation of the US sanctions at the end of July 1941, talk of war intensified in Japan. At a meeting of the chiefs of the army and navy's Military Affairs Bureaus on 16 August, the navy presented "A Plan for Implementation of National Policies." It called for a parallel development of war preparations and diplomatic efforts aimed toward late October; if there were no prospects for a diplomatic resolution by mid-October, then Japan would resort to forcible measures. The army was dissatisfied with this, arguing that a decision for war needed to come first. After considerable debate, a unified plan was finally arrived at on 3 September, which would be approved at an Imperial Conference on 6 September. Titled "Guidelines for Implementation of National Policies," it contained the following key points:

1. Our Empire, in order to ensure its self-preservation and self-defense, and with the resolve not to shrink from war with the United States (as well as Great Britain and the Netherlands), will proceed with war preparations, to be completed by sometime in late October.
2. [omitted by author]
3. If there is no prospect for achieving our demands by early October through the diplomatic negotiations mentioned in the previous item, we will immediately decide to initiate hostilities against the United States (as well as Great Britain and the Netherlands).

For an Imperial Conference to have approved a decision in which war was seriously anticipated was a grave matter. The day before, Prime Minister Konoe had met with the emperor to inform him in advance of the nature of the proposal, in the course of which the emperor observed that it gave the impression that war was the priority and diplomacy an afterthought, and questioned whether this was true. Konoe responded that diplomatic negotiations would be pursued to the end, and Army Chief of Staff Sugiyama and Navy Chief of Staff Nagano gave similar reassurances. In the Imperial Conference the following day, Hara Yoshimichi, president of the Privy Council, raised the same question, and was offered the same response, but this time only by Minister of Navy Oikawa. At this point, the emperor suddenly commented that it was regrettable that the Supreme Command (the army and navy chiefs of staff) had nothing to say, and read a poem written by his father, Emperor Meiji:

> On all four seas
> I thought all men were brothers
> Yet in this world
> Why do winds and waves
> Now rise and stir?

Following this, he said, "Whenever I read this poem, I am moved to try to embody my late grandfather's peace-loving spirit." The entire room fell silent.

However, as an appendix to the "Guidelines for Implementation of National Policies," there was a list of minimum requirements to be presented in the negotiations with the United States, which included demands that the United States and Britain not obstruct or intervene in Japan's efforts to handle the Sino-Japanese War; that they close the Burma route and offer no further assistance to Chiang Kai-shek; that they acknowledge Japan's special relationship with French Indochina; and that they cooperate with Japan in its acquisition of necessary materials. In return, the maximum concessions Japan was willing to accede to were an offer not to use Indochina as a base for further military advances; to withdraw its troops from Indochina after the establishment of peace in the Far East; and to guarantee the neutrality of the Philippines. With such conditions set, it was difficult to see how compromise was going to be possible.

Konoe was eager to move forward with negotiations, but there was little reason to expect a positive US response. On 2 October, Hull sent a reply noting that the Japanese position was even less forthcoming than before, reiterated the four principles he had enunciated previously, and demanded specific conditions with regard to withdrawal of Japanese troops from China and Japan's position toward the Axis alliance. Minister of Army Tōjō Hideki showed no sign of being willing to make any such concessions, particularly regarding troop withdrawal from China. As war drew ever closer, Konoe's restless impatience peaked. He met repeatedly with Tōjō to try to get the army to back off of its insistence on terminating negotiations, but was unable to budge him on the issue of troop withdrawals. On 12 October, Konoe convened at his private residence in Ogikubo what amounted to a final conference with the army and navy ministers, the foreign minister, and the president of the Cabinet Planning Board. The day before, Oka Takazumi, chief of the Navy Military Affairs Bureau, had conveyed a message to Konoe through Chief Cabinet Secretary Tomita Kenji that the navy wanted negotiations to continue, but because it could not officially express this, it recommended that the decision be left to the discretion of the prime minister; the real intention of the navy was to avoid war. But at the meeting in Ogikubo, Tōjō would not concede on the troop issue, and argued for going to war, saying that the previous Imperial Conference was the time and place to have debated prospects for war, and that he could not accept Konoe's reservations about it now.

On 14 October, a cabinet meeting was held. On that day, Mutō Akira, chief of the Army Military Affairs Bureau, reported that he asked the chief cabinet secretary to tell the navy that if it would say that it was not ready for war, the army would accept this, but the chief of the Navy Military Affairs Bureau, Oka Takazumi, responded that all the navy could do was to say that the decision should be left to the prime minister. Thus, when the deadline of 15 October arrived without any positive prospects on the diplomatic front, Konoe resigned the next day. His opportunity to take seriously the outstanding issues between the two countries and exert himself to resolve them should have come prior to 6 September; now it was too late. The navy should have honestly admitted there was no prospect for victory in a war with the United States and Britain. And the army should have thought about whether the troops it had stationed in China really needed to be there.

The Tōjō Cabinet

There were a variety of proposals for a successor to Konoe. One was a member of the imperial family, who might be able to act as a restraint upon the army. But there was no concrete evidence that this would actually work, and if a war broke out with a member of the imperial family as the head of the cabinet, the imperial house itself might be threatened.

On 17 October, a conference of elder statesmen (*jūshin kaigi*) was convened. Wakatsuki Reijirō suggested Ugaki. He argued that the decision of the Imperial Conference of 6 September was being understood too legalistically, and that such a grave matter of national policy needed to be approached with more political consideration. On the other hand, Kido Kōichi nominated Tōjō. He believed, paradoxically, that if anyone was going to be able to return the 6 September decision to a blank slate, and restrain the army, it would have to be the main culprit, a military man. Wakatsuki said a prime minister drawn from the military would give a dangerous impression overseas, and Okada Keisuke agreed with him, but in the end, Kido heeded his own counsel. At this point, the *jūshin kaigi* had devolved into not much more than an advisory body to the lord keeper of the privy seal.

Emperor Shōwa remarked, "You can't catch a tiger cub without entering the lair," and on the afternoon of 17 October gave the imperial order to form a new cabinet to General Tōjō Hideki. This was the first cabinet headed by an active-duty army officer since that of Terauchi Masatake in 1916. But Terauchi was a highly experienced military politician—a field marshal, backed by the Chōshū clique, who had served as army minister for nine and a half years and had spent five years as governor-general of Korea. In contrast, Tōjō was only a lieutenant-general who had been army minister for a year and three months, after the creation of the second Konoe cabinet. He was a vivid illustration of the shift from the clique-centered army of the Meiji and early Taishō eras to the bureaucratized organization of Shōwa.

Speaking with Tōjō about the formation of the new cabinet, Kido urged him not to be bound by the decision of 6 September, and to continue to pursue diplomatic negotiations. Tōjō was a very earnest individual, even to the point of being rigid and inflexible, and he was sincerely faithful to what he believed to be the emperor's will. It was these traits that Kido pinned his hopes on.

Tōjō simultaneously held the offices of minister of the army and minister of home affairs, as well as that of prime minister. In other words, he commanded both the police and the military police. Such a concentration of power in one man's hands had never occurred before. But this was only an attempt to conceal gaping divisions in national policy.

Tōjō began to reexamine the 6 September decision. But the Supreme Command were not enthusiastic about this. War was their profession. And as long as there was a possibility of war, they wanted to go into it with the most advantageous conditions. An Imperial Conference on 1 November 1941 deliberated on three different proposals: (1) avoid war at all costs, even if it means "enduring hardship and adversity" (*gashin shōtan*); (2) decide immediately to initiate hostilities, and concentrate all efforts and measures to this end; and (3) after resolving for war, continue diplomatic efforts while completing all operational preparations, in an effort to achieve a compromise. The Supreme Command, navy included, was leaning toward war. Minister of Foreign Affairs Tōgō Shigenori and Minister of Finance Kaya Okinori favored "enduring hardship and adversity," but it was the third proposition—which might be described as the moderate proposal— that carried the day. The attempt to return to a blank slate had ended in little more than an extension of the decision of 6 September. The deadline for deciding to go to war was set for 1 December. Approval for the third proposal and for this timetable was confirmed in an Imperial Conference on 5 November. Thus, in less than a month's time, war would be inevitable, barring a major shift in the diplomatic situation.

At this stage, Japan prepared two final proposals for presentation to the United States. The first was in essence a slightly more conciliatory version of the proposal approved on 6 September. With regard to the key issue of troop withdrawal, Japan was offering to withdraw troops from China within two years of the conclusion of a peace settlement, except in certain areas of North China, Mongolia-Xinjiang, and Hainan Island; and to withdraw from French Indochina as soon as peace was established. Concerning the timeframe for stationing troops in North China and other specified areas, Ambassador Nomura was instructed by Minister of Foreign Affairs Tōgō to say twenty-five years. When Tōgō had discussed this point with the army, he had proposed five years. The army countered with ninety-nine years, then fifty, and then finally agreed to twenty-five. It was as if they were negotiating a leasehold.

The second of the two proposals was more in the nature of a provisional agreement. There were four main points: that both Japan and the United States would refrain from any military advance into Southeast Asia or the Pacific except for the part of French Indochina where Japanese troops were already stationed; that the two nations would cooperate in securing necessary commodities from the Dutch East Indies; that commercial relations between the two nations would be restored to those prevailing prior to the US freezing of Japan's assets, with the United States providing oil to Japan; and that the United States would not obstruct endeavors toward peace between China and Japan.

The United States had no interest in compromising with the first proposal, with which it was presented separate from and before the second. The concessions Japan was making on troop withdrawals were inadequate. The United States also knew, having cracked the code used for Japan's diplomatic correspondence, that there was a second proposal in the works. It also knew from intercepted cable traffic that these were being referred to by the Japanese as "last proposals" and "final proposals," and that 25 November had been set as a deadline of some sort. If the final proposal were not accepted, what then? The only answer was war.

But Hull wanted to delay that eventuality at least a little longer. So on 22 November he proposed a three-month interim (modus vivendi) agreement in which Japan would agree to withdraw its troops from southern Indochina, restore the situation in northern Indochina to that prevailing prior to 26 July, and limit the number of troops stationed there to 25,000 or fewer. In return, the United States would suspend the freeze on Japanese assets and offer

Inauguration of the Tōjō Hideki cabinet (18 October 1941–22 July 1944)
Tōjō's cabinet was unusual in that he served concurrently as prime minister and army minister (and initially as home minister). He searched for a way out of the deadlock in negotiations with the United States, but they soon fell apart, leading to war. Photo courtesy of Kyodo News Images Inc.

other concessions. Later a pledge to provide a specified amount of oil to Japan was included. In short, this was a plan that was attempting to restore the status quo existing prior to Japan's advance into southern Indochina. From the Japanese point of view, it was an attractive proposal. The final version of the US interim proposal was completed on 25 November.

However, China expressed strong objections to this. The most powerful person in the US State Department concerning Far Eastern issues was Stanley Hornbeck. He had been strongly pro-China for many years and believed that Japan was exhausted and close to capitulating. The result was that the United States decided to scrap the interim proposal.

Instead, on 26 November, Secretary of State Hull handed Ambassador Nomura the document that has come to be known as the Hull Note. It contained ten specific measures to be taken, including a demand for the withdrawal of Japanese forces from China and French Indochina; that neither the United States nor Japan would support any government in China other than the one in Chongqing; and a virtual renunciation of the Tripartite Pact. There are a number of theories as to why, on 25 November, the United States suddenly shifted from the more conciliatory interim proposal to the Hull Note, but the decisive reason remains unclear. The Americans, too, were having difficulty making up their minds.

War with the United States

Many on the Japanese side, seeing the Hull Note, felt this meant war. Tōgō recalled feeling faint. He must have had great difficulty bearing the news that all of the complex machinations and long bitter negotiations with the army and navy that he had endured to date had all been for naught. Hull, too, was distraught, and said to Secretary of War Stimson, "I have washed my hands of it and it is now in the hands of you and [Navy Secretary] Knox, the Army and the Navy." In Tokyo an Imperial Conference was convened on 1 December, and the decision for war was made. The Supreme Command informed operational units that hostilities would commence on 8 December. The war began with Japanese landings on the Malay Peninsula, followed somewhat later by the attack on Pearl Harbor.

There is a theory with regard to the outbreak of war between Japan and the United States that Roosevelt was aware of Japan's plans for the surprise attack on Pearl Harbor, and allowed it to happen. This interpretation, which has surfaced repeatedly in the United States, holds that in order to overcome the isolationist sentiment of the American people and bring the United States into the war against Germany, Roosevelt deliberately used the "back door to war" opened by the Japanese attack. However, despite years of searching by scholars and obsessives alike, no solid evidence has been produced to substantiate the idea that the president had foreknowledge of the timing of the Japanese attack. Various intelligence hinting at Pearl Harbor as a target must have reached him, and there is a variety of evidence to indicate that he should have been aware of it. But the president must have been presented with a mountain of intelligence: intelligence that suggested Pearl Harbor, but also intelligence suggesting other targets, intelligence pointing to Southeast Asia, intelligence hinting at later dates, intelligence indicating the softening of the Japanese position, and so on. Amid it all, there was none that clearly indicated to the president the time and place of the surprise attack.

One must also think carefully about why the "back door to war" theory has had such traction. Roosevelt had repeatedly gone on record saying that the United States would not fight, and then led it into the war. Doubts about this, and doubts about whether he might have had prior knowledge of the attack, are deeply rooted in democracy. It is whether or not the president deceived the people that is being called into question.

If we pursue a similar question with regard to Japan, it might be framed in terms of asking why Japan did not give a formal notification of its intentions, and instead delayed its declaration of war until after the fact, resulting in the Japanese people being saddled with an undeserved reputation for cowardice and treachery for many decades to come. The fundamental question here becomes: Who was responsible?

The first issue that was addressed was whether, in fact, prior notification should be given. The navy wanted no prior notice; the foreign ministry initially wanted to break off negotiations and give twenty-four hours' advance warning. The navy strongly objected to this, and in the end it was agreed to deliver notification of the attack thirty minutes before it commenced. Whether or not that truly represents prior notification is quite debatable. Second, the delayed cable did not, in fact, really amount to an ultimatum. Originally, it contained a number of phrases that gave it the character of an ultimatum—an announcement of the breaking off of negotiations, an assertion of freedom of action, and an accusation that responsibility for what was to happen lay with the United States—but these were struck from the final version. Even if the text, vague in content after being stripped of such language, had arrived when it was supposed to, it is likely that the accusations of a "sneak attack" would still have been made. Third, the text of the cable was poorly written, elliptical, verbose, disorganized—and quite long. It had to be divided into fourteen parts for transmission, and the portion announcing the termination of negotiations was not sent until quite some time after the other parts. Moreover, since it was marked neither "urgent" nor "extremely urgent," the decryption and typing of this crucial document were not completed at the Japanese embassy in Washington, D.C., until around 11:30 A.M. This was a fatal error on the part of the foreign ministry.

The Japanese embassy also made major mistakes. The rumor that the staff had all gotten drunk at a going-away party for a colleague the night before is actually groundless, but neither did Japan's diplomatic representatives in Washington, D.C., seem to have an adequate grasp of the fact that they were on the eve of war. Their teletype operator was not on duty that evening, and when the order came in from Tokyo to destroy the code machines, the staff, instead of realizing that war was imminent, struggled with typing out a fair copy (when a handwritten document would have sufficed)—and strangely refused to use native-English-speaking typists to speed the process.

Moreover, there could have been other methods to relay the information. Ambassador Grew could have been informed in Tokyo; even a radio announcement could have been made. Any of these would have been timed immediately before the attack, which still would have been criticized as devious, but it would have been better than the embarrassingly delayed final memorandum.

In broad outline it is true that the United States let the Japanese strike first, enabling it to unite its people and enter the war. And there are some who might regard this as a dirty trick. But to a great extent international politics is the art of bargaining and, in some cases, mutual deception. There's no point in accusing the United States of being deceitful. The blame falls on those who allow themselves to be deceived. The United States was a tough adversary, which the best and brightest of Japan's bureaucrats and politicians engaged in the fierce arena of international politics with a fixation on the details of diplomatic rhetoric and an excessive concern for organizational honor and reputation. They were simply not up to competing with the United States.

Yet there were some exceptions. Yoshida Shigeru was one who did not abandon hope, even after the Hull Note. He noted that the Hull Note mentioned no specific date, and therefore did not constitute an ultimatum. Concerned first and foremost with avoiding war with the United States, he urged Minister of Foreign Affairs Tōgō to resign. We must be circumspect in introducing counterfactual hypotheses into historical analysis, but if Tōgō had resigned, throwing the cabinet into disarray and delaying any important decisions, the timing for the Pearl Harbor attack would have become problematic, because the weather in the northern Pacific is violent and winter navigation difficult. The next opportunity for such an attack would have been after spring 1942, by which time Germany was thrown on the defensive. No matter how rash the Japanese Imperial Army might have been, its desire to enter the war was predicated on German victory. If it were clear that Germany's advantage was slipping, then that would have been quite a different matter. Moreover, the text of the Hull Note demanded a withdrawal of Japanese forces from China, which was quite shocking to the Japanese, but did not explicitly state whether that demand included Manchuria. In such cases, there was room for further consultation, and in fact one might even read the deliberate vagueness in this regard as a sign that the other side wished to avoid a complete breakdown of negotiations. Japan might well have decided to interpret this as not including Manchuria, and continued negotiations on that basis.

All of Yoshida's actions at this time were focused on an effort to avoid war. He maintained a close relationship with US ambassador Joseph Grew, frequently providing him with confidential information—some of sufficient significance that he would have been in grave danger if this had been

Above, US battleships in flames at Pearl Harbor after the Japanese attack; *below,* front page of the *New York Times* reporting the attack.
(© Pacific Press Service)

discovered. This was something that no ordinary organization man or typical bureaucratic overachiever could have been capable of risking.

Epilogue: Toward the Postwar Era

About six months after the outbreak of war with the United States, Kiyosawa Kiyoshi published a book titled *Gaiseika toshite no Ōkubo Toshimichi* (Ōkubo Toshimichi as a diplomatist). Kiyosawa had built his career as a commentator on diplomacy and foreign affairs, but restrictions on freedom of speech were making this increasingly difficult. Even so, he persevered for some time, until the Axis alliance rendered it impossible for him to write freely on European affairs. From that point onward, Kiyosawa began to try his hand at diplomatic history. Diplomacy without knowledge of history, he wrote, was like a rootless flower. His book on Ōkubo was published in May 1942. It is a superb piece of historical research, but at the same time it is a pointed critique of the diplomacy of his times. When he wrote of how Ōkubo shouldered full responsibility for diverting Japan from war with Korea in the early years after the Meiji Restoration, and in dealing with the aftermath of Japan's Taiwan Expedition in 1874, he was no doubt thinking of the contrast with contemporary figures like Konoe and Hirota.

Kiyosawa sent copies of the book to a number of friends and acquaintances, among them Yoshida Shigeru. Perhaps because Yoshida was Ōkubo's grandson by marriage (having wed the daughter of Ōkubo's second son, Makino Nobuaki), he responded quickly with a letter conveying his impressions of the book. He praised Ōkubo's refusal to evade responsibility, no matter what the circumstances, and said that Japan needed leaders like that. Yoshida probably had no way of knowing that in a few years' time, he would find himself in such a position of leadership. But it was certainly true that for its recovery Japan would need a statesman with just such a keen sense of responsibility.

But a keen sense of responsibility alone was insufficient. In a letter to Kiyosawa dated 2 February 1940, Yoshida wrote scathingly of the farce of Nagatachō politics, saying that the problem was less with the cast than with the script, which was awful. For Yoshida, the proper script was cooperation with the United States and Great Britain, which he consistently advocated during the entire period covered by this book. As noted many times, this meant the Open Door principle in China, and free trade and an open market economy in Japan itself. These principles of liberalism would also support the institution of party politics.

I opened this book with the years surrounding the death of Hara Takashi, and I will close it with an anticipation of Yoshida's rise to prominence in

Kiyosawa Kiyoshi (1890–1945)
Journalist and political commentator of the Taishō and early Shōwa periods. Kiyosawa traveled to the United States at the age of sixteen; he worked while studying at Whitworth College and, after reporting for a Japanese-language newspaper in the United States, returned to Japan in 1923, where he became the foreign affairs editor of Chūgai shōgyō shinpōsha *(present-day financial news organization Nihon Keizai Shinbunsha) and made his debut as a commentator. He was a strong proponent of a liberal diplomacy of international cooperation.*

the postwar era. Both of these men were decisive party leaders, criticized for strong-arm tactics. And both shared an unswerving commitment to cooperation with the United States and Britain. It is true that party politics in their time was corrupt, inefficient, and rife with problems. But its essential nature was that of free competition, and there was room within it for the appearance of outstanding political debate, such as that of Saitō Takao. Freedom of speech was severely restricted, but in the space that remained, figures like Yoshino Sakuzō, Kiyosawa Kiyoshi, and Ishibashi Tanzan were still able to deliver exceptional commentary.

The era of Taishō democracy may have seemed hopeless in many respects: saddled with political corruption and waste and the concentration of wealth in the great zaibatsu. Dissatisfaction with this created the politics of the early Shōwa era, characterized by militarism, war, and totalitarianism. In pursuit of total wartime mobilization, social equality was promoted and new types of organization were brought to all levels of society. This social leveling and reorganization came to be known as the "1940 System" and laid the foundation for postwar development. On the other hand, in the prewar period the liberal thought represented by figures such as Yoshida formed a powerful undercurrent. With the addition of a single character, one can alter the wartime slogan "Luxury is the Enemy!" (*Zeitaku wa teki da*) to read "Luxury is Wonderful!" (*Zeitaku wa suteki da*), and many people would probably agree with the latter sentiment. The postwar recovery and economic development would arise out of a confluence of this type of liberalism and freedom of spirit with the egalitarianism and social organization that had been forged in prewar and wartime Japan.

Notes

1. Stalin was a very shrewd geopolitical strategist. He had always feared fighting a war on both the western and eastern fronts. The main reason he supported the Kuomintang was to keep Japan occupied in China. Stalin had initiated the idea of a neutrality agreement (or nonaggression treaty) with Japan in 1932, twice with Yoshizawa Kenkichi and also with Ishiwara Kanji.

Chronology

~

Japan	International

1921 (Taishō 10)
Hara Takashi Cabinet

4 Nov.	Prime Minister Hara (age sixty-five) assassinated at Tokyo Station by Nakaoka Kon'ichi
5 Nov.	Cabinet resigns en masse

	International
9 Nov.	Fascist Party forms in Italy

12 Nov.	Washington Conference convenes (through 6 Feb. 1922)

Takahashi Korekiyo Cabinet

13 Nov.	Cabinet formed
25 Nov.	Crown Prince Hirohito appointed regent

1922

1 Feb.	Yamagata Aritomo (age eighty-three) dies
6 Feb.	Naval Arms Limitation Treaty and Nine-Power Treaty concerning China signed at Washington Conference

	International
27 Feb.	Sun Yat-sen initiates Northern Expedition from Guilin

3 Mar.	Zenkoku Suiheisha (National Levelers Association) formed for human rights protection

	International
28 Apr.	First Zhili-Fengtian War (though 27 June)

6 June	Reorganization of Takahashi cabinet fails; cabinet resigns en masse

Japan	International

Katō Tomosaburō Cabinet
12 June   Cabinet formed
4 July   Army announces Yamanashi arms
          reduction plan
15 July   Japanese Communist Party illegally
          established

| | 22 Oct.   King of Italy appoints |
| | Mussolini as prime minister |

8 Nov.   Inukai Tsuyoshi and associates form
          Kakushin Kurabu

| | 30 Dec.   Formation of the Union of |
| | Soviet Socialist Republics |

1923

| | 11 Jan.   French and Belgian forces |
| | occupy Ruhr |

2 Feb.   Women's Suffrage League formed
          in Tokyo
24 Aug.   Katō Tomosaburō (age sixty-two) dies
25 Aug.   Cabinet resigns en masse
1 Sept.   Great Kantō Earthquake
2 Sept.   Amid rumors of violence by Korean
          residents, large numbers of Koreans
          massacred

August   Hyperinflation leads to
          collapse of German
          currency

Yamamoto Gonnohyōe Cabinet
3 Sept.   Second Yamamoto cabinet formed
4 Sept.   Kameido Incident (murder of militant
          laborers)
16 Sept. Amakasu Incident (murder of
          Ōsugi Sakae)

29 Oct.   Republic of Turkey
          declared
8 Nov.   Munich Putsch fails;
          Hitler arrested

10 Nov.   Imperial Rescript on Revival of National
          Morale (addressing social disturbances
          after the Great Kantō Earthquake)

14 Nov.   Italian parliament approves
          Mussolini's reform of
          election law

27 Dec.   Toranomon Incident (assassination
          attempt on Crown Prince Hirohito)
          Yamamoto cabinet resigns

1924
Kiyoura Keigo Cabinet
7 Jan.   Cabinet formed
10 Jan.   Second Movement to Protect
          Constitutional Government (Seiyūkai,
          Kenseikai, and Kakushin Kurabu unite
          in effort to topple Kiyoura cabinet)

Japan	International

15 Jan. Seiyūkai splits (one faction forms Seiyū Hontō)	
	20 Jan. First United Front between Kuomintang and Chinese Communist Party
	22 Jan. Labour cabinet formed in Britain under Prime Minister Ramsay MacDonald
26 Jan. Crown Prince Hirohito marries Princess Nagako	
	1 Feb. Britain recognizes the Soviet Union
7 Feb. Yoshino Sakuzō joins Asahi Shinbunsha	
	6 Apr. Fascist Party wins absolute majority in Italian elections
10 Apr. Japanese ambassador Hanihara Masanao's letter to the US secretary of state protesting anti-Japanese immigration legislation upsets American public opinion	
April Ōkawa Shūmei and associates found right-wing nationalist organization Kōchikai (later Kōchisha)	
	15 May US Congress passes new immigration act (including a ban on immigration from Japan and other Asian countries)
7 June Cabinet resigns en masse	
	16 June Whampoa Military Academy opens (Chiang Kai-shek, commandant; Zhou Enlai, political department director)

Katō Takaaki Cabinet

Japan	International
11 June Cabinet formed (Goken Sanpa three-party coalition cabinet) Shidehara Kijūrō becomes foreign minister	
	17 June Comintern Fifth World Congress convenes in Moscow
21 Aug. Finance and home ministers issue fiscal austerity orders to local governors	
	18 Sept. Second Zhili-Fengtian War
	7 Nov. Stanley Baldwin forms Conservative cabinet in Britain

Japan	International
24 Nov. Sun Yat-sen delivers speech in Kobe on "Pan-Asianism," questions Japanese policy toward China	**24 Nov.** Duan Qirui appointed acting chief executive of Republic of China

1925

20 Jan. Soviet-Japanese Basic Convention signed (establishes diplomatic relations between the two countries)

11 Feb. Nationwide demonstrations opposing enactment of Peace Preservation Law, Labor Dispute Arbitration Act, and Labor Union Act

19 Feb. Peace Preservation Bill introduced (revised and enacted 7 Mar.)

12 Mar. Sun Yat-sen (age fifty-eight) dies in Beijing

29 Mar. Universal Manhood Suffrage Act enacted

30 Mar. Makino Nobuaki appointed lord keeper of the privy seal

14 Apr. Tanaka Giichi becomes president of the Seiyūkai

22 Apr. Peace Preservation Law promulgated

26 Apr. Field Marshal Paul von Hindenburg elected president of Germany

5 May Universal Manhood Suffrage Act promulgated

10 May Kakushin Kurabu decides to merge with the Seiyūkai

31 July Katō cabinet collapses due to internal dissension

Katō Takaaki Cabinet

2 Aug. Second Katō cabinet formed

5 Oct. Locarno Conference convenes (on 16 Oct., Locarno Pact signed by seven nations, including Britain, France, Italy, and Germany)

20 Oct. Park Yeol Incident

1926 (Taishō 15/Shōwa 1)

4 Jan. Second National Congress of the Kuomintang convenes in Guangdong; party effectively controlled by Wang Jingwei, Chiang Kai-shek, and others

21 Jan. Shidehara Kijūrō delivers speech on nonintervention in China's domestic affairs

Japan	International

Japan

28 Jan.   Katō Takaaki (age sixty-six) dies; cabinet resigns en masse

Wakatsuki Reijirō Cabinet
30 Jan.   Cabinet formed
28 Feb.   Matsushima red-light district bribery incident
5 Mar.   Rōdō Nōmintō formed (Sugiyama Motojirō, chairman)

10 June   Anti-Japanese Mansei demonstrations in Korea
24 June   Reorganization of prefectural, municipal, and local government administration (adoption of universal manhood suffrage, expansion of local autonomy)

25 Dec.   Emperor Taishō (age forty-seven) dies; Crown Prince Hirohito becomes emperor; era name is changed to Shōwa

1927

15 Mar.   Run on Tokyo Watanabe Bank and other financial institutions; beginning of 1927 financial crisis
24 Mar.   Nanjing Incident

3 Apr.   Hankou Incident
5 Apr.   Trading company Suzuki Shōten in Kobe suspends new transactions (goes out of business 31 July)

International

20 Mar.   Chiang Kai-shek declares martial law and seals off Guangzhou, arrests Communist Party members in the Nationalist army (Canton Coup or Zhongshan Incident)
1 May   Coal miners' strike in Britain (on 3 May, develops into nationwide general strike)

9 July   Chiang Kai-shek launches Northern Expedition
23 Oct.   Central Committee of the Soviet Union purges Leon Trotsky from Politburo

21 Feb.   Wuhan Kuomintang government established under Wang Jingwei

24 Mar.   National Revolutionary Army occupies Nanjing; British and US gunboats shell the city

Japan	**International**
	12 Apr. Chiang Kai-shek initiates anti-Communist purge in Shanghai
17 Apr. Cabinet resigns en masse	
	18 Apr. Chiang Kai-shek establishes a Nationalist government in Nanjing, rivaling the Wuhan government

Tanaka Giichi Cabinet

20 Apr.   Cabinet formed
22 Apr.   Three-week moratorium on bank payments implemented
28 May   First Shandong Intervention
1 June   Kenseikai and Seiyū Hontō merge to form Rikken Minseitō (Hamaguchi Osachi, president)
27 June   Officials of Ministry of Foreign Affairs, Ministry of Army, and Kwantung Army convene the Eastern Conference (Tōhō Kaigi)

15 July   Comintern approves 1927 Theses on Japan
1 Aug.   Chinese Communist forces initiate Nanchang Uprising
6 Sept.   Wuhan government merges with Nanjing government
1 Nov.   Kemal Atatürk elected president of Turkey

1 Dec.   Japanese Communist Party deliberates on rebuilding itself in line with the 1927 Theses

Note: Significant drop in birth rate this year

1928

2 Feb.   Kuomintang National Congress in Nanjing votes to resume Northern Expedition

20 Feb.   Sixteenth general election (first under universal manhood suffrage)
15 Mar.   Nationwide mass arrests of Japan Communist Party members
19 Apr.   Second Shandong Intervention

3 May   Combat between Northern Expedition forces and forces of Japan's Shandong Intervention

Japan	International
	10 May Nationalist government protests Japan's Shandong Intervention at the League of Nations
4 June Assassination of Zhang Zuolin	
29 June Revision of Peace Preservation Law promulgated	
11 Aug. Tokyo municipal government bribery scandal	
	27 Aug. Kellogg-Briand Pact signed in Paris
	1 Oct. Soviet Union initiate first five-year plan
10 Nov. Enthronement ceremony for Emperor Shōwa	

1929

	11 Feb. Mussolini signs Lateran Treaty with Vatican
28 Mar. Japan and China sign agreement resolving Jinan Incident	
16 Apr. Nationwide mass arrest of Japan Communist Party members	
2 May Japan and China sign agreements resolving Nanjing and Hankou Incidents	
19 May Isseki-kai formed by officers of the Imperial Japanese Army	
	30 May Second Ramsay MacDonald cabinet formed in Britain
3 June Japan recognizes Nationalist government as official government of China	
2 July Cabinet resigns en masse	

Hamaguchi Osachi Cabinet

2 July Cabinet formed; Inoue Junnosuke appointed finance minister (implements fiscal policy of austerity, return to gold standard, no new public bond issues); Shidehara Kijūrō becomes foreign minister (initiating second period of "Shidehara diplomacy")	
29 July Government announces an austerity budget	
8 Aug. Ōyama Ikuo and others propose reorganizing Rōdō Nōmintō (as a way of uniting the legal left-wing parties)	
	4 Oct. New York stock market collapse (beginning of worldwide Great Depression)

Japan	**International**
1 Nov. Founding conference for Rōnōtō (Ōyama Ikuo, chairman)	
3 Nov. Anti-Japanese demonstrations in Gwangju, South Jeolla province, Korea (Gwangju Student Movement)	
29 Nov. Ministry of Finance issues ordinance lifting gold embargo	
	31 Dec. Meeting of Indian National Congress party in Lahore resolves for complete independence from Britain

Note: This year marked by many political corruption scandals; industrial rationalization policies enforced; "Tokyo March" a pop music phenomenon

1930

21 Jan. London Naval Conference	21 Jan. Five-nation (Japan, Britain, United States, France, Italy) naval arms limitation conference in London (on 22 Apr., London Naval Treaty signed)
26 Feb. Nationwide roundup of Japan Communist Party members	
22 Apr. London Naval Treaty signed	
25 Apr. Seiyūkai attacks government with accusations that London Naval Treaty constitutes an infringement on the imperial right of supreme command	
25 Aug. Special session of the National Association of Town and Village Mayors approves "Declaration on Relief for Agricultural Villages" and presents it to the central government	
Sept. Hashimoto Kingorō and associates form the Sakurakai	1 Sept. Wang Jingwei, Yan Xishan, Feng Yuxiang, and others establish anti-Chiang government in Beijing
4 Nov. Prime Minister Hamaguchi shot and gravely wounded by Sagoya Tomeo at Tokyo Station	
	27 Dec. Chiang Kai-shek launches First Anti-Communist Annihilation Campaign

Note: Effects of Great Depression start to impact Japan this year (Shōwa Depression begins)

1931

23 Jan. Matsuoka Yōsuke argues in the House of Representatives that Manchuria and Mongolia represent Japan's "lifeline" (*seimeisen*)	
March Hashimoto Kingorō and other Sakurakai Army officers join with Ōkawa Shūmei and associates in plotting an abortive coup d'état (March Incident)	4 Mar. Gandhi-Irwin Pact signed in Delhi

Japan	International
13 Apr. Hamaguchi's condition worsens; cabinet resigns en masse	

Wakatsuki Reijirō Cabinet

Japan	International
14 Apr. Second Wakatsuki cabinet formed	14 Apr. Alfonso XIII of Spain flees the country; provisional government of Niceto Alcalá-Zamora established
16 May Cabinet resolution to cut salaries of government officials	16 May Chiang Kai-shek launches Second Anti-Communist Annihilation Campaign
	28 May Wang Jingwei, Li Zongren, and others form an anti-Chiang coalition and establish a new Nationalist government in Guangzhou
4 Aug. Minister of Army Minami Jirō instructs a conference of staff officers and divisional commanders that a "positive" resolution must be found for the issue of Manchuria and Mongolia	
	25 Aug. Ramsay MacDonald heads national unity cabinet in Britain
18 Sept. Liutiaohu bombing incident (Manchurian Incident begins)	
	21 Sept. China appeals the Liutiaohu Incident to the League of Nations
24 Sept. Government announces policy of nonexpansion with regard to Manchurian Incident	
17 Oct. Abortive military coup by Hashimoto Kingorō and associates (October Incident)	
	24 Oct. League of Nations passes resolution urging withdrawal of Japanese troops from Manchuria
10 Nov. Puyi, last emperor of Qing dynasty, flees Tianjin for Dalian	
	27 Nov. Soviet Republic of China (Jiangxi Soviet) founded with Mao Zedong as chairman
	10 Dec. Lytton Commission, a five-member body headed by Lord Lytton, created by League of Nations to investigate Manchurian Incident

Japan	**International**

11 Dec.   Cabinet resigns as a result of internal
dissension

Inukai Tsuyoshi Cabinet
13 Dec.   Cabinet formed; Takahashi Korekiyo
appointed finance minister, launches new
fiscal policies
First cabinet meeting decides to reinstate
gold embargo

*Note: This year the rate of labor unionization
reached 7.9 percent (highest in prewar era)*

1932

1 Jan.   Chiang Kai-shek and Wang Jingwei collaborate to form a new Nationalist government in China

4 Jan.   Indian National Congress declared illegal; Gandhi arrested

 8 Jan.   Lee Bong-chang, a Korean activist, throws hand grenade at the emperor's carriage outside Sakuradamon gate of imperial palace (Sakuradamon Incident)
28 Jan.   Shanghai Incident
 9 Feb.   Former finance minister Inoue Junnosuke assassinated by League of Blood member

16 Feb.   League of Nations Council cautions Japan to cease hostilities in the Shanghai area

29 Feb.   Lytton Commission begins on-site investigations
 1 Mar.   Founding of Manchukuo
 5 Mar.   Mitsui holding company's director-general, Dan Takuma, assassinated by League of Blood member

13 Mar.   Hindenburg reelected as president of Germany

15 May   Prime Minister Inukai Tsuyoshi (age seventy-six) assassinated in May Fifteenth Incident; cabinet resigns en masse

Saitō Makoto Cabinet
26 May   Cabinet formed
10 July   *Akahata* (Red Flag) publishes Kawakami Hajime's translation of the 1932 Comintern Theses on Japan

Japan	International

		30 July	Tenth Olympic Games held in Los Angeles
		31 July	Elections in Germany make the Nazi Party the largest in the Reichstag
25 Aug.	Minister of Foreign Affairs Uchida Kōsai gives "scorched earth" speech on Manchurian issue		
15 Sept.	Japan-Manchukuo Protocol signed		

1933

		30 Jan.	Hitler appointed chancellor of Germany
17 Feb.	Cabinet opposes League of Nations recommendations to withdraw Japanese troops from Manchuria		
		24 Feb.	League of Nations General Assembly approves Lytton Report
		4 Mar.	Franklin D. Roosevelt inaugurated president of United States
		23 Mar.	German Reichstag passes Enabling Act (Hitler's dictatorship begins)
27 Mar.	Announcement of Japan's withdrawal from League of Nations delivered to secretary-general		
1 Apr.	Manchukuo closes doors to countries that will not recognize it		
10 Apr.	Kwantung Army incursion into North China		
		2 May	Hitler abolishes labor unions
21 May	Japanese forces occupy Tongzhou		
31 May	Tanggu Truce signed between Kwantung Army and Chinese forces		
		12 June	London Economic Conference convened
3 Oct.	Five Ministers Conference (prime, finance, army, navy, foreign)		
		14 Oct.	Germany announces withdrawal from Geneva Disarmament Conference and League of Nations
		17 Nov.	United States recognizes the Soviet Union

Note: This year, 4,288 individuals arrested under Peace Preservation Law

Japan	International

1934

	26 Jan.　Germany signs nonaggression pact with Poland
1 Mar.　Manchukuo becomes an empire (with its chief executive, Puyi, taking the throne as Emperor Kangde)	
	10 Apr.　Chinese Communists issue "A Statement to the People of the Whole Country," proposing an anti-Japanese United Front and a six-point program for resistance to Japan and national salvation
18 Apr.　Teijin stock scandal	
17 May　Konoe Fumimaro, president of the House of Peers, visits the United States and meets with President Roosevelt and Secretary of State Cordell Hull	
3 July　Cabinet resigns en masse as result of the Teijin scandal	

Okada Keisuke Cabinet
8 July　Cabinet formed

	2 Aug.　German president Hindenburg dies
	19 Aug.　Hitler simultaneously assumes offices of both chancellor and president
	18 Sept.　Soviet Union joins League of Nations
1 Oct.　Ministry of Army distributes pamphlet titled "Fundamental Principles of National Defense and Proposals for Its Reinforcement"	
	4 Oct.　Right-wing cabinet of Alejandro Lerroux takes power in Spain
20 Nov.　Muranaka Takaji, Isobe Asaichi, and other young officers arrested on suspicion of plotting a coup	

Note: This year marked by a cold summer and crop damage in the Tōhoku region of northern Japan; rightward political turn of zaibatsu business interests intensifies

1935

	13 Jan.　Mao Zedong cements his leadership of the Chinese Communist Party at an enlarged session of Politburo (Zunyi Conference)

Japan	International
24 Jan. Saitō Takao attacks army in a speech in the House of Representatives	
18 Feb. Kikuchi Takeo attacks Minobe Tatsukichi's emperor-as-organ theory in the House of Peers	
	16 Mar. Germany announces it will rearm, ignoring arms limitations imposed by Versailles Treaty and reintroducing military conscription
23 Mar. House of Representative passes resolution for "clarification of the national polity"	
6 Apr. Manchukuo emperor Kangde (Puyi) visits Japan	
9 Apr. Announcement of an impending ban on Minobe Tatsukichi's *Basics of the Constitution* and two other works causes a run on bookstores and copies sell out	
1 May Sixteenth May Day in Japan (last in prewar period)	
	25 July Seventh World Congress of the Comintern opens in Moscow
	1 Aug. Chinese Communists propose a United Front for national salvation and resistance to Japan
3 Aug. Government makes declaration on "clarification of the national polity"	
18 Sept. Minobe Tatsukichi resigns from House of Peers	
	3 Oct. Italy invades Ethiopia (Second Italo-Ethiopian War)
	11 Oct. League of Nations passes economic sanctions against Italy
25 Nov. East Hebei Anti-Communist Autonomous Government declares independence from Nationalist government	
	9 Dec. Anti-Japanese demonstrations in Beijing
18 Dec. Hebei-Chahar Political Council established	

Note: Crop damage due to cold weather worsens in Tōhoku region this year

Japan	International

1936

21 Jan. Minister of Foreign Affairs Hirota Kōki announces in the Diet three principles of China policy: Sino-Japanese cooperation, Chinese recognition of Manchukuo, and anti-Communist partnership

16 Feb. Popular Front victorious in Spanish parliamentary elections

26 Feb. February Twenty-Sixth Incident; cabinet resigns en masse

27 Feb. Martial law declared in Tokyo

5 Mar. Hirota Kōki given imperial order to form new cabinet

7 Mar. Germany abrogates Locarno Pact, reoccupies Rhineland

Hirota Kōki Cabinet

9 Mar. Cabinet formed

5 May Association for the Restoration of the Fatherland organized by Koreans in Manchuria

9 May Italy proclaims annexation of Ethiopia

12 May De Wang organizes Inner Mongolian Military Government with backing of Kwantung Army

18 May Official announcement that army and navy ministers and vice ministers must be active-duty officers

17 July Military revolt in Spain (Spanish civil war begins)

1 Aug. Eleventh Olympic Games open in Berlin

7 Aug. Four Ministers Conference (prime, foreign, army, navy) decides "Imperial Foreign Policy" and Five Ministers Conference (joined by finance minister) approves "Fundamental Principles of National Policy"

9 Sept. Committee of twenty-seven nations formed in London declaring policy of nonintervention in Spanish civil war

1 Oct. Generalissimo Franco proclaims himself Caudillo (chief of state) in Spain

25 Nov. Japan signs Anti-Comintern Pact with Germany

Japan	**International**
	12 Dec. Chiang Kai-shek held captive by Zhang Xueliang (Xi'an Incident)

1937

23 Jan. Cabinet resigns en masse
25 Jan. Ugaki Kazushige receives imperial order to form new cabinet (unable to do so, he gives up on 29 Jan.)

Hayashi Senjūrō Cabinet

2 Feb. Cabinet formed

	15 Feb. Kuomintang agrees to United Front with Chinese Communists
	26 Apr. German Luftwaffe bombs Guernica in Spain

31 May Cabinet resigns en masse

Konoe Fumimaro Cabinet

4 June Cabinet formed
7 July Lugouqiao Incident (Second Sino-Japanese War begins)

	17 July Chiang Kai-shek and Zhou Enlai hold talks at Lushan

28 July Japanese forces commence general offensive in North China
15 Aug. Japan declares it will "punish" the Nanjing government; expansion into full-scale warfare begins

	21 Aug. Sino-Soviet Non-Aggression Pact signed in Nanjing
	23 Sept. Second Nationalist-Communist United Front established

2 Nov. Trautmann mediation begins

	20 Nov. Chiang Kai-shek announces relocation of capital to Chongqing
	11 Dec. Italy withdraws from League of Nations

13 Dec. Japanese forces occupy Nanjing (Nanjing Massacre)
14 Dec. Provisional Government of the Republic of China established in Beiping (headed by Wang Kemin)
15 Dec. 400 people, including members of the Rōnō-ha, arrested (First Popular Front Incident)

Note: This year, displays of popular support (good-luck charms, care packages) for troops are common

Japan	**International**

1938

11 Jan. Imperial Conference (*gozen kaigi*)
by heads of armed services and
the government

16 Jan. Declaration of nonrecognition (*aite to
sezu*) of Nationalist government in China

4 Feb. Hitler takes supreme
command of the German
armed forces

3 Mar. Lieutenant-Colonel Satō Kenryō of
Ministry of Army creates an incident by
shouting at Diet representatives heckling
him during legislative committee testimony
on the proposed National Mobilization Act

13 Mar. Germany annexes Austria

29 Mar. Kuomintang Extraordinary
National Congress in
Hankou: Chiang Kai-shek
elected president; Wang
Jingwei, vice president

1 Apr. National Mobilization Act promulgated

6 Apr. Electrical Power Management Act promulgated (nationalization of electrical power)

29 Sept. Munich Conference (Britain,
France, Germany, Italy);
Munich Agreement allows
German annexation of
Sudetenland

27 Oct. Japanese forces occupy Wuhan (the three
cities of Wuchang, Hankou, and Hanyang)

3 Nov. Prime Minister Konoe proclaims the
construction of a "New Order" in
East Asia

18 Nov. Minister of Foreign Affairs Arita Hachirō
sends written reply to US protests
concerning Japanese actions in China

22 Dec. Prime Minister Konoe declares three
principles for readjustment of Sino-
Japanese relations: neighborly amity,
anti-Communist cooperation, and
economic collaboration

1939

1 Jan. Kuomintang permanently
expels Wang Jingwei

4 Jan. Cabinet resigns en masse

Hiranuma Kiichirō Cabinet

5 Jan. Cabinet formed

Japan	International
	26 Jan. Franco's forces occupy Barcelona
	24 Feb. Hungary joins Anti-Comintern Pact
9 Mar. Revision of Military Service Act promulgated (length of military service extended, short-term active service system abolished)	
	15 Mar. Germany occupies Bohemia and Moravia (dissolution of Czechoslovakia)
	28 Mar. Franco's forces enter Madrid (end of Spanish civil war)
	7 Apr. Italy occupies Albania
30 Apr. Seiyūkai splits into two factions	
12 May Border clash between armies of Manchukuo and Outer Mongolia (beginning of Nomonhan Incident)	
	23 Aug. Soviet-German Non-Aggression Pact signed in Moscow
28 Aug. Cabinet resigns en masse, saying it is baffled by developments in European situation surrounding the German-Soviet Non-Aggression Pact	

Abe Nobuyuki Cabinet
30 Aug. Cabinet formed

Japan	International
	1 Sept. German armies invade Poland (World War II begins)
	3 Sept. Britain and France declare war on Germany
	5 Sept. United States declares neutrality in the war in Europe
4 Nov. Minister of Foreign Affairs Nomura Kichisaburō meets with Ambassador Joseph Grew in talks aimed at adjusting Japan–United States relations	
8 Dec. At meeting of Asia Development Board, agreement is reached to engineer establishment of a new central government in China	
26 Dec. Governor-general of Korea orders Koreans to adopt Japanese-style names (sōshi kaimei)	

Japan	**International**

1940

14 Jan.   Cabinet resigns en masse

Yonai Mitsumasa Cabinet

16 Jan.   Cabinet formed
2 Feb.   Minseitō member Saitō Takao criticizes conduct of China war in the House of Representatives (from which he is expelled on 7 Mar.)
9 Mar.   House of Representatives passes resolution calling for carrying the "Holy War" to a successful conclusion

12 Mar.   Wang Jingwei issues a declaration on peace and national reconstruction in Shanghai
10 May   Winston Churchill heads coalition cabinet in Britain
10 June   Italy declares war on Britain and France
18 June   General Charles de Gaulle orders continued war of resistance against Germany in a radio broadcast from London

24 June   Konoe Fumimaro resigns as president of the Privy Council, resolving to promote the New Order Movement
6 July   Shakai Taishūtō disbands
16 July   Cabinet resigns en masse
        Seiyūkai Kuhara faction disbands

Konoe Fumimaro Cabinet

22 July   Second Konoe cabinet formed
26 July   Cabinet meeting approves "Outline of Fundamental National Policy" (policies for building New Order in East Asia, national defense state)
27 July   Liaison conference of Imperial General Headquarters and Japanese government approves a "southern advance" involving use of military force if necessary
30 July   Seiyūkai Nakajima faction disbands
15 Aug.   Minseitō disbands

3 Sept.   "Destroyers for Bases" defense agreement between United States and Britain
7 Sept.   German Luftwaffe bombs London

Japan	International
22 Sept. Japan moves troops into northern French Indochina	
	25 Sept. United States provides Chiang Kai-shek government with $25 million loan
27 Sept. Tripartite Pact signed by Japan, Germany, and Italy (Minister of Foreign Affairs Matsuoka Yōsuke)	
12 Oct. Imperial Rule Assistance Association inaugurated	
	5 Nov. Franklin D. Roosevelt elected for third term as US president

Note: This year, intensification of controls on publication; 2,600-year anniversary of imperial rule celebrated; considerable debate over the new economic order

1941

Japan	International
8 Apr. Cabinet Planning Board Incident	
13 Apr. Soviet-Japanese Neutrality Pact signed	
16 Apr. Ambassador Nomura Kichisaburō begins talks with US secretary of state Cordell Hull	
	6 May Joseph Stalin appointed premier of Soviet Union
	27 May Roosevelt declares a state of national emergency
	22 June Germany invades Soviet Union (German-Soviet War begins)
25 June Japan moves into southern French Indochina	
	1 July Germany and Italy recognize Wang Jingwei government in China
16 July Cabinet resigns en masse	

Konoe Fumimaro Cabinet

Japan	International
18 July Third Konoe cabinet formed	
1 Aug. United States embargoes oil exports to Japan	**1 Aug.** United States embargoes oil exports to all aggressor nations
	11 Sept. United States approves attacks on Axis vessels entering waters deemed vital to US defense
	2 Oct. German army begins attack on Moscow
16 Oct. Cabinet resigns en masse	

Japan	International

Tōjō Hideki Cabinet

18 Oct. Cabinet formed

5 Nov. Imperial Conference approves proposals (A and B) and guidelines for implementation of national policies
Kurusu Saburō sent as special envoy to the United States

7 Nov. Ambassador Nomura presents Proposal A to Secretary Hull

20 Nov. Nomura and Kurusu present Proposal B to Secretary Hull

26 Nov. Hull rejects Proposal B, presents Nomura and Kurusu with the Hull Note

1 Dec. Imperial Conference decides for war with the United States (and Great Britain and Netherlands)

8 Dec. Pearl Harbor attacked
Nomura and Kurusu deliver final Japanese communiqué to Hull
Imperial rescript declaring war on United States and Britain

8 Dec. United States and Britain declare war on Japan

11 Dec. Germany and Italy declare war on United States

References

Chronologies and Handbooks

Gaimushō, ed. *Nihon gaikō nenpyō narabi ni shuyō bunsho, ge* [Chronological table and key documents relating to Japanese diplomacy]. 2 vols. Hara Shobō, 1965.

Gikai seido hyakunenshi [A centennial history of the parliamentary system]. Ōkurashō Insatsukyoku, 1990.

Hata Ikuhiko, ed. *Nihon riku kai gun sōgō jiten* [Encyclopedia of the Japanese army and navy]. Tokyo Daigaku Shuppankai, 1991.

Katei Sōgō Kenkyūkai, ed. *Shōwa kateishi nenpyō* [A chronology of Shōwa household history]. Kawade Shobō Shinsha, 1990.

Kindai Nihon seijishi hikkei [Essential guide to modern Japanese political history]. Iwanami Shoten, 1961.

Kindai Nihon sōgō nenpyō, dai-3 pan [Comprehensive chronology of modern Japan, 3rd ed.]. Iwanami Shoten, 1991.

Momose Takashi. *Jiten Shōwa senzenki no Nihon: Seido to jittai* [Encyclopedia of prewar Shōwa Japan: Institutions and realities]. Yoshikawa Kōbunkan, 1990.

Nihon gaikōshi jiten, shinpan [Dictionary of Japanese diplomatic history, new ed.]. Yamakawa Shuppansha, 1992.

Primary Source Materials, Biographies, and Memoirs

Andō Yoshio, ed. *Shōwa keizaishi eno shōgen, jō, chū, ge* [Testimonies on Shōwa economic history]. 3 vols. Mainichi Shinbunsha, 1965.

Funaki Shigeru. *Shina hakengun sōshireikan Okamura Yasuji taishō* [General Okamura Yasuji, commander in chief of the China Expeditionary Army]. Kawade Shobō Shinsha, 1984.

Gaimushō, ed. *Nihon gaikō bunsho* [Documents on Japanese foreign policy]. (At time of this writing, published through *Shōwaki* [Shōwa period] II [1931–1937]; other volumes to follow.)

Harada Kumao, as transcribed by Konoe Yasuko. *Saionji kō to seikyoku* [Prince Saionji and political events]. 9 vols. Iwanami Shoten, 1950–1956.

347

Hatano Sumio and Kurosawa Fumitaka, eds. "Nara Takeji jijū bukanchō nikki (shō)" [Selections from the diary of Nara Takeji, chief imperial aide-de-camp]. *Chūōkōron,* September–October 1990.

Hayashi Shigeru and Oka Yoshitake, eds., *Taishōdemokurashī-ki no seiji: Matsumoto Gōkichi seiji nisshi* [The politics of Taishō democracy: The political diary of Matsumoto Gōkichi]. Iwanami Shoten, 1959.

Honjō Shigeru. *Honjō nikki* [The Honjō diary]. In *Meiji hyakunenshi sōsho* [Meiji centennial history series]. Hara Shobō, 1967.

Ishibashi Tanzan. *Ishibashi tanzan zenshū* [Collected works of Ishibashi Tanzan]. Tōyō Keizai Shinpōsha, 1970–1972.

Ishii Itarō. *Gaikōkan no isshō* [My life as a diplomat]. Chūkō Bunko, 1986.

Itō Takashi and Hirose Yoshihiro, eds. *Makino Nobuaki nikki* [Diary of Makino Nobuaki]. Chūōkōron-sha, 1990.

Itō Takashi and Liu Jie, eds. *Ishii Itarō nikki* [Diary of Ishii Itarō]. Chūōkōron-sha, 1993.

Itō Takashi and Shiozaki Hiroaki, eds. *Ikawa Tadao Nichi-Bei kōshō shiryō* [Papers of Ikawa Tadao on the Japan–United States talks]. Yamakawa Shuppansha, 1982.

Itō Takashi and Suetake Yoshiya, eds. *Hatoyama Ichirō, Kaoru nikki, jō* [Diaries of Hatoyama Ichirō and Kaoru, vol. 1]. Chūōkōron-Shinsha, 1999.

Itō Takashi and Watanabe Yukio, eds. *Shigemitsu Mamoru shuki* [Memoirs of Shigemitsu Mamoru]. Chūōkōron-sha, 1986.

———, eds. *Zoku Shigemitsu Mamoru shuki* [Memoirs of Shigemitsu Mamoru, pt. 2]. Chūōkōron-sha, 1988.

Itō Takashi et al., eds. *Honjō Shigeru nikki* [Diary of Honjō Shigeru]. 2 vols. Yamakawa Shuppansha, 1982.

Itō Takashi et al., eds. *Masaki Jinzaburō nikki* [Diary of Masaki Jinzaburō]. 6 vols. Yamakawa Shuppansha, 1981–1987.

Kido Nikki Kenkyūkai, ed. *Kido Kōichi kankei monjo* [Papers of Kido Kōichi]. Tokyo Daigaku Shuppankai, 1966.

———, ed. *Kido Kōichi nikki, jō, ge* [Diary of Kido Kōichi]. 2 vols. Tokyo Daigaku Shuppankai, 1966.

Koiso Kuniaki. *Katsuyama kōsō* [Memoirs of Koiso Kuniaki]. Marunouchi Shuppan, 1968.

Kokka sōdōin [National mobilization]. 2 vols. In *Gendaishi shiryō* [Documents on contemporary history]. Misuzu Shobō, 1970, 1974.

Kokkashugi undō [The Nationalist movement]. 3 vols. In *Gendaishi shiryō* [Documents on contemporary history]. Misuzu Shobō, 1963, 1974.

Manshū jihen [The Manchurian Incident]. In *Gendaishi shiryō* [Documents on contemporary history]. Misuzu Shobō, 1964.

Mitarai Tatsuo, ed. *Minami Jirō.* Minami Jirō Denki Kankōkai, 1957.

Nagai Kafū. *Danchōtei nichijō* [Diary of Nagai Kafū]. 7 vols. Iwanami Shoten, 1980–1981.

Nihon Kindai Shiryō Kenkyūkai, ed. *Suzuki Teiichi-shi danwa sokkiroku, jō, ge* [Transcripts of conversations with Mr. Suzuki Teiichi]. 2 vols. 1971–1974.

Nitchū sensō [The Second Sino-Japanese War]. 5 vols. In *Gendaishi shiryō* [Documents on contemporary history]. Misuzu Shobō, 1964–1966.

Ogawa Heikichi Monjo Kenkyūkai, ed. *Ogawa Heikichi kankei monjo* [Papers of Ogawa Heikichi]. Misuzu Shobō, 1973.

Okada Keisuke and Okada Sadahiro, ed. *Okada Keisuke kaikoroku* [Memoirs of Okada Keisuke]. Chūkō Bunko, 1987.

Rikugun: Hata Shunroku nisshi [The army: Diary of Hata Shunroku]. In *Zoku gendaishi shiryō* [Documents on contemporary history, pt. 2]. Misuzu Shobō, 1983.

Sanbō Honbu, ed. *Sugiyama memo, fukyūban* [The Sugiyama memo, popular ed.]. Hara Shobō, 1994.

Shidehara Kijūrō. *Gaikō gojūnen* [Fifty years of diplomacy]. Chūkō Bunko, 1987.

Taiheiyō sensō [The Pacific War]. 5 vols. In *Gendaishi shiryō* [Documents on contemporary history]. Misuzu Shobō, 1968, 1969, 1972, 1975.

Tanaka Giichi Denki Kankōkai, ed. *Tanaka Giichi denki, jō, ge* [Biography of Tanaka Giichi]. 2 vols. In *Meiji hyakunenshi sōsho* [Meiji centennial history series]. Hara Shobō, 1981.

Terasaki Hidenari et al., eds. *Shōwa tennō dokuhakuroku: Terasaki Hidenari goyō-gakari nikki* [Emperor Shōwa's soliloquy: The diary of liaison officer Terasaki Hidenari]. Bungei Shunjū, 1991.

Tsunoda Jun, ed. *Ishiwara Kanji shiryō: Kokubō ronsaku, shinsōban* [Papers of Ishiwara Kanji: On national defense policy, new format ed.]. Hara Shobō, 1994.

———, ed. *Ishiwara Kanji shiryō: Sensōshi ron, shinsōban* [Papers of Ishiwara Kanji: On the history of warfare, new format ed.]. Hara Shobō, 1994.

———, ed. *Ugaki Kazushige nikki* [Diary of Ugaki Kazushige]. 3 vols. Misuzu Shobō, 1968, 1970, 1971.

Uehara Yūsaku Kankei Monjo Kenkyūkai, ed. *Uehara Yūsaku kankei monjo* [Papers of Uehara Yūsaku]. Tokyo Daigaku Shuppankai, 1976.

Ugaki Kazushige Bunsho Kenkyūkai, ed. *Ugaki Kazushige kankei bunsho* [Papers of Ugaki Kazushige]. Fuyō Shobō Shuppan, 1995.

US Department of State. *Foreign Relations of the United States.* Washington, D.C.: Government Printing Office.

Wakatsuki Reijirō. *Kofūan kaikoroku, kaiteiban* [Memoirs of Wakatsuki Reijirō, rev. ed.]. Yomiuri Shinbunsha, 1975.

Woodward, E. L., and Rohan Butler, eds. *Documents on British Foreign Policy, 1919–1939.* 2nd series. London: His Majesty's Stationery Office, 1946.

Yamamoto Jōtarō-ō Denki Hensankai, ed. *Yamamoto Jōtarō.* In *Meiji hyakunenshi sōsho* [Meiji centennial history series]. Hara Shobō, 1982.

Yamaura Kan'ichi. *Mori Kaku.* In *Meiji hyakunenshi sōsho* [Meiji centennial history series]. Hara Shobō, 1982.

Yoshida Shigeru Kinen Jigyō Zaidan, ed. *Yoshida Shigeru shokan* [Letters of Yoshida Shigeru]. Chūōkōron-sha, 1994.

Yoshino Sakuzō senshū [Selected works of Yoshino Sakuzō]. Iwanami Shoten, 1995–1997.

Zoku Manshū jihen [The Manchurian Incident, pt. 2]. In *Gendaishi shiryō* [Documents on contemporary history]. Misuzu Shobō, 1965.

Secondary Sources

General Reference

Andō Yoshio. *Burujowajī no gunzō* [Group portrait of the bourgeoisie]. Vol. 28 in *Nihon no rekishi* [History of Japan]. Shōgakkan, 1976.

Asada Sadao. *Ryōtaisen-kan no Nichi-Bei kankei: Kaigun to seisaku kettei katei* [Japan–United States relations between the two world wars: The navy and the policymaking process]. Tokyo Daigaku Shuppankai, 1993.

Awaya Kentarō. *Shōwa no seitō, shinsōban* [Shōwa political parties, new format ed.]. Vol. 6 in *Shōgakkan raiburarī: Shōwa no rekishi* [Shōgakkan Library: Shōwa history]. 1994.

Baba Akira. *Nitchū kankei to gaisei kikō no kenkyū* [A study of Sino-Japanese relations and the foreign policy apparatus]. In *Meiji hyakunenshi sōsho* [Meiji centennial history series]. Hara Shobō, 1983.

Bōeichō Bōei Kenshūjo Senshishitsu. *Senshi sōsho* [War history series]. 102 vols. Asagumo Shinbunsha, 1966–1980.

Crowley, James. *Japan's Quest for Autonomy: National Security and Foreign Policy, 1930–1938.* Princeton: Princeton University Press, 1966.

Duus, Peter, Mark Peattie, and Ramon Meyers. *The Japanese Informal Empire in China, 1895–1937.* Princeton: Princeton University Press, 1989.

Fujiwara Akira. *Gunjishi* [Military history]. Tōyō Keizai Shinpōsha, 1961.

Gaimushō Hyakunenshi Hensan Iinkai, ed. *Gaimushō no hyakunen, jō, ge* [One Hundred Years of the Foreign Ministry]. 2 vols. In *Meiji hyakunenshi sōsho* [Meiji centennial history series]. Hara Shobō, 1969.

Hosoya Chihiro, ed. *Nichi-Ei kankeishi 1917–1949* [A history of Anglo-Japanese relations, 1917–1949]. Tokyo Daigaku Shuppankai, 1982.

Ikeda Michiko. *Tai-Nichi keizai fūsa* [The economic encirclement of Japan]. Nihon Keizai Shinbunsha, 1992.

Iriye Akira. *The Globalizing of America, 1913–1945.* Vol. 3 in *The Cambridge History of American Foreign Relations.* Cambridge: Cambridge University Press, 1993.

Iriye Akira and Aruga Tadashi, eds. *Senkanki no Nihon gaikō* [Japanese foreign policy in the interwar period]. Tokyo Daigaku Shuppankai, 1984.

Iriye Akira and Warren Cohen, eds. *American, Chinese, and Japanese Perspectives on Wartime Asia, 1931–1949.* Wilmington, DE: SR Books, 1990.

Itō Takashi. *Jūgonen sensō* [The Fifteen-Year War]. Vol. 30 in *Nihon no rekishi* [History of Japan]. Shōgakkan, 1976.

———. *Shōwa-ki no seiji* [Politics of the Shōwa period]. Yamakawa Shuppansha, 1983.

———. *Zoku Shōwa-ki no seiji* [Politics of the Shōwa period, pt. 2]. Yamakawa Shuppansha, 1993.

Katō Yōko. *Mosaku suru 1930-nendai* [Groping through the 1930s]. Yamakawa Shuppansha, 1993.

Kindai Gaikōshi Kenkyūkai, ed. *Hendōki no Nihon gaikō to gunji: Shiryō to kentō* [Japanese foreign policy and military affairs in an era of transition: Documents and analysis]. Hara Shobō, 1987.

Kindai Nihon Kenkyūkai, ed. *Nenpō kindai Nihon kenkyū: Shōwa-ki no gunbu* [Annual research on modern Japan: The military in the Shōwa period]. Yamakawa Shuppansha, 1979.

Kitaoka Shinichi. *Kanryōsei toshite no Nihon rikugun* [The Japanese army as a bureaucracy]. Chikuma Shobō, 2012.

———. *Kiyosawa Kiyoshi: Gaikō hyōron no unmei, zōhoban* [Kiyosawa Kiyoshi: The fate of foreign policy commentary, expanded ed.]. Chūkō Shinsho, 2004.

Kojima Noboru. *Tennō* [The emperor]. 5 vols. Bungei Shunjū, 1981.

Kurihara Ken. *Tennō* [The emperor]. Hara Shobō, 1985.

Kusayanagi Daizō. *Shōwa tennō to sanma* [Emperor Shōwa and sauries]. Chūkō Bunko, 1999.

Masumi Junnosuke. *Nihon seitōshi ron* [Narrative history of Japanese political parties, vols. 5–8]. Tokyo Daigaku Shuppankai, 1965–1980.

Matsumoto Seichō. *Shōwa-shi hakkutsu* [Unearthing the Shōwa period]. 13 vols. Bunshun Bunko, 1978–1979.

Mikuriya Takashi. *Baba Tsunego no menboku* [The honor of Baba Tsunego]. Chūōkōronsha, 1997.

Mitani Taichirō. *Kindai Nihon no sensō to seiji* [War and politics in modern Japan]. Iwanami Shoten, 1997.

Miyake Masaki et al., eds. *Shōwa-shi no gunbu to seiji* [The military and politics in Shōwa history]. 5 vols. Daiichi Hōki Shuppan, 1983.

Nagai Kazu. *Kindai Nihon no gunbu to seiji* [The military and politics in modern Japan]. Shibunkaku Shuppan, 1993.

Nakamura Takafusa, ed. *Kakeibo kara mita kindai Nihon seikatsushi* [A history of every-day life in modern Japan as seen from household account books]. Tokyo Daigaku Shuppankai, 1993.
———. *Shōwa-shi*. 2 vols. Tōyō Keizai Shinpōsha, 1993. Translated by Edwin Whenmouth as *A History of Shōwa Japan, 1926–1989*. Tokyo Daigaku Shuppankai, 1998.
Neumann, William L. *America Encounters Japan: From Perry to MacArthur.* Translated by Honma Nagayo et al. as *Amerika to Nihon: Perī kara Makkāsā made.* Kenkyūsha Shuppan, 1986.
Nish, Ian, ed. *Britain & Japan: Biographical Portraits*, vol. 1, Folkstone, Kent: Japan Library, 1994.
———. *Japanese Foreign Policy, 1869–1942: Kasumigaseki to Miyakezaka.* Translated and supervised by Miyamoto Moritarō as *Nihon no gaikō seisaku, 1869–1942: Kasumigaseki kara Miyakezaka e.* Minerva Shobō, 1994.
Nomura Kōichi. *Shō Kaiseki to Mō Takutō* [Chiang Kai-shek and Mao Zedong]. Vol. 2 in *Gendai Ajia no shōzō* [Portraits of Contemporary Asia]. Iwanami Shoten, 1997.
Ōe Shinobu. *Nihon no Sanbō Honbu* [The Japanese General Staff]. Chūkō Shinsho, 1985.
———. *Tennō no guntai, shinsōban* [The emperor's army, new format ed.]. Vol. 3 in *Shogakkan raiburarī: Shōwa no rekishi* [Shogakkan Library: Shōwa history]. 1994.
———. *Tōsuiken* [Right of supreme command]. Nippon Hyōron Sha, 1983.
Oka Yoshitake. *Oka Yoshitake chosakushū* [Works of Oka Yoshitake]. Iwanami Shoten, 1992–1993.
Saitō Makoto and Hosoya Chihiro, eds. *Nichi-Bei kankeishi: Kaisen ni itaru jūnen (1931–41)* [A history of Japan–United States relations: The decade leading to war (1931–41)]. 4 vols. Tokyo Daigaku Shuppankai, 1971–1972.
Shidehara Kijūrō. Shidehara Heiwa Zaidan, 1955.
Shinsōban: Taiheiyō sensō eno michi [New format edition: The road to the Pacific War]. 7 vols. plus 1 vol. supplement. Asahi Shinbunsha, 1987–1988.
Shōda Tatsuo. *Jūshintachi no Shōwa-shi, jō, ge* [Shōwa history through its senior statesmen]. 2 vols. Bunshun Bunko, 1984.
Tadai Yoshio. *Tairiku ni watatta en no kōbō, jō, ge* [The rise and fall of the yen on the Asian continent]. 2 vols. Tōyō Keizai Shinpōsha, 1997.
Takahashi Kamekichi. *Taishō Shōwa zaikai hendōshi* [History of fluctuations in the world of finance in Taishō and Shōwa Japan]. 3 vols. Tōyō Keizai Shinpōsha, 1954–1955.
Titus, David. *Palace and Politics in Prewar Japan.* Translated by Ōtani Kenshirō as *Nihon no tennō seiji.* Simul Shuppankai, 1979.
Tobe Ryōichi. *Gyakusetsu no guntai* [The paradoxical military]. Vol. 9 in *Nihon no kindai* [A history of modern Japan]. Chūōkōron-sha, 1998.
Yamada Akira. *Gunbi kakuchō no kindaishi* [A modern history of military expansion]. Yoshikawa Kōbunkan, 1997.
Yomiuri Shinbunsha, ed. *Shōwa-shi no tennō* [The emperor in Shōwa history]. 30 vols. 1967–1976.

Chapter 1 and Chapter 2

Borg, Dorothy. *American Policy and the Chinese Revolution, 1925–1928.* New York: Octagon, rep. 1968, c. 1947.
Hara Takeshi. *"Minto" Ōsaka tai "Teito" Tōkyō: Shisō toshite no Kansai shitetsu* [The "people's capital" of Osaka versus the "imperial capital" of Tokyo: The private railways of the Kansai region as an ideology]. Kōdansha, 1998.
Harada Kumao. *Tōan-kō seiwa* [Memoirs of Prince Saionji]. Iwanami Shoten, 1943.
Hosokibara Seiki. *Gendai sesō manga* [Caricatures of contemporary culture]. Vol. 1 in *Gendai manga taikan* [A General Survey of Modern Caricatures]. Ōzorasha, 1928.

Hosoya Chihiro and Saitō Makoto, eds. *Washinton taisei to Nichi-Bei kankei* [The Washington treaty system and Japan–United States relations]. Tokyo Daigaku Shuppankai, 1978.

Inoue Mitsusada et al., eds. *Dai ichiji sekai taisen to seitō naikaku* [World War I and party cabinets]. Vol. 16 in *Nihon rekishi taikei (fukyūban)* [Japanese history series (popular ed.)]. Yamakawa Shuppansha, 1997.

Iriye Akira. *Kyokutō Shinchitsujo no mosaku* [The search for a New Order in the Far East]. Hara Shobō, 1968.

Itō Takashi. *Shōwa shoki seijishi kenkyū* [A study of the political history of the early Shōwa period]. Tokyo Daigaku Shuppankai, 1969.

———. *Shōwa-ki no seiji* [Politics of the Shōwa period]. Yamakawa Shuppansha , 1983.

Itō Yukio. *Taishō demokurashī to seitō seiji* [Taishō democracy and party politics]. Yamakawa Shuppansha, 1987.

Kamimura Shinichi. *Chūgoku nashonarizumu to Nikka kankei no tenkai* [Chinese nationalism and the development of Sino-Japanese relations]. Vol. 17 in *Nihon gaikōshi* [History of Japanese foreign relations]. Kajima Kenkyūjo Shuppankai, 1971.

Kindai Nihon Kenkyūkai, ed. *Nenpō kindai Nihon kenkyū: Seitō naikaku ki no seiritsu to hōkai* [Annual research on modern Japan: The establishment and dissolution of the era of party cabinets]. Yamakawa Shuppansha, 1984.

Kokkai Shūgiin and Kokkai Sangiin., eds. *Me de miru gikai seiji hyakunenshi* [Visual history of a century of parliamentary politics]. Ōkurashō Insatsukyoku, 1990.

Kurata Yoshihiro. *Nihon rekōdo bunka shi* [A history of Japanese records]. Iwanami Shoten, 2006.

MacMurray, John. *How the Peace Was Lost: The 1935 Memorandum—Developments Affecting American Policy in the Far East.* Edited by Arthur N. Waldron. Translated by Kinugawa Hiroshi under the supervision of Kitaoka Shinichi as *Heiwa wa ikani ushinawareta ka*. Hara Shobō, 1997.

Mitani Taichirō. *Kindai Nihon no shihōken to seitō: Baishinsei seiritsu no seiji shi* [Judicial power in modern Japan and political parties: The political history of the creation of the jury system]. Hanawa Shobō, 1980.

Nakamura Takafusa. *Keizai seisaku no unmei* [The fate of economic policy]. Nihon Keizai Shinbunsha, 1967.

———. *Shōwa kyōkō to keizai seisaku* [The Shōwa depression and economic policy]. Kōdansha Gakujutsu Bunko, 1994.

———. *Shōwa shi*. Vol. 1. Translated (abridged) by Edwin Whenmouth as *A History of Shōwa Japan*. Tokyo: University of Tokyo Press, 1998.

Nihon Kindaishi Kenkyūkai. *Zusetsu kokumin no rekishi, dai-15* [Illustrated history of the Japanese people, vol. 15]. Kokubunsha, 1964.

Nishimura Shigeo. *Chō Gaku-ryō: Nitchū no haken to "Manshū"* [Zhang Xueliang: Sino-Japanese struggle for hegemony and "Manchuria"]. Vol. 3 in *Gendai Ajia no shōzō* [Portraits of contemporary Asia]. Iwanami Shoten, 1996.

Ogawa Heikichi Monjo Kenkyūkai, ed. *Ogawa Heikichi nikki* [Diary of Ogawa Heikichi], 8 December 1928.

Oka Yoshitake. *Tenkanki no Taishō* [Taishō: Period of transition]. Iwanami Shoten, 1997.

Sakai Tetsuya. *Taishō demokurashī taisei no hōkai* [The collapse of the institutions of Taishō democracy]. Tokyo Daigaku Shuppankai, 1992.

Sasaki Tōichi. *Aru gunjin no jiden* [Autobiography of a soldier]. Keisō Shobō, 1967.

Satō Motoei. *Shōwa shoki tai-Chūgoku seisaku no kenkyū* [A study of policy toward China in the early Shōwa period]. In *Meiji hyakunenshi sōsho* [Meiji centennial history series]. Hara Shobō, 1992.

Suzuki Hiroyuki. *Toshi e* [To the cities]. Vol. 10 in *Nihon no kindai* [A history of modern Japan]. Chūōkōron-Shinsha, 1999.

Takahashi Hiroshi. *Heika, otazune mōshiagemasu* [Your highness, a question please]. Gendaishi Shuppankai: Hatsubai Tokuma Shoten, 1982.

Takamura Naosuke. *Kindai Nihon mengyō to Chūgoku* [The modern Japanese cotton industry and China]. Tokyo Daigaku Shuppankai, 1982.
Tokyo Daigaku Hōgakubu Kindai Rippō Katei Kenkyūkai, ed. *Araki Sadao kankei monjo* [Papers of Araki Sadao]. 1976.
Tonedachi Masao. *Asahi Jūtaku zuan-shū* [Collection of housing designs submitted to *Asahi shinbun*]. Asahi Shinbunsha, 1931.
Usui Katsumi. *Nihon to Chūgoku* [Japan and China]. Hara Shobō, 1972.
———. *Nitchū gaikōshi: Hokubatsu no jidai* [Sino-Japanese diplomacy: The era of the Northern Expedition]. Hanawa Shobō, 1971.
Wakatsuki Reijirō. *Kofūan Kaikoroku* [Memoirs of Wakatsuki Reijirō]. Yomiuri Shinbunsha, 1950.
Waldron, Arthur N. *From War to Nationalism: China's Turning Point, 1924–1925*. Cambridge: Cambridge University Press, 1995.

Chapter 3

Bōei Kenshūjo Senshibu. *Rikugun gunsenbi* [Imperial Japanese Army war preparedness]. In *Senshi sōsho* [War history series]. Asagumo Shinbunsha, 1979.
Borg, Dorothy. *The United States and the Far Eastern Crisis of 1933–1938: From the Manchurian Incident Through the Initial Stage of the Undeclared Sino-Japanese War*. Cambridge: Harvard University Press, 1964.
Coble, Parks M. *Facing Japan: Chinese Politics and Japanese Imperialism, 1931–1937*. Cambridge: Harvard University Press, 1991.
Hata Ikuhiko. *Gun fashizumu undōshi, shinsōban* [A history of the military fascist movement, new format ed.]. Hara Shobō, 1980.
Hosoya Chihiro. *Nihon gaikō no zahyō* [Coordinates of Japanese foreign policy]. Chūōkōron-sha, 1979.
———. *Ryōtaisen-kan no Nihon gaikō* [Japanese foreign policy between the two world wars]. Iwanami Shoten, 1988.
Hosoya Chihiro and Aruga Tadashi, eds. *Kokusai kankyō no hen'yō to Nichi-Bei kankei* [The changing international environment and Japan–United States relations]. Tokyo Daigaku Shuppankai, 1987.
Inoue Mitsusada et al., eds. *Kakushin to sensō no jidai* [An era of innovation and war]. Vol. 17 in *Nihon rekishi taikei (fukyūban)* [Japanese history series (popular ed.)]. Yamakawa Shuppansha, 1997.
Inoue Toshikazu. *Kiki no naka no kyōchō gaikō* [Cooperative diplomacy in the midst of crisis]. Yamakawa Shuppansha, 1994.
Ishii Osamu. *Sekai kyōkō to Nihon no "keizai gaikō" 1930–1936* [The world depression and Japan's "economic diplomacy," 1930–1936]. Keisō Shobō, 1995.
Kennedy, M. D. *The Estrangement of Great Britain and Japan, 1917–35*. Manchester: Manchester University Press, 1969.
Kitaoka Shinichi. *Nihon rikugun to tairiku seisaku: 1906–1918 nen* [The Imperial Japanese Army and continental policy: 1906–1918]. Tokyo Daigaku Shuppankai, 1985.
———. "Rikugun habatsu tairitsu (1931–35) no saikentō: Taigai, kokubō seisaku o chūshin toshite" [A reevaluation of army factional conflict (1931–35): Centering on foreign and national defense policies]. In Kindai Nihon Kenkyūkai, ed., *Nenpō kindai Nihon kenkyū: Shōwa-ki no gunbu* [Annual research on modern Japan: The military in the Shōwa period]. Yamakawa Shuppansha, 1979.
———. "Shina-ka kanryō no yakuwari" [The role of the China Section bureaucrats]. In Nihon Seiji Gakkai, ed., *Nenpō seijigaku 1989: Kindaika katei ni okeru seigun kankei* [Political science annual 1989: Politico-military relations in the modernization process]. Iwanami Shoten, 1990.

Kokkai Shūgiin and Kokkai Sangiin., eds. *Me de miru gikai seiji hyakunenshi* [Visual history of a century of parliamentary politics]. Ōkurashō Insatsukyoku, 1990.

Kubo Tōru. *Senkanki Chūgoku: Jiritsu eno mosaku* [China in the interwar period: The quest for independence]. Tokyo Daigaku Shuppankai, 1999.

Kawakami Sumio. *Shin Tōkyō hyakkei* [New one hundred views of Tokyo]. Heibonsha, 1978.

Li, Lincoln. *The Japanese Army in North China, 1937–1941: The Politics of Collaboration.* Tokyo: Oxford University Press, 1975.

Mikuriya Takashi. *Seisaku no sōgō to kenryoku* [Policy synthesis and power]. Tokyo Daigaku Shuppankai, 1996.

Nakamura Takafusa. *Senkanki no Nihon keizai bunseki* [An analysis of the Japanese economy of the interwar period]. Yamakawa Shuppansha, 1981.

———. *Senzenki Nihon keizai seichō no bunseki* [An analysis of economic growth in prewar Japan]. Iwanami Shoten, 1971.

NHK Shuzaihan, ed. *Fōdo no yabō o kudaita gunsan taisei* [The military production system that shattered Ford's ambitions]. Vol. 3 in *Nihon no sentaku* [Japan's choices]. Kadokawa Bunko, 1995.

Office of the Historian. "The Japanese Minister for Foreign Affairs (Arita) to the American Ambassador in Japan (Grew)," November 18, 1938. https://history.state.gov /historicaldocuments/frus1931-41v01/d608.

Ōtani Keijirō. *Shōwa kenpeishi, shinsōban* [History of the Shōwa military police, new format ed.]. Misuzu Shobō, 1979.

Peattie, Mark. *Ishiwara Kanji and Japan's Confrontation with the West.* Princeton: Princeton University Press, 1975.

Tajima Nobuo. *Nachizumu gaikō to "Manshūkoku"* [Nazi diplomacy and "Manchukuo"]. Chikura Shobō, 1992.

Takahashi Masae. *Ni ni-roku jiken, zōhokaiban* [The February Twenty-Sixth Incident, rev. and expanded ed.]. Chūkō Shinsho, 1994.

———. *Shōwa no gunbatsu* [Shōwa military factions]. Chūkō Shinsho, 1969.

Takamiya Tahei. *Gunkoku taiheiki* [A chronicle of militarism]. Kantōsha, 1951.

Thorne, Christopher. *The Limits of Foreign Policy: The West, the League, and the Far Eastern Crisis of 1931–1933.* Translated by Ichikawa Yōichi as *Manshū jihen towa nan datta no ka, jō, ge.* 2 vols. Sōshisha, 1994.

Toyota Jidōsha Kabushiki Kaisha. *Sōzō kagirinaku: Toyota Jidōsha 50-nen shi* [Unlimited creation: A fifty-year history of Toyota Motor Corporation]. 1987.

Trotter, Ann. *Britain and East Asia, 1933–1937.* Cambridge: Cambridge University Press, 1975.

Tsutsui Kiyotada, *Ni ni-roku jiken to sono jidai* [The February Twenty-Sixth Incident and those times]. Chikuma Shobō, 2006.

———. *Shōwa-ki Nihon no kōzō* [The structure of Shōwa Japan]. Yūhikaku, 1984.

Ueyama Kazuo and Sakata Yasuo, eds. *Tairitsu to dakyō: 1930-nendai no Nichi-Bei tsūshō kankei* [Conflict and compromise: Japan–United States trade relations in the 1930s]. Daiichi Hōki Shuppan, 1994.

Usui Katsumi. *Chūgoku o meguru kindai Nihon no gaikō* [Modern Japanese diplomacy concerning China]. Chikuma Shobō, 1983.

———. *Manshū jihen* [The Manchurian Incident]. Chūkō Shinsho, 1974.

———. *Manshūkoku to Kokusai Renmei* [Manchukuo and the League of Nations]. Yoshikawa Kōbunkan, 1995.

———. *Nitchū gaikōshi kenkyū: Shōwa zenki* [Research on the history of Sino-Japanese diplomacy: Early Shōwa period]. Yoshikawa Kōbunkan, 1998.

Vagts, Alfred. *A History of Militarism: Civilian and Military.* New York: Meridian Books Inc., 1959.

Yamamuro Shinichi. *Kimera: Manshūkoku no shōzō* [Chimera: Portrait of Manchukuo]. Chūkō Shinsho, 1993.

Chapter 4

Bōeichō bōeikenshūjo senshishitsu, *Shina jihen rikugun sakusen* [Army operations in the China Incident], vol. 1. *Senshi sōsho* [War History Series]. Asagumo Shinbunsha, 1975.

Chang, Iris. *The Rape of Nanking.* New York: Basic Books, 1997.

Coox, Alvin D. *The Anatomy of a Small War: The Soviet-Japanese Struggle for Changkufeng-Khasan, 1938.* Translated by Iwasaki Hirokazu and Iwasaki Toshio as *Mō hitotsu no Nomonhan: Chōkohō jiken.* Hara Shobō, 1998.

———. *Nomonhan: Japan against Russia, 1939.* Translated by Iwasaki Toshio and Yoshimoto Shin'ichirō, under the supervision of Hata Ikuhiko, as *Nomonhan, jō, ge.* 2 vols. Asahi Shinbunsha, 1989.

Gaimushō, ed., with explanatory notes by Hosoya Chihiro. *Nichi-Bei kōshō shiryō* [Sources on the Japan–United States talks]. In *Meiji hyakunenshi sōsho* [Meiji centennial history series]. Hara Shobō, 1978.

Hata Ikuhiko. *Nankin jiken* [The Nanjing Incident]. Chūkō Shinsho, 1986.

———. *Nitchū sensō shi, zōhokaiteiban* [A history of the Second Sino-Japanese War, rev. and expanded ed.]. Kawade Shobō Shinsha, 1972.

———. *Rokōkyo jiken no kenkyū* [Research on the Marco Polo Bridge Incident]. Tokyo Daigaku Shuppankai, 1996.

Hatano Sumio. *Bakuryō-tachi no Shinjuwan* [Pearl Harbor from the perspective of the staff officers]. Asahi Shinbunsha, 1991.

Heinrichs, Waldo. *American Ambassador: Joseph C. Grew and the Development of the United States Diplomatic Tradition.* Translated by Asada Sadao as *Nichi-Bei gaikō to Gurū.* Hara Shobō, 1969.

———. *Threshold of War: Franklin D. Roosevelt and American Entry into World War II.* New York: Oxford University Press, 1989.

Higashinakano Shūdō. *"Nankin gyakusatsu" no tettei kenshō* [A complete examination of the evidence for the "Nanjing Massacre"]. Tendensha, 1998.

Hosoya Chihiro et al., eds. *Taiheiyō sensō* [The Pacific War]. Tokyo Daigaku Shuppankai, 1993.

Itō Takashi. *Konoe Shintaisei* [Konoe's New Order]. Chūkō Shinsho, 1983.

Kasahara Tokushi. *Nankin jiken* [The Nanjing Incident]. Iwanami Shinsho, 1997.

Kindai Nihon Kenkyūkai, ed. *Nenpō kindai Nihon kenkyū: Taiheiyō sensō* [Annual research on modern Japan: The Pacific War]. Yamakawa Shuppansha, 1982.

Kita Hiroaki. *Nitchū kaisen* [The beginning of the Second Sino-Japanese War]. Chūkō Shinsho, 1994.

Kurihara Ken, ed. *Satō Naotake no menboku* [The honor of Satō Naotake]. Hara Shobō, 1981.

Kusayanagi Daizō. *Saitō Takao kaku tatakaeri* [Saitō Takao's struggle]. Bungei Shunjū, 1981.

Liu Jie. *Nitchū sensō ka no gaikō* [The diplomacy in the Second Sino-Japanese War]. Yoshikawa Kōbunkan, 1995.

Matsumoto Shigeharu. *Shanhai jidai, jō, ge* [Shanghai days]. 2 vols. Chūkō Bunko, 1989.

Matsumoto Shigeharu and Rōyama Yoshirō, eds. *Konoe jidai, jō, ge* [The Konoe era]. 2 vols. Chūkō Shinsho, 1986.

Matsuura Masataka. *Nitchū sensō ki ni okeru keizai to seiji: Konoe Fumimaro to Ikeda Shigeaki* [Economics and politics in the period of the Second Sino-Japanese War: Konoe Fumimaro and Ikeda Shigeaki]. Tokyo Daigaku Shuppankai, 1995.

Miller, Edward S. *War Plan Orange: The U.S. Strategy to Defeat Japan, 1897–1945.* Translated by Sawada Hiroshi as *Orenji keikaku.* Shinchōsha, 1994.

Moriyama Atsushi. *Nichi-Bei kaisen no seiji katei* [The political process leading to the Japan–United States war]. Yoshikawa Kōbunkan, 1998.

Nakamura Takafusa. *Senji Nihon no Kahoku keizai shihai* [Japan's wartime domination of the North China economy]. Yamakawa Shuppansha, 1983.

Nakashizuka Michi. *Iryō hoken no gyōsei to seiji 1895–1954* [Administration and politics of medical insurance, 1895–1954]. Yoshikawa Kōbunkan, 1998.

Nakatogawa Yōkō (Tenshin). *Shina jihen shussei kinen shashin chō* [A commemorative photo album of the China expedition]. Self-published, 1938.

Nihon Seiji Gakkai, ed. *Nenpō seijigaku 1972: "Konoe Shintaisei" no kenkyū* [Political science annual 1972: Research on Konoe's New Order]. Iwanami Shoten, 1973.

Nomura Kōichi. *Shō Kaiseki to Mō Takutō* [Chiang Kai-shek and Mao Zedong]. Iwanami Shoten, 1997.

Nomura Minoru. *Taiheiyō sensō to Nihon gunbu* [The Pacific War and the Japanese military]. Yamakawa Shuppansha, 1983.

———. *Yamamoto Isoroku saikō* [A reexamination of Yamamoto Isoroku]. Chūkō Bunko, 1996.

Ōsugi Kazuo. *Nitchū jūgonen sensōshi* [A History of the Sino-Japanese Fifteen-Year War]. Chūkō Shinsho, 1996.

Ozaki Hotsumi and Imai Seiichi, eds. *Kaisen zen'ya no Konoe naikaku* [The Konoe cabinet on the eve of the war]. Aoki Shoten, 1994.

Sanekisha. *Chūshi no tenbō* [Perspectives on central China]. Shanghai, 1938.

Shibata Shinichi. *Shōwa-ki no kōshitsu to seiji gaikō* [The imperial house and the politics of diplomacy in the Shōwa period]. Hara Shobō, 1995.

Shiozaki Hiroaki. *Nichi-Ei-Bei sensō no kiro: Taiheiyō no yūwa o meguru seisenryaku* [Crossroads of Japan's war with Britain and the United States: Political strategies surrounding appeasement in the Pacific]. Yamakawa Shuppansha, 1984.

Slavinskii, Boris. *A Documentary Study of the Soviet-Japanese Neutrality Pact.* Translated by Takahashi Minoru and Ezawa Kazuhiro as *Kōshō Nisso Chūritsu Jōyaku.* Iwanami Shoten, 1996.

Sudō Shinji. *Haru Nōto o kaita otoko* [The man who wrote the Hull Note]. Bunshun Shinsho, 1999.

———. *Nichi-Bei kaisen gaikō no kenkyū* [A study of Japan–United States diplomacy at the outbreak of the war]. Keiō Tsūshin, 1986.

Takagi Sōkichi. *Jidenteki Nihon kaigun shimatsu ki* [An autobiographical account of the last days of the Japanese navy]. Kōjinsha, 1971.

———. *Takagi Sōkichi nikki: Nichi-Doku-I sangoku dōmei to Tōjō naikaku datō* [The diary of Takagi Sōkichi: The tripartite alliance among Japan, Germany, and Italy and the overthrow of the Tōjō cabinet]. Mainichi Shinbunsha, 1985.

Tobe Ryōichi. *Pīsu fīrā* [Peace feeler]. Ronsōsha, 1991.

Usui Katsumi. *Nitchū sensō* [The Second Sino-Japanese War]. Chūkō Shinsho, 1967.

Utley, Jonathan. *Going to War with Japan: 1937–1941.* Translated by Gomi Toshiki as *Amerika no tai-Nichi senryaku.* Asahi Shuppansha, 1989.

Watt, Donald Cameron. *How War Came: The Immediate Origins of the Second World War, 1938–1939.* New York: Pantheon, 1989.

Yabe Teiji. *Konoe Fumimaro.* Jiji Tsūshinsha, 1986.

———. *Yabe Teiji nikki* [Diary of Yabe Teiji]. 4 vols. Edited by Nikki Kankōkai. Yomiuri Shinbunsha, 1974–1975.

Yamaguchi Yoshiko and Fujiwara Sakuya. *Ri Kōran: Watakushi no hansei.* Shinchō Bunko, 1990. Translated by Chia-ning Chang as *Fragrant Orchid: The Story of My Early Life.* Honolulu: University of Hawaii Press, 2015.

Index

About the Book

The years in Japan between June 1924, when a coali-
tion cabinet of three political parties was established, and December 1941,
when the country declared war on the United States and Britain, were characterized first by nearly a decade of domestic and international cooperation—
and then a period of oppressive militarism. Kitaoka Shinichi captures the
essence of these years in Japan's political history, stressing not only the dis-
continuities, but also the connections, between the two periods.

Kitaoka pays particular attention to the interaction of domestic and foreign affairs. He equally explores the conflicts between political parties and
the military—as well as those among internal factions in both spheres. Con-
necting political issues to economic and social developments, his book
serves as a comprehensive history of the period, a history that, in his words,
"exemplifies the horrific damage that can result when a modern nation-state
goes off course."

Kitaoka Shinichi was born in Nara prefecture in 1948. After graduating
from the University of Tokyo (B.A. 1971, Ph.D. 1976), he taught at Rikkyo
University (1976–1997) and his alma mater (1997–2004, 2006–2012) and
also served as ambassador extraordinary and plenipotentiary and deputy
permanent representative of Japan to the United Nations (2004–2006). He
later became a professor at the National Graduate Institute for Policy Studies
(GRIPS, 2012–2015), was president of the International University of Japan
(IUJ, 2012–2015), and is currently president of the Japan International
Cooperation Agency (2015–).